Praise for *The Religious Cr*

The Religious Crisis of the 1960s, quite sin
persuasive account of the complex changes i

The best book in this field ... a magisterial assembly of facts, preferably statistics, about the changing status of Churches; and it carries on a dialogue with
other scholars who have reached other conclusions while handling the same
subject in the mode of sociology. *Church Times*

McLeod makes effective use of oral testimony to shed light on the many
ways in which Christians changed their religious practice, created their own
patchwork of values and beliefs or simply lost interest in church affairs.
History Today

The strength of McLeod's history is first, that it uses the oral-history
experiences of ordinary people, in a variety of national cultures, who lived
through these years, and second ... that it takes seriously the complexity of
the changes that came and the significance of their sequencing and social
contexts. *Sofia*

Religious Crisis is detailed and comprehensive, yet is also engagingly written.
Moreover, a great deal of important new source material, especially from
unpublished personal testimonies, is incorporated into the text ... a very valuable book indeed. *Journal of Ecclesiastical History*

... a fascinating piece of research on the "long 1960s" (1957–1974), combining
quantitative data (statistics) with qualitative data (oral history)
Methodist Recorder

Lucidly written [and] admirably concise ... Professor McLeod has produced a
work that is likely to remain the starting point for new research into the period
for many years, perhaps for a generation. *Reviews in History*

This excellent book provides further evidence of a recent historiographical
shift in the treatment of the 1960s... furnishing a more complex and nuanced
portrait of change in the sixties and providing a reliable platform for further
work on the part of sociologists and historians as they attempt to assess the
recent history of the churches in the West. *Theology*

What is particularly impressive about this book-and one reason why it will not
easily be superseded-is its remarkable international scope
20th Century British History

The Religious Crisis of the 1960s

HUGH McLEOD

OXFORD
UNIVERSITY PRESS

OXFORD
UNIVERSITY PRESS

Great Clarendon Street, Oxford OX2 6DP

Oxford University Press is a department of the University of Oxford.
It furthers the University's objective of excellence in research, scholarship,
and education by publishing worldwide in

Oxford New York

Auckland Cape Town Dar es Salaam Hong Kong Karachi
Kuala Lumpur Madrid Melbourne Mexico City Nairobi
New Delhi Shanghai Taipei Toronto
With offices in
Argentina Austria Brazil Chile Czech Republic France Greece
Guatemala Hungary Italy Japan South Korea Poland Portugal
Singapore Switzerland Thailand Turkey Ukraine Vietnam

ISBN 978-0-19-9582020-0

Printed in the United Kingdom by
the MPG Books Group Ltd

Acknowledgements

This book began as the 2004 Vonhoff Lectures at the University of Groningen. I would like to thank all those whose attendance at the lectures, participation in discussion, and provision of generous hospitality helped to make it such an enjoyable experience for me. In particular, I would like to thank Mr Henk Vonhoff, who as Queen's Commissioner in the Province of Groningen was instrumental in the establishment of the lectures and after whom they are named; Jan Bremmer and Arië Molendijk, who as, respectively, Dean of the Faculty of Theology and Professor of Church History, were principally responsible for inviting me and for organizing the lectures; and Mathilde van Dijk, who introduced me to the province of Groningen.

There are three other individuals or groups of people I would like especially to thank. First, I want to acknowledge the inspiration and stimulus provided by Callum Brown: we have often reached different conclusions, but without the stimulus derived from Callum's books and from conversations with him it is quite possible that the book would never have been written. Second, I have been greatly helped by Jeff Cox, Moira Harnett, and Mike Snape, who read and commented on drafts. Third, I have been very fortunate in having had an outstanding set of colleagues, past and present, at the University of Birmingham, most of them in the Departments of Modern History or Theology and Religion, but some from other departments too, who have discussed the book with me or lent me their own books. They include, as well as Mike Snape, already mentioned, Mike Butler, Andrew Chandler, Hera Cook, Clive Field, Ian Jones, Gordon Lynch, Peter Marsh, Stephen Pattison, Werner Ustorf, Markus Vinzent, Sarah Williams, and all the members of the History of Religion Seminar.

I also owe a lot to the many other friends and colleagues who have discussed the book with me or sent copies of unpublished papers. Here I would specially like to mention Daniel Alvunger, Ashley Rogers Berner, Jim Bjork, Steve Bruce, Hilary Carey, Wilhelm Damberg, Grace Davie, Janet Eccles, Stefan Gelfgren, Friedrich Wilhelm Graf, Angela Hager, Paul Heelas, Mary Heimann, David Hempton, David Hilliard, Gerd-Rainer Horn, Anders Jarlert, Aila Lauha, Hartmut Lehmann, Bernice Martin, David Martin, Jim Obelkevich, Thomas Schmidt-Lux, Erik Sidenvall, Jo Spaans, Pamela Taylor, Peter van Rooden, Graham Willett, Linda Woodhead, Benjamin Ziemann. Sections of the book have been presented as papers at the universities of Birmingham, Boston,

Chichester, Lancaster, Leipzig, Paris, and Umeå, at the Church of England Record Society, at the Arbeitskreis für Sozialgeschichte in Bochum, at conferences held at the Evangelische Akademie in Tutzing and at the Katholische Akademie in Weingarten, at a workshop held by the Lund-based 'Religion and Masculinity' project, at a conference in Wuhan University and at the International Historical Congress in Oslo (2000) and Sydney (2005). I would like to thank all those who made helpful comments on these occasions.

I would like to thank David Lodge for permission to quote from his novel, *How Far Can You Go?* and for the pleasure I got from rereading his novels while working on this book. I would also like to thank Robert Perks, Director of the National Sound Archive, for permission to quote from transcripts of oral history interviews in the archive; Elizabeth Roberts for permission to quote from transcripts of interviews by herself and Lucinda Beier at the Centre for North-West Regional Studies; Paul Heelas, Linda Woodhead, and Benjamin Seel for allowing me to consult and quote from interviews conducted as part of the Kendal project; the Mistress and Fellows, Girton College, Cambridge, for permission to refer to information contained in the 'University and Life Experience' questionnaires, and Kate Perry and Pat Thane for telling me about the project and assisting me in the use and interpretation of the questionnaires.

Contents

List of Tables   viii
Abbreviations   ix

Introduction   1

1. The Decline of Christendom   6

2. Late Christendom   31

3. The Early 1960s   60

4. Aggiornamento   83

5. Affluence   102

6. New Worlds   124

7. 1968   141

8. Sex, Gender, and the Family   161

9. The Crisis of the Church   188

10. From 'Christian Country' to 'Civilized Society'   215

11. The End of Christendom?   240

Conclusion   257

Bibliography   266
Index   283

List of Tables

1. Church of England Easter communicants, 1934–1973   39
2. Church of England confirmations, 1934–1974   40
3. Church of England Sunday School enrolments, 1934–1960   63
4. Church of England infant baptisms, 1934–1973   63
5. Church of England electoral rolls, 1934–1964   65
6. Membership of Nonconformist churches in England, 1934–1970   66

Abbreviations

ALRA	Abortion Law Reform Association
BBC	British Broadcasting Corporation
BC	'Birth Control', transcripts of interviews, National Sound Archive, British Library
FSMA	'Families, Social Mobility and Ageing, a Multi-Generational Approach', National Sound Archive, British Library
IVF	Inter-Varsity Fellowship
JEC	Jeunesse étudiante chrétienne
MP	Member of Parliament
MPNSA	Millennium Project, recordings held at National Sound Archive, British Library
SCM	Student Christian Movement
SFL	'Social and Family Life 1940–1970', Oral History Archive, Centre for North-West Regional Studies, University of Lancaster
SGR	'1968: A Student Generation in Revolt', transcripts of interviews, National Sound Archive, British Library
SNCC	Student Non-Violent Coordinating Committee
WSCF	World Student Christian Federation
YMCA	Young Men's Christian Association
YWCA	Young Women's Christian Association

Introduction

The 1960s were a period of decisive change in the religious history of the Western world—including not only western Europe, but the United States, Canada, Australia, and New Zealand. Historians disagree as to when the '1960s' began and ended, but here I will use Arthur Marwick's concept of a 'long 1960s', lasting from about 1958 to 1974.[1] In the religious history of the West these years may come to be seen as marking a rupture as profound as that brought about by the Reformation.

The seventeenth, eighteenth, and nineteenth centuries had seen the gradual introduction of religious toleration and a trend towards greater religious pluralism. But in the 1950s the great majority of the people in all Western countries were at least nominal members of one of the Christian churches; the numbers of those professing other religions or none at all were in most countries very small; the churches remained extremely powerful institutions; the clergy of the larger Christian denominations generally enjoyed high status and considerable influence.

In the 'long 1960s' all of this was changing. Nearly every Western country saw a drop in church-going, and in some cases the drop was dramatic. In these years large numbers of people lost the habit of regular church-going. In some countries there was a substantial drop in the proportion of couples marrying in church or having their children baptized. There was also a considerable decline in the numbers of clergy, both because of a fall in ordinations and in the case of the Catholic Church because of resignations. There was a modest increase in the numbers of those professing other religions, such as Buddhism, Hinduism, or Islam, or stating that they had no religion. The main novelty here was that those who rejected Christianity were increasingly ready to say so loudly and openly.

In describing and explaining these changes I will highlight four major themes. First, from the 1950s to the 1970s there was an enormous increase in the range of beliefs and world-views accessible to the majority of the population. By the 1970s the options had widened strikingly to include not only new

[1] Arthur Marwick, *The Sixties: Cultural Revolution in Britain, France, Italy and the United States, c.1958–1974* (Oxford, 1998), 7.

forms of Christianity and new political faiths, but many other religions and 'alternative spiritualities'. Indeed, by the 1980s and 1990s, the fashion would be for eclecticism—a deliberate mixing of elements drawn from different belief-systems, or a casual assumption that the boundaries between them were irrelevant.

Second, there was a change in the way that people in most Western countries understood the religious identity of their own society. In the 1940s and 1950s they still tended to assume that they lived in a 'Christian country'—though they also often commented that most people's Christianity was rather superficial. In the 1960s, and even more in the 1970s, it was increasingly said that Western societies were 'pluralist', 'post-Christian', or 'secular'. This had important implications for the laws relating to such contentious issues as abortion or divorce. Laws which purported to be based on Christian moral principles might no longer be appropriate in a society where there was no consensus on key ethical questions, and where the rights of a variety of groups, Christian and non-Christian, needed to be recognized.

Third, there was a serious weakening of the process by which the great majority of children were socialized into membership of a Christian society and in particular were given a confessional identity and a basic knowledge of Christian beliefs and practices. Fewer parents were decorating the home with religious pictures, teaching their children prayers, or talking to them about God and Jesus; and fewer parents were sending their children to learn about these things at Sunday School or catechism class. At the same time, parents who were atheists or agnostics were readier to discuss their unbelief with their children.

Fourth, in the wake of the Second Vatican Council, Catholics and Protestants moved closer together. But as the divisions between the Christian churches were narrowing, the divisions within each of the churches were deepening. This was a time of intense conflict between conservatives, moderates, liberals, radicals, especially in the Roman Catholic Church, but in many of the Protestant churches too.

By the end of the twentieth century, these changes had gone much further. The trends established in the 'long 1960s' set the pattern for the rest of the century. According to the European Values Survey in 1999, 54 per cent of the population in the Netherlands said they had no religion, and 43 per cent in France, though elsewhere in western Europe and North America 15–20 per cent was a more typical figure. The proportion of the population claiming to attend church at least once a month was down to 9 per cent in Sweden, 10 per cent in Denmark, 12 per cent in France, and 19 per cent in Great Britain, though some countries, including Ireland, Italy, and probably the United States, showed much higher figures.[2] In most countries the majority of babies were being baptized, but in nearly all there had been a substantial fall in the ratio of baptisms to births. This was partly because of immigration by Muslims and Hindus—but only partly, as the proportion of the population adhering to non-Christian faiths was still quite small.

By the end of the twentieth century it had become common to contrast European 'secularity' with American 'religiosity'. The contrast is certainly often exaggerated, and it also glosses over the considerable differences both within the United States and within western Europe. However, it is true that in the 1970s the patterns of religious development in Europe and the USA did diverge. In the 1960s trends on the two sides of the Atlantic were very similar. However in the middle and later 1970s, while levels of Christian practice continued to fall in Europe, those in the United States stabilized, albeit at a level considerably lower than those obtaining in the 1950s. Moreover, the emergence in the later 1970s of the American 'Religious Right' meant that the political profile of religion and the churches was rising in the United States at a time when it was tending to fall in western Europe. The end of the 'long 1960s' did therefore see at least a temporary parting of the ways between America and western Europe, which will be discussed in the latter part of the book. However, for most of the 'long 1960s' it is the similarities between American and European trends that were most conspicuous and which will be most emphasized here.

The '1960s' were an international phenomenon. The Civil Rights Movement and the Vietnam War were of course central to the history of the United States in this period, but the impact of the Vietnam War, in particular, was felt throughout the Western world. The same is true of the events of May 1968 in Paris; of the contraceptive pill, which became available in the United States in 1960 and in Europe in 1961; and of developments in pop music, fashion, or the use of drugs which started in Britain or the United States, but were very quickly adopted in many other countries. The religious history of the decade is equally international. This is most obviously true of the Second Vatican Council, an event with enormous implications for Catholics everywhere. But it is also true of books such as *Honest to God*, John Robinson's theological bestseller, published in England in 1963 and soon translated into numerous languages. Other religious trends of the decade, such as the drop in church-going and the movement of

---

[2] Yves Lambert, 'New Christianity, Indifference and Diffused Spirituality', in McLeod and Ustorf (eds.), *Decline of Christendom*, 71.

resignations from the Catholic priesthood, were also remarkably international, though of course there are differences from country to country in their scale.

This book will focus exclusively on the democratically governed countries of western and northern Europe, on North America, and on Australasia. It will stress the similarities between the trends in most of these countries. The situation in the Communist-ruled countries of eastern Europe, with their official atheism, or in the right-wing dictatorships of Spain or Portugal, was sufficiently different to demand a separate book, or a much longer one. Similarly, the completely different political, as well as economic and social situation in Latin America or South Africa precludes their inclusion here, in spite of some points of similarity. Perhaps more arbitrarily the book will contain very little discussion of the distinctive situation in Ireland, the country where Christian observance was highest, and the only one where there was no substantial decline in this period. The principal focus will be on England and the secondary focus on the United States and France, though significant attention will also be given to other countries. Sections relating to England will draw heavily on primary sources, while those on other countries will depend mainly on secondary sources. Every country has its own history, and, as I shall indicate, some of the characteristic trends of this period went much further in certain countries than in others. However it is not my purpose to provide a comprehensive account of the religious history of each country. I have two main objectives. First, I want to identify the main religious changes across the Western world, explaining why these changes were happening, and suggesting which common factors meant that the patterns of change in different countries were often so similar. Second, I want to understand how these changes were experienced by 'ordinary people'. In order to do this I have drawn wherever possible on personal testimony, and especially on unpublished personal testimony. Other historians in this field have often used published personal testimony. Useful as this can be, however, it suffers from the double drawback that the authors tend to be celebrities or activists, whose experiences may be quite unrepresentative of the wider population, and that writing for publication requires concern for such matters as self-presentation and literary effect. There is a danger in taking such works too much at face value. Here I have been able to draw on the largest and most varied body of unpublished personal testimony yet used in the exploration of this subject, and I believe that it has been important both in adding depth and detail to the familiar picture in some areas, and in other respects suggesting that the familiar picture is wrong. Names assigned to those giving unpublished testimony are always pseudonyms. Where I have quoted from books by oral historians, I have used the names assigned to interviewees by the authors of these books, which in some cases are pseudonyms, and in some cases are their real names.

The 1960s were a revolutionary era—a time of cultural revolution, and of largely unsuccessful attempts at political revolution. To convey the distinctive atmosphere of the time and the impact of specific events, as well as the gathering dynamic of change which developed as the decade progressed, a narrative structure, with an emphasis on certain key events and personalities, is needed. At the same time, these events cannot be understood without reference to underlying social changes. Moreover, changes of a more mundane kind may have affected more people than the great events and personalities. The basic framework of this book will be chronological, beginning in the period after the Second World War and ending around the middle of the 1970s. At the same time the narrative will be interwoven with sections focusing on broader social change or on topics that do not lend themselves to narrative treatment. Switches in focus between different countries will reflect not only the availability of sources, but also the fact that different countries are central to different aspects of the story.

1

The Decline of Christendom

This chapter will begin by discussing some of the main theories advanced by historians and sociologists to explain the religious crisis of the 1960s. It will then go on to suggest an historical framework within which the dramatic developments in that decade can be understood.

INTERPRETING RELIGIOUS CHANGE

There is now quite a large body of literature by historians and sociologists which attempts to describe and interpret the religious crisis of the 'long 1960s'. A few writers have concentrated specifically on that decade, but most have included the events of that period within a longer narrative.

Among the accounts focusing specifically on that period, the only one to provide an overview is an essay by Patrick Pasture.[1] However, there are general accounts of developments in France, the United States, Quebec, and Australia,[2] as well as more specialized studies on such topics as the impact of Vatican II on the Netherlands, alienation from the church in that country, the impact of social and economic change on religion in rural France, or the decline of popular religion in England.[3] In the United States sociologists have given a lot of attention to the distinctive religious approach of the

---

[1] Patrick Pasture, 'Christendom and the Legacy of the Sixties: Between the Secular City and the Age of Aquarius', *Revue d'histoire écclésiastique*, 99 (2004), 82–117.

[2] Denis Pelletier, *La crise catholique: Religion, société et politique en France (1965–1978)* (Paris, 2002); Robert S. Ellwood, *The Sixties Spiritual Awakening: American Religion Moving from Modern to Postmodern* (New Brunswick, NJ, 1994); Michael Gauvreau, *The Catholic Origins of Quebec's Quiet Revolution, 1931–1970* (Montreal and Kingston, Ontario, 2005); David Hilliard, 'The Religious Crisis of the 1960s: The Experience of the Australian Churches', *Journal of Religious History*, 21 (1997), 209–27.

[3] John A. Coleman, *The Evolution of Dutch Catholicism, 1958–1974* (Berkeley, Calif., 1978); Peter van Rooden, 'Oral History and the Strange Demise of Dutch Christianity', www.xs4all.nl/pvrooden (accessed 14 Apr. 2005); Yves Lambert, *Dieu change en Bretagne* (Paris, 1985); Richard Sykes, 'Popular Religion in Decline: A Study from the Black Country', *Journal of Ecclesiastical History*, 56 (2002), 287–307.

'baby-boomers', the generation coming to maturity in the 1960s and 1970s.[4] There are numerous histories of religion in the twentieth century, the later twentieth century, or even 'the modern world' which give significant attention to the 1960s. These include works focused specifically on the nature and causes of secularization, such as the books on Britain by Alan Gilbert and Callum Brown, the comparative study of Catholic Europe by Jean-Louis Ormières, and various publications by the Belgian sociologists Karel Dobbelaere and Liliane Voyé.[5] They also include more general religious histories, with a strong emphasis on narrative,[6] and works of interpretation where the emphasis is as much on innovation and adaptation as on crisis.[7]

Sociologists whose understanding of religion in the modern world is founded on the classical theories of secularization as propounded around 1900 by Weber and Durkheim see the events of the 1960s as a perfect illustration of the general secularizing trends in modern societies, but they have seldom addressed the specificity of that decade. Thus the most uncompromising champion of this tradition, Steve Bruce, argues strongly for a general 'erosion of the supernatural' in the modern Western world, and offers numerous examples of the diminution over time of religious belief and behaviour, but he provides very generalized explanations of these trends and does not try to identify specific periods as being especially significant.[8] However, a growing number of sociologists, and more especially of historians, have seen the speed

---

[4] Wade Clark Roof, *A Generation of Seekers: The Spiritual Journey of the Baby-Boom Generation* (New York, 1993); Robert Wuthnow, *After Heaven: Spirituality in America since the 1950s* (Berkeley, Calif., 1998); and a collection of essays on various countries, Wade Clark Roof *et al.* (eds.), *The Post-War Generation and Establishment Religion: Cross-Cultural Perspectives* (Boulder, Colo., 1998).

[5] Alan D. Gilbert, *The Making of Post-Christian Britain: A History of the Secularization of Modern Society* (London, 1980); Callum G. Brown, *The Death of Christian Britain* (London, 2001) and *Religion and Society in Twentieth-Century Britain* (London, 2006); Jean-Louis Ormières, *L'Europe désenchantée: La fin de l'Europe chrétienne? France, Belgique, Espagne, Italie, Portugal* (Paris, 2005); Karel Dobbelaere, 'Secularization, Pillarization, Religious Involvement and Religious Change in the Low Countries', in Thomas M. Gannon (ed.), *World Catholicism in Transition* (New York, 1988), 80–115; Karel Dobbelaere and Liliane Voyé, 'Western European Catholicism since World War II', in Ebaugh (ed.), *Vatican II and U.S. Catholicism*, 205–31.

[6] Gérard Cholvy and Yves-Marie Hilaire (eds.), *Histoire religieuse de la France contemporaine 1930–1988* (Toulouse, 1988); Adrian Hastings, *A History of English Christianity 1920–1985* (London, 1986); Callum G. Brown, *Religion and Society in Scotland since 1707* (Edinburgh, 1997); D. Densil Morgan, *The Span of the Cross: Christian Religion and Society in Wales 1914–2000* (Cardiff, 1999); Sydney Ahlstrom, *A Religious History of the American People* (New Haven, 1972); Patrick Allitt, *Religion in America since 1945: A History* (New York, 2003).

[7] Robert Wuthnow, *The Restructuring of American Religion* (Princeton, 1988); Amanda Porterfield, *The Transformation of American Religion: The Story of a Late-Twentieth-Century Awakening* (Oxford, 2001).

[8] Steve Bruce, *Religion in the Modern World: From Cathedrals to Cults* (Oxford, 1996) is the fullest statement of his position.

of religious change in the 1960s, and especially the contrast between that decade and those immediately preceding as a problem.

Here I will look at the ways in which they have tried to answer three key questions of interpretation. First, should the religious crisis of the Sixties be seen as the culmination of a long historical evolution, or as a period of revolutionary rupture from the past? Second, what was the relationship, if any, between the decline in church-going and in the numbers of clergy during the Sixties and the movements of church reform and theological modernisation taking place at the same time? And third, which social or religious groups were the key agents of religious change in this period?

Evolution or Revolution?

This question is complicated by the fact that the 1960s followed a period, between about 1945 and 1960, when the institutional strength and levels of popular involvement in the churches were growing in many parts of the Western world, most notably the United States. One of the key issues for historians of the 1960s is the relationship between that decade of spectacular change and the more staid 1950s. Some enthusiasts for the 1960s, such as Callum Brown, have a positive dislike for the period preceding, and frequently draw comparisons—always to the disadvantage of the earlier decade.[9] On the other hand, Gérard Cholvy and Yves-Marie Hilaire, doyens of French Catholic history, who dislike most aspects of the later 1960s, present a highly positive image of the period 1930–60, which they term the 'Thirty Glorious Years' of French Christianity, marking 'the apogee of the role of Christians in society'.[10] So historians of the 1960s need to consider not only the long-term roots of developments in that decade, but also the impact of the more immediate past.

At one extreme stands Alan Gilbert, a historian with a quantitative bent, strongly influenced by sociology, and especially by the theories of secularization, who simply ignores evidence for a religious upturn in the 1940s and 1950s. For him the 1960s were a culmination of a long-term process of secularization, going back to the Renaissance and Reformation. The early industrial period in Britain had seen a temporary interruption of this process, but the evangelical movements of that time were running out of steam by the 1850s. Since that time there had been a progressive marginalization of religion and the churches—gradual in the later nineteenth century, more rapid since the First World War, and very rapid since the 1960s. The 1960s merely represented

[9] Brown, *Religion and Society in Twentieth-Century Britain*, 202 and *passim*.
[10] Cholvy and Hilaire, *Histoire religieuse*, 7 and *passim*.

a more acute phase of this long-term crisis, arising from inexorable processes of modernization and rationalization, as more and more areas of life become subject to human knowledge and control. Essentially the same position is argued by Dobbelaere and Voyé, though in focusing especially on Flanders they have a different chronology: they argue that 'modernization' in the 1960s delivered the coup de grace to Flemish Catholicism.[11]

At the opposite pole stands Callum Brown, a cultural historian, strongly influenced by postmodernism, and critical of 'social science history', who sees the churches principally as agents of moral discipline. Brown and Gilbert agree that by the later twentieth century Britain was overwhelmingly secularized, but they have very different explanations as to how this situation had come about. According to Brown, the dominance of Christian— and specifically 'evangelical'—discourses continued right into the 1950s. One of the most important developments of the early 1800s was the 'feminisation of piety'. From the Methodist revivals right up to the Billy Graham Crusades of the 1950s, it was women, especially young women and teenage girls, who were the first to be saved, and who put pressure on their menfolk to follow their example. Throughout this period, being religious was for large numbers of women an essential part of their feminine identity.

Brown is unusual in the degree to which he places gender at the centre, though it has played an increasingly large role in the most recent literature, partly under the influence of Brown's much-debated book.[12] But the historian of Dutch religion, Peter van Rooden, whose approach is in most respects quite different, goes even further in sharply contrasting the 1950s and 1960s. Like Brown, in respect of Britain, van Rooden completely rejects the secularization narrative as a way of summarizing the evolution of Dutch religion from the 1790s to the 1950s. He detects no process of long-term decline, but rather a series of major, and often rather sudden, changes in the relationship between religion and the social order. He specially highlights the 'pillarization' of Dutch society in the later nineteenth century (to which I will return later in this chapter) and the prominence this gave both to Catholics and to orthodox Protestants. Both 'pillars' still appeared very solid in the 1950s and, he suggests, Dutch church-going may even have peaked in that decade. At the same time, the power of the churches provoked an underlying resentment and the tight-knit Catholic or orthodox Protestant milieu could be claustrophobic. Thus, while for Gilbert the losses suffered in the 1960s were simply the logical conclusion of a long period of decline, for Brown, and even more for van

[11] Gilbert, *Post-Christian Britain*; Dobbelaere and Voyé, 'Western European Catholicism'.
[12] Brown, *Death*.

Rooden, it is the power of the churches in the 1940s and 1950s which partly explains the force of the subsequent reaction.[13]

In contrast to those studies which see the 1950s and 1960s as polar opposites, Mark Ruff's history of the decline of the Catholic milieu in West Germany sees gentle rebellion in the 1950s preparing the ground for more open revolt in the 1960s. He convincingly challenges the stereotype of the 1950s as a period of dreary conformity.[14] Here I will argue that the relationship between these two decades is double-sided. However excitingly and terrifyingly new the 1960s seem now—and indeed seemed at the time—they were made by people whose formative experiences came in earlier decades. Both positively and negatively the 1950s prepared the way. In some respects the 1950s led into the 1960s, while in other ways the 1960s were an escape from the 1950s.

Most historians have mixed the 'evolutionary' and 'revolutionary' interpretations, while usually avoiding the teleology which is often implied in the evolutionary approach. So, for instance, Cholvy and Hilaire emphasize the sudden and drastic nature of the crisis experienced by the French churches in the later 1960s, though they also note that the roots of the crisis can often be traced back to the later 1950s.[15] But as specialists in the nineteenth century they could scarcely be unaware of the multiple crises faced by French Catholicism in that century or of the progress of 'dechristianization' in certain regions. In speaking of 1930–60 as the 'Thirty Glorious Years' they were contrasting this period with what came before as well as what came after.

In this book I will attempt to give due attention both to the long-term preconditions for and the short-term precipitants of the 1960s crisis, as well as providing a narrative of the events in those years. My approach is similar to that of the Dutch sociologist, Leo Laeyendecker[16] who, in discussing the dramatic changes of the 1960s and 1970s in the Netherlands, argues that they need to be understood at three levels: those of long-term processes, developing over a century or more; of medium-term processes developing over maybe two or three decades; and of 'catalysts', among which he includes the Second Vatican Council (Vatican II)—to which I would add, to name only the most significant, the Vietnam War.

---

[13] Peter van Rooden, 'Secularization, Dechristianization and Rechristianization in the Netherlands', in Hartmut Lehmann (ed.), *Säkularisierung, Dechristianisierung, Rechristianisierung im neuzeitlichen Europa* (Göttingen, 1997), 231–53.

[14] Mark Edward Ruff, *The Wayward Flock: Catholic Youth in Post-War West Germany, 1945–1965* (Chapel Hill, NC, 2005), 195–7 and *passim*.

[15] Cholvy and Hilaire, *Histoire religieuse*, 255, 303–4.

[16] Leo Laeyendecker, 'The Case of the Netherlands', in Roof *et al.* (eds.), *Post-War Generation*, 131–49.

The Impact of Church Reform

The 1960s were, as David Hilliard points out, not only a 'watershed' but also a 'seedbed' in modern religious history.[17] As well as many new religious movements, this period also saw major efforts at church reform and theological modernization. Of these by far the most important was the Second Vatican Council of the Roman Catholic Church, meeting in Rome from 1962 to 1965. But the decade also saw many widely read works by liberal Protestant theologians, of which the most influential were probably John Robinson's *Honest to God* (1963), Harvey Cox's *Secular City* (1965), and Joseph Fletcher's *Situation Ethics* (1966). (Robinson and Cox are sometimes misleadingly linked with the so-called 'Death of God' theologians, who became a media sensation in the United States in 1966. Robinson and Cox were not advocating a Christian atheism: on the contrary they were trying to find more meaningful ways of writing about God which would resonate with contemporaries in ways that some of the older language failed to do.)

Here we enter controversial territory, as historians' and sociologists' evaluation of these developments is frequently and sometimes very obviously influenced by their own ideological commitments. This is especially true of Catholic scholars, who like Catholics generally, continue to be deeply divided by the events of the 1960s, and especially by Vatican II. If anything, these divisions have become even deeper as Catholics have reacted very differently to the papacy of John Paul II (1978–2005) and to the key role played in that papacy by Cardinal Josef Ratzinger, now Benedict XVI. Some conservative Catholics blame the Council for the decline in Catholic church-going since the 1960s and the fall in the numbers of priests and nuns. Others, including Cholvy and Hilaire, blame not the Council itself, but the ways in which it was misinterpreted by many of those in positions of influence in the French church. They criticize those clergy (including some bishops), as well as many lay militants, who took the ideas generated by the Council to harmful extremes, who engaged in ill-founded pastoral experiments, or who were seduced by the spirit of 1968. These authors suggest that the utopianism of that fateful year, the hatred of institutions and structures, the love affair of many radical Catholics with Marxism, and their idealization of the Third World in general, and of certain Marxist dictators in particular, all had devastating effects on the Catholic Church. The results included bitter internal divisions, a weakening of the rhythms and disciplines of Catholic life, and disillusion when the unrealistic hopes of those years inevitably came to nothing.[18] Also, like a number of other writers, including some liberal and radical Catholics, they regret the

---

[17] Hilliard, 'Crisis', 227.   [18] Cholvy and Hilaire, *Histoire religieuse*, 287–90, 328–30.

undermining of an allegedly superstitious 'popular religion' in the wake of the Council.[19]

Authors with a liberal Catholic perspective have questioned these arguments. Many have blamed the Church's problems in the wake of the Council not on the Council itself, but on the failure of Pope Paul VI to carry through the reforms to which the Council was pointing: Catholics whose hopes for reform had been fired up by the Council, now left in droves as they found them disappointed.[20] Another line of argument, of which Wilhelm Damberg and Martine Sevegrand are leading exponents, focuses not so much on the merits or otherwise of the reforms envisaged at the Council as on their inevitability. They see the Council as an attempt to address the serious problems that the Church was already facing in the 1950s, especially the shortage of priests: the idea that the Church could have simply carried on as it was simply shows a lack of realism.[21]

Scholars writing in a more secular style have sometimes agreed with the religious conservatives in criticizing the modernizers. Thus Alan Gilbert who, as already mentioned, sees secularization as a very long-term process, nonetheless blames the specific crisis of the 1960s on the reformers, and especially John Robinson. *Honest to God*, he suggests, was 'a vital event in the making of post-Christian Britain'. According to Gilbert, all religious groups are, and are likely to remain, small minorities in the modern world. But those with the best survival chances are Evangelicals and, to a lesser extent conservative Catholics, who are able to establish tightly knit subcultures with highly distinctive and dogmatic beliefs and moral rules. Liberals like Robinson fatally opened the way for doubt and a massive growth in agnosticism. The debates which he sparked off enabled doubters 'actually to admit their unbelief' and alienated many of those who had accepted Christianity in a passive and unreflecting way. He quotes one ex-church-goer as saying that 'now the parsons are contradicting everything they have said'.[22]

Since this is an area where everyone—even those professing neutrality—has some kind of polemical agenda, I will say that my sympathies are with the church reformers and the theological modernizers. What they were trying to do was right, indeed necessary—which is not to say that the answers that they came up with were always convincing. However, I will argue that

---

[19] Ibid. 287, 315–24. Cf. Andrew Greeley, *The Catholic Revolution: New Wine, Old Wineskins and the Second Vatican Council* (Berkeley, Calif., 2004), 131–49.

[20] Ibid. 34–40.

[21] Martine Sevegrand, *Les enfants du bon Dieu: Les catholiques français et la procréation au XXe siècle* (Paris, 1995); Martine Sevegrand, *Vers une Église sans prêtres: La crise du clergé seculier en France* (Rennes, 2004); Wilhelm Damberg, *Abschied vom Milieu? Katholizismus im Bistum Münster und in den Niederlanden, 1945–1980* (Paderborn, 1997).

[22] Gilbert, *Post-Christian Britain*, 121–3, 133–57.

both reformers and traditionalists—and indeed the conflict between them—contributed in different ways to the crisis that the Christian churches faced in these years. Especially in the wake of Vatican II, hopes for change were raised to unrealistically high levels, only for disillusion to follow when it became clear that these hopes would not be realized; equally, many radicals, Catholic and even more Protestant, were too contemptuous of institutions, structures, and procedures, and their commitment to rapid and thorough-going change often led to intolerance of anyone who thought differently and a one-sided stress on the political to the neglect of other aspects of life. On the other hand, even more damage, at least in the Catholic Church, was done by those at the top or near the top. In particular, in spite of much that was admirable in the papacy of Paul VI, his two encyclicals *Sacerdotalis Caelibatus* and *Humanae Vitae* (reaffirming respectively compulsory clerical celibacy and the ban on contraceptives) have had disastrous effects, both short-term and long-term.

The Drivers of Change

One major difference is between scholars like Cholvy and Hilaire who see religious change being driven principally by developments within the religious world and those, like Brown, who see it as mainly the result of wider social changes. For Cholvy and Hilaire the 1960s were largely a tragedy and the villains of the piece were the over-zealous reformers. Brown, on the other hand is as enthusiastic as they are pessimistic. For him the 1960s mark a blissful dawn, and the heroines of his story are the millions of women (mostly young) who rejected the definitions of femininity, the moral rules, and the career options prescribed by the churches, and abandoned the task of passing on religious beliefs and customs to the younger generation.[23] The details of how and why this came about still need fuller elaboration. But Brown has identified a crucial dimension of religious change. Previous religious crises, like those of the 1790s or the late nineteenth century, influenced men much more than women and did not seriously affect the process by which religion was transmitted by women to the younger generation.[24] In the 1960s, for the first time, those rejecting religion included as many women as men. (More recently Brown has gone further: arguing that secularization is 'a woman's thing' and that those who have left the church include far more women than men.[25])

[23] Brown, *Death*, 176–9.
[24] Hugh McLeod, *Secularisation in Western Europe 1848–1914* (Basingstoke, 2000), 124–36.
[25] Callum Brown, lecture at Anglo-American Historical Conference, London, 6 July 2006.

Here Gilbert's position is in complete contrast to Brown's. While Brown consistently argues that gender has played a much bigger part than class in Britain's modern religious history, Gilbert ignores gender, while placing class close to the centre. For Gilbert a key part in secularization has been played by a 'dechristianized' working class. Since Gilbert's book was published in 1980 a flood of revisionist literature has questioned the extent of working-class dechristianization in the nineteenth century, or even in the twentieth. So it would be difficult for Gilbert today to present his case in quite such blunt terms. The argument is nonetheless an interesting one. He suggests that, although the British working class was thoroughly dechristianized in the nineteenth century, the full significance of this did not become apparent until the twentieth. With the advent of democracy after the First World War and then with rising working-class incomes since the Second World War, first politicians, and then advertisers, and especially newspapers and television, were forced to take the working class increasingly seriously. Right up to the 1960s the working class comprised the great majority of the British population. To stay in business, the mass media had to reflect the values of the largest part of their customers—including a lack of interest in religion, and (in the prosperous 1960s) an increasing hedonism. In so far as the mass media and the worlds of sport have an appeal that transcends differences of class, and have thus become the arbiters of national culture, irreligion and hedonism have become characteristic features of this national culture.[26]

In discussing more generally the background to the 1960s, Marwick reaches a similar conclusion by a different route. While he is careful to give weight to a range of factors, he suggests that the principal catalyst of change in the later 1950s and early 1960s was the emergence of a rebellious youth culture, focused above all on popular music, but also attuned to the latest fashions in clothes and ready to defy the restrictions placed by adults on sex or the use of drugs. He relates this to the fact that young people had more money in their pockets, with working-class youth having most, since they tended to start earning much earlier than their middle-class counterparts.[27] A somewhat similar argument is presented by Mark Edward Ruff, in explaining the decline of the Catholic subculture, and indeed of Catholicism, in such countries as West Germany, Switzerland, and the Netherlands. The 'Catholic milieu', he argues, was constructed in the second half of the nineteenth century as a defensive weapon against the dominant Protestants and Liberals. It became irrelevant as

---

[26] Gilbert, *Post-Christian Britain*, 86–94. The extensive revisionist literature on British working-class religion includes Brown, *Death*; S. C. Williams, *Religious Belief and Popular Culture in Southwark, c.1880–1939* (Oxford, 1999); Richard Sykes, 'Popular Religion in Dudley and the Gornals, c.1914–1965' (Ph.D. thesis, University of Wolverhampton, 1999).

[27] Marwick, *Sixties*, ch. 3.

Catholics entered the 'social mainstream' and even enjoyed political power, and the authoritarian leadership provided by the clergy was increasingly resented. With rising earnings in the 1950s, the availability of commercial alternatives to the activities provided by the church, and the emergence of a democratic and individualistic mentality focused on consumption, working-class youth became increasingly detached from the church, preparing the way for the later defection of other social groups.[28]

Most commentators on the United States would agree on the importance of youth in this period, but they usually identify the key agents of change as being middle-class youth, and especially students and young professionals. For these writers the most important factor in social change in this period was the expansion of higher education. The sociologist Robert Wuthnow showed that in the 1960s and early 1970s the drop in church-going was greatest among the college-educated. The college-educated were also more likely to have participated in the counter-culture or in new religious movements, to support such causes as women's rights or gay rights, and to reject a literalist understanding of the Bible. They thus pioneered new ways of thinking and behaving which filtered through more gradually to wider sections of the population.[29]

One thing which many writers in this field share, in spite of their numerous differences, is the search for a master-factor which will explain a cultural revolution that is both momentous and mysterious. I believe that this search is mistaken. The 1960s were explosive not because of one key ingredient, but precisely because so many currents of change, initially separate, interacted with one another. Most important was the impact of affluence, because the changing economic climate affected so many other aspects of people's lives, and opened up new possibilities. However, this affluence is not in itself a sufficient explanation of what happened in that decade. At least five other factors made an essential contribution to the story. There was the decline from the later 1950s of the ideologically based subcultures which had been central to life in many parts of Europe since the later nineteenth century. There was the theological radicalization beginning in the early 1960s. There was the 'sexual revolution', gathering pace from the mid-1960s. There was the political radicalization of the mid- and late 1960s, stimulated above all by opposition to the Vietnam War. There was women's search for greater freedom, self-fulfilment, and independence.

I will return to each of these themes later in the book. In the remainder of this chapter I will place the religious crisis of the 1960s in the context of longer term changes in Western religion and society.

---

[28] Ruff, *Wayward Flock*, 187–202.   [29] Wuthnow, *Restructuring*, 154–72.

LONG-TERM RELIGIOUS CHANGE

In 1968 a member of the German New Left and former theology student, Joachim Kahl, published a polemic entitled *Das Elend des Christentums* (an English translation was published by Penguin in 1971 with the title *The Misery of Christianity*). Kahl expressed surprise that Christianity had survived the criticisms of philosophers, scientists, and biblical scholars from the time of Voltaire onwards. He himself added little that was new to this critique, relying heavily on arguments drawn from Marx, Nietzsche, and Freud. The only original aspect of his book was a political attack, focusing on Christianity's social role rather than its intellectual viability, and highlighting especially Christian anti-Semitism and oppression of women. This illustrates a more general point about religious controversy and innovation in the 1960s. Most of the ideas that became fashionable in that decade were not new—indeed many of them went back to the early twentieth century, the nineteenth century, or even earlier. But the 1960s provided the social context in which ideas which had previously been relatively esoteric could gain a mass audience, and other ideas which had often been talked about but seldom practised could be made a reality.

The 1960s were a time when history moved faster, and in which a dynamic of change built up which old institutions and traditions were powerless to withstand. But this revolution did not come as a bolt from the blue. The ground was prepared by earlier changes, some relatively recent, others beginning much further in the past.

The most familiar interpretative framework for the history of religion in the modern West is that of a progressive secularization. The concept of secularization has been the subject of a large literature and of often intense debate, especially among sociologists, but to a lesser extent among historians and theologians too.[30] One fundamental divide is between those who use this concept to *explain* religious change, and those who use it merely to *describe* religious change. According to proponents of the 'secularization thesis' there is an intimate connection between processes of secularization and modernization, and there is a general tendency for religion to become increasingly marginalized in modern societies.[31] Others, including myself, have used 'secularization' as a useful descriptive terms to summarize religious trends since the later seventeenth century in the Western world, but have denied that the 'secularization thesis' provides a convincing explanation of how and why this has happened, or that examination of past trends enables us to predict the

---

[30] McLeod, *Secularisation*, 1–12.

[31] The classic statement is Peter Berger, *The Social Reality of Religion* (Harmondsworth, 1972)—though Berger himself now no longer accepts the secularization thesis. Other leading exponents include Dobbelaere and Bruce (see nn. 5 and 8 above).

religious future, either in Europe or in other parts of the world. Discussion of secularization has been bedevilled by the fact that the term has been used to mean quite different things: different understandings of secularization often reflect different understandings of religion. In my book, *Secularisation in Western Europe 1870–1914*, I distinguished between secularization at the level of individual belief and practice, at the social and political level, and at the cultural level. I argued that in the nineteenth century secularization was most in evidence at the individual level, reflected, for instance, in declining levels of church-going in many countries and in the growth of agnosticism, especially among intellectuals and political radicals. On the other hand, at the social and political level the picture was mixed, and at the cultural level secularization was very limited. I went on to suggest that in the first half of the twentieth century 'a fine balance between the forces of religion and secularity remained characteristic of western Europe' and that this continued until the 1960s. 'Only then did the balance tip more decisively in a secular direction.'[32]

   As this suggests, one way of placing and interpreting the religious history of the 1960s is to see the events of this time as part of a longer history of religious decline. However, there is no one uniquely valid way of telling the story of religion in the modern West. Different historical frameworks have their own strengths and limitations, and useful as the concept of secularization is when used in a sufficiently nuanced way, it has often obscured more than it has illuminated. First, secularization is a loaded word, and its use as an apparently neutral scientific term often conceals a polemical agenda. David Martin once made the famous claim that it was used as 'a tool of counter-religious ideologies'.[33] And while the term has by no means been used only by secularists, and indeed it has been deployed in aid of many other ideologies,[34] it is frequently far from neutral. Second, adoption of secularization as an interpretative key has often led to a one-sided emphasis on symptoms of religious decline to the exclusion of equally significant religious innovations. Third, what is categorized as 'secularization' may sometimes be better understood as 'religious change'. A good example is that of changing Christian attitudes to homosexuals and to the laws relating to homosexuality. One may argue as to whether these changes were justified, but, as I show in Chapter 10, to describe such changes as symptoms of secularization is at best a gross oversimplification and at worst another example of the use of an apparently neutral scientific term to conceal a polemical agenda. Fourth, there is the question

---

[32] McLeod, *Secularisation*, 13, 285–9.

[33] In his 1965 essay, 'Towards Eliminating the Concept of Secularisation', repr. in David Martin, *The Religious and the Secular* (London, 1969), 9.

[34] For instance in E. R. Norman, *Secularisation* (London, 2002), it is used in support of a conservative Christian critique of liberalism.

of how to interpret the growth of 'alternative spiritualities', as well as of non-Christian religions, in the later twentieth century. They may be taken as an aspect of dechristianization, but hardly of secularization—unless one adopts an artificially narrow definition of religion. While granting, then, that one way of placing the 1960s is as part of a longer term history of secularization, and that the concept of secularization remains a useful one if used in a sufficiently nuanced and discriminating way, it remains true that most historians and sociologists who have used secularization as an organizing concept have fallen into one or more of the traps mentioned above.

The historical framework which I have chosen here is that of 'the decline of Christendom'. This emphasizes a qualitative rather than a quantitive approach to the relationship between religion and society, and an emphasis on religious change as much as religious decline. This does not preclude discussion of secularization, and in later chapters I will indicate the important role which more secular ideals and lifestyles played in the 1960s. But it also allows both for the emergence of new forms of religion or spirituality beyond Christianity, and for the ways in which Christians tried to adapt to a changing society. Christian reform movements and Christian radicalism were indeed central aspects of the religious drama of the decade—though ones that are often trivialized, or even ignored, in those accounts which are focused on secularization.

The gradual decline of Christendom is one of the central themes in the history of western Europe and North America during the last three centuries.[35] Christendom may be described as a society were there are close ties between leaders of the church and secular elites; where the laws purport to be based on Christian principles; where, apart from certain clearly defined outsider communities, everyone is assumed to be Christian; and where Christianity provides a common language, shared alike by the devout and by the religiously lukewarm. In the 1940s and 1950s aspects of Christendom survived, though with varying degrees of vigour, in all parts of the Western world. But for more than two centuries there had been a process of erosion, as Christian doctrine and moral teachings faced significant challenge, as a variety of religious options became available, and new secular ideologies (sometimes with state backing) tried to take the place of Christianity and the church.

In the eighteenth century the states of western Europe and most of the European colonies in the Americas were confessionally based. In spite of constitutional differences, differences in social structure, and differences between

---

[35] See McLeod and Ustorf (eds.), *Decline of Christendom*. The following section is based on my own earlier work. For fuller elaboration, see my *Piety and Poverty: Working Class Religion in Berlin, London and New York, 1870–1914* (New York, 1996); *Religion and the People of Western Europe, 1789–1989* (Oxford, 1997); *Secularisation*; 'Introduction', in McLeod and Ustorf (eds.), *Decline of Christendom*, 1–26.

those that were Catholic, Lutheran, Reformed, or Anglican, there were major similarities between the religious situations in these countries. Nearly all had an established church, subject to considerable state controls, but also possessed of extensive powers and privileges, and a ubiquitous social presence. Such churches were protected by blasphemy laws, often by censorship, and by laws which excluded Christian minorities from public office and obstructed or even prohibited their worship and evangelism. In many countries there were laws requiring attendance at church and observance of Sunday or other religious holidays, or imposing penalties on those failing to receive communion. Jews also suffered disabilities of various kinds, and in a few cases were still confined to ghettos. Hierarchy and regulation were general characteristics of these societies, and by no means limited to religion. In large parts of Europe, landowning aristocracies dominated the lives of the countryside, and merchant patriciates the cities. Economic activity was frequently limited by guild monopolies. Sexual morality was controlled by church courts.

While the established churches were very powerful and levels of popular participation were high, there were, as at any time, areas of tension between clergy and laity, and between religious and secular values. Widespread anti-clericalism is to be expected in any society where the church is wealthy and influential, and resentment of the clergy is quite compatible with high levels of devotion. But more radical deviations from the church's teachings were also common. For instance, especially among the aristocracy, an overriding concern with personal and family honour was a powerful alternative to religiously based morality, and found expression in feuds, duels, and marriages based entirely on status or financial considerations. Equally contrary to any Christian ethic was the double standard of sexual morality, widely accepted and practised by upper class men. Among the poor the overriding concern was with survival, and this sometimes led to infanticide, as well as to theft and prostitution. 'Secularity' is an essential element of apparently very 'religious' societies, just as religion may play a significant part in apparently very secular societies.

The decline of Christendom has been a long drawn out process, and the historian can distinguish between several distinct stages. First there was the toleration by the state of a variety of forms of Christianity. Second there was the open publication of anti-Christian ideas. Third was the separation of church and state. The fourth and most complex stage has been the gradual loosening of the ties between church and society.

The first two of these changes were already taking place in the seventeenth and eighteenth centuries. *De facto* religious toleration allowed a variety of religious groups to flourish in seventeenth-century Holland, and the Act of Toleration of 1689 in England and Wales recognized that many Dissenting bodies were already in existence and that attempts to suppress them had failed. The abolition of censorship in England in 1694 was almost immediately followed by books of unorthodox theology. At about the same time underground literature of a similar kind began to circulate in France, though for another fifty years or so it could not be openly published in that country. In spite of continuing restrictions, deistic and later atheistic ideas spread widely in eighteenth-century Europe, though before 1789 they remained the preserve of small educated elites. However, the declining ability or willingness of the elites to enforce general attendance was already leading to a decline in churchgoing, at least in some countries or regions. The speed with which heterodox publishing or falling church attendance followed the relaxation of controls suggests that the religious unanimity of earlier periods had been deceptive: increased freedom inevitably led to greater religious pluralism.

The separation of church and state came first in the United States in 1791, with France and the Netherlands following in 1795 and 1796. In France church and state would be reunited in 1801, but in the second half of the nineteenth century separation became a normal part of Radical, and later Socialist, programmes. It was enacted in Ireland in 1869, in France in 1905, Geneva in 1907, Portugal in 1911, Germany in 1919, Wales in 1920, and Spain in 1931. In spite of the great symbolic significance which has often attached to the relationship between church and state, the formal relationship has been less significant than the practical relationship in areas such as education and welfare. Even more important have been the different ways in which religion and the churches have related to the processes of political and social emancipation.

Since the French Revolution of 1789 the central theme of European history has been emancipation from the old social order, based on hierarchy, privilege, and the regulation of every area of life. Religion and secularization have been integral parts of the story. This emancipation was at first and for long mainly collective. Subordinate social groups and religious or ethnic minorities claimed the rights of full citizenship. They formed political parties and pressure groups, and published their own newspapers. They organized mass meetings and demonstrations, and took part in riots or even uprisings. First the middle class, and then workers, the lower middle class, and peasants challenged the political order that privileged a tiny elite. Jews and Christian minorities challenged the privileges of established churches and the link between citizenship and religious orthodoxy. From about the 1860s women began to challenge their exclusion from the public sphere. The nineteenth century and the first half of the twentieth was an era of organizations, of banners, of charismatic orators, of marches through the streets with bands playing and flags flying. It was a time when large numbers of people found their sense of who they were, their concept of the good life, their hopes for the future, embodied in churches, freethought societies, political parties, or trade unions—or in a combination of these, since such organizations were often linked with one another.

Political change was closely bound up with social and economic change. Beginning in the late eighteenth century, first Britain, and then every other west European country, was transformed by mechanized industry, a revolution in communications, and the growth of cities. These developments presented established churches, deeply rooted in the old order, with enormous challenges, and potentially they prepared the way for sweeping religious change. However, nothing was inevitable. Emancipation from the old order took very different forms in different countries, and in particular the role of religion varied considerably. One can, for instance, distinguish between societies that were (*a*) polarized, (*b*) pillarized, (*c*) pluralist, or (*d*) characterized by religious nationalism. These differences had their roots in the early modern period, and especially in the religious order established in the aftermath of the Reformation and the 'religious' wars of the sixteenth and seventeenth centuries.

In 'polarized' societies, of which the classic example would be France, emancipation from the old order came to be identified with militant secularism. The result in the nineteenth century was a polarization between those social groups and regions which remained loyal to the Catholic Church and those which rejected it. Levels of mobilization on both sides were exceptionally high, so that for instance France included areas with some of the highest and others with the lowest levels of church-going in western Europe. At least up to the time of the First World War, Catholics and secularists each aspired to remake the nation in their own image. Each regarded the other as 'the enemy'. This confrontation took even more extreme and very violent forms in Spain.

In 'pillarized' societies, such as the Netherlands, with four or five major religious or anti-religious groups, none strong enough to dominate the others, emancipation came through the formation of Protestant, Catholic, and Socialist subcultures, each with its own institutions, each dominant in particular districts or regions, but each compelled at the national level to negotiate with one another and to reach some degree of compromise. These, together with the Liberals, were the 'pillars' holding up the Dutch state and society— each separate, but each contributing to supporting the structure. In the Netherlands, though the link between secularism and progressive politics was less clear-cut than in France, most Socialists and many Liberals were also secularists.

In 'pluralist' societies, such as Great Britain, Nonconformist religion became the principal agent of emancipation. Although Dissenters continued to face certain forms of discrimination, and this helped to keep their political radicalism alive, they had been free to organize and to build their own places of worship from 1689 in England and Wales and from 1712 in Scotland. By 1851 Protestant Dissenters accounted for 80 per cent of those attending church services in Wales, 60 per cent in Scotland, and 44 per cent in England. They had a key role in Liberal politics, and in certain industries they were leaders in the formation of trade unions. They also had an important influence on the emerging Labour Party in the early twentieth century. From the 1790s onwards British radicalism also had a significant secularist wing, but by comparison with the huge numbers of Methodists and other Nonconformist Protestants, this was very much a minority option, and often highly localized. On the other hand it was probably easier in a 'pluralist' society than in one that was 'polarized' or 'pillarized' to be more or less neutral. There were many areas of nineteenth-century Britain where nearly everyone belonged at least nominally to a Christian denomination, but church attendance was low.

Religious nationalism was especially characteristic of eastern Europe, with its multinational monarchies, in which the numerous subject peoples often claimed the support of their church for the national cause, and found their national identity most strongly expressed in their religion with its saints and its sacred sites. A similar situation existed in Ireland, where nationalism was closely linked with Catholicism and loyalism with Protestantism. In such situations, secularism tended to be marginalized, and the situation of religious minorities could also become problematic, as they could be seen as being outside the religiously defined nation.

The degree to which collective emancipation promoted secularization or intensified religious loyalties thus varied considerably from country to country. The link between emancipation and secularization was strongest in 'polarized' countries. It was weakest in those countries where religious nationalism was the dominant political force. In 'pillarized' and 'pluralist' societies there was an intermediate situation, with secularism as one means of emancipation, but generally less significant than Protestant Dissent or a revitalized Catholicism.

In the United States and in the British settler colonies of Canada, Australia, and New Zealand, the political situation was different. For instance there was no aristocracy, and there either was no monarch, or else she was living thousands of miles away. By the later nineteenth century church and state had been formally separated in all these countries. Manhood suffrage came early and New Zealand, Australia, and some American states were pioneers in women's suffrage. Many of the issues which impassioned European Liberals were of limited relevance in North America or Australasia. Moreover the racial diversity of these countries was a fundamental area of difference from Europe. Yet all of these countries, including the United States, had a lot in common religiously with the British Isles from which so many settlers had come. There were similarities between the religious nationalism in Quebec and in Ireland. The religious pluralism and sectarianism of English-speaking Canada, the United States, Australia, and New Zealand had much in common with that of Great Britain as well as of the north of Ireland. The United States stood apart both in its extreme ethnic diversity and in the religious inventiveness of the people. Yet there was also much that they shared religiously with the other English-speaking countries, especially in the case of those belonging to Protestant denominations of British origin, such as the Episcopalians, Presbyterians, Congregationalists, Methodists, and Baptists.[36]

Except where it was propelled by a militantly secularist ideology, the secularization of public institutions in nineteenth- and twentieth-century Europe was a slow, uneven, and far from universal process. In the nineteenth century the classic example of ideological secularism was France between 1879 and 1914. In these years the dominant Republicans, as well as separating church and state in 1905, stopped religious teaching in state schools, banned members of religious orders from teaching even in private schools, exiled the members of some orders, removed religious symbols from public places, and discriminated against practising Catholics in public employment. Twentieth-century examples include the secularizing programmes of the Portuguese and Spanish Republicans, and of the Nazis and, later, Communists in Germany.

In the longer run, even governments not motivated by secularist ideology have had a tendency to extend their powers into areas formerly controlled by the church, whether in response to demands for equity between different religious communities, or because of the belief that only the state has sufficient resources to provide an adequate system of education or welfare. In England, for instance, one can speak of a 'creeping secularization' in the later nineteenth and early twentieth centuries as central or local government gradually replaced the churches in many areas. On the other hand, governments may deliberately assign churches a significant role in the education or welfare system, in the hope that they will promote social harmony, build up national morale, or foster civic virtues.

In Germany church and state were separated in 1919, but until then the relationship had been as close as in England. Even after separation, the Protestant and Catholic churches retained important privileges. In particular, the two 'big' churches in Germany were much stronger financially than the many

[36] Richard Carwardine, 'Religion and Politics in Nineteenth-Century Britain: The Case Against American Exceptionalism', in Mark Noll (ed.), *Religion and American Politics: From the Colonial Period to the 1980s* (New York, 1990), 225–52; George A. Rawlyk and Mark A. Noll (eds.), *Amazing Grace: Evangelicalism in Australia, Britain, Canada, and the United States* (Montreal and Kingston, Ontario, 1994).

smaller churches in England. This was partly because of the 'church tax' system in many German states in the later nineteenth century, whereby a proportion of income tax went to the tax-payer's church. As a result the churches were able to build up an extensive network of hospitals, orphanages, parish nurses, social workers, and so on, with subsidies from local authorities.

There was thus no irresistible logic leading to institutional secularization on the French model. The role of religion in public institutions already varied widely in the later nineteenth century, and there was further divergence with the growth of democracy in the twentieth century. In some countries, such as Ireland or the Netherlands, or Italy after 1945, a mainly church-going electorate was able to vote into power parties favourable to the church. (The enfranchisement of women played a part in strengthening Christian Democracy after the Second World War.)

Moving from the political dimensions of religion and the churches to their broader social role, there are three areas in which we can see a long-term trend away from an explicitly Christian society towards one in which a variety of other beliefs and value-systems have a significant influence.

First there was the emergence of rival systems of belief. Religious heterodoxy was popularized in the 1790s, and it spread more widely from about the 1850s onwards. During the second half of the nineteenth century an increasingly wide range of world-views became available to the mass of the population, rather than being limited to small intellectual elites. In 1900, and indeed in 1950, Christianity was still the greatest influence on the world-view of the majority of people. But at least four major alternatives had a significant following. First, there was science. Of course many eminent scientists were themselves religious believers. The two world-views were not mutually exclusive. But there were also those like the German medical scientist, Rudolf Virchow, who claimed in 1860 that the sciences had taken the place of the church, and in 1865 that 'science has become a religion for us'. This view was particularly attractive to middle-class Liberals like Virchow, who believed that through science and education most of humanity's problems could be solved without the need for any kind of social revolution. The German zoologist, Ernst Haeckel, wrote an international bestseller, *The Riddle of the Universe* (1899), which was one of several popular books published at the time arguing that science held the key to the understanding of the world and had thus superseded all forms of supernatural religion. In the 1960s faith in science was still very much alive, though now it was the human and social sciences which carried the highest hopes. Sociologists, economists, and psychologists were the new gurus. Second, there was Socialism, which in the Germany of the 1870s was compared to the Protestant revivals of earlier decades. By the early twentieth century, Socialism had a large and often passionate following in working-class communities in most of western Europe. In Germany there was a huge subculture based on the Social Democratic Party. Full integration into this milieu required rejection of the churches and adoption of Socialism as a complete world-view—though most Socialist voters continued to keep a foot in both camps. In the 1960s expectations of world transformation through Socialism briefly reached a new high—though the new believers were students and young professionals, rather than factory workers.

Two other kinds of alternative faith won a significant following in these years. First, there was belief in salvation through art, literature, and music. This was especially typical of the educated middle class in Germany, and it appealed to women as much as to men. Here Beethoven, Wagner, and, above all, Goethe and Schiller, acquired the status of prophets. Their writings provided the basis for a religion of freedom, self-fulfilment, creativity, and belief in humanity. Their equivalents in the 1960s were popular singers, such as Bob Dylan, whose songs were treated with a reverence similar to that accorded by nineteenth-century Germans to the poems of Goethe and Schiller. Second, there was what might be termed a 'spiritualist' current, which influenced people in all social classes in the later nineteenth century. They were looking for a 'third way' between orthodox religion and orthodox science, both of which they regarded as excessively rigid and dogmatic. They usually believed in God, but not necessarily the God of Christianity and Judaism. They were open to the influence of Eastern religions, and they also believed that there were powers inherent in human beings which had been lost with their increasing distance from nature. The vogue for Hinduism in the 1960s can in fact be traced back to the later nineteenth century and to such figures as Madame Blavatsky, who in 1875 founded Theosophy and in 1879 made a pilgrimage to India; it goes back also to the World's Parliament of Religions in Chicago in 1893.

By the second half of the nineteenth century Christianity and Judaism were thus in an increasingly competitive situation in which rival views of the world and rival systems of ethics were making themselves heard and attracting a significant following. This was reflected in declining levels of attendance at church and participation in religious rites, though the extent to which this happened, and its chronology, varied considerably from country to country. The patterns cannot be correlated in any straightforward way with levels of modernization. In France there were by the later nineteenth century huge regional differences in the degree to which people practised the Catholic faith. At one extreme there were many parts of Brittany where over 90 per cent of the population went to church every Sunday. At the other extreme, there were equally remote and 'backward' areas of the Limousin where less than 5 per cent of the adult population went to church and where in many villages no men did so. In Germany there were big differences between Protestants and Catholics.

The Protestant church suffered a crisis in many parts of Germany in the 1860s and 1870s. In 1881 one clergyman claimed that Berlin was regarded as 'the most irreligious city in the world'. On the other hand, the Catholic Church in Germany was much more successful in retaining the loyalty of its members, and levels of Catholic religious practice remained high until after the Second World War.

Political and social factors conditioned the climate in which these new ideas were received, as did the ecclesiastical structure of each country and the strategies adopted by the various churches. Over western Europe as a whole the group most alienated from the churches was the working class—especially in the cities and in mining districts, but sometimes in rural areas too. In some cases this was because of the adoption of Socialism or Anarchism as a rival 'religion'. More often it reflected consciousness of a separate working-class identity, leading to resentment of other classes and of links between churches and employers. Or it might simply reflect the constraints imposed by poverty, in which the struggle for survival took precedence. Again, all of this had little to do with modernity or modernization. Alienation from the church took its most extreme forms in some of the most backward regions of western Europe, such as southern Spain. Political and social factors also played a part in the varying middle-class receptivity to religious heterodoxy. For instance, in Germany the main proponents of the materialist and anti-religious science fashionable in the 1850s were political liberals and radicals who regarded the churches as strongholds of conservatism and wanted to undermine their influence. As a result, the ground was well prepared for the reception of Darwinism in the 1860s, and for many years Darwinist influence was stronger in Germany than in England, where middle-class Liberals were often devout members of Nonconformist chapels. In Germany secularization was linked with urbanization, and though there were certainly 'irreligious' rural areas, urban culture was markedly more secular than that of the countryside. In Britain no such sharp contrasts can be drawn. Most cities had a flourishing religious life, and although in England average levels of church-going were somewhat higher in rural areas, in Scotland the average was higher in the towns.

A second area where the influence of the church was potentially undermined was the rise of professions claiming exclusive jurisdiction over certain areas of life because of their unique expertise, and often using a specialist language incomprehensible to outsiders. The clergy gradually found their own sphere of competence narrowed down, as 'experts' took over many of the areas where priests and pastors had once been the main authorities. Religious heterodoxy could gain a willing audience in certain emerging professions, which found themselves in rivalry with the clergy, either because their fields of competence overlapped, or because of the pretensions of the clergy to regulate their activities. Frank Turner has shown that the professionalization of science was a key dimension of the 'conflict between science and religion' in Victorian Britain.[37] An even more striking example was the teaching profession in France. With the secularization of the French school system in 1882, the teacher took on the role of missionary for the Republic in the countryside. In thousands of French villages, priest and teacher were locked in battle—each trying to shape the mentality and the morality of the common people, and to undermine the influence of the other. In the 1960s a questionnaire sent to thousands of retired French teachers who had been in schools before 1914 found that only 11 per cent had been church-goers during that period, while 32 per cent had been freethinkers.[38]

While priest and teacher disagreed radically on theology and politics, they were often much closer in their views on questions of ethics, and especially sexual ethics, which were of more immediate concern to many of their parishioners or pupils. Priest and teacher were likely to agree on the central importance of morality, of clearly defined moral rules, and of self-discipline. They were likely to agree on marriage, the family and work as foundations of a healthy society, on the fact that the proper place for sex was within marriage, and on the dangers of drunkenness and gambling. However, important changes of thinking about morality, and especially about sex, were beginning around the end of the nineteenth century, and this is the third area where the relationship between church and society was gradually loosening. These changes would ultimately have a huge influence on the thinking and behaviour of wide sections of the population—culminating in the 1960s.

One aspect of this was the reaction against 'puritanism', against 'cant', or against what came to be called 'Victorianism'.[39] 'Victorianism' had been most powerful in the English-speaking and the Nordic countries, and it was there that this reaction was most virulent in the period from about 1890, as novelists and dramatists, such as Ibsen, Strindberg, and Shaw, artists, such as Munch, and journalists led the assault on what were seen as the taboos, the rigid and repressive morality and the stifling social conventions that had regulated large areas especially of middle-class life in the nineteenth century. While 'puritanism' had never been as powerful in Germany or France, Germans such

[37] Frank M. Turner, *Contesting Cultural Authority: Essays in Victorian Intellectual Life* (Cambridge, 1993).

[38] McLeod, *Secularisation*, 109.

[39] This paragraph is based on Hugh McLeod, *Class and Religion in the Late Victorian City* (London, 1974), 254–5; Cate Haste, *Rules of Desire: Sex in Britain. World War I to the Present* (London, 1992); Marcus Collins, *Modern Love: An Intimate History of Men and Women in Twentieth-Century Britain* (London, 2003); Hera Cook, *The Long Sexual Revolution: English Women, Sex and Contraception* (Oxford, 2004).

as Wedekind and above all Nietzsche were among the most outspoken critics. Bernard Shaw in 1891 defined the leitmotiv of this literature as 'acceptance of the impulse to greater freedom as sufficient ground for the repudiation of any customary duty, however, sacred that conflicts with it'. For a variety of reasons, religious, political, and above all economic, relatively few people were yet ready for this message. But a process had started by which the thinking at least of the well-educated or well-to-do was gradually changing. In 1894 one of the lesser known prophets of anti-puritanism, the English novelist Grant Allen, coined the term 'The New Hedonism' to define his creed, and he identified sex as a crucial area of debate. Certainly the most controversial aspect of the work of such professional iconoclasts as Ibsen, Shaw, or Wedekind, as well as the more restrained Thomas Hardy, was their questioning of conventional sexual mores. The literary attacks coincided with pioneering scientific researches which would have an equally powerful long-term influence. As was most often the case in the nineteenth century, the German-speaking countries led the way in pioneering new areas of research. Sexologists and psychoanalysts changed the thinking first of the educated middle class and more gradually of wider sections of the population, both by establishing the central part played by sexuality in human psychology and by revising conceptions of 'normal' sexual behaviour. Freud was the biggest single influence on the thinking of the educated middle class in most Western countries from the 1920s to the 1950s. As Auden wrote at Freud's death in 1939, 'To us he is no more a person Now but a whole climate of opinion, Under whom we conduct our differing lives'.[40] Christian thinking struggled to keep pace with the changes which were under way from about the 1880s and were moving fast by the 1920s. By this time the avant-garde of Christian opinion recognized the importance of sex as part of a happy marital relationship, rather than simply as the means for producing children, and accordingly favoured open discussion of sex, the use of contraceptives, and the elimination of the continuing sense of shame and prudery. The evidence collected by Kinsey in the 1940s suggested that the 1920s had seen an increase in pre-marital sex in the United States, which continued in subsequent decades.[41] The same period also saw the beginnings of a more sympathetic attitude to homosexuality, though this change was very slow and gradual, and the whole subject was still surrounded with taboos. And it was in 1927 that Wilhelm Reich's *The Function of the Orgasm*, which was to be a key text of the 'sexual revolution' was first published in Germany. Once again the 1960s provided the context in which much older ideas could come

---

[40] 'In Memory of Sigmund Freud', in W. H. Auden, *Collected Shorter Poems, 1927–1957* (London, 1969), 168.

[41] Christie Davies, *Permissive Britain* (London, 1975), 9–11.

fully into their own. Gradual processes of change over a much longer period of time provided the long-term preconditions for the more rapid changes in that decade

CONCLUSION

In the 1950s the great majority of people living in Western countries were nominally Christian; the majority of the younger generation were still being socialized into membership of a Christian society; links between religious and secular elites were often close. Yet the foundations on which the edifice of Christendom was built were far from solid. A small but influential section of the population had broken away entirely from Christianity, including many intellectuals, writers, and political radicals. There was a much larger section of the population, including a large part of the working class, whose involvement in the church was limited to participation in rites of passage. There was a growing tension between the sexual ethics taught by the churches and the messages which had been coming over several decades from literature and films and from the writings of psychologists; there was also a wide, and probably increasing, divergence, between church teaching and what people, including church-goers, were actually doing.

The ground was already well prepared for the crisis of Christendom in the 1960s. The most important of the immediate precipitants of the crisis was the wide-ranging impact of the unprecedented affluence enjoyed by most Western countries from the later 1950s. In particular the new economic and social climate had major effects on political parties as well as churches, in that it favoured a trend towards greater individualism and weakened the collective identities which had been central to the processes of social emancipation in the nineteenth century and the first half of the twentieth. The powerful ideologically based subcultures which had been a central feature of life in most Western countries since the later nineteenth century were, by the 1950s, beginning to seem both oppressive and indeed redundant. This affected Communist and Socialist parties as much as Catholic or Protestant churches, and the former often suffered a more severe drop in membership. However, high wages, full employment, and the mass production of what had formerly been luxury items, changed people's thinking and behaviour in many different ways, sometimes directly, but very often indirectly.

But to understand the unique atmosphere of the 1960s one also has to take account of specific events and movements. In particular, three stand out as being of pivotal significance in the political and religious radicalization and polarization during that decade, namely the US Civil Rights Movement, the Vietnam War, and the Second Vatican Council. Even if none of these had happened, the economic and social changes would in any case have had far-reaching consequences. But the utopian hopes of some and the militant conservatism of others, the atmosphere of intense expectation alternating with bitter despair, gave the 1960s their unique flavour, and helped to define the distinctive character of the religious crisis.

2

Late Christendom

In the 1940s and 1950s it was still possible to think of western Europe and North America as a 'Christendom', in the sense that there were close links between religious and secular elites, that most children were socialized into membership of a Christian society, and that the church had a large presence in fields such as education and welfare, and a major influence on law and morality. That did not mean that all, or even most of the population were devout believers: this chapter will look at the wide-ranging role played by Christianity and the churches in Western societies in the 1940s and 1950s, but will also consider the limits of their influence and the new challenges which they were facing.

WORLD WAR AND COLD WAR

In June 1940 it seemed that Hitler was on the brink of becoming master of Europe. During the previous two months Germany had invaded Belgium, the Netherlands, Denmark, and Norway. Now France had agreed to humiliating peace terms. At this greatest crisis in the nation's history, the United Kingdom's new Prime Minister, Winston Churchill, declared: 'The Battle of Britain is about to begin. Upon this battle depends the survival of Christian civilisation.' Churchill was not himself a professing Christian, though he claimed to act as a flying buttress on the edifice of the Church of England—supporting it from outside.[1] But this identification of the British cause with the cause of Christianity had become a commonplace, proclaimed in public and in private, by doubters as well as by believers, by politicians, generals, and journalists, as much as by churchmen. No one made the connection more frequently or with greater conviction than Britain's principal military commander, Field-Marshal Bernard Montgomery.[2] It was also a central theme of British propaganda. Thus the Religious Division of the Ministry of Information had

---

[1] Keith Robbins, *History, Religion and Identity in Modern Britain* (London, 1993), 195.

[2] Michael Snape, *God and the British Soldier: Religion and the British Army in the First and Second World Wars* (London, 2005), 72–6.

the task of imparting 'a real conviction of the Christian contribution to our civilisation and of the essential anti-Christian character of Nazism'. Meanwhile the British Broadcasting Corporation (BBC) increased by several times the number of radio programmes devoted to religious topics (while excluding any speaker who was known to be a pacifist).[3] Christianity, it was hoped, would give comfort to the anxious and the bereaved and would strengthen the waverers in their belief in the national cause. It could also point to the possibility of a new and better world that would be built after the war was over.

The war years were full of schemes for a new national and international order. The most widely read contribution to this debate was *Christianity and the Social Order* (1942), by William Temple, who had recently become archbishop of Canterbury, but would not live to see the post-war extension of the welfare state which he had advocated. Temple was also one of many who were calling for a greater emphasis on religion in the nation's education system. In 1940 *The Times* had called for a 'national system of education which is definitely Christian' and which would produce 'Christian children who in due course will become Christian parents'.[4] The 1944 Education Act made religious education a compulsory part of the curriculum in state schools (subject to a conscience clause, allowing individuals to opt out), and also decreed that the school day should begin with an act of common worship.[5]

Some of the same discussions were taking place in Germany at this time—though obviously in strict secrecy. Thus the Kreisau Circle, which brought together anti-Nazi politicians and intellectuals of varying political, religious, and social backgrounds, agreed on the important role of a revitalized Christianity in a new post-Hitler Germany.[6] Like other dreamers and plotters in Nazi Germany most members of this circle fell victims to Hitler's hangmen. But with the fall of the Nazis and the Allied occupation of Germany, many Christians believed that the time of 'rechristianisation' had come.[7] In the years immediately following the war the churches enjoyed considerable prestige and influence in Germany, and they were determined to take advantage of

---

[3] Kenneth Wolfe, *The Politics of Religious Broadcasting* (Canterbury, 1984), 10–11.

[4] Robbins, *History, Religion and Identity*, 202.

[5] Gerald Parsons, 'There and Back Again? Religion and the 1944 and 1988 Education Acts', in Parsons and Wolffe (eds.), *Religious Diversity*, ii. 165–9.

[6] Terence Prittie, *Germans Against Hitler* (London 1964), 212–18.

[7] Martin Greschat, *Die evangelische Christenheit und die deutsche Geschichte nach 1945: Weichenstellungen in der Nachkriegszeit* (Stuttgart, 2002), 310–14; Damian van Melis, ' "Strengthened and Purified through Ordeal by Fire": Ecclesiastical Triumphalism in the Ruins of Europe', in Bessell and Schumann (eds.), *Life After Death*, 231–41.

this situation. The leadership of the Catholic Church was even in a self-congratulatory mood: they had survived the Nazis, while keeping their distance from and even on occasion being critical of the regime. In the British and American zones the churches enjoyed the support of the occupying authorities, as both British and American officials tended to believe that Christianity and democracy were synonymous and that strong churches would provide a firm foundation for the new Germany; at the same time the churches gained credit with their own people by protests against abuses or unpopular policies by the occupiers.[8] A pastoral letter from the Catholic bishops immediately after the end of the war declared that the only hope for Germany lay in a return to God's commands and a conversion of society as well as of individuals. Similarly many Protestant leaders denied the possibility of establishing a stable moral order on secular foundations: Nazism was a supreme example of the evil consequences of secularization. Education was seen as one crucial arena, and there was much discussion of the need to strengthen the quantity and quality of religious teaching in schools. Women would also have a crucial role in the home in bringing up the new generation as Christians.[9]

And across large parts of Europe, as the German occupation ended and the process of reconstruction began, Christian parties emerged as major political players. The period from about 1945 to 1965 was the golden age of Christian Democracy. Confessional parties had for long had a leading political role in Belgium and the Netherlands. In the post-war era Christian Democratic Parties dominated the politics of Italy and West Germany, and for a time had an important place in France. The success of the Christian Democratic *Mouvement républicain populaire* was relatively brief, but more significant was the accepted role which Catholics enjoyed in French public life, including a range of political parties, after the sixty years of discrimination which they had faced under the Third Republic.[10] Meanwhile, in Italy, even the Communist Party believed that it was politically necessary to accept a privileged role for the Catholic Church in the post-Fascist era. The new Italian constitution, voted in 1946, retained the ban on divorce enacted by Mussolini and the role of the church in the education system.[11]

In 1947 and 1948, as the split between Europe's Soviet-dominated east and American-dominated west became increasing clear-cut, the role of Christianity and the churches as an integral part of Western identity was further emphasized. The cold war, as Dianne Kirby points out, was also a religious

---

[8] Greschat, *Evangelische Christenheit*, 30–40.   [9] Ibid. 310–14.

[10] Gérard Cholvy and Yves-Marie Hilaire (eds.), *Histoire religieuse de la France contemporaine 1930–1988* (Toulouse, 1988), 127–37.

[11] A. C. Jemolo, *Church and State in Italy, 1850–1950* (English tr. Oxford, 1960; 1st publ. 1955), 291–304.

war.[12] In the United Kingdom, which had no confessional parties, and where many of the ministers in Attlee's Labour government were agnostics, Foreign Secretary Ernest Bevin attached a lot of importance to gaining support from the churches for his anti-Communist policies.[13] In Italy, the 1948 election was above all a battle between the Communist Party and the Catholic Church. Pope Pius XII, in spite of earlier reservations about the new party, gave emphatic support to the Christian Democrats, who emerged with 48 per cent of the votes. That same year saw a record number of Marian apparitions in Italy, some of which led to well-publicized conversions of Communists, though the attitude of church authorities to these reported visions was often ambivalent. While being potentially a weapon in the battle against the Communists, they also gave status and influence to uneducated lay people who were not under effective church control, and many of whom were in the church's eyes 'bad Catholics'.[14]

Not only did Christianity gain a higher political profile in these years: there were also signs of a wider Christian reawakening. These signs were most evident in the United States, where the years between about 1945 and 1960 were known as the time of 'the religious revival'. Will Herberg wrote in 1955: 'Whether we judge by religious identification, church membership, or church attendance, whether we go by the best-seller lists, the mass media, or the writings of intellectuals, the conclusion is the same: there is every sign of a notable "turn to religion" among the American people today'.[15] Herberg's intention was not to celebrate the revival, but to point out its ambiguities and limits. We will return to those later. But at this stage I want to emphasize that most people at the time thought they were living through a religious revival, that the signs of this revival were highly visible, and that some of the same phenomena were to be seen in many other Western countries.

The most obvious signs of this revival were the facts that more and more churches were being built and that more people were worshipping in these churches. According to the Gallup polls 38 per cent of Americans questioned in 1946 claimed to have attended a service in church or synagogue during the previous week; this figure then gradually rose to peak at 49 per cent in

[12] Dianne Kirby, 'Religion and the Cold War: An Introduction', in Kirby (ed.), *Religion and the Cold War* (Basingstoke, 2003), 1.

[13] Philip Coupland, 'Western Union, "Spiritual Union", and European Integration, 1948–51', *Journal of British Studies*, 43 (2004), 366–94.

[14] William Christian Jr, 'Religious Apparitions and the Cold War in Southern Europe', in Eric R. Wolf (ed.), *Religion, Power and Protest in Local Communities: The Northern Shore of the Mediterranean* (Berlin, 1984), 239–66.

[15] Will Herberg, *Protestant, Catholic, Jew: An Essay in American Religious Sociology* (2nd edn. Garden City, NY, 1960; 1st publ. 1955), 2.

1955.[16] The church-building boom was an integral part of the massive shift of population to the suburbs during the same period. Meanwhile politicians were making displays of piety that reflected the new national mood. In 1952, General Eisenhower decided that if he was to run for president he needed a religion, and announced that he was a Presbyterian. In 1954 Congress agreed to inscribe the words 'In God we trust' on the currency. Religious intellectuals, of whom the most famous was Reinhold Niebuhr of New York's Union Theological Seminary, enjoyed a high profile at this time, and it has been argued that the 1950s was the last period in which theologians were generally recognized public figures.[17] In 1950 *Partisan Review* had published a symposium on 'Religion and the Intellectuals'. Referring to 'the new turn towards religion among intellectuals and the growing disfavor with which secular attitudes and perspectives are regarded in not a few circles that lay claim to the leadership of culture', the editor added that 'at present many thinkers sound an insistent note of warning that Western civilization cannot hope to survive without the re-animation of religious values'. A sceptical contributor to the symposium added that 'religion now has its fellow-travellers', who, though not personally convinced, believed that religion helped to produce a healthy society.[18] As the reference to 'Western civilization' suggests, part of the context was the threat to this civilization posed first by Nazi Germany and then by Soviet Communism. As Silk argues, two accompanying considerations contributed to the mood of the times. One was the fear of nuclear annihilation: Silk, borrowing from W. H. Auden, calls the 1940s an 'Age of Anxiety'. Second, there was a resulting decline in faith in progress, and a corresponding vogue for the Neo-Orthodox theologians, whose stark realism rang true to the experience of that generation.[19]

Even bigger was the impact of popular preachers like the evangelist Billy Graham, the Catholic radio bishop Fulton J. Sheen, or the provider of 'peace of mind', Norman Vincent Peale. Peale was only one of several writers who mixed insights from theology and psychology in providing reassurance to a troubled generation. Graham had been catapulted to fame by the Los Angeles Crusade of 1949, assisted by the Hearst newspapers, instructed by their owner to 'Puff Graham'—apparently because of his value as an anti-Communist. After a false start with Harry Truman, Graham established a rapport with Eisenhower— and, to his subsequent regret, struck up a long-lasting relationship with

---

[16] Dean Hoge, *Commitment on Campus: Changes in Religion and Values over Five Decades* (Philadelphia, 1974), 166.

[17] Patrick Allitt, *Religion in America since 1945: A History* (New York, 2003), 26–31.

[18] Mark Silk, *Spiritual Politics: Religion and America since World War II* (New York, 1988), 31.

[19] Ibid. 22–39.

Richard Nixon.[20] Whether or not Graham had any success in influencing their policies, he was able to establish a mutually advantageous relationship with successive presidential candidates and presidents, whereby their friendship with the evangelist helped to secure their credentials as Christians and men of integrity, while their recognition of him helped to confirm the belief that being religious was part of being a good American. As Silk suggests, Graham's unique popularity arose not only from his personal charisma and from the celebrity status endowed by the media, but also from certain specific features of his message. He acknowledged the fears of his audiences that America faced multiple dangers both from without and from within, and yet he was also a patriot, who thanked God for 'this greatest nation on earth', and he promised that each individual conversion would play its part in the redemption of the nation.[21]

At the height of the post-war church-going boom in 1957, young people in their twenties were going to church slightly more often than their elders—a situation in glaring contrast to the one that would emerge in the 1960s and 1970s. In the early and middle 1950s religious activity was increasing on university campuses and students were also becoming more orthodox in their beliefs. The *New York Times* in 1955 and *Newsweek* in 1957 both ran features on the religious boom on campus. The University of Michigan, which asked new students about their religious affiliation, found that the proportion claiming an affiliation had risen from 68 per cent in 1924 to 78 per cent in 1952–5—before dropping very fast to 40 per cent in 1968.[22]

While the increase in church-going was probably biggest in the United States, many other aspects of the religious boom were duplicated elsewhere. In the 1950s new churches were springing up everywhere. In many parts of Europe this was primarily an attempt to make good the damage done by wartime bombing. But these were also the years of the 'baby-boom', when every family that could afford it was moving into bigger accommodation, and new housing estates were being built on the outskirts of the cities, with every gradation of amenity, from privately owned detached houses with large gardens, to the most basic municipal flat. In Canada and Australia, where the population was swollen by immigrants from Europe, the church-building boom in these years was as conspicuous as in the United States.[23] In the Nordic

[20] William Martin, *The Billy Graham Story: A Prophet with Honour* (London, 1991), 117–18, 131–2, 146–9, 208–10, and *passim*.

[21] Silk, *Spiritual Politics*, 68.

[22] Robert Wuthnow, *Experimentation in American Religion: The New Mysticisms and their Implications for the Churches* (Berkeley, Calif., 1978), 130–1; Hoge, *Campus*, 51, 140–1.

[23] David Hilliard, 'The Religious Culture of Australian Cities in the 1950s', *Hispania Sacra*, 42 (1990), 469–81; Brian Clarke, 'English-Speaking Canada from 1854', in Murphy and Perin (eds.), *Christianity in Canada*, 355–7.

countries, where overwhelmingly high levels of church membership contrasted with low levels of attendance at services, relatively rich state churches were able to build extensive church complexes, in which a variety of social services could be provided.

In Britain the post-war revival was certainly more modest and less widely spread than in the United States. The clearest signs of growing interest in religion were on university campuses. Student religious societies were booming, and the number of prominent intellectuals and writers who were professing Christians was higher than it had been in the early twentieth century or would be in the later twentieth century.[24] The poet and novelist, John Wain, who was a student at Oxford in the years around the end of the Second World War, and for whom at the time 'Christianity was a kind of poetry', recalled that many of the most inspiring personalities at the time seemed to be Christians. He especially highlighted the wide-ranging influence of C. S. Lewis, not only as a teacher, but as the leading figure in the Socrates debating club and a very popular broadcaster on radio:

For Christianity (as everyone knows who lived through those years in England, or has read about them) was just then enormously powerful. The war had made normal life an affair of constant crisis and suffering. The anti-clerical and rationalistic left-wing generation were dispersed and—as it seemed to many—discredited, and a suitably presented Christianity met with no real opposition among either the uneducated or the intelligentsia.[25]

In 1950 a writer in the University magazine, *Isis*, claimed that 'Christianity in Oxford is very evidently more lively than it is almost anywhere else in the country'. About 15 per cent of students were members of a religious society, and many more attended services on Sundays. The bishop of Bristol, who was conducting a university mission at the time, contrasted the current situation with that in the days when he had been vicar of the university church. In the 1930s 'political ideology, largely Left-wing, was the supposed alternative to Christianity in Oxford'. Now, he suggested, opposition to Christianity had 'lost its dynamic' and was 'largely negative'—taking the form mainly of logical positivist philosophy. The bishop had accordingly recruited four Anglican philosophers for his mission team.[26]

A questionnaire sent to former students at Girton, a Cambridge women's college, found that no less than 70 per cent of those responding who had entered the college between 1950 and 1954 said that religion had been 'important' to them during their time at university; among those entering between

[24] Adrian Hastings, *A History of English Christianity 1920–1985* (London, 1986), 288–301, 491–504.

[25] John Wain, *Sprightly Running: Part of an Autobiography* (London, 1962), 139–40.

[26] *Church Times* (3 Feb. 1950).

1955 and 1959 the proportion fell to a still very substantial 49 per cent. Out of thirteen respondents who had entered in 1953 and 1954, four were sufficiently committed to join the Student Christian Movement (SCM) or the Catholic Society.[27] A survey of students at Sheffield University in 1961 found that 46 per cent claimed to be regular church-goers—which, even allowing for a little exaggeration, would probably make students the most church-going group in the English population; 15 per cent of Sheffield students belonged to one of the campus religious societies, such as the liberal and ecumenical SCM, the conservative evangelical Christian Union (CU), which was affiliated to the Inter-Varsity Fellowship (IVF), or one of the denominational societies. John Robinson, the later bishop of Woolwich, who was dean of Clare College, Cambridge, from 1951 to 1959, claimed to have experienced a religious boom in his years at Cambridge, which for a time made him believe that the religious tide had turned.[28]

/ The evidence for any more general religious boom in this period is less clear. Callum Brown claims that 'the later 1940s and 1950s witnessed the greatest growth in church membership that Britain had experienced since the mid-nineteenth century'.[29] Whether or not this is true of Scotland, it would be hard to justify this claim in respect of England or Wales. In Wales the four main Nonconformist denominations suffered substantial losses between 1945 and 1962. In England, though the evidence is incomplete, it is clear that any increase in church-going was quite small. The proportion of English adults receiving communion in an Anglican church at Easter rose from 5.8 per cent in 1947 to 7.2 per cent in 1956—though this was still below the pre-war figure. (See Table 1.) Anglican statistics generally show a substantial drop during the war years, followed by a recovery in the later 1940s and early 1950s, reaching a peak some time in the 1950s, but below the level of the later 1930s. The exception is confirmations which in the period 1952–60 returned to the level which had obtained in the 1930s. (See Table 2.) Brown may be right then in suggesting that the revival in this period was principally affecting young people, and especially teenage girls—though the difference between boys and girls was not dramatic: between 1948 and 1957 male confirmations increased by 22 per cent and female confirmations by 27 per cent. Meanwhile Methodist membership was static, and the Baptists and Congregationalists had both

[27] 'University and Life Experience', Girton College Archives, Cambridge. The questionnaires were sent to a 10% sample of those who had studied at Girton between 1930 and 1989, and more than 70% of the questionnaires were completed.

[28] David Bebbington, 'The Secularization of British Universities since the Mid-Nineteenth Century', in George M. Marsden and Bradley J. Longfield (eds.), *The Secularization of the Academy* (New York, 1992), 268; Eric James, *A Life of John A. T. Robinson: Scholar, Pastor, Prophet* (London, 1989; 1st publ. 1987), 111.

[29] Brown, *Death*, 170.

Table 1. England: Church of England
Easter Communicants per 1,000 estimated population aged 15 and over,
1934–1973

1934	80
1938	78
1947	58
1950	62
1953	65
1956	72
1960	70
1964	62
1968	56
1973	47

Source: R. F. Neuss, *Facts and Figures about the Church of England*, iii (London, 1965), 60; *Official Yearbook of the Church of England*.

suffered a modest decline. (See Table 6 in Chapter 3.) Very probably the numbers of Roman Catholic worshippers increased in this period because of immigration from Ireland, Poland, and other mainly Catholic countries. However, since Catholics were no more than about 10–12 per cent of the population, the impact of such an increase on overall levels of church-going would have been small.[30]

Brown is on firmer ground in arguing that, in spite of the decline in church-going since the later nineteenth century, Britain retained a 'Christian culture'.[31] It was still a generally accepted commonplace that Britain was 'a Christian country', that the laws and national institutions should reflect this fact, and that the Christian churches should have a major voice on any public issue which had a religious or moral dimension. Most people had experienced some degree of religious upbringing, including attendance at Sunday School and sometimes the learning of prayers or other kinds of religious teaching from parents, and an awareness of being a Protestant or a Catholic, and if Protestant, of belonging to a particular denomination. The previously mentioned survey of Sheffield students found that no less than 94 per cent of those questioned in 1961 claimed to have had some kind of religious upbringing.[32]

---

[30] Ronald F. Neuss (ed.), *Facts and Figures about the Church of England*, iii (London, 1965), 54–61; Robert Currie, Alan Gilbert, and Lee Horsley, *Churches and Churchgoers: Patterns of Church Growth in the British Isles since 1700* (Oxford, 1977), 128–234; D. Densil Morgan, *The Span of the Cross: Christian Religion and Society in Wales 1914–2000* (Cardiff, 1999), 206–12.

[31] Brown, *Death*, 9–15.   [32] Bebbington, 'Universities', 268.

Late Christendom

Table 2. England: Church of England confirmations per 1,000 estimated population aged 12–20, 1934–1974

	female	male
1934	39.2	30.8
1938	36.8	28.9
1948	33.6	27.3
1950	34.5	27.6
1953	39.1	27.8
1956	40.8	28.1
1958	40.6	27.6
1960	40.9	27.6
1962	36.7	24.7
1964	31.3	20.7
1966	27.8	18.8
1968	26.1	16.9
1970	24.2	15.3
1972	22.4	13.8
1974	19.6	12.1

Source: Neuss, *Facts and Figures*, 55; *Official Yearbook of the Church of England*.

The monarchy was closely linked with the Church of England, of which the sovereign was Supreme Governor, and the archbishop of Canterbury crowned the monarch in the Coronation ceremony. While the link between church and monarchy was symbolic, of more practical import was the role of the BBC. The first Director-General, Sir John Reith (later Lord Reith) was a Presbyterian, keenly aware of the Corporation's religious responsibilities. In 1948 his successor, Sir William Haley, referred to Britons as 'citizens of a Christian country', and affirmed that 'the BBC—as an institution set up by the State—bases its policy upon a positive attitude towards Christian values'. As well as broadcasting a daily radio service and a short religious talk (*Lift up your Hearts*) on weekdays, the BBC provided an extensive menu of religious programmes on radio and television on Sundays, and in the case of television the period from 6 to 7.30 on a Sunday evening was preserved as a 'God slot'. The BBC did indeed experiment tentatively with giving non-Christians a chance to make their views heard. In 1948 there was a radio debate between the Jesuit Fr Coplestone and Britain's most famous agnostic, Bertrand Russell. In 1955 a series of broadcasts on *Morals without Religion* by the Humanist Margaret Knight caused many protests from Christians who felt that the BBC was abandoning its responsibilities. *Meeting Point*, BBC television's long-running Sunday evening religious discussion programme introduced in 1956, frequently favoured a debate format, in which for instance a Christian confronted a Humanist, or a theologian and a psychiatrist were invited to present alternative perspectives on a moral issue.[33]

BBC radio's Third Programme, directed at the most highly educated sectors of the public, was given greater scope than more popular channels. For instance in October 1957 the philosopher Stephen Toulmin gave a talk with the title 'On Remaining an Agnostic'. This led to considerable discussion in the pages of the BBC journal, *The Listener,* which provided transcripts of programmes. Toulmin complained that agnostics had frequently failed to make their case heard, especially 'at times like the present when a religious revival has been—officially at least—in progress'. The subsequent correspondence reflected the ambiguities in the current situation and the fact that two people with completely opposite views could both feel that their own view was not being given a sufficient airing. Thus Britain's second most famous agnostic, the novelist E. M. Forster, objected to the BBC's tendency to allow freethinkers to have their say only if there was a Christian around to answer back; while the philosopher of religion H. D. Lewis suggested that Bertrand Russell and Margaret Knight gained extensive newspaper coverage for their views, while equally cogent expressions of Christian theology were ignored by the press. However, a fair summary of the situation at the time was probably the comment by another writer that:

the BBC is scared stiff of causing a rumpus over religion. Although it is probably fair to say that many of the people who give serious talks on the Third Programme are rationalists in religious matters, it is not considered proper that this basis to their thinking should be given uninhibited hearing. And in this the BBC merely accepts the feeling of society in general . . . [34]

This last comment pointed to a feature of British society inherited from the nineteenth century, and still in force in the 1950s, namely the sharp distinction between 'private' and 'public'. In the 1950s there were still strict conventions regarding the language that could be used, the subjects discussed or the opinions expressed in books, newspapers, films, theatre, radio, and television. For instance there was a concept of 'bad language' and some words that were in common use in everyday speech were either discouraged or totally excluded from these public media. Explicit descriptions of sex were regarded as 'obscene' and any discussion at all of either homosexuality or abortion was

---

[33] Asa Briggs, 'Christ and the Media: Secularisation, Rationalism and Sectarianism in the History of British Broadcasting, 1922–1976', in E. Barker *et al.* (eds.), *Secularization, Rationalism and Sectarianism* (Oxford, 1993), 280; Hastings, *English Christianity*, 495–6; *Radio Times* (17 Feb. 1957, 9 Feb. 1958).

[34] *Listener* (17 Oct., 31 Oct., 26 Sept. 1957).

potentially objectionable. The theatre censor had a list of forbidden topics, which until 1957 included any presentation of homosexuality on the stage. The forty-two plays refused a licence between 1945 and 1954 included eighteen banned for 'sexual impropriety', fourteen for mention of homosexuality, described by the censor as 'the forbidden subject', and one for irreverent treatment of Christianity. When the novel *Saturday Night and Sunday Morning*, an uncompromisingly 'realist' account of working-class life in Nottingham, was made into a memorable 'new wave' film in 1960, the censor insisted on an abortion scene being changed so that the attempted abortion failed, and the woman decides to have the baby.[35] To some extent religious doubt belonged among the tabooed topics. Although books representing every conceivable religious or anti-religious opinion were readily available, radio, television, and newspapers were much more cautious in their handling of this topic.

The debate on homosexuality in the 1950s provides a good example both of the continuing influence of the idea that Britain was 'a Christian country', of the distinction between private and public, and the taboos which continued to surround public debate of some sensitive topics.[36] Sodomy had been a capital offence until 1861, though the last execution was in 1835. In 1885 the 'Labouchere Amendment' criminalized all forms of male homosexual activity. Oscar Wilde, who was jailed for two years in 1895, was the first high-profile victim. However, by the 1920s homosexuality was so widespread among students at Oxford and Cambridge that Noel Annan speaks of a 'cult of homosexuality', including a large proportion of the most distinguished writers, actors, musicians, and academics of the inter-war years.[37] This was not widely known among the general public, and was certainly not a subject of comment in the press. Thus few people would have realized when W. H. Auden married Erika Mann that he was homosexual and she a lesbian, and most readers of Auden's famous love poem, 'Lay your sleeping head, my love', assumed that the person addressed was female. The relatively small numbers of homosexuals who went to prison in the inter-war period were mainly drawn from the working class and were arrested while seeking or practising sex in public places. The same remained broadly true after the Second World War, but the numbers of arrests increased, and some of the victims came from a completely different background. Most notably, in 1953, one of Britain's most famous

---

[35] Dominic Shellard, *Kenneth Tynan: A Life* (New Haven, 2003), 101–2, 218–22; Marwick, *Sixties*, 129–33.

[36] This paragraph is based on Peter G. Richards, *Parliament and Conscience* (London, 1970); Jeffrey Weeks, *Coming Out: Homosexual Politics in Britain from the Nineteenth Century to the Present* (2nd edn. London, 1990); Patrick Higgins, *Heterosexual Dictatorship: Male Homosexuality in Postwar Britain* (London, 1996).

[37] Noel Annan, *Our Age: The Generation that Made Post-War Britain* (London, 1990), 134–69.

actors, Sir John Gielgud, was arrested, though he escaped with a fine. In 1953, a Labour MP, convicted of importuning, was forced to resign; and in 1954 the Montagu trial resulted in prison sentences for the high-profile accused. Defenders of these laws in the 1950s and 1960s still saw them as reflecting the nation's Christianity, though this was not their only or their most frequently used argument. When in 1954 the government appointed the Wolfenden Committee to review the laws on homosexuality and prostitution, the members included an Anglican and a Presbyterian clergyman, as well as doctors, lawyers, and academics. Wolfenden himself was a committed Anglican. Most strikingly, the British Medical Association (BMA), in condemning homosexuality and opposing any relaxation of the law, claimed that 'the weakening of personal responsibility with regard to social and national welfare in a significant proportion of the population may be one of the causes of the apparent increase of homosexual practices and prostitution'. Their evidence to the Wolfenden Committee urged that: 'There should ... be a recognition of the fact that homosexuals can acquire a new direction in their lives through religious conversion, and opportunities should be available to them to discover for themselves a basis of life that proves a reality to many people.' The BMA also provided case-studies of men whose religious conversion had cured them of homosexuality.[38] In 1957 the Committee issued its report, including the historic recommendation that homosexual acts between consenting adults in private should be legal. But Macmillan's Conservative government refused to implement this recommendation, arguing that it was too far in advance of public opinion.[39]

In fact it had been the Church of England's Moral Welfare Council which in 1954 became the first religious or political body to call for legalization, and the Council's secretary, the Revd D. Sherwin Bailey restated this view in evidence to the Committee. When in 1960 the House of Commons defeated a motion for legalization, one of the major arguments used by the advocates of reform was the fact that the Anglican, Methodist, and Roman Catholic churches all supported a change in the law.[40] During the parliamentary debates of 1965–7 which ended with legalization in 1967, defenders of the status quo fiercely attacked the churches for failing to stand up for these allegedly Christian laws.[41]

[38] Higgins, *Dictatorship*, 34–5.

[39] Mark Jarvis, *Conservative Governments, Morality and Social Change in Affluent Britain, 1957–64* (Manchester, 2005), 96–9.

[40] Richards, *Parliament*, 63–84.

[41] Lord Dilhorne, a leading Conservative, stated that homosexuality was simply 'a vice' and made sarcastic references to the support of 'the most reverend Primates and the right reverend Prelates' for a bill that would encourage vice. *House of Lords Debates*, 10 May 1966, col. 619.

What is striking in the 1950s, and continued to a lesser extent to be so in the 1960s, is the embarrassment and discomfort which surrounded the whole discussion. Wolfenden was concerned that women members of his committee should be protected from what he regarded as the more unpleasant evidence: ideas of the demarcation between public and private were of course bound up with assumptions about gender, of female sensitivity and the respect due to it. Wolfenden frequently resorted to euphemism, homosexuals becoming 'Huntleys' and prostitutes 'Palmers' (referring to the famous Huntley & Palmers biscuit firm in his home town of Reading).[42]

All Western states in the 1950s tried to promote moral behaviour, and all had a range of laws punishing what they saw as immoral behaviour. There were differences between predominantly Protestant and predominantly Catholic countries both in concepts of morality and in the forms of immorality which they chose to punish. Thus mainly Catholic countries tended to be more restrictive of divorce and the sale of contraceptives. Mainly Protestant countries went further in restricting drinking and gambling and requiring Sunday observance, and they tended to be stricter in their treatment of homosexuality.[43] Denmark and Sweden had in fact repealed their anti-homosexual laws in 1932 and 1944 respectively; however, not only Britain, but also Norway, Canada, New Zealand, the Australian states, and the states of the USA retained these laws in the 1950s. The strictest laws in western Europe were those in Germany and Austria, enacted under the Nazis and retained after the Second World War. On the other hand, France, Belgium, Italy, and Spain had no ban. Among Catholic countries the relationship between religion and the law was a lot closer in, for instance, Ireland than in France. But even in 'secular' France there were still in the 1950s strict limits on abortion. In fact the main distinction was between countries which allowed abortion only in cases where the mother's life or health was endangered, and those where it was totally prohibited. A few countries, such as Italy and Ireland, prohibited divorce; most allowed divorce, but only in strictly defined circumstances. Sale of contraceptives was prohibited in Ireland, but restricted in other mainly Catholic countries, including France, where 'Malthusian propaganda' and even providing information about methods of contraception were banned. Many Western countries had obscenity laws, which limited the explicit presentation of sex in books

[42] Higgins, *Dictatorship*, 17.
[43] Home Office and Scottish Home Department, *Report of the Committee on Homosexual Offences and Prostitution* [The Wolfenden Report] (London, 1957), 149–51, summarized legislation in other countries.

and magazines, or in films and plays. Some countries still had blasphemy laws.[44]

The climate of opinion in the 1940s and 1950s tended to favour the retention of these laws. This was partly because conservative and/or confessional parties were predominant in most Western countries at this time and that at least in the immediate post-war period economic reconstruction and international tensions had a much higher priority in the minds of government than changes in the law of morals. However, there were also deeper causes for the moral conservatism of the time—and these deeper causes also played a part in the post-war religious revival. First there was the impact of the Second World War and then of the cold war. In Britain the war had revived a flagging sense of Christian national identity.[45] In many of the countries of continental Europe the church or churches emerged from the war with enhanced authority, partly because of the role they were seen as playing in the rebuilding of Europe's moral and spiritual foundations after the horrors of Nazism. The connection between Christianity, national identity, and moral revival was reinforced by the cold war with the atheist Soviet Union.[46] The cause of the West was linked with Christianity, and often with specific forms of Christianity. These were often, though not necessarily, politically conservative—after all, most Social Democrats were fervently anti-Communist too. More particularly it was a morally and theologically traditionalist Christianity.[47] These tendencies were further strengthened by another aspect of the post-war years, namely a desire to return to 'normal' after the disruptions and horrors of the war years. This 'normality' was defined especially in terms of the restoration of family life, preferably of a kind where the father was the breadwinner and the mother had responsibility for the home and the bringing up of children. Religion and science combined to support this model of family life. Preachers exalted the family and the role of the mother; criminologists blamed the post-war crime wave on the disruptions of family life cause by the war; and

---

[44] Arthur Marwick, *The Sixties: Cultural Revolution in Britain, France, Italy and the United States, c.1958–1974* (Oxford, 1998), 115–18, 700–16; Sevegrand, *Enfants*, gives the history of the French anti-contraception law from enactment in 1920 to repeal in 1967.

[45] Tom Lawson, *The Church of England and the Holocaust: Christianity, Memory and Nazism* (Woodbridge, 2006), 11–15.

[46] See Kirby (ed.), *Religion and the Cold War*.

[47] Thus Martin Greschat, 'Kirche und Öffentlichkeit in der deutschen Nachkriegszeit', in A. Boyens *et al* (eds.), *Kirchen in der Nachkriegszeit* (Göttingen, 1979), 100–24, stresses the continuities between German Protestant thinking in the period after the Second World War and in earlier periods—the biggest changes in Protestant thinking came in the 1960s. A similar point with regard to the Catholics is made in van Melis, 'Ecclesiastical Triumphalism', 241.

psychoanalysts like John Bowlby pointed to the dire consequences of 'maternal deprivation'.[48]

CHRISTIAN SOCIALIZATION

Except in a few anti-clerical strongholds, the great majority of children growing up in the 1950s were being socialized into membership of a Christian society—through day school (except in France and the United States), through Sunday School or catechism classes, and often in the home as well, though families varied greatly in their relationship with the national religion. Two contrasting examples will illustrate some of the ways in which this Christian socialization was experienced. The first is from an overwhelmingly Catholic environment in rural France; the second is from a much more pluralistic and also more secularized English industrial district.

The village of Limerzel in the Morbihan department of western France was the subject of an invaluable local study by Yves Lambert illustrating the religious changes in Catholic Brittany in the course of the twentieth century.[49] In 1958 it was estimated that 92 per cent of adults in this large village attended mass regularly—though the figure had been even higher in the 1930s. In the 1950s, according to Lambert, Limerzel was still a 'quasi-Christendom', in which a single overwhelmingly dominant world-view was learnt in church, Catholic school, and home. A central theme was 'fideism'—'that is to say the total confidence which the believer must have in the church'. Religious symbols dominated the houses and also the topography of the village: the crucifix had the place of honour above the fireplace, and was surrounded by images of saints, as well as by family photographs and military citations. The intensely physical and material character of Catholicism meant that it was more easily communicated to children than Protestantism. Catholics did not only attend services, learn prayers, listen to sermons, and read religious books. They were initiated into membership of the Catholic community through the highly popular First Communion, a great occasion requiring special clothing; they wore crosses and medallions, and carried pictures of saints; and they also took part in processions and pilgrimages. With rising incomes in the period after the Second World War more people could afford a pilgrimage to Lourdes, as well as visits to the more easily accessible local shrines. From an early age

[48] Pat Thane, 'Family Life and "Normality" in Postwar British Culture', in Bessell and Schumann (eds.), *Life After Death*, 193–210.

[49] Yves Lambert, *Dieu change en Bretagne: La religion à Limerzel de 1900 à nos jours* (Paris, 1985), 7–98.

children learnt that priests were special: when a priest visited, adults behaved with respect and children were afraid. Priests were well aware of their authority and their responsibilities. Noting a (relatively modest) drop in attendance in 1962, the rector issued mass-missers with a grave warning, concluding: 'The presence of man here below has no other reason than preparation for the eternal salvation of which the church has charge.'[50]

Interviews conducted in the later 1980s by Elizabeth Roberts and Lucinda Beier from the University of Lancaster offer a wealth of material on childhood and youth in and around Preston, Lancaster, and Barrow, three industrial towns in the north-west of England.[51] Church attendance was much lower than in Limerzel, and the people belonged to a variety of denominations, including Catholic, Anglican, and Methodist, as well as many other branches of Protestantism. One could not speak of a dominant world-view of the kind existing in Limerzel, but the great majority of young people had some contact with organized Christianity in their early years, and at the very least they were made aware of belonging to the Protestant majority or to the substantial Catholic minority. Even those who had little contact with the church as adults often continued to emphasize that they were Christians and believed in God—though they might admit that their religion did not play a large part in their lives. Men and women brought up in working-class and lower middle-class families nearly all had attended Sunday School for at least part of their childhood; many went on to join church youth clubs as teenagers; some attended church day schools; and those with more devout parents learnt prayers at home. They also learnt at home the importance of being a Protestant or a Catholic, as well as hostile stereotypes of those on the other side, the importance of various rituals such as the churching of mothers after childbirth, and a variety of moral precepts, relating especially to sex.

Among twenty-three interviewees born between 1931 and 1937, at least nineteen had attended church or Sunday School as children; at least six had belonged to a church youth club; and six mentioned the religious teaching received at day school. Among twenty-two interviewees born between 1940 and 1950, at least nineteen had attended church or Sunday School as children; at least eight had belonged to a church youth club; and four mentioned religious teaching at day school. Some of them had loved Sunday School, while others went unwillingly, but it was generally agreed that it was something you had to do. George Nixon (born 1937, Lancaster) and his brothers

---

[50] Ibid. 246–7.

[51] 'Social and Family Life 1940–1970' (henceforth SFL), Oral History Archive, Centre for North-West Regional Studies, University of Lancaster. All references are to the paginated transcripts; all names assigned to respondents are pseudonyms.

were taken to church by their mother, while their labourer father stayed at home: 'You never missed Sunday School, that was one thing we never ever got away with.'[52] Anne Kelly (born 1945, Preston) was the daughter of strongly Catholic working-class parents. Her father was 'Victorian' and until she married and left home in 1965 she was obliged to go to church regularly, and every day in Lent.[53] Janice Porter (born 1947, Lancaster), who got 'fed up' with Sunday School and dropped out early, was a harbinger of a pattern that would become more common in the 1970s. Janice had never known her father, and her mother's complicated love life may have limited the time available for directing her daughter's behaviour, so her family situation was untypical of those interviewed in this project.[54] For most, the parting of the ways came around the early teens, when some joined a church youth group or started regularly going to the main church services, while others gave up any church involvement: many parents, especially the less religiously committed, accepted that they were now old enough to decide for themselves.

It is less clear what the respondents learned directly from their parents—mainly, perhaps, because the interviewers seldom directly questioned them about this. Parents (and sometimes grandparents) taught by example, taking children to services with them, and participating in a wide range of church activities. Mothers and grandmothers sometimes taught children prayers. Derek Allen (born 1946, Lancaster), with an Anglican mother and a non-church-going father, said 'we was just brought up to believe in God and all that'[55]—apparently meaning that they were given a basic and standard religious belief, of a kind that was more or less universal, rather than any fancy doctrines or specially devout practices. The religious atmosphere could become all-embracing in Catholic homes, where the symbols of faith were part of the household furniture. Irene Wells (born 1931, Lancaster), the daughter of a bus conductor and a shop assistant, recalled that there was a statue of Jesus on their sideboard, round which the family would gather in the evening for prayers led by her father.[56] The one religious message which families seem to have conveyed very successfully in this confessionally mixed region was that Catholics were very different from Protestants and that each growing child should remain loyal to his or her own community. As Irene Wells commented:

I think in them days people were rather bigoted towards other religions, weren't they. I know when I used to go dancing when I was about 16 or 17 I went with my friend whose mother felt that way about Catholics and although she was never nasty to me

[52] SFL, interview with Mr G3L, 32. [53] SFL, interview with Mrs R1P, 19–22.
[54] SFL, interview with Mrs L3L, 21. [55] SFL, interview with MrF2L, 20.
[56] SFL, interview with Mrs H5L, 15–16.

about it, she used to get little digs in about me being a 'left footer' as they called them.... We were always sort of singled out in our street as being Catholics.... My dad did feel that we should set an example because we were Catholics, because we knew better than them sort of thing, we're the real religion type of thing, so we let them see that because we're Catholics we've got to be gentle and good.[57]

When she married a Protestant, her father-in-law refused to attend the ceremony, because it was in a Catholic church. She would later have a big row with her own father, as her Protestant husband was adamant that their children should not go to a Catholic school.

In Britain, Catholics were no more than about 10–12 per cent of the total population. Confessional rivalries only became a major part of life in those regions such as Lancashire and the west of Scotland with a large Catholic minority. However, in West Germany, Switzerland, and the Netherlands, where Catholics and Protestants were more nearly equal in numbers, as well as in Australia, which had a large Catholic minority, most aspects of life had a confessional dimension.[58] Partly because of regional concentrations, but also because so much of life was organized on confessional lines, many people would reach adulthood before they consciously met a person belonging to the other faith. Mutual stereotyping was rife.

Christel Köhle-Hezinger studied relations between Catholics and Protestants in Württemberg between 1803, when the previously all-Lutheran state first acquired a large Catholic population, and the 1970s. At the latter date, most people said that confessional differences were a thing of the past. But not very far below the surface, the sense of difference, sometimes exacerbated by prejudices and grievances, was still there. Three points were especially noted by Protestants as summing up the difference: Catholics knelt during their worship, which to Protestants seemed undignified; they venerated saints, whom Protestants saw as little better than heathen idols; and above all the central role of Mary in Catholic life embodied all that Protestants regarded as 'kitsch' and 'sickly-sweet'. For Catholics, on the other hand, their self-perception strongly emphasized piety and devotion to the church. The Protestant Church was still seen by them as little more than an adjunct of the state—it could never inspire the kind of affection that they felt for their 'Mother' Church. Protestantism was also equated with secularization and moral decline, and Protestants were accused of monopolizing positions of power, and using them to oppress Catholics.[59] In Germany, Switzerland,

---

[57] Ibid. 17.

[58] Olaf Blaschke (ed.), *Konfessionen im Konflikt: Deutschland zwischen 1800 und 1970. Ein zweites konfessionelles Zeitalter* (Göttingen, 2001); Michael Hogan, *The Sectarian Strand: Religion in Australian History* (Ringwood, Victoria, 1987).

[59] Christel Köhle-Hezinger, *Evangelisch-Katholisch* (Tübingen, 1976), 99–110.

and the Netherlands, there were religiously mixed regions and cities, but also others that were relatively homogeneous. Confessional stereotypes strongly shaped the ways in which north Germans and Bavarians, or people from the north and south Netherlands, saw one another. The situation was not so different in Belgium, though there the split was between Catholics and anti-clericals, with the Dutch-speaking north being seen as more Catholic, while the French-speaking south was perceived as more inclined to anti-clericalism. Even in the Nordic countries, which were homogeneously Protestant, and mainly Lutheran, national identities were partly shaped by a sense of being different from the Catholics further south. Thus a Swedish historian who examined images of 'Europe' in the Social Democratic press between 1949 and 1972 found that it was repeatedly presented as 'Capitalistic, Conservative, corrupted and Catholic'. The strongest anti-Catholics often came from the ranks of what have been termed 'secularized Lutherans', who had little involvement in their own church, but who regarded Catholicism as intolerant, undemocratic, crudely emotional, and therefore un-Swedish.[60]

In summary, young people growing up in the 1940s and 1950s in many parts of Europe learnt at home, at school, at church, through membership of youth organizations, a whole set of assumptions about what it meant to be a Catholic or a Protestant or a secularist. Nor was this awareness limited to those who were strongly committed: the overwhelming majority of people knew what their religion was, however little they may have practised it, and most had some idea of what made other confessions, or secularists, different. Hostile stereotyping was seldom far below the surface and, in particular, marriages across confessional lines were always potentially problematic. The situation was not very different in the United States, where there were still mutual suspicions between the Protestant majority and the large Catholic minority. There were no confessional parties, and the multiplicity of ethnic and racial, as well as religious, cleavages within American society meant that Catholic/Protestant conflicts could not be as central or all-pervasive as they were in some European societies. The favourable depiction of Catholic priests in Hollywood films of the 1930s and 1940s reflected the assumption that Catholics were now an accepted part of American society—and in the 1950s the constant references to America's 'Judeo-Christian' culture blurred the distinctions between Christian and Jew, as well as between Catholic and Protestant.[61] However, there were still a lot of people who were less eirenic. Conservative Protestants continued to deny that Catholics were Christians and liberal

[60] Daniel Alvunger, 'A Secularised Lutheran Kingdom of the Swedish Nation?', paper delivered at the Modern History Seminar, University of Birmingham, 19 May 2004.

[61] Silk, *Spiritual Politics*, 50.

Protestants questioned the compatibility between Catholic teachings and the separation of church and state.[62] Catholics often retained a sense of being an embattled minority, for whom loyalty to one's own community was a supreme virtue. 'On every side,' wrote one lay activist in the early 1950s, 'Catholics are subjected to a sea of secularism. We are assailed by a paganism which probably ranks in some respects with the most flagrant paganism of Greece and Rome.'[63]

PATTERNS OF CHURCH-GOING

In spite of this shared 'Christian culture', levels of active involvement in the church varied radically between countries and between regions of the same country.[64] Around 1960 the proportion of the adult population attending church in a given week ranged from about 90 per cent in the Irish Republic to less than 10 per cent in the Scandinavian countries. At the upper end of the scale, with figures between about 35 and 50 per cent, were Northern Ireland, the United States, Canada, Belgium, the Netherlands, Italy, and Austria. Figures between about 20 and 35 per cent were recorded in France, West Germany, Australia, and New Zealand, and probably Scotland and Switzerland. In England and probably Wales it was between 10 and 20 per cent. There were also huge variations within particular countries—especially in Catholic countries, where the polarization between the 'faithful' and the militant anti-clericals was much sharper than in a mainly Protestant environment.

These patterns of religious observance and non-observance were studied in great detail in France, where Gabriel Le Bras, the founder of 'religious sociology', had since the 1930s been measuring the regional, class, and gender differences in Catholic practice. In rural areas there were huge regional variations in religious behaviour. Towns also varied by region, with those in the west and the east being the most strongly Catholic. However, the biggest differences were those of class. Bourgeois districts were often Catholic strongholds, while the church had much less of a following in working-class districts, and least of all in those working-class districts which were politically

[62] Allitt, *Religion in America*, 9, 65–7.

[63] Leslie Woodcock Tentler, *Catholics and Contraception: An American History* (Ithaca, NY, 2004), 139.

[64] My main source for this paragraph is Hans Mol (ed.), *Western Religion* (The Hague, 1972).

dominated by Communism.[65] This needs to be emphasized, because this fact which was obvious to most contemporary observers has tended to be obscured both by an influential tradition in the sociology of religion and by recent developments in cultural history. The older tradition, of which the German sociologist Thomas Luckmann was the most trenchant representative, argued that the survival of 'church-oriented religion' in western Europe was to be explained by the survival of groups 'peripheral to the structure of modern society' ('the peasantry, the remains of the traditional bourgeoisie and petite bourgeoisie').[66] More recently the overriding emphasis by cultural historians on gender differences has tended to obscure the even greater role of class differences.[67] The exhaustive work of French sociologists of religion in the 1950s and early 1960s demonstrated that, in spite of the continuing importance of gender differences, class was still by far the most important factor in explaining the patterns of religious practice in French cities, and that the upper bourgeoisie was the most religiously observant section of the urban population. For instance in Lille 51 per cent of the upper bourgeoisie and 6 per cent of the working class attended church on a census Sunday; in Bordeaux 32 and 3 per cent.[68] Gérard Cholvy, who conducted a census of attendance at mass throughout the diocese of Montpellier on 2 December 1962 found that professionals were those most likely to attend, while fishermen and miners were those least likely to do so. Gender differences were certainly important, but less so than those of class. Among professionals 47 per cent of women and 34 per cent of men attended; among workers 11 per cent of women and 4 per cent of men did so.[69] In the France of the Fourth and early Fifth Republics Catholicism was a religion not of the marginalized or the survivors from an earlier epoch, but of the powerful and the well-educated— the more so in that Catholics no longer suffered the discrimination that they had sometimes encountered under the Third Republic. Hilaire illustrates this point well in referring to the Catholic student centres in post-war Paris which provided 'a solid spiritual and theological formation for thousands of future lawyers, teachers and doctors'.[70]

In 1943 a famous book by the priests Henri Godin and Yvan Daniel had asked whether France was 'a mission territory'.[71] They concluded that the religious situation varied hugely as between different regions and different

[65] Fernand Boulard and Jean Rémy, *Pratique religieuse urbaine et régions culturelles* (Paris, 1968).

[66] Thomas Luckmann, *The Invisible Religion* (English tr. New York, 1967), 30.

[67] See esp. Brown, *Death*, 149–61 and *passim*.

[68] Boulard and Rémy, *Pratique*, 122–38.

[69] Gérard Cholvy, *Géographie religieuse de l'Hérault contemporain* (Paris, 1968).

[70] Cholvy and Hilaire, *Histoire religieuse*, 191.

[71] Henri Godin and Yvan Daniel, *La France, pays de mission?* (Lyon, 1943).

social milieux, but that the working-class suburbs of many cities, as well as some rural areas, *could* rightly be described as mission territories. One result of this conclusion was the worker priest movement, which flourished between about 1945 and 1954.[72] Worker priests lived in tenements, rather than presbyteries, and took jobs in factories or on building sites. They mixed more conventional forms of evangelism with engaging fellow workers in religious discussions, inviting them to celebrations of mass in the priest's home, and performing baptisms, weddings, and funerals. They often shared the political interests and hopes of their fellow workers, and some became active in the Communist-dominated trade union, the CGT—leading Vatican officials to fear that the conversion that was taking place was not of Communists to Catholicism, but of Catholic priests to Communism. These and other concerns caused the Vatican to impose restrictions that led to the gradual breakdown of the movement (though it was started again after Vatican II).

England had only a small Communist Party and no tradition of militant anti-clericalism to compare with that of France. But the differences between the religious life in a student town and in the working-class districts of south London were seen very clearly by John Robinson, when he moved from being dean of Clare College, Cambridge, to being bishop of Woolwich in 1959. Robinson (1919–83) was a key figure of the 1960s in England, and indeed throughout the English-speaking world, and he will appear in several subsequent chapters. While best known as a theologian and would-be modernizer of the Church of England, he was also actively and often outspokenly involved in numerous liberal campaigns, including those for reform of the laws on homosexuality and abortion, and against nuclear weapons and the death penalty. His famous book, *Honest to God*, which would try to restate the Christian gospel in terms more accessible to his contemporaries, arose partly out of his experiences in south London. As his biographer writes:

Above all there was the all but total alienation of the urban working class from the institutional church. John was aware that in Southwark he was experiencing *The Secular City* ... as he had never experienced it before, not even in Bristol, and in complete contrast to the 'religious boom' he had come from in Cambridge.[73]

---

[72] Oscar L. Arnal, *Priests in Working Class Blue: The History of the Worker Priests, 1943–1954* (New York, 1986).
[73] Eric James, *A Life of John A. T. Robinson: Scholar, Pastor, Prophet* (paperback edn. London, 1989), 111.

In 1957 E. R. Wickham, the Anglican bishop of Middleton published a history of 'church and people' in Sheffield, which observed similar contrasts:

It will be claimed that at the present there is evidence of a return to the churches by the middle classes. It is true, and replenished churches can turn it to creative purpose. Despite the losses, the middling groups are still more easily embraced by churches of all denominations than working-class groups. Every industrial city proves the point. The well-attended churches are generally in the pleasant, middle-class suburban and dormitory areas—and there are many such churches; and the struggling, denuded churches, those in the old downtown and slum areas, the 'East-ends', and on the huge new housing estates where industrial workers live.[74]

Wickham's book was primarily an attempt to identify the historical roots of present-day alienation from the church. He was pioneering a field of historical investigation which was to develop much further in the 1960s and 1970s, and which continued to generate new ideas in the later years of the century.[75] More recent work has suggested that Wickham underestimated the significance of those forms of religion which cannot be measured by church attendance. Nonetheless, he was right to emphasize that involvement in the church was strongly related to social class.

While England had been highly industrialized and urbanized for several generations, the process was still ongoing in many other parts of Europe. For instance, West Germany's 'economic miracle' of the 1950s was partly founded on migration from the countryside to work in newly established factories. On the Lower Rhine in north-west Germany, where large numbers of villagers were either moving to industrial areas or taking part in a weekly migration, returning to the village for Saturday evening and Sunday, there were fears that many of these workers were losing contact with the church. Part of the problem lay in shortages of churches and clergy in these fast-growing areas, and the difficulty of ministering to a population swollen by the influx of refugees from Poland and Czechoslovakia. An article in 1956 claimed that half the rural migrants to industrial areas immediately gave up going to church, and that they were also giving up the old traditions of hanging crosses and religious pictures on the walls.[76]

Working-class religious alienation had been a major concern of the churches since the first half of the nineteenth century, and by the 1950s it was often simply taken for granted. Attacks on Christianity by some sections of the intelligentsia had been a familiar phenomenon since the

---

[74] E. R. Wickham, *Church and People in an Industrial City* (London, 1957), 219.

[75] See esp. S. C. Williams, *Religious Belief and Popular Culture in Southwark, c.1880–1939* (Oxford, 1999).

[76] Wilhelm Damberg, *Abschied vom Milieu? Katholizismus im Bistum Münster und in den Niederlanden 1945–1980* (Paderborn, 1997), 173–84.

eighteenth century, but in the post-war years these were relatively muted by comparison with many earlier periods. The major exception was Sweden, where in 1949 the Professor of Philosophy at Uppsala University, Ingemar Hedenius, published a book, *Tro och Vetande* (*Faith and Reason*), which attacked religion on a mixture of psychological, linguistic philosophical, and logical grounds. He was especially critical of his colleagues in the Theology Faculty, whom he accused of teaching a meaningless subject. The unique feature of this debate was the support Hedenius enjoyed from Herbert Tingsten, editor of Sweden's leading newspaper, *Dagens Nyheter*. Tingsten made Hedenius a celebrity, and turned the local debate into a nation-wide controversy over the truth of Christianity. Church-going was already very low in Sweden, but the debate encouraged atheists and agnostics to 'come out' in a way that in other countries happened more often in the 1960s and 1970s. Indeed, one Swedish journalist claimed in 1964 that 'The debate on religion may to a certain extent be said to have ceased since the beginning of the 1950s', to be replaced by a debate about new moral norms in ' "the vacuum after Christianity" '. One may speculate that Sweden, as one of the very few European countries to be neither a combatant nor a victim of foreign occupation during the Second World War, was less affected by the post-war mood of moral traditionalism.[77]

Meanwhile 'Christendom' was facing not only attacks from outside, but also challenges from within. The intellectuals who were troubling Catholic hierarchies in the 1950s were not so much the atheist or agnostic enemies of Christianity as the liberal Christians who were demanding greater intellectual and political freedom, and were contesting the rights of bishops to regiment the faithful. In 1950 Pope Pius XII's encyclical *Humani Generis*, condemned the (mainly French) *nouvelle théologie*, as well as various non-Christian philosophies which were thought to have influenced it. This was linked with a purge of Catholic teaching institutions in which several French theologians, including Yves Congar and Henri de Lubac, who would come to prominence at the Second Vatican Council, lost their jobs. The theological writings of the French Jesuit, Pierre Teilhard de Chardin, another intellectual hero of the later 1950s and 1960s had to be circulated in samizdat form, as his superiors would not allow their publication.[78] Politics were also a potential source of conflict. The Pope and bishops frequently tried to direct the faithful towards voting for one party or not voting for another; they wished to establish control over the various 'Catholic Action' organizations,

[77] *Wikipedia* article on Hedenius; R. F. Tomasson, *Sweden: Prototype of Modern Society* (New York, 1970), 62–3; information from Anders Jarlert.

[78] Jacques Prévotat, *Être chrétien en France au XXe siècle*, 144–8; Michael Walsh in Hastings (ed.), *Catholicism*, 23.

which mobilized Catholics belonging to specific social groups or working in a specific environment; and they hoped to avoid the divisions between Catholics which political controversy could cause. Pius XII's decree of 1949 threatened excommunication not only to Communists but to those who 'collaborated' with Communists—which was likely to include a large proportion of French and Belgian worker priests. And though most French bishops tried to avoid interference from the Vatican, there were persistent tensions from the 1940s through to the 1970s between the French hierarchy and a section of the lower clergy and lay activists who had strong left-wing sympathies. Another focus of disagreement was the Algerian war. While the bishops had a tendency to sit on the fence, the Catholic student organization (JEC) strongly supported the nationalist cause. In 1957 there was a mass resignation by the JEC leadership after the bishops tried to clamp down on their political activities. In 1954 the Dutch Catholic bishops issued a pastoral letter condemning membership of socialist organizations, while also attacking liberals and humanists. This was bitterly resented by Catholic intellectuals, who in the latter part of the decade were increasingly critical of the system of pillarization in their country and the rigid communal loyalties which it engendered. There were similar trends in Quebec, which also had a history of strong confessional identities and episcopal authoritarianism. Here the liberal Catholic journal *Cité libre*, founded in 1951 and edited by the future Prime Minister Pierre Trudeau, was a principal forum for Catholic professionals and managers, critical of the excessive power of the clergy.[79]

The ideal of a clerically controlled Catholicism was not only facing attack from militant laypeople: it was also being undermined by declining recruitment to the clergy. Wilhelm Damberg has shown in his study of the Catholic diocese of Münster that the shortage of vocations to the secular clergy and to female orders was already a key concern of the bishop in 1952. The 'lay apostolate' was not an invention of Vatican II, but was already regarded as a practical necessity at the diocesan synod in 1958, where it was a major theme.[80] In France too there was a sharp decline in ordinations in the 1950s, which will be discussed in Chapter 10. Probably most people were unaware of the extent of the decline in the 1950s. It was however all too evident to Catholic bishops. In this, as much else, the 1960s, which seemed at the time a period of radical new departures, grew out of as much as in reaction to the 1950s.

One final example of change in the 1950s: sex. The 1960s are synonymous with the 'sexual revolution', of which the availability of the contraceptive

---

[79] Cholvy and Hilaire, *Histoire religieuse*, 254; John A. Coleman, *The Evolution of Dutch Catholicism, 1958–1974* (Berkeley, Calif., 1978), 48–57; Kenneth McRoberts, *Quebec: Social Change and Political Crisis* (3rd edn. Toronto, 1988), 90.

[80] Damberg, *Abschied?*, 184–91.

pill from 1960–1 is often taken to be the catalyst. Sex in the 1960s will be discussed in Chapter 8. My point here, however, is that much of the ground was being prepared in the 1950s (and indeed earlier). One of the most talked about aspects of sex in the 1960s was the increase in sex before marriage. In Britain and the United States this was a continuation of a trend already well-established, going back to the 1920s. This is admittedly a subject on which it is very hard to obtain accurate information. However, the proportion of English married women in two surveys who reported pre-marital coitus rose steadily from 19 per cent of those born before 1904, to 43 per cent of those born 1924–34, 62 per cent of those born 1931–45, and 86 per cent of those born 1946–55.[81] In Germany, levels of pre-marital sex may have declined somewhat in the 1950s, but these remained very high (and higher than in Britain or the United States).[82] More importantly, in Britain and the United States certainly, though the situation no doubt varied between countries, attitudes to sex were evolving in ways that helped to prepare the way for the more radical changes in the following decade. Since the 1920s a growing body of advice literature dwelt on the joys of married love and the importance of sex for a happy relationship. Much of this literature also pointed out the advantages of contraception, and in Britain the post-war years saw a big growth in the number of clinics run by the Family Planning Association from 61 in 1938 and 65 in 1948, to 400 in 1963.[83] According to Hera Cook, married couples were following the advice in the literature and having sex more often. She argues that the rise in fertility between 1933 and 1964 was principally due to increasing frequency of marital intercourse at a time when contraception was widely used but not always reliable. Similar trends are seen in the United States and Australia.

At the same time a variety of intellectual and cultural influences were reinforcing the message that romantic love is the principal source of personal fulfilment and that a happy sexual relationship is crucial to health and well-being. Freudian psychology emphasized the dangerous consequences of repression. Alfred Kinsey's studies of human sexual response, published in 1948 and 1953, delivered a somewhat similar message by a different route, showing that all sorts of practices condemned by official morality were much more widespread than most people realized. 'If so many other people are doing it, why shouldn't I try it too?' was probably the response of many readers—or perhaps 'If so many other people are doing it too, why should I feel guilty?' Another

---

[81] Cook, *Contraception*, 326.

[82] Dagmar Herzog, *Sex after Fascism Memory and Morality in Twentieth-Century Germany* (Princeton, 2005), 96–100.

[83] Elizabeth Wilson, *Only Half Way to Paradise: Woman in Postwar Britain* (London, n.d.), 95–100.

important influence were the novels of D. H. Lawrence, highly popular in the 1950s, principally because of their central focus on sexual relationships. In the world of popular culture no influence was as big as Hollywood, the central themes of whose films were romantic love and the physical attractions of its leading actors and actresses. Most of the pundits in the 1950s still felt that the right place for sex was within heterosexual marriage. But it was not long before people started asking 'If sex is so good for you, why should it only be available to the married? And why should it always be with the same partner?' Herzog notes the example of German literature on marriage from the 1950s which strongly emphasized, and presented an idealized view of, marital sex. This was 'an important precedent for the celebration of sex so often associated with the 1960s: in this way the sexual culture of the later 1960s might be interpreted not just as backlash against 1950s culture but also as an extension and expansion of several of its elements'.[84] Meanwhile, references to sex in the media were becoming increasingly frequent, and film directors and advertisers were extending little by little the limits of what was permissible in references to sex and depiction of the naked body. Betty Friedan quoted a study of the American media which found that references to sex increased by two and a half times between January 1950 and January 1960.[85] As Pat Thane writes of Britain, 'The "swinging sixties" can be said to have grown out of, rather than to represent a reaction to the 1950s, although even then Britain was a long way from mass abandonment of sexual restraint.'[86]

CONCLUSION

The years of the Second World War and then of the cold war boosted the sense of Christian national identity in many Western countries. The church-building boom was accompanied by a relatively brief boom in church-going, which was probably strongest in the middle classes and among students. Confessional parties enjoyed exceptional electoral success and laws regulating morality were widely accepted. The great majority of children and adolescents were receiving a Christian socialization, and whether or not they gained an understanding of Christian doctrine or ethics, they internalized a sense of confessional identity. Christendom appeared to be intact, and

[84] Herzog, *Sex after Fascism*, 118–19.
[85] Betty Friedan, *The Feminine Mystique* (Harmondsworth, 1965; 1st publ. 1963), 229.
[86] Thane, 'Normality', 199.

even enjoying a revival. However, appearances were in some ways deceptive. The biggest problem faced by most of the churches was still the lack of involvement, or even alienation, of the working class. There were admittedly significant exceptions—in some countries, for instance in Britain, the Catholic Church was much more successful than the Protestants in retaining the loyalty of its working-class members. On the other hand, the tight-knit Catholic subcultures which had flourished in such countries as Germany and the Netherlands and in Quebec were facing two areas of impending crisis. One was the drop in vocations to the priesthood. Another was the discontent among Catholic intellectuals and the declining membership of Catholic youth organizations.

3

The Early 1960s

When did 'The 1960s' begin? You can make out a reasonable case for saying '1960', but many other dates have been suggested. In a contemporary polemic, designed to discredit the decade before it had even ended, the satirist Christopher Booker proposed 1956. Arthur Marwick starts the 'long 1960s' in 1958. Callum Brown distinguishes between a 'Long Sixties' starting in 1956 and a 'Short Sixties' starting in 1963. David Hilliard dates the Australian 1960s from the arrival of the Beatles in 1964.[1] And many historians have attributed special significance to the year 1965.[2] Here I will take the concept of a 'long 1960s', developing in several distinct stages, and without wishing to argue about a precise chronology I will suggest that there is a period between about 1958 and 1962, which might be termed the 'early 1960s'. This is a period of cautious questioning, of still tentative new beginnings, in which some of the ideas and movements and trends that were to be characteristic of the years following began to be heard and seen. The 'Christendom' of the post-war years was still intact, but it was being undermined by satirists who laughed at all established institutions; by those who wanted more individual freedom and so objected both to rigid moral codes and to the regulation of morality by the state; by church reformers critical of the power of the clergy and ecclesiastical hierarchy.

This chapter will look at the trends towards greater moral and religious pluralism; at the undermining of respect and deference, which affected all established institutions, including the churches; at the signs of discontent within the various ideologically based subcultures which had been a major aspect of life in most west European countries in the first half of the twentieth century; at demands for reform in the church and at the radicalization of Christian students; at the changes in the relationship between 'public' and 'private'; and at the still modest decline in church-going that was under way in the United States and probably Britain, France, and West Germany.

[1] Christopher Booker, *The Neophiliacs* (London, 1969); Callum G. Brown, *The Death of Christian Britain* (London, 2001), 188; Arthur Marwick, *The Sixties* (Oxford, 1998); David Hilliard, 'The Religious Crisis of the 1960s', *Journal of Religious History*, 21 (1997), 210.

[2] e.g. Sydney Ahlstrom, 'The Radical Turn in Theology and Ethics: Why it Occurred in the 1960s', *Annals of the American Academy of Political Science*, 387 (1970), 2; Henri Mendras, *La Seconde Révolution française* (Paris, 1988).

THE END OF THE 'RELIGIOUS BOOM'

In the United States, the post-war religious boom was beginning to fade by the late 1950s. A poll in 1939 had found that 41 per cent of Americans claimed to have attended church or synagogue during the previous week. The figure dropped during the Second World War, but then rose to reach a peak of 49 per cent in 1955, oscillating around the peak between 1956 and 1958, before gradually declining between 1959 and 1971, when the figure was 40 per cent. Religious books as a proportion of all books published peaked in 1958, and spending on religion as a proportion of income peaked in 1961. The really big changes were in the religious behaviour of the young. In 1957 there was hardly any difference between the church-going habits of Americans in different age-bands; but by 1972, when only 28 per cent of men and women in their twenties reported church attendance during the previous week, this was far below the average for all adults. It seems that affluent and well-educated youth were those most likely to give up church-going in this period. In the 1950s the college-educated were far more likely to be church-goers than their less educated compatriots; in the 1960s the gap narrowed considerably. And though it was in the later 1960s that universities became notorious as strong-holds of nonconformity, it seems that the proportion of religiously active students was already dropping in the later 1950s. Declining interest in the church among the new generation of parents was also perhaps reflected in the fact that enrolment in Sunday Schools fell behind population growth between 1955 and 1960, before declining absolutely in most denominations in the 1960s.[3]

In Britain levels of church-going were much lower than in the United States, but trends were similar. Callum Brown sees the religious statistics marching in step, with a general decline from 1956, and 'free fall' from 1963.[4] But the picture is more complicated. By the later 1960s all of the larger Protestant denominations in Britain were suffering serious losses, and nearly all forms of measurable religious activity were affected. However, in the period between 1945 and 1965 there were considerable differences between denominations and between different kinds of religious activity. Here I will focus on those denominations which were based entirely or mainly in England, and will not attempt to say how far Scotland was different. So far as the Church of England was concerned, the decline was most marked and started earliest in the case

---

[3] Dean Hoge, *Commitment on Campus* (Philadelphia, 1974), 165–6; Robert Wuthnow, *Experimentation in American Religion: The New Mysticisms and their Implications for the Churches* (Berkeley, Calif., 1978), 117–23; Ruth T. Doyle and Sheila M. Kelly, 'Comparison of Trends in Ten Denominations, 1950–75', in Hoge and Roozen (eds.), *Growth and Decline*, 144–59.

[4] Brown, *Death*, 188.

of those religious activities which were practised not only by the devout, but also by those on the margins of the churches; the decline was most delayed in the case of those activities that required the highest level of commitment. Around 1950 large numbers of non-church-going parents were still bringing their infants to be baptized and subsequently sending them to Sunday School. Both practices were already declining in the 1950s. Sarah Williams in an oral-history-based study of the south London borough of Southwark has argued that Christian identity and commitment to Christian ethics and some aspects of Christian doctrine persisted at least up to the time of the Second World War, in spite of infrequent attendance at church services.[5] As she and others have noted, one of the reasons for this was the fact that so many working-class children went to Sunday School. However, this was beginning to change in the 1950s. Sunday School enrolments as a percentage of British children aged 5–14 had peaked before the First World War, but remained high in the inter-war period. After a big drop during the Second World War, all of the larger Protestant denominations in Britain saw a rise after the war in the numbers of children enrolled, followed by a serious decline in the later 1950s. The Methodists reached their post-war peak as early as 1952; for the Baptists and maybe the Church of England (though the Anglican figures are incomplete) it came in 1953. (See Table 3.) For the Congregationalists it came in 1954, and for the Church of Scotland in 1956.[6]

Anglican baptisms per 100 live births reached a post-war peak of 67 in 1950, which was similar to the pre-war level.[7] There was then a drop to 60.2 per cent in 1956, 55.4 per cent in 1960, and 52.6 per cent in 1964. (See Table 4.) Part of the Anglican decline can be attributed to the growing proportion of the population who were Catholics—9.5 per cent of weddings in England and Wales had been Catholic in 1952, rising to 12.3 per cent in 1962—but the majority of the decline must be explained in other ways. The diocesan statistics show a strongly regionalized pattern. Between 1956 and 1964 the proportion of babies baptized in the Church of England fell by 12.6 per cent. By far the greatest decline was in the two principal cities, London and Birmingham, and in the highly urbanized northern diocese of Bradford. In all of these, non-Christian or non-Anglican immigration was likely to have been a significant factor, though, more speculatively, it can be suggested that those who were prepared to defy established conventions were disproportionately concentrated in the largest cities and that it was also in certain districts of the largest cities that community controls were weakest. Above average levels

[5] S. C. Williams, *Religious Belief and Popular Culture in Southwark* (Oxford, 1999).

[6] Robert Currie *et al.*, *Churches and Churchgoers* (Oxford, 1977), 167, 170, 187, 191.

[7] The Anglican statistics discussed in this section are all drawn from Neuss, *Facts and Figures*, or the *Official Yearbook of the Church of England*.

Table 3. England: Church of
England Sunday School children
per 1,000 estimated population
aged 3–14, 1934–1960

1934	232
1938	220
1953	177
1956	169
1958	149
1960	133

Source: Neuss, *Facts and Figures*, 61.

of decline were found in southern dioceses close to London, and sometimes including London suburbs, such as Guildford, Chelmsford, Rochester, Oxford, Ely, and St Edmundsbury and Ipswich. All of these dioceses had above average rates of population growth, and they included some of the fastest-growing areas in the whole of England. It seems likely that a highly mobile population was less amenable to the kind of pressures which still influenced behaviour in more stable communities. At the other extreme, there were several dioceses where the decline in baptisms in these years was very slight. All of them except for Worcester had below average levels of population growth. These included some rural dioceses, but most were northern and highly industrialized, with

Table 4. England: Infant Baptisms in Church of
England per 1,000 live births 1934–1973

1934	687
1938	669
1947	631
1950	672
1953	601
1956	602
1960	554
1964	526
1968	490
1973	465

Note: Between 1956 and 1964 the baptismal rate fell by 12.6%. The highest rates of decline were in the dioceses of London 25.4%, Birmingham 24.9, Southwark 24.3, Bradford 19.5, Ely 19.0, Guildford 18.3, Chelmsford 17.8, St Edmundsbury and Ipswich 17.1, Rochester 16.6, Oxford 15.7. The lowest rates were in the dioceses of Derby 0.4%, Sheffield 2.7, Sodor & Man 3.0, Worcester 3.2, Durham 4.1, Wakefield 4.2, Lincoln 4.3, Norwich 4.5, York 5.0, Liverpool 5.2.

Source: Neuss, *Facts and Figures*, 54; *Official Yearbook of the Church of England*.

a large working-class population, employed in factories or mines. These latter dioceses all had low levels of Anglican church-going but, it would seem, a high attachment to traditional rites.

One other traditional rite was also declining in the 1950s, namely the churching of mothers after childbirth. It was interpreted by some as an act of thanksgiving, and by others as a rite of purification. It had been strongly opposed by some militant Protestants, who saw it as a 'popish superstition'. Many people refused to let a new mother into their house until she had been churched, claiming that all kinds of ill-fortune might otherwise befall those living there. A survey of the diocese of Southwark in 1951 showed that this rite was widely practised, especially in the poorer working-class areas of inner south London, but that a substantial proportion of parishes reported that it was declining. Evidence from a mixture of urban and rural parishes in Berkshire and Staffordshire suggests that the peak in churching may have come before the First World War, but that in the 1950s there were still about 60 churchings to 100 baptisms. This rite declined rapidly in the 1960s and 1970s, partly because many women saw the rite as demeaning, superstitious, or old-fashioned, partly because of the lack of enthusiasm of many of the clergy, and partly because of the impact of social changes which weakened the processes by which conformity was enforced.[8]

Baptisms and Sunday School enrolments were declining sharply at a time when other religious statistics showed a more mixed picture. Very probably the decline in the proportion of children attending Sunday School in the 1950s prepared part of the way for the declining participation in the churches by adolescents and young adults in the 1960s. Most Anglican statistics show a pattern of a post-war increase, reaching a peak some time in the 1950s, followed by a period of stabilization, and then a decline in the 1960s. For instance, confirmations as a percentage of the teenage population reached a plateau between 1954 and 1960, and then declined from 1961 (see Table 2, in Chapter 2). Easter communions as a percentage of adult population peaked between 1956 and 1962, but declined steadily from 1964 (see Table 1, in Chapter 2). The Church of England enjoyed a boom in ordinations, with a continuous rise from 455 in 1955 to a peak of 636 in 1963, and clear decline coming only in 1967. There are signs however that, whereas active commitment was increasing in the post-war years and remained at a relatively high level in the later 1950s and early 1960s, the wider constituency of those with a looser attachment to the Church of England was already declining. I have noted the case of Sunday School attendance. The numbers of those

---

[8] Margaret Houlbrooke, 'The Churching of Women in the Twentieth Century' (Ph.D. thesis, University of Reading, 2006).

Table 5. England: Church of England
electoral rolls, enrolment rate per 1,000
estimated population aged 18 and over
(or from 1957 aged 17 and over), 1934–
1964

1934	132
1938	123
1947	98
1950	96
1953	95
1956	93
1958	91
1960	89
1962	85
1964	81

Source: Neuss, *Facts and Figures*.

on the church's electoral roll showed a slow but continuous decline from 1947 through to 1964 (see Table 5). In England it would seem that the post-war religious boom involved more intensive religious involvement by one section of the population—probably those already to some extent involved with the churches—at a time when there was also a growing section of the population which had little or no connection with the churches, and the number of those receiving a religious socialization was also diminishing. In Chapter 2, I mentioned the example of students, the great majority of whom came from middle-class families, and who were probably the most religiously active section of the English population in the 1950s. Richard Sykes reaches a similar conclusion in his study of the mainly working-class industrial town of Dudley. The Anglican diocesan mission of 1951 which included house-to-house visitation, was followed by a rise in the number of communicants between 1951 and 1954:

However, these local missionary efforts seem to have had the effect of strengthening the faithful (as several local clergy observed), revitalising for a time practices of worship which had been 'neglected', but generally failed to have any apparent impact on the habits of the wider constituency of those who, evidence from the late nineteenth century onwards would suggest, viewed Christian duties in ways which were much less concerned with regular church worship.[9]

English Catholics went to church in much greater numbers than their Protestant neighbours, and the decline in numbers seems to have started somewhat later. According to official figures, 52.4 per cent were attending mass regularly

[9] Richard Sykes, 'Popular Religion in Decline', *Journal of Ecclesiastical History*, 56 (2002), 292.

Table 6. England: membership of major Nonconformist denominations 1934–1970 (000s)

	Methodists	Congregationalists	Baptists
1934	763	280	253
1938	740	263	244
1947	682	221	215
1950	684	210	207
1953	684	203	202
1956	684	200	204
1958	680	196	203
1960	673	193	199
1962	665	190	195
1964	649	185	189
1966	629	180	183
1968	603	165	180
1970	572	151	173

Source: Robert Currie *et al. Churches and Churchgoers* (Oxford, 1977), 143–4, 150–1.

in 1960, and 47 per cent were still doing so in 1970. But there was then a more rapid drop to 38.6 per cent in 1980.[10] In the free churches the post-war decline started earlier than it did in the Church of England (see Table 6). Methodist membership was more or less static in absolute numbers between 1946 and 1956, and then dropped, at first slowly and then more rapidly, from 1963. The Baptists and Congregationalists were declining through most of the post-war period, though in the case of the Baptists with some temporary respites. In the case of the Congregationalists the decline started slowly but became precipitous in the later 1960s.[11]

In West Germany the picture in these years is also one of a modest decline in church-going, but a more severe decline in some aspects of the religious socialization of the young. Thus the percentage of Catholics attending mass on Sunday rose in the immediate aftermath of war and peaked at 51 per cent as early as 1949. It then fell slowly to 46 per cent in 1960 and 43 per cent in 1965, before dropping more precipitously to 37 per cent in 1970 and 27 per cent in 1980. However, the membership of parish youth organizations fell much more drastically, from 860,000 in 1953 to 450,000 in 1964. In the diocese of Münster the proportion of Catholic youth aged between 10 and 25 who belonged to a Catholic youth organization fell from 30 per cent in 1953 to 18 per cent in 1963

[10] Michael Hornsby-Smith, *The Changing Parish: A Study of Parishes, Priests and Parishioners after Vatican II* (London, 1989), 2.

[11] Currie *et al.*, *Churchgoers*, 164–5.

and 11 per cent in 1973, though there was then a slight increase.[12] Estimates of French Catholic church-going in this period vary considerably. However, Yves-Marie Hilaire, who may be regarded as an outstanding authority, suggests that, after a long period of stability, average attendance levels fell from 30 per cent to 25 per cent between 1961 and 1965, stabilized between 1965 and 1969, and then fell to 14 per cent by 1975.[13]

PUBLIC AND PRIVATE

One of the biggest revolutions in Western societies during the 1960s involved a redrawing of the boundaries between public and private. In the 1950s, concepts of decency and discretion ensured that much that was normal in private was excluded from the public sphere, and some forms of behaviour which were regarded as abnormal, but were nonetheless known to be widespread, were surrounded with secrecy and taboo. At the same time, the state penetrated the private sphere in order to punish these widespread, yet morally unacceptable and seldom openly discussed practices, including most notably homosexuality and abortion. Attacks on religion and open expressions of religious doubt lay on a borderline. On the one hand the Western world had a long and widely known history of religious scepticism going back to the seventeenth century; on the other hand the idea continued to be widely accepted that in a Christian country it was bad manners to air one's religious doubts publicly, and that at the very least the convictions of what were assumed to be the believing majority should be treated with respect. There was also a suspicion that those who openly attacked religion were likely to be political subversives or crazed fanatics. In the 1960s all of these assumptions were called in question. Already in the later 1950s elite opinion was being converted to the idea that there ought to be a sphere of private behaviour within which the individual should be guided only by conscience, and where the law ought not to intervene. Meanwhile, especially in the early 1960s, various *causes célèbres* or controversial books, plays, and films forced taboo topics into the public sphere. Then, from the mid-1960s, members of the counter-culture were flouting conventions of decency in a way that shocked many respectable citizens, but also accustomed them to new ways of thinking.

[12] Mark Edward Ruff, *The Wayward Flock* (Chapel Hill, NC, 2005), 86, 200–1; Wilhelm Damberg, 'Pfarrgemeinden und katholische Verbände vor dem Konzil', in Günther Wassilowsky (ed.), *Zweites Vatikanum: vergessene Anstösse. Gegenwärtige Fortschreibungen* (Freiburg, 2004), 13; Wilhelm Damberg, *Abschied vom Milieu? Katholizismus im Bistum Münster und in den Niederlanden 1945–1980* (Paderborn, 1997), 417–21.

[13] Yves-Marie Hilaire, 'La sociologie religieuse du catholicisme français au vingtième siècle', in Chadwick (ed.), *Catholicism*, 255–6.

In October 1960 Penguin Books, Britain's most prestigious paperback publisher, were prosecuted for obscenity.[14] In a new edition of the works of D. H. Lawrence, timed to mark the thirtieth anniversary of his death, they had included *Lady Chatterley's Lover*, renowned for its lavish use of 'four letter words', hitherto taboo in print, and its graphic descriptions of sex between the aristocratic heroine and her husband's gamekeeper. The novel had been published in Italy in 1928, and many copies were subsequently smuggled into Britain, but hitherto no British publisher had dared to risk the inevitable obscenity prosecution. The way was opened by the 1959 Obscene Publications Act which protected works of literary or scientific merit from such prosecutions, and Penguin successfully pleaded literary merit, as well as persuading various educationalists, psychologists, and theologians, including the bishop of Woolwich, to testify to the value of Lawrence's view of sex. The trial provoked enormous amounts of public discussion, and the acquittal of Penguin, as well as enabling them to sell some two million copies of the book, precipitated a flood of sexually explicit literature in the years following.

The Lady Chatterley trial provided an appropriate beginning to Britain's 1960s, introducing as it did many of the themes characteristic of that decade. The prosecuting counsel Mervyn Griffith-Jones presented *Lady Chatterley* as an immoral book, while the many witnesses called by Gerald Gardiner for the defence frequently emphasized that Lawrence was a moralist, even a puritan. Discussion of sexual morality and the desirability or otherwise of a 'new' morality was to be a constant preoccupation of those at all points on the moral and religious spectrum in the years following. One of the most sensational aspects of the trial was the appearance of John Robinson, Anglican bishop of Woolwich, as a witness for the defence and the rebuke which he subsequently received from Geoffrey Fisher, archbishop of Canterbury, who accused him of condoning adultery. Church leaders and theologians, as well as many Christian laypeople, were to play key roles on both sides of the debates in those years. Griffith-Jones accepted that 'four-letter' words were in common use in private conversation, but he did not think them appropriate in print, whereas defence witnesses wanted authenticity rather than compliance with artificial conventions. The redrawing of the boundaries between 'public' and 'private' would be a major theme of the decade. Griffith-Jones provoked laughter by some of those in the court and ridicule by numerous commentators, most notably when he asked the jury if this was a book that they would like their wife or servants to read. This was to be a decade in which figures in authority, and later the whole principle of authority, were to be under constant criticism, first through satire, but later through more direct attack.

[14] C. H. Rolph, *The Trial of Lady Chatterley* (Harmondsworth, 1961) is a transcript of the proceedings with brief commentary. Marwick, *Sixties*, 143–9, provides contextualization.

The breaking of taboos was a key theme of the early 1960s. A series of other *causes célèbres* played an important part in shaking complacency and calling in question familiar orthodoxies. The most dramatic example was the publication in Moscow in 1962 of Aleksandr Solzhenitsyn's concentration camp novel, *One Day in the Life of Ivan Denisovich*—an exercise in taboo-smashing by comparison with which Lawrence's four-letter words seem pretty tame. Perhaps the nearest to a west European Solzhenitsyn was Rolf Hochhuth whose play *Der Stellvertreter* (The Representative) was first performed in West Berlin in February 1963. The central characters of the play were a Jesuit priest (modelled on Provost Lichtenberg of Berlin, who died while being transported to a concentration camp) and Pope Pius XII. A major theme was the priest's unavailing attempts to persuade the Pope to abrogate the Concordat that had been signed with Nazi Germany in 1933 and to protest strongly and explicitly against the deportation and murder of Jews by the Nazis. Within three months the text of the play had sold 40,000 copies, as well as provoking a protest from Cardinal Montini (the future Pope Paul VI) and an apology from the German Foreign Minister. According to one commentator, the resulting discussion 'placed all previous scandals of the post-war period in the shadow'.[15] At a time when the prestige of the Catholic Church was high, and the Catholics were still congratulating themselves on their creditable role during the Nazi period, Hochhuth was the first influential writer to accuse Pope Pius XII of 'silence' in the face of Nazi crimes. Many Catholics were of course angered by what they saw as a travesty of history. But the book acted as a catalyst for criticism of the record of the churches more generally during the Third Reich, which in turn fed into criticism of their continuing authority in contemporary Germany. According to one account it was a major step towards the cultural revolution of the later 1960s, gaining approval from many journalists and students, as well as Catholic intellectuals, such as the novelist Heinrich Böll.[16]

In Quebec a book published in 1960, *Les Insolences du Frère Untel* (The Insolences of Brother Such and Such) had a similar role. The anonymous author, a brother teaching in a Catholic school, was critical of many aspects of the contemporary church, and especially of the hierarchy. Criticism that might have been ignored if made by a professed atheist or political radical were taken the more seriously because of their authorship and the book was one of those which became a best-seller by articulating ideas which many people had half-consciously thought.[17]

[15] Hermann Glaser, *Deutsche Kultur 1945–2000* (Munich, 1999), 379.

[16] Dennis L. Bark and David R. Gress, *Democracy and its Discontents* (Oxford, 1989), ii. 73–4; Egon Schwarz, 'Rolf Hochhuths "Der Stellvertreter"', in Walter Hinck (ed.), *Rolf Hochhuth: Eingriff in die Zeitgeschichte* (Reinbek bei Hamburg, 1981), 117–45.

[17] Gregory Baum, *The Church in Quebec* (Ottawa, 1991), 23.

In Britain the new mood was represented by the 'satire' movement, at its peak between 1960 and 1963. It began with the revue *Beyond the Fringe* which opened in 1960; then in 1961 came the magazine *Private Eye* and the Soho night club, The Establishment; and in 1962–3 what might have seemed a rather esoteric brand of humour was brought to an audience of millions through the television series *That Was The Week That Was* (often abbreviated to *TW3*). According to one of the satirists, their main objection was to 'the unthinking attitudes of respect' still prevalent in the United Kingdom.[18] David Frost, the programme's compère, wrote that '*TW3* started from the then revolutionary starting-point that public men were in fact the same as private men—though with more power to create havoc—and should be measured by the same criteria, without the traditional *cordon sanitaire* of sanctimony that still surrounded them'.[19] Politicians, especially Conservative politicians, were the principal targets. 'Didn't they understand', Frost questioned, 'that Fifties discipline, order and authority were, in the England of the early 1960s, not only stifling, but discredited as well. And getting more discredited with every week that *TW3* was on the air ...'[20] But the monarchy, the military, the empire, and national icons such as Winston Churchill received their share of satire—as did the Church of England, and sometimes the Roman Catholic Church. Anglicanism was attacked mainly via the clergy, especially those who were pompous, bland, or unduly trendy. Criticism of the Catholic Church focused mainly on its teachings on birth control.

Only occasionally did *TW3* venture into humorous treatment of religion in general. The most famous example was 'Why? A Consumer Guide to Religions', broadcast on 12 January 1963, which provoked a record number of complaints from viewers. After analysing the costs and benefits involved in adherence to Judaism, Buddhism, Islam, Protestantism, Roman Catholicism, and Communism, the authors of the sketch concluded by recommending the Church of England: 'All in all we think you get a jolly good little faith for a very moderate outlay and we have no hesitation in proclaiming it the Best Buy'.[21] The programme's producer, Ned Sherrin, who was himself an Anglican, argued, quite reasonably, that the programme was not attacking religion as such, but satirizing 'religion as product'. But many viewers were unconvinced. They regarded even the most apparently harmless jokes about religion (or, many would add, the royal family) as inappropriate. They were horrified by the deliberate breaking of taboos and

[18] Humphrey Carpenter, *That was Satire that was* (London, 2000), 119–20.
[19] David Frost, *An Autobiography, Part One: From Congregations to Audiences* (London, 1993), 47.
[20] Ibid. 79.
[21] David Frost and Ned Sherrin, *That Was The Week That Was* (London, 1963), 78–81.

the undermining of respect for national institutions and figures of authority. The programme on 8 December 1962, which included a particularly innocuous piece of humour at the expense of cardinals attending the Second Vatican Council, provoked an outburst by the Conservative *Daily Mail*, which claimed that: 'RELIGION was ridiculed...THE PRIME MINISTER was insulted...BERNARD LEVIN...was rude to Mr Charles Forte'.[22] In fact, several leading figures in the satire movement were Christians or Christian fellow-travellers, and though they certainly claimed the right to laugh at religion and the churches as much as anything else, their religious humour tended to lack the barbs that sometimes made their attacks on politicians so lethal. However, they played an important part in establishing a climate of criticism, in which the venerability of a tradition, the respectability of an institution, or the status carried by a figure of authority were all prima facie evidence that they ought to be rejected.

TW3 enjoyed at least for a time the protection of Hugh Carleton Greene (1910–87), who had been appointed Director General of the BBC in 1960, and who was one of the key figures in 1960s Britain because of his support for the new ethos of questioning, taboo-breaking, and lack of respect for established institutions. When Greene was appointed in 1960, he believed that there was a new mood with which the BBC should be identified. He wanted to drag it 'kicking and screaming into the Sixties'.[23] As well as professionalism and 'lively broadcasting', he wanted 'relevance', 'debate', 'provocation', and 'healthy scepticism'. He was particularly famous for the *Wednesday Play*, which specialized in frank treatment of sexual themes, damning indictments of contemporary social conditions, and plenty of 'bad language'. Critics claimed that, as well as ignoring all rules of propriety, these plays acted as a self-fulfilling prophecy: in focusing on violence, drunkenness, drug-taking, and sexual promiscuity to the exclusion of other aspects of contemporary society, they presented these forms of behaviour as 'normal' and so increased their social acceptability.[24] Greene, and others who thought like him, believed that older styles of broadcasting had presented an equally biased picture of life by suppressing those aspects which were unacceptable to guardians of official morality. Greene was said by his biographer to have had very little interest in religion. It is a reflection of the degree to which religious scepticism was still regarded as a private matter that when the chairman of the BBC governors, Sir Arthur fforde, sounded Greene out about his possible appointment as Director General, he first asked him

[22] Carpenter, *Satire*, 235, 244–7.

[23] Hugh Greene, *The Third Floor Front: A View of Broadcasting in the Sixties* (London, 1969), 13–14.

[24] Mary Whitehouse, *Who does she Think she is?* (London, 1971), 72 and *passim*. See also Michael Tracey and David Morrison, *Whitehouse* (London, 1979).

if he was a Catholic (presumably because his more famous brother, Graham Greene, was a well-known Catholic). Greene said that he would describe himself as 'a respectful agnostic', to which fforde replied: 'Well, that's alright then. Have a drink, you will be DG.'[25] Greene did not have any anti-religious agenda as Director General, and he was even responsible for introducing the highly popular Sunday evening hymn-singing programme, *Songs of Praise*. In a speech of 1965 he praised the range of religious broadcasting, 'unrivalled anywhere in the world, because of, rather than in spite of the increasingly secular nature of our society'. He agreed that the BBC should not seek to cause offence, but he added:

This does not mean that in our broadcasting on religious matters we avoid the difficult or controversial questions. The BBC long ago added religious controversy to the other forms of controversy which it is prepared to broadcast. It regards it as its duty too, to broadcast views of unbelief as well as differing beliefs. We do not, for example, think it wrong to allow broadcasting opportunities to Humanists. We believe in fact that it is our duty to remove blinkers from believers—and unbelievers too—who may be inclined to wear them.[26]

An increasingly open approach to religious broadcasting was indeed already being established before Greene became Director General. By the later 1950s, the need for cohesion and strongly defined moral and religious values with which to confront the Nazi and then Communist dangers no longer seemed so evident, and the costs of such cohesion in terms of loss of freedom, and some-times of human suffering, were becoming more apparent. Moreover the real diversity of British religion was also becoming increasingly recognized—not because of the still very small numbers of Muslims and Hindus, but because of the significant minorities of agnostics and atheists, as well as the majority of non-church-going Christians. The new approach to religious broadcasting was pioneered by the BBC's Sunday evening religious television programme, *Meeting Point*, so-called because it would 'seek to bring together those who believe that man is a spiritual being and those who believe no such thing'.[27] It started in 1956 and ran right through to 1968, providing, in the view of its crit-ics, a vehicle for the liberal theology and 'New Morality' of the decade. While programmes became more frankly provocative as time went on, right from the beginning they were based on the formula of picking a controversial issue and then presenting two or more opposing views. For instance, in February 1957 a theologian and a zoologist were discussing the 'cruelty of nature', which 'presents the Christian with one of his toughest problems', and in the following

---

[25] Michael Tracey, *A Variety of Lives: A Biography of Sir Hugh Greene* (London, 1983), 180.
[26] Greene, *Third Floor*, 108.   [27] *Radio Times* (12 Oct. 1956).

year a Christian and an atheist were discussing 'Humanism and Morals'.[28] The 'religion and' or 'religion versus' science formula remained popular, though science was most often represented by 'A Doctor' or 'A Psychiatrist'—reflecting not only the respect still enjoyed by scientists, at a time when all other forms of authority were being called in question, but also the practical nature of the issues which the programme liked to highlight.[29]

THE DECLINE OF COLLECTIVE IDENTITIES

One of the most important social changes at this time was the weakening of the collective identities rooted in confessional and ideological subcultures, which had dominated many Western societies in the period from about the 1880s to the 1950s. The full consequences of this became apparent in the 1970s and 1980s, but signs of change were already there in the 1950s and especially the 1960s. These included the blurring of boundaries between ideological communities, the effects of social mobility, and the tendencies towards greater individualism.[30]

The blurring of ideological boundaries arose primarily because of the realization by political parties and churches that they had alienated specific social or confessional groups, and that any advance in membership or influence would depend on a broadening of their appeal. Thus the Dutch Social Democrats, reinvented in 1946 as the Labour Party, tried to win the support of church-goers who had been alienated by the party's image of doctrinaire Marxism; the German Social Democrats tried to do the same with their Bad Godesberg Programme in 1959. In Belgium, the 'School Pact' of 1958 brought to an end the long-running conflict between the Catholic party and the traditionally anti-clerical Liberals and Socialists over the place of religion in the school system. In France in 1964 the 'Christian' trade union redefined itself as 'Democratic'—a code-word for 'non-Communist', but also a means of tapping new sources of support. The election of John F. Kennedy as the first Catholic president of the United States in 1960 marked a breakthrough in inter-confessional relations in a country where Protestant traditions were still strong. In this instance the cold war, and the impeccably anti-Communist stance of the Catholic Church, had helped to promote references to 'the Judeo-Christian tradition' as a much broader definition of the insiders in

---

[28] *Radio Times* (17 Feb. 1957, 9 Feb. 1958). For criticism, see Whitehouse, *Who?*, 45.

[29] See e.g. *Radio Times* (12 Feb. 1961, 17 Feb. 1963, 29 Nov. 1964).

[30] Similar points are made by Ruff, *Wayward Flock*, 192–5, in discussing the decline of the Catholic and Socialist milieux in Germany.

American society. But, with the election in 1958 of Angelo Roncalli (1881–1963) as Pope John XXIII, the Catholic Church itself was increasingly open to dialogue. John's social encyclicals of 1959 and 1963 modified the old anti-Socialism and anti-Communism by focusing on the need for joint action in pursuit of peace and the common good. Pope John's move towards dialogue was probably influenced mainly by the recognition that the division of the world into two hostile camps could end in nuclear war. Political parties were motivated chiefly by the need to increase their vote by appealing to new constituencies. In either case this more pragmatic approach marked a move towards the recognition of a *de facto* pluralism, and away from the conception of a world divided into two irreconcilably opposed camps.

In countries like Belgium and the Netherlands with their extensive confessional subcultures there were signs of strain by the later 1950s. In Netherlands a focus of tension lay in the attempts by the bishops to control many aspects of Catholic life, including telling Catholics how they should vote. After the Labour Party increased its vote in Catholic industrial districts in 1952, the bishops responded in 1954 with their anti-socialist pastoral letter. Catholic bishops defended the system of 'pillarization', which they saw this as a means of protecting Catholics from harmful Protestant or secularist influences; many Catholic intellectuals, including theologians, partly under the influence of French *nouvelle théologie*, rejected this 'ghetto' mentality, demanding more freedom of thought, more lay autonomy, and freedom to work with Protestants and secularists. Some also claimed that pastoral needs were being neglected, because so large a part of the church's resources was being devoted to maintaining the national network of Catholic institutions.[31] In Belgium, Cardinal Van Roey continued until his death in 1961 to instruct Catholics how they should vote, and he enjoyed a last success in 1955 when Catholics united to oppose the school reforms proposed by the Liberal–Socialist government. Like his anti-clerical and freethinking enemies, Van Roey assumed that the fundamental division in Belgian society was between Catholics and non-Catholics. But in 1958 the School Pact brought the long religious war to an end, and both Catholic unity and anti-clerical unity soon collapsed under the weight of other differences. Above all, the 1960s would be dominated by the language conflict, in which Walloon and Flemish solidarities overrode the old differences of religion.[32]

Edgar Morin's study in 1965 of a Breton rural commune which he named 'Plodémet' included a long section on 'The Red and the White'. Since the

[31] John A. Coleman, *The Evolution of Dutch Catholicism 1958–1974* (Berkeley, Calif., 1978), 48–57.

[32] Martin Conway, 'Belgium', in Tom Buchanan and Martin Conway (eds.), *Political Catholicism in Europe 1918–1965* (Oxford, 1996), 214–17.

1870s the commune had been polarized between a Republican majority, traditionally Radical but now mainly Communist, and a Catholic minority, which voted for right-wing parties. The conflicts were at their most intense before the First World War when, as in many parts of rural France, there were 'two networks for marriage, mutual help, suppliers, customers, tradesmen, craftsmen and *buvettes*; there were even two doctors, two garages and two hotels'.[33] In the 1960s there was still a 'red' doctor and the political and religious affiliations of the various shopkeepers and tradesmen were well-known. But except at election times the conflicts had lost a lot of their urgency, and many of those aged under 40 had scant interest in them. The attempt to found a village youth club foundered on differences of social class, but 'red' and 'white' was not an issue—while most of the youngsters came from 'red' families, they elected two Catholics as the chief officers of the club. 'Mixed' marriages between young people from 'red' and 'white' families were regarded with growing acceptance. A 'red' girl broke off her engagement when her fiancé insisted on her going to mass; but the issue was not his religion, but the threat to her personal autonomy.[34] Tolerance and compromise increasingly determined the relations between those on either side, and indeed Morin noted a tendency for the values of 'reds' and 'whites' to converge. In the early twentieth century teachers were like a secular priesthood, imbued with a sense of mission, carrying the values of Enlightenment, militant secularism, and a glorious future to be achieved through education, culture, and science. In the 1950s and 1960s teachers were still the leaders in the dwindling company of left-wing activists, but most people had a more narrowly instrumental view of education, and few people regarded teachers with veneration. Indeed, parents who voted Communist were quite happy to send their children to a Catholic school if they thought it would offer better opportunities and more up-to-date teaching methods. On the Catholic side, the nostalgia for the past which had still been strong in the earlier part of the century had long gone by the 1960s. In fact Catholic organizations had been in the forefront of the modernization of agriculture through the formation of co-operatives. The clergy were enthusiasts for education, science and technology, and 'the modern world'. In summary both sides had come to terms, however reluctantly, with the reality of a pluralist society.[35]

Meanwhile, at the local level, changes in social structure were also having an impact. One of the best-documented cases is that of Quebec, where from the mid-nineteenth century to the mid-twentieth, the Catholic Church had enjoyed a dominant role, underpinned by the close links between Catholicism

---

[33] Edgar Morin, *Plodémet* (English tr. London, 1971; 1st publ. 1967), 168.
[34] Ibid. 200.   [35] Ibid. 165–209.

and French-speaking identity in a mainly English-speaking Canada, and reinforced between 1936 and 1959 by ties between the church and the dominant
political party. In a mainly rural society, in which much of the economic
elite belonged to the English-speaking minority, the clergy were for long
the largest body of relatively well-educated people. The Liberal Party, which
came to power in 1960, introduced what came to be known as the 'Quiet
Revolution', which weakened the power of the church, notably by secularizing
the health and welfare systems, and extended state control over education, the
other former bastion of church power. The new government also fostered a
much more aggressive Quebec nationalism, which would eventually issue in
demands for separation from Canada. It has been argued that the impetus for
this 'revolution' came from a 'new middle class', including academics, social
workers, officials, and journalists, which had been growing in numbers in the
1940s and 1950s and was resentful of what they saw as the excessive power
both of English speakers and of the clergy.[36] The leaders of this 'new middle
class' included liberal Catholics, as well as those more distanced from the
church, but both could agree in criticism of the Catholic hierarchy and of
clericalism more generally, specific bones of contention being censorship and
the hierarchy's support for employers during labour disputes. In fact liberal
Catholics were key players in this revolution. The most influential journal of
the critical intelligentsia, *Cité libre*, was founded in 1951 by a group which
included the later Prime Minister, Pierre Trudeau. They were strongly influenced by Emmanuel Mounier, the French Catholic personalist and advocate of
Christian–Marxist dialogue, and many of them had a background in Catholic
Action. As Gauvreau shows, the Quiet Revolution is better understood not so
much as a movement of secularization, but as a readjustment of church–state
relations, based on the assumption that Catholicism would continue to provide the moral cement of Quebec society, though in a context where the role of
the laity was to be extended and the territory controlled by the clergy narrowed
down. Gauvreau notes, for instance, that confessional teaching continued to
be provided in state schools and that innovations such as the provision of sex
education were approved by the church. Indeed, some militant secularists were
bitterly disappointed at the limited extent of the changes.[37]

Somewhat similar changes were taking place in Belgium, and especially in
the Flemish strongholds of political Catholicism. Conway notes 'the emergence of a more educated and self-confident laity reluctant to accept uncrit-
ically the guidance of the ecclesiastical hierarchy' and the development of
'a more integrated and fluid society in which the isolation of the Catholic

---

[36] McRoberts, *Quebec*, 147–57.

[37] Michael Gauvreau, *The Catholic Origins of Quebec's Quiet Revolution, 1931–1970* (Montreal
and Kingston, Ontario, 2005), 3–13, 247–251.

community no longer seemed to many Catholics to be either feasible or desirable'.[38] It is a commonplace that in the later twentieth century declining religious practice weakened the base for confessional parties. But in Belgium, as in the Netherlands, the decline in support for Catholic parties started in the early and mid-1960s, *before* the big drop in Catholic church-going in the later 1960s and early 1970s. Thus in 1958 46.5 per cent of Belgian voters chose the Social Christians, but this then dropped to 41.4 per cent in 1961 and 34.4 per cent in 1968. The Socialists were suffering similar losses, while both Liberals and regionalist parties gained. In the Netherlands votes for the Catholic People's Party fell from 31.7 per cent in 1963 to 26.5 per cent in 1967.[39]

In scarcely perceptible ways, social mobility was also undermining the cohesion of political parties founded on class solidarity. The clearest examples of this were the Communist Parties, which emerged greatly strengthened from the Second World War because of their role in the resistance to the Nazis and Fascists and the great prestige which the Soviet Union then enjoyed. In most countries of western and northern Europe Communist membership peaked in the later 1940s,[40] though in France, Italy, and Finland they retained the support of a large part of the electorate for much longer. In Britain the two main parties, Labour and the Conservatives, suffered serious membership losses in the later 1950s and 1960s, and these continued in subsequent decades. In the Netherlands membership of political parties fell from 15 per cent of the adult population in 1945 to 10 per cent in 1963 to 3 per cent in 1994.[41] While there were a variety of reasons for this, including rejection of specific party policies, it seems likely that social changes played a part, including most notably the weakening of the class identities and the loosening of the community ties which made a mass membership possible. Certainly the activists and enthusiasts remained—and in the later 1970s and 1980s the perception of the British Labour Party as dominated by small numbers of militants had disastrous effects on its electoral fortunes. But, as with the churches, it was becoming harder to recruit the much larger numbers who in earlier times had joined the party as an expression of membership of a particular class or community (the community sometimes having a religious as well as a geographical and occupational dimension).

---

[38] Conway, 'Belgium', 214, 216; Hans Martien ten Napel, 'Christian Democracy in the Netherlands', in Lamberts (ed.), *Christian Democracy*, 55–8.

[39] R. E. M. Irving, *The Christian Democratic Parties of Western Europe* (London, 1979), 189, 213.

[40] S. Bartolini, *The Political Mobilisation of the European Left* (Cambridge, 2000), 268.

[41] Stuart Ball, 'Local Conservatism and Party Organisation', in Anthony Seldon and Stuart Ball (eds.), *Conservative Century: The Conservative Party since 1900* (Oxford, 1994), 290–2; David Howell, *British Social Democracy* (London, 1976), 280; Ruud A. Koole, 'The Societal Position of Christian Democracy in the Netherlands', in Lamberts (ed.), *Christian Democracy*, 145.

Oral history suggests some of the ways in which this was happening. Respondents born in the 1940s frequently contrast the political fervour, even fanaticism, of their parents with their own more relaxed, even indifferent, attitude. This was particularly typical of the many members of that generation who had enjoyed some degree of social mobility. One man who had been born in 1946 in a working-class family, but now had a managerial job and voted Conservative, stated that 'I think me father had sort of had Labour beaten into him'. Typical of the move from a politics based on identity and loyalty to one based on pragmatic assessment of a particular situation was a Brighton man, born 1950 in a working-class family and now manager in a small business. His parents always voted Labour, while he tended to vote Labour in local elections and Conservative in national elections. But 'there's not one particular party that we can sorta say "Yes. Definite." You can say "Well, there's a bitta that one and a bitta that one." ' Admittedly, these interviews were conducted in the 1980s, and it is not always clear when the respondents began to adopt their ultra-pragmatic attitude.[42] However, interviews in 1965 in Plodémet, an area historically polarized between a Catholic right and an anti-clerical (and by then mainly Communist) left found the same phenomenon. There were increasing numbers of floating voters, who were said to want 'competence and efficiency' rather than ideological commitment.[43]

Meanwhile official thinking was moving towards the concept of a pluralist society in which a variety of religious and ethical standpoints were recognized, and none could claim a position of privilege. Thus in 1962 the Swedish parliamentary commission on educational reform recommended a switch from confessional to 'objective' religious education: 'Today different conceptions of questions about outlooks on life manifest themselves within our people, and old normative systems, which many people still consider valid, have by others been replaced by new ones.'[44]

In Britain, important changes in ways of thinking were also indicated by the Wolfenden Report of 1957. Their recommendations with regard to the laws on male homosexuality represent a turning-point in the development of British official thinking on the relationship between law and morality and had a big influence throughout the English-speaking world.[45] In recommending

---

[42] 'Families, Social Mobility and Ageing, a Multi-Generational Approach' (henceforth FSMA), transcripts of interviews 98 and 77 (no pagination), National Sound Archive, British Library, London.

[43] Morin, *Plodémet*, 206.

[44] Daniel Alvunger, 'A Secularised Lutheran Kingdom of the Swedish Nation?', 12.

[45] G. I. T. Machin, *Churches and Social Issues in Twentieth Century Britain* (Oxford, 1998), 157; Owen Chadwick, *Michael Ramsey: a Life* (Oxford, 1990), 146; Graham Willett, 'Homosexuality in the "British World", 1945–70', paper delivered at the conference on 'Empires of Religion', Dublin, 22 June 2006, noted the considerable influence of Wolfenden in Canada, Australia, and New Zealand.

that homosexual acts 'between consenting adults in private' should no longer be punished by law, the committee made a distinction between the sphere of morality which concerns all areas of human behaviour and the sphere of law, which is much narrower, and which should only embrace those forms of immoral or irresponsible behaviour that disturb public order. Although the proposed reforms were not in fact enacted for another ten years, there was a rapid change in elite opinion, including that of many church leaders. For instance, Geoffrey Fisher, the archbishop of Canterbury, agreed with the recommendations, although he continued to regard homosexual acts as sinful. Michael Ramsey, then archbishop of York, claimed never to have given the issue any thought before, but to have been immediately converted by the report.

POINTERS TO THE 1960s

In the later 1960s the range of religious options seemed to be widening day by day. But some of the new possibilities were already emerging in the more staid 1950s.

San Francisco, the international hippie capital of the later 1960s, was known in the 1950s as the home of the Beats. They were the role models for the 'Beatniks', the avant-garde of youthful nonconformity around 1960, and according to one version they also inspired the name chosen by a obscure group of young Liverpool musicians in early 1960—The Beatles. Zen Buddhism was emerging as the religion in fashion in San Francisco. Expounded in more academic fashion in the books of D. T. Suzuki and Alan Watts, it received poetic treatment in the novels of Jack Kerouac, such as *Dharma Bums* (1958) and the poems of Allen Ginsberg. Other early pointers to the new religious world of the late 1960s came in 1960: a Belgian Benedictine published a book on Christian Yoga, and the Harvard psychologist Timothy Leary began his experiments with psychedelic drugs.[46]

In Cambridge a group of theologians started meeting in 1957.[47] They had noted that 1960 would mark the centenary of *Essays and Reviews*, the book which had introduced modern German biblical criticism to the Anglican public, and had led to the (ultimately unsuccessful) prosecution of two contributors for heresy. The Cambridge theologians, of whom the most prominent was Alec Vidler, dean of King's College, believed that any attempt

[46] Robert S. Ellwood Jr, *Alternative Altars: Unconventional and Eastern Spirituality in America* (Chicago, 1979), 136–67; Jay Stevens, *Storming Heaven: LSD and the American Dream* (New York, 1987), 121–35.

[47] This account is based on Keith W. Clements, *Lovers of Discord: Twentieth-Century Theological Controversies in England* (London, 1988), 143–77.

at a new theological synthesis would be premature, but that there was an urgent need for questioning of existing orthodoxies. They were particularly concerned at what seemed the current mood of complacency in the Church of England (to which they all belonged). The result was a collection of essays entitled *Soundings*, which caused a lot of controversy in that church when it was published in 1962, and which anticipated some of the ideas which become common currency by the middle of the decade. The book also established the reputation and notoriety of Cambridge as the main centre of new theological thinking in England, which would remain throughout the 1960s. One reason for the interest in the volume was simply the authors' insistence that Christian theology, rather than consisting of unchangeable orthodoxies, should always be open to questioning in the light of new knowledge and new experience. An important influence on their thinking was Dietrich Bonhoeffer, executed by the Nazis in 1945, who was to become the principal theological hero of the 1960s, partly because of his heroic life and death, and partly because of the resonance of some of the ideas contained in his posthumously published prison writings. They were especially attracted by his idea of a 'religionless Christianity'.

One line of criticism by the Cambridge group focused on the church: they complained that it was imprisoned within a religious subculture and was not relating to the needs of contemporary society or speaking in a language which contemporaries understood. This aspect of the book gained special publicity when Vidler appeared on a television programme about the Church of England in which, much to the dismay of many fellow Anglicans, he devoted most of his efforts to attacking his church. A second aspect of the book, and the one that caused the most controversy, was a chapter by Harry Williams, dean of Trinity College, drawing on insights from Freudian psychology in order to criticize conventional Christian ethics, and especially sexual ethics. In particular he condemned the undue emphasis on sin and guilt in the Book of Common Prayer, which in his view had damaging psychological effects and actually proved ethically counterproductive. Williams, it later emerged, was drawing on the experience of painfully coming to terms with his own homosexuality. However, his call for an ethics based on love rather than law anticipated a theme that would be repeated many times in the years following, and which would deeply divide Christians.

Meanwhile Christian students were getting increasingly involved in social action. The United States offers a striking example. Sporadically in the later 1950s, and then in a concentrated wave from February 1960, African American students, with white students sometimes supporting, defied segregation by non-violent direct action. The most common form of protest was to sit down in an all-white restaurant and demand to be served. But other protesters picketed discriminatory employers, took a 'freedom ride' on a segregated bus, or staged a 'pray-in' in an all-white church. It was in keeping with the community-leadership role which the black church played in the southern states that divinity students were often among the leaders in these protests. So for instance in Nashville, Tennessee, the protests were led by students from Vanderbilt Divinity School, including most notably James Lawson, a Christian pacifist, who was expelled from the university, and went on to found the Student Non-Violent Co-ordinating Committee (SNCC), a key civil rights player in the following years, and a stronghold of radicalism.[48]

American Christian students were also being radicalized by participation in the large international conferences organized by the Student Volunteer Movement (SVM), which brought them into contact with students from Asia, Africa, Latin America, and the Caribbean, many of whom gave the North Americans their first encounter with anti-Americanism. The SVM had started in the later nineteenth century with the aim of recruiting students for overseas missions. By the 1950s the movement had a very broad conception of mission which included a keen political and social awareness, and often a very critical view of Western imperialism. One of the main organizers of these conferences, Ruth Harris, had been a missionary in China and remained very sympathetic to the Communist revolution, although the Communists eventually expelled her. The 1955 conference had concluded that 'A primary task of the church in the modern world is to smash the barriers of racial segregation and prejudice everywhere'. But it was the conference at Athens, Ohio, in December 1959, where Martin Luther King Jr was among the speakers, which had a more immediate impact. When the sit-in movement began a month later in North Carolina, soon spreading to ten other states, and leading to some two thousand arrests, it was claimed that every demonstration included at least one student who had been at the Athens conference.[49]

In France the catalyst was the Algerian War of 1954–62. The French bishops condemned the use of torture by the French forces, but the Catholic student organization (JEC) went much further, openly supporting the independence movement. In a complaint that would often be heard in the 1960s, the archbishop of Bourges criticized the Catholic students for their excessive concern with the political, and consequent neglect of the spiritual. As Gérard Cholvy comments, the bishops were taking the position traditionally argued by French anti-clericals, according to which religion and politics must be separated, whereas the student radicals championed the traditionally

---

[48] Silk, *Spiritual Politics*, 108–35.
[49] Sara M. Evans, *Journeys that Opened up the World* (New Brunswick, NJ, 2003), 17.

'clericalist' position that true Christianity leads inevitably to political action.[50]

And most important of all the new religious developments in these years was the election of Pope John XXIII in November 1958, and his decision, announced in January 1959, to call a council. Some Vatican officials hoped that the council would concentrate on reaffirming disputed teachings and condemning modern errors.[51] Some bishops promised the faithful that nothing would change. Others were consciously or unconsciously preparing the ground for reform. In the Netherlands a new generation of modernizing bishops was appointed around 1960, and older bishops were adapting to changing times. Cardinal Alfrink, who had endorsed the controversial Pastoral Letter of 1954, was now talking of a more decentralized and less rigorously disciplined church, and of the need for 'pluriformity'. Two new bishops appointed in that year, Bekkers at Den Bosch and van Dodewaard at Haarlem, stressed the role of the laity and the need for a non-authoritarian style of leadership. The bishops' Christmas letter of 1960 was the first official document to air the idea of collegiality. It also called for the whole church to be involved in the council discussions, and this theme was often repeated by the Dutch bishops in the years following.[52]

CONCLUSION

The 'early 1960s' from about the later 1950s to 1962 or 1963 had a distinctive atmosphere. They provide a bridge between the post-war years, with their urgent demands to 'return to normality' and the all-embracing spirit of experiment and iconoclasm in the late 1960s; between the coldest years of the cold war and the utopian hopes of '1968'. Major religious changes were already under way, even if as yet their extent could not be known, and even if their direction was not entirely clear. The post-war church-going boom had come to an end, and in some countries congregations were already shrinking, albeit slowly. The power and prestige which the churches had often enjoyed in the years after the war and the associated atmosphere of moral conservatism were increasingly resented and were coming under attack—often in indirect ways. These were the years of satire and of the *causes célèbres* which forced previously taboo topics into the public domain. It was also a time when reformers and radicals were making their voices heard again within the churches.

---

[50] Gérard Cholvy and Yves-Marie Hilaire, *Histoire religieuse de la France contemporaine 1930–1988* (Toulouse, 1988), 243, 254–5; Michael Kelly, 'Catholicism and the Left in Twentieth-Century France', in Chadwick (ed.), *Catholicism*, 158–9.

[51] Peter Hebblethwaite, *John XXIII, Pope of the Council* (London 1984), 401–2.

[52] Coleman, *Dutch Catholicism*, 102–7.

4

Aggiornamento

Pope John said that the task of the Second Vatican Council would be *aggiornamento*—a bringing up to date, or renewal, of the church. The same spirit was also sweeping through the Protestant churches at this time. Religious reform was important news for the media and for considerable sections of the general public. The middle 1960s were a time of intense, but also critical, religious interest[1]—a time when every tradition and convention was open to question, and a reforming consensus seemed to be emerging. John Robinson liked to speak of a 'New Reformation' in the making.

THE NEW REFORMATION

The fact that large numbers of people, young as well as old, were keenly interested in new approaches to Christianity, had already been shown in February 1963, when some 1,500 Cambridge students regularly trudged through the snow to hear a series of open lectures on 'Objections to Christian Belief'. The lecturers were not humanists, but Christian theologians. The leaders of the 'Soundings' group, Alec Vidler and Harry Williams, were joined by Donald MacKinnon and J. S. Bezzant. 'Belief in Christianity, or in anything else,' argued Vidler, 'if it is to be mature, must want to face the worse that can be said against it and evade no difficulties.' Indeed the book of the lectures (subsequently published as a Penguin paperback) set a fashion for self-criticism, with similar volumes being produced by teams of Catholics and of Humanists—though one reviewer accused the latter of 'praising' their creed 'with faint damns'. Such charges could not have been laid against the Cambridge Anglicans who laid about their own faith with a vigour that won the admiration of some readers, while disgusting others—though their target

[1] The latest general history of Britain in the 1960s, Dominic Sandbrook, *White Heat: A History of Britain in the Swinging Sixties* (London, 2006), 432, rightly notes that 'Although the sixties are often seen as a secular, even post-religious, age, in few decades of the twentieth century were religious issues so hotly and enthusiastically debated.'

was not so much 'Christian belief' as the ways in which it had been interpreted and practised. They lambasted dogmatism, legalism, and 'cosy ecclesiasticism'. Vidler claimed to have more sympathy with sceptics who possessed a sense of the mystery of life than with cocksure believers. Williams, who felt that too many Christians had a damaging and exaggerated sense of guilt, suggested that those condemned by conventional morality were often closer to the heart of Christianity than the routinely pious. MacKinnon was hostile to any form of Christian triumphalism: he objected to portrayals of 'Christ the King' and wanted Christians to focus on 'the crucified'. Many of the typical themes of 1960s Christianity were stated or implied here: a critical view of the church (and indeed of institutions generally); an insistence that the best practical Christianity was often to be found outside the church; the rejection of a legalistic code of morality in favour of situation ethics; the claim that the true place of Christians is with the marginalized, and a consequent suspicion of any kind of respectability or recognized status; a horror of dogma.[2]

A month later new theology became front page news. On 17 March 1963 the headline in the review section of London's Sunday *Observer* declared 'OUR IMAGE OF GOD MUST GO'. The author was John Robinson, and the article was a trailer for his book, *Honest to God*. On publication the following week the book was an instant best-seller. It was translated into twelve languages, and by 1967 it had sold over a million copies. The book arose out of Robinson's conviction that his church was failing to teach Christianity in a way that made sense to contemporary men and women. He had three main answers to the problem. The largest part of his slim volume, and the part that seems to have caused the greatest controversy, was concerned with updating Christian language and imagery to make it more meaningful to a scientific age. But secondly he was very impressed by Dietrich Bonhoeffer's *Letters and Papers from Prison*, and his concept of 'religionless Christianity'. Robinson feared that instead of entering into every aspect of life, including those deemed most 'secular', Christianity had been separated off into a compartment labelled 'religion', which had little relationship with the rest, and might even offer a means of escape from the tragic or the merely mundane. Thirdly, he advocated a 'new morality', based on love, applied creatively to the needs of the actual situation, rather than on a legalistic ethical code. He was fond of quoting

[2] D. M. MacKinnon *et al.*, *Objections to Christian Belief* (Harmondsworth, 1965; 1st publ. 1963). For comments on the interest attracted by these lectures, see Keith W. Clements, *Lovers of Discord* (London, 1988), 168. At the same time, 'day by day from February 10 to 17, the big hall of the Examinations Schools was full' for the Oxford University mission led by Trevor Huddleston: see *Church Times* (22 Feb. 1963).

St Augustine's injunction to 'love, and then do as you will' (or to 'love God, and then do as you will', as it is sometimes interpreted).

About four thousand people wrote to Robinson, some to condemn what he had written, but many to tell him that this was the book that they had been waiting for. The critics tended to accuse Robinson of abusing his position as a bishop in order to shake the simple faith of ordinary believers. According to one letter which, according to David Edwards, who edited the correspondence, 'represents many':

I always thought it was the parson's job to get people to go to church, but if there are many like you nobody will go. The parsons have always spoken of a God up there, but now the parsons are contradicting everything they have said. therefore the working man has started talking thus, 'If the parsons say everything they have taught us is wrong, how can they be right as to what they tell us now?'[3]

Some of the clergymen who wrote to Robinson agreed that he was making their task more difficult. One claimed that his parishioners needed 'not the strong meat of the advanced theologian, but the simple milk of the Gospel'.[4]

On the other hand, most of those who wrote to Robinson were sympathetic,[5] and many expressed relief or joy at having read his book. This was partly because they were more critical of the church and more pessimistic about the contemporary religious situation. They decried the notion of a mass of 'simple believers' wedded to traditional doctrines and practices: on the contrary, they argued that urgent action was needed to stem a rising tide of religious doubt. For instance, an Oxford undergraduate wrote:

Many prominent men in the Church of England have allowed their unmeditated reaction to your ideas to appear in print. Such men are unaware of the urgency of the need for a new image, and of the harmful contempt for the Christian religion which the old mythological image arouses amongst the younger generation, both at university and in the ordinary grammar school.[6]

The typical correspondent had despaired of Christianity as s/he had heard it taught in church or school, but praised Robinson for providing a version that made sense. It was not always clear what they liked about the book, though worries about 'mythology', conflicts between religion and science, or particular doctrines (for instance, the virgin birth, divinity of Christ, or life after death) bulked large. None of the correspondents quoted by Edwards referred to Robinson's 'New Morality', though it was mentioned, usually critically, in some of the reviews in newspapers and journals. A later analysis by Robert Towler of some 200 letters found that 12 focused mainly on questions of ethics

---

[3] John A. T. Robinson and David L. Edwards, *The Honest to God Debate* (London, 1963), 49.
[4] Ibid. 50.   [5] Ibid. 48.   [6] Ibid. 62.

but that the largest category (36 letters) focused on 'questions of belief'. It seems to have been Robinson's attempt to find new ways of thinking about God that caused most excitement.[7] The correspondents included many clergy and teachers, who complained of their difficulties in presenting Christianity to their parishioners or pupils, and welcomed Robinson's book as offering a way forward. One public school headmaster shared some of the qualms expressed by Robinson's critics, but also argued that the break with the past was necessary and inevitable:

I agree that this is a tremendously exciting time to be alive in the history of the Church—though we may well be coming to a sort of end of the history of the Church. This is a revolution of far greater consequence than Luther's and Calvin's. Of the same order of consequence as Constantine's. But this means that we must now go into a period of ferment, and the worrying thing is that while intelligent and thoughtful people can clearly accept the *sturm und drang* which is about to descend on the Church, or well up from it, what is going to happen to the admiring believer? What happens to our school chapel in what may easily be 50 years of redefinition?[8]

This mixture of a keen interest in religious questions with a refusal to accept prepackaged answers was noticed by David Frost, one of the leading figures in British television in the 1960s. Frost first made his name as presenter of *That Was The Week That Was* and other satirical programmes. He went on to specialize in discussion programmes where a panel, or sometimes a single interviewee, interacted with an audience. He introduced this format in *The Frost Programme*, which started in the autumn of 1966. He later wrote: 'As the series progressed we found ourselves wanting to give more and more attention to matters of morality and faith'. When in October of that year a working party of the British Council of Churches stated that 'In the field of sexual relations, rules in themselves are not an adequate guide to morality', Frost responded by staging a discussion between a conservative Christian, a liberal Christian, a humanist, and the author of a popular sex manual. Particular interest was aroused by a debate between the bishop of Kingston and the Manchester academic, John Allegro, as to whether Jesus was a historical figure. Frost commented:

The reaction to the programme confirmed a belief I had held, that despite the growth in scepticism—or perhaps because of it—religion and everything that went with it was still a subject of consuming interest, provided that the questions asked were those that the public wanted to hear answered, and not imposed from above by dogma.[9]

[7] Robinson and Edwards, *Debate*, 99, 104, 117, 178–80; and positively 124; Robert Towler, *The Need for Certainty: A Sociological Study of Conventional Religion* (London, 1984), 120–6.

[8] Edwards and Robinson, *Debate*, 71.

[9] David Frost, *An Autobiography* (London, 1993), 222–3.

He later interviewed the archbishop of Canterbury, Michael Ramsey:

The programme that resulted was in some ways a statistical phenomenon. While the Archbishop held immense prestige and respect I was told by everybody that we could not expect our usual level of ratings for such a programme. In fact, these fears proved unjustified because, I think, of the audience's deep concerns as well as the Archbishop's charismatic and lucid performance.[10]

While *Honest to God* polarized the British religious world, similar ideas were developed and taken much further by theologians in the United States. Robinson's 'new morality' drew on the ideas of Joseph Fletcher, and Fletcher was to go on to publish the standard exposition of *Situation Ethics* (1966). 'Religionless Christianity' found its fullest expression in Harvey Cox's *Secular City* (1965). And the 'Christian atheism' of which Robinson was perversely accused (mostly by people who had not read his book) was advocated by some of the American 'Death of God' theologians (though they differed among themselves in the meaning they gave to this much quoted phrase). Again, the media played a big role in acquainting a wider public with the new thinking. 'IS GOD DEAD?' asked *Time* magazine in giant capitals on the cover of its Easter 1966 issue.[11] The question was inspired by a recently published book, *Radical Theology and the Death of God* by Thomas Altizer and William Hamilton, as well as by the works of Gabriel Vahanian and Paul van Buren. Hamilton took to extremes the progressivist optimism which flourished in the early and middle years of the decade. He claimed that the death of God could be dated precisely to 4 January 1965, which saw the death of T. S. Eliot, poet of alienation, as well as Lyndon Johnson's expansive State of the Union address, in which he invited his fellow-countrymen 'to enter the world of the twentieth century'. Hamilton saw signs of hope everywhere—from the progress of social science to the music of the Beatles. In terms which still seemed just credible, but would very soon appear absurd, he proclaimed America's messianic role as pioneer of a new civilization.[12]

There was thus a highly profiled Protestant avant-garde in the mid-1960s sharing certain key ideas, though also with major differences. The hopes of these years were well represented by the British journal, *New Christian*, founded in October 1965, with an Anglican editor and an editorial board deliberately composed of members of different Christian denominations ranging from Catholic to Baptist to Quaker—all of them men, except for the business manager. The editorial team largely represented what might be called the liberal establishment. (The only one who would have strongly objected to such a description was the Catholic Marxist, Neil Middleton.) The

[10] Ibid. 223–4.   [11] Patrick Allitt, *Religion in America since 1945* (New York, 2003), 75.
[12] Ibid. 74.

chairman, Kenneth Slack, had been General Secretary of the British Council of Churches and the two Anglicans went on to be canons of Westminster. Two of the most frequent contributors were John Robinson and the dissident Catholic theologian Charles Davis.

The opening editorial declared that '*New Christian* is published to-day to meet an obvious need. At a time of ferment and reformation in the Church, there is need for a channel of communication which is open to new thought and action coming from many different quarters'. Their approach would be thoroughly ecumenical, and they would focus on 'world affairs', going beyond 'traditional "moral issues",' and on 'the interpretation of the Christian faith in language and ideas which are appropriate to the twentieth century'.[13] This was a fair description of what the journal provided. The standard of journalism was superior in terms of the quality of writing, the thoroughness with which issues were discussed, and the lack of any denominational axe to grind, to any of the other British Christian papers of the times. The intended reader was a highly literate church-going Christian, probably of relatively liberal theological views and left of centre politics, though the letters column suggested that they were also attracting readers with more conservative tendencies. Bonhoeffer was the theological hero of many of the contributors. A typical example was a long article by the Revd Chad Varah, the London clergyman who founded the Samaritans, the telephone helpline for the suicidal:

In many situations, communication by speech alone is ineffective. One can only usefully *be*, or *act*, or *suffer*.... The new Christian knows he is called to be Christ in his world, to let Christ act and suffer in and through him. He seeks opportunities to take the form of a servant. He finds more and more of these opportunities in our day outside the church premises and the normal parochial activities, and, most significant of all, he finds himself working in mutual respect alongside colleagues who do not profess his faith.

The Samaritans was the wrong place both for 'the militant atheist' and for 'the compulsive evangeliser', since neither had any respect for beliefs other than their own. But Christians, Jews, Buddhists, Humanists could work together, and each could see this work as a practical application of their own beliefs.[14]

In November 1965 the theatre critic, Kenneth Tynan, became the first person to say 'fuck' on British television—leading his biographers to regret that other more notable aspects of his career have been eclipsed by this one piece of notoriety. *New Christian* responded with an editorial denouncing censorship, and concluding that 'the real obscenities are being enacted in Vietnam and Rhodesia'.[15] Current politics, including especially Vietnam and

---

[13] *New Christian* (7 Oct. 1965).   [14] *New Christian* (4 Nov. 1965).

[15] *New Christian* (2 Dec. 1965).

Rhodesia, but also race relations, nuclear weapons, and religious persecution in the Soviet bloc were a central concern of the paper. At the same time they gave a lot of attention to theology, from a position that might be termed liberal orthodox. For instance, David Edwards, a member of the editorial board who was an Anglican clergyman, wrote a long article on 'Seeing Jesus Now: Can an Educated Person be a Christian To-day?' in which he deplored undue stress on abstract dogmas, rather than 'the real Jesus': he believed in the resurrection, but he did not think that those who were unable to do so should thereby be excluded from the church.[16] While Callum Brown has argued that the churches in the 1960s were in a constant state of panic about sex, *New Christian* not only gave far more attention to other issues, but showed a complete lack of panic when it did turn its attention to sex. It strongly supported decriminalization of male homosexuality, though one reader criticized the paper for being insufficiently enthusiastic about gay sex. Soon after, however, the paper published a very positive article about lesbianism.[17] An interview with Mary Whitehouse, leader of the campaign to 'Clean Up TV', though it gave a fair summary of her views, was clearly critical of what she was saying. It prompted only one reader's letter in her defence—which suggests that few readers of the paper supported her campaign. (Controversial articles often provoked many responses and a prolonged correspondence.) As I will suggest in Chapter 10, Whitehouse represented the conservative end of the spectrum of Christian opinion at the time, and was far from being representative. Even the moderately conservative Anglican *Church Times*, which was more sympathetic to her stance than *New Christian*, presented a measured and unpanicked response to contemporary sexual mores, and gave far more attention to other contemporary issues, ranging from evangelism, to church union schemes, to race relations in Rhodesia, South Africa, and Britain, to the Vietnam War.[18]

Meanwhile many clergy were convinced of the need for 'relevance' and 'action'—sometimes to the extent of abandoning their ministry in favour of some form of social work, which seemed to be practising Christ's injunction

---

[16] Ibid.

[17] Callum Brown, lecture at the Anglo-American Historical Conference, London, 6 July 2006; *New Christian* (24 Feb., 10 Mar., 7 Apr. 1966).

[18] *New Christian* (24 Mar. 1966). A typical example of the *Church Times* approach was an article 'Our Morals—Then and Now' by P. A. Welsby (13 Aug. 1965), which regretted some contemporary trends, but denied that sexual morality had been superior in the past, and criticized undue emphasis on sex rather than on other equally or more important aspects of morality. See also articles by their regular columnist, Margaret Duggan. For instance, 'Letter to my Daughter' (2 Feb. 1968), prompted by the news that her daughter was to study *Lady Chatterley's Lover* as an 'A' Level text, was a thoughtful, and in many respects sympathetic, Christian critique of Lawrence.

to 'feed the hungry and clothe the naked' in a more direct way. A drop in Anglican ordinations in 1967 led to the following observations:

So powerful is the attraction of this social welfare work and the pressure to share in it that it is easy in the modern world to feel on the shelf and socially redundant if one is not actively and completely committed to it. . . . These doubts have not produced many withdrawals from the ministry of men already ordained (though there have been a few) but they have had great influence in steering men away from ordination into more effective channels of professional social work. . . . So great is the contemporary emphasis on this social work that it becomes almost impossible to bring oneself to make the assertion that the first task of the priest is not social work and the development of social betterment. The atmosphere of the times makes that sound like a contemporary obscenity or blasphemy.[19]

The Revd Nicholas Stacey, rector of Woolwich in south-east London, gained a lot of media attention in the 1960s through his attempts to make his church a multipurpose community centre. In 1965, he was recommending that 'most of the clergy now engaged in parochial work should leave their parishes and take secular jobs, especially in the welfare and social services run by the State'. He also wanted a 'structural slimming down', with most of the money spent on clerical salaries and maintenance of buildings being diverted to what a reporter called 'new social experiments', and a similar doctrinal slimming down, allowing for more freedom of belief. He later left his parish to work for Oxfam and then to become a director of social services.[20]

Probably the two groups most strongly affected by the new theologies of the 1960s were religious professionals and students. In liberal Christian student organizations like the SCM the tension between 'Christianity' and 'religion' would become a cliché in the 1960s. Sara Evans, introducing a collection of memories of women who had been active in the American Christian student movement of the 1960s, recalls:

Most of us arrived on college campuses in the 1950s and 1960s to find an energetic, intellectually lively student Christian movement. Some of us found that the challenges shook us to our roots, forcing a confrontation between deeply held values of our Christian heritage and the realities of social injustice. Others were thrilled finally to have a language (existential theology, for the most part) that released us from attention to dogma and focused instead on action, on living a life in response to the injunction to 'love thy neighbour'.[21]

---

[19] *Church Times* (23 Feb. 1968).
[20] *Church Times* (28 May 1965); Paul A. Welsby, *A History of the Church of England 1945–1980* (Oxford, 1984), 105. For similar views in Australia around this time, David Hilliard, 'The Religious Crisis of the 1960s', *Journal of Religious History*, 21 (1997), 213.
[21] Sara M. Evans, *Journeys that Opened up the World* (New Brunswick, NJ, 2003), 9–10.

Campus ministers played a part in their radicalism by introducing students to new theologies, above all those of Dietrich Bonhoeffer and Paul Tillich, who provided alternatives to the conservative evangelical theologies on which many of them had been brought up. Some were introduced to activism through the YWCA which, in 1970, would adopt the 'One imperative' of 'the elimination of racism, wherever it exists and by any means necessary'.[22] Participation in national and especially international Christian student conferences also made a big impact, as young Americans who had been brought up in a spirit of intense patriotism and anti-communism were exposed to harsh criticism of their country's international role and a much more positive view of some of America's enemies, notably Cuba. Above all it was the Civil Rights Movement which provided an unquestionably just cause, and one whose most prominent leaders were Christians, insisting that the battle be fought with the 'Christian weapons' of non-violent direct action. The experience of a generation of Christian activists was summed up in the story of M. Sheila McCurdy, who had been born in Alabama in 1944, the daughter of a Methodist minister, and who in 1963 was a student at a small Methodist college in Montgomery. Hearing that Martin Luther King was going to preach at Dexter Avenue Baptist Church, she determined to hear him, although the church was one of many places declared out of bounds by the college authorities. She entered the church 'terrified'. 'All the taboos of my childhood in a segregated society were there'. But she was calmed by the singing of 'We shall overcome':

I was amazed that my own sense of powerlessness began to be replaced by strength within that gathered community. Then Dr King began to preach, and I began to see the vision that he so powerfully proclaimed. As I heard his prophetic words, I knew that my life would never be the same again. When I reflect on that evening, I realize that it was a conversion experience, a time in which I experienced the liberating spirit of the God of Exodus in a new way. My understanding of the church as the community of the faithful would be deeply strengthened as I experienced the courage and commitment of countless persons in the civil rights movement.[23]

Alabama in 1963 was, as McCurdy writes, 'a police state', and those who fought against segregation would need faith, courage, and commitment in ample measures. But, as her account indicates, the movement also offered comradeship, moments of exaltation, a sense of being present as history was being made, and a new sense of purpose, based on a more authentic understanding of Christianity. Many people experienced these emotions most intensely during the march from Selma to Montgomery in March 1965, which in retrospect could be seen as Martin Luther King's last great victory before the movement began to fragment. Ruth Harris who had been a missionary in

---

[22] Ibid. 254.   [23] Ibid. 158.

China was one of many who responded to King's call for volunteers to join a second march after the first had been stopped by Alabama state troopers. The two weeks of preparation in an African American district of Selma was one of the great memories of her life:

We had inspired preaching, glorious singing, laughing and weeping, eating, and some-times sleeping—and through it all, courage, deep joy, and the power of the Spirit. For the first time the reality that I had experienced in China... was apparent in my own country. I was part of the church ALIVE![24]

In Selma she 'experienced power in a melding together of political action and religious faith and morality':

This was Dr King's way. He refused to let politics and religion be separated. For him it was not whether they mix, but rather how to establish as great a degree of congruence as possible between the nature of the God we worship and the nature of the human action that we undertake in God's name.[25]

Typical of the new orthodoxies of these years was the opening in 1966 of a non-denominational school and community centre in Roxbury, an African American district of Boston. According to the Catholic nuns who worked there it would 'eliminat[e] the barriers which separate Negro and white, the inner city and suburb, Catholic and non-Catholic, the sacred and secular. Such endeavours seem logical outcomes of Vatican II and of the Constitution on the Church and the Decree on Christian Education'.[26] Of all these oppositions it was the separation between sacred and secular which was most offensive to the progressive Christians of the 1960s. The Christian gospel was relevant to every area of life, but it was not dependent on Christian institutions, or even on the presence of professing Christians. Institutions too often became an end in themselves, and their leaders too readily became preoccupied with power, status, and money. The atheist who 'fed the hungry and clothed the naked' was more truly a follower of Christ than those Christians who failed to get involved in the great political and social struggles of the day.

VATICAN II

The most dramatic expression of the spirit of reform which seemed to be dominant in the mid-1960s was the Second Vatican Council.[27] It met in four

---

[24] Evans, *Journeys*, 40.   [25] Ibid. 43.

[26] John T. McGreevy, *Parish Boundaries: The Catholic Encounter with Race in the Twentieth-Century Urban North* (Chicago, 1996), 177.

[27] The literature on Vatican II is vast. A good overview of the Council and its impact is Adrian Hastings (ed.), *Modern Catholicism* (London, 1991).

sessions between October 1962 and December 1965. The Council Fathers comprised some two thousand bishops and abbots with the right to speak and vote, but many of the bishops had brought with them theologians or other expert advisers. There were also in attendance large numbers of observers, including official representatives of other churches, not to mention numerous journalists. Of the latter the most famous was an American priest with the pseudonym Xavier Rynne whose talents for digging up gossip and uncovering behind the scenes manœuvring helped both to demystify the proceedings and to maintain public interest at a high level. Pope John XXIII presided over the first session, ensuring that the reforming agenda of many of the bishops from northern Europe would be addressed, and defeating efforts by conservative curial officials to pre-empt debate. Pope John died in June 1963. But the election of Giovanni Battista Montini (1897–1978), archbishop of Milan, as Pope Paul VI ensured that the voices of moderate reform would remain in the ascendant. The Council had the challenging task of producing a series of documents which would restate each aspect of Catholic teaching in terms more relevant to the contemporary world, but without changing its substance. The main immediate consequence was the change from the mass in Latin— the sacred language understood by only the best-educated of the laity—to the mass in the local vernacular. But the Council documents presented Catholics with many new concepts, some with potentially revolutionary implications, the practical application of which would be the business of the following years.

Three aspects of the Council documents were particularly significant. First, in stressing that the leadership of the church should be 'collegial', in affirming the 'apostolate of the laity', and in declaring that the whole church was 'the people of God', the Council Fathers seemed to be pointing towards a more decentralized and less hierarchical church, all of whose members could exercise a responsible role. Second, the declaration on 'Religious Liberty' emphasized the rights of the individual conscience, and moved away from the long-established principle that the Catholic Church as the only teacher of the truth, should seek special (and even exclusive) privileges wherever secular authority was willing to grant them. Third, in emphasizing that there is a 'hierarchy of truths' among which only some were essential, they prepared the ground for closer relations with other Christian churches and specifically for full participation in the ecumenical movement, which previous popes had condemned. Furthermore, the new enthusiasm for 'dialogue' allowed for a more positive view of non-Christian religions, and even of atheists. In particular, the Constitution on the Church in the Modern World, *Gaudium et Spes*, presented a mainly positive view of contemporary culture and was optimistic about the possibilities for collaboration between Catholics and others in the common interests of humanity. Many enthusiastic reformers saw *Gaudium et Spes* as the crowning achievement of the Council; those who were more sceptical about the Council's legacy directed their fire especially at this constitution and what they saw as its excessive optimism about human nature in general and the contemporary world in particular.[28]

It soon became apparent that putting into practice the principles enunciated in the Council documents would be a difficult, and sometimes very controversial task. Two of the biggest problems were inherent in the whole exercise: *aggiornamento* had to be reconciled with maintaining the essential continuity of Catholic teaching; and, while presenting Catholics with many radical new concepts, the Council did nothing to change the church's very hierarchical structures. For instance, bishops continued to be nominated by the pope, and there was no requirement that in doing so he should take any account of the views of priests or laypeople in the diocese. Pastors of parishes were nominated by the bishop who, equally, might ignore the views of those living in the parish. Pastors might choose to consult assistant priests, religious sisters, and lay parishioners, but if they chose not to do so, there was very little anyone could do about it, beyond complaining to the bishop. Furthermore, some of the concepts emanating from the Council—for instance the church as 'People of God'—while hugely resonant, lacked a clearly defined meaning. Very soon it became apparent that Catholics were divided into three broad tendencies. Paul VI, probably supported in this by most of the bishops, saw the Council as a warrant for moderate reform. However, there were some Catholics who had never wanted the Council, or had wanted a different kind of Council, and they were soon joined by others who thought that change was going too fast. The former French colonial archbishop, Marcel Lefebvre, emerged as the leading ultra-conservative, and there were many others who, without taking their protests to such extremes, shared some of Lefebvre's concerns. At the other end of the church there were Catholics, including both laypeople and many priests, especially those belonging to such orders as the Jesuits and Dominicans, who wanted a rapid and whole-hearted implementation of Vatican II, as well as further reforms not even discussed at the Council, such as allowing priests to marry.

When the Council ended in 1965 this third group seemed to be in the ascendant. Some bishops returned from Rome full of enthusiasm for the new ideas. Dearden of Detroit, for instance, was said to have been 'transformed' by the Council.[29] Seminarians and younger priests had closely followed the proceedings, and confidently expected that big changes were under way. Most Americans priests believed that compulsory celibacy would soon be ended.

---

[28] John W. Allen Jr, *Pope Benedict XVI: A Biography of Cardinal Ratzinger* (London, 2005), 81.
[29] Leslie Woodcock Tentler, *Catholics and Contraception* (Ithaca, NY, 2004), 257.

Many lay Catholics were equally hopeful that the official teaching on contraception was about to be revised. Both among the lower clergy and among the laity there were many who were looking for a new style of leadership at every level.[30]

Interest in the Council and support for reform was particularly intense in the Netherlands. The archbishop of Utrecht, Cardinal Alfrink, had been one of the most prominent 'progressives' at Vatican II. Having come from a relatively conservative background he had undergone something of a conversion in the period immediately before the Council. During the Council Bishop Bekkers of Den Bosch initiated joint lay–clergy discussion groups to talk about the issues under consideration in Rome. These were at their peak in the later 1960s, when similar groups were also set up in other dioceses. The year 1966 saw the publication of a *New Catechism*, which became one of the classic documents of post-Vatican II Catholicism. It was written in an accessible style and according to Coleman 'exudes an atmosphere of ecumenism, respect for human rights and a collegial church'. It was translated into many other languages—and provoked criticism from the Vatican, which insisted on the addition of a supplement. The same year also saw the beginning of the Dutch Pastoral Council, which was notable for the large representation both of nuns and of lay men and women. It started in a mood of high excitement—at least so far as Catholic progressives were concerned.[31]

One big change which followed the Council was the move towards closer relations with other Christians. The first major steps had taken place before the Council, with the establishment in 1960 of a Secretariat for Christian Unity, and the sending of five Catholic observers to the Assembly of the World Council of Churches in 1961. Some forty observers from other churches were invited to the opening session, and by the end of the Council the number had risen to eighty. Admittedly their understanding of the proceedings was often limited by ignorance of Latin, but they had frequent contacts with the bishops and their theological advisers outside the formal sessions.[32] As the Council ended, Catholics and Protestants in various parts of the United States were taking the initiative in organizing joint services. Official 'dialogues' between Catholics and many other Christian denominations were also already under way. In the Netherlands local councils of churches started appearing from 1967. A national council came in 1968, one of its first tasks being to propose changes to the rules relating to mixed marriages. In 1969 the Catholic

---

[30] Ibid. 229–30; Andrew Greeley, *The Catholic Revolution* (Berkeley, Calif., 2004), 64; Sevegrand, *Vers une église sans prêtres* (Rennes, 2004), 165–7.

[31] John A. Coleman, *The Evolution of Dutch Catholicism* (Berkeley, Calif., 1978), 107–14, 247–61.

[32] Michael J. Walsh, 'The History of the Council', in Hastings (ed.), *Modern Catholicism*, 36.

and Protestant overseas aid agencies merged. Similar changes were taking place in Australia. In 1966 the Catholic archbishop of Sydney attended the enthronement of his Anglican counterpart, and in 1968 the Anglican bishop was preaching in Hobart's Catholic cathedral, while the Catholic bishop was taking part in an Anglican service. By 1971 the Catholics were full members of eleven national councils of churches.[33]

In the light of four centuries of mutual anathema these steps were significant enough. But at the local level there were plenty of people who wanted to take fraternization further, notably through joint communion services. This was a step too far for the church authorities. But barriers between Catholics and Protestants were fast breaking down, as was indicated by the increasing frequency of shared worship, Bible study, or social action. Especially significant was the rising rate of inter-marriage. In some cases more frequent inter-marriage simply reflected the diminishing importance of religious identities of whatever kind. But other factors were also involved. One was the fact that in the face of secularizing trends, especially at the end of the 1960s and in the 1970s, a shared Christianity seemed more significant than denominational differences. Another was the affinity between liberal or radical Christians of different denominations in the face of common opposition to conservatives within their own denomination. Perhaps most important was the fact that as 'ordinary' Catholics and 'ordinary' Protestants came into more frequent contact many of the old stereotypes simply lost their meaning.

Meanwhile the Council, together with the social encyclicals of John XXIII, followed in 1967 by Paul VI's *Populorum Progressio*, gave a fillip to 'left' Catholicism. In Britain a group of Catholic Marxists had founded the journal *Slant* in 1964. In France the Franciscan journal *Frères du monde*, in pleading the cause of Third World revolutionaries, increasingly argued that identification with the poor meant acceptance of Marxism. In Quebec the Dominican journal, *Maintenant*, founded in 1962, wanted the church to drop any claim to a privileged voice, and to ally with secular radicals in a common struggle to build a more democratic and humane society: this would be more truly Christian than the so-called 'Christian civilization' in which the church had enjoyed a position of power while accepting all kinds of injustices.[34] Again younger clergy and students were those most attracted by the vision of a

---

[33] Robert Wuthnow, *The Restructuring of American Religion* (Princeton, 1988), 93–4; Coleman, *Dutch Catholicism*, 215–21; Hilliard, 'Crisis', 216; George H. Tavard, 'Ecumenical Relations', in Hastings, *Modern Catholicism*, 404.

[34] Adrian Hastings, *A History of English Christianity* (London, 1986), 571–3; G. Cholvy and Y.-M. Hilaire (eds.), *Histoire religieuse de la France contemporaine* (Toulouse, 1988), 282–6; Michael Gauvreau, *The Catholic Origins of Quebec's Quiet Revolution* (Montreal and Kingston, Ontario, 2005), 307–22.

new kind of church. Activist clergy were nothing new. The American 'labor priest', the German 'rote Kaplan', or the French 'prêtre démocrate' go back to the later nineteenth century. But probably never before had the activists been so widespread or the spheres of their activity so varied. By the later 1960s, especially, but by no means only, in the United States, protests against the Vietnam War were a major field of action for clerical radicals, as for radicals everywhere. The most famous anti-war priests, the Berrigan brothers, ended up in prison because of their involvement in direct action at a draft office. A Catholic layman, Roger LaPorte, inspired by the example of Buddhist monks in Vietnam, burned himself to death outside the United Nations building in New York. However, the biggest impact of activist clergy and other church-based militants was probably at the local level. There they could use their local knowledge, and draw upon their local networks and reputation, in order to organize rent strikes, pickets and boycotts of unfair or discriminatory employers, promote neighbourhood improvement schemes, or protest against segregated housing or factory closures.[35]

Paul VI was broadly supportive of the social radicalism inspired by the Council. But here the opposition came mainly at the local level—especially from more conservative laypeople, who wanted their priests and nuns to 'keep out of politics', and who were sometimes supported by bishops who wanted to avoid anything that might divide the Catholic community. For instance, as the American Civil Rights Movement went north in 1966, Catholics were bitterly divided between those, including many priests and nuns, who took part in civil rights marches and championed the right of African Americans to live in mainly white neighbourhoods and to attend all-white schools, and the many laypeople, with support from Catholic politicians and some priests, who wanted their neighbourhood and its institutions to stay all white. A Cleveland priest noticed hostility to any sermon on the theme of 'loving your neighbour'.[36] Civil rights demonstrators were stoned, and African Americans who moved into previously all-white districts sometimes found their homes vandalized. Many white Catholics were particularly indignant at what they saw as the disloyalty of their clergy who seemed to be more concerned about the rights of outsiders than those of their own parishioners. In July 1966 a nun was hit by a stone as she marched, and when she fell the crowd cheered. As the archdiocesan paper commented: 'For the first time in the history of this city, a nun was attacked in the streets of Chicago in a public demonstration. And the attack came from a mob of howling Catholics.'[37] While physical

---

[35] Maurice Isserman and Michael Kazin, *America Divided: The Civil War of the 1960s* (2nd edn. New York, 2004), 258; James Hennesey, *American Catholics* (Oxford, 1981), 318–20, 326–7; Evans, *Journeys*, 166–7.

[36] McGreevy, *Boundaries*, 183.   [37] Ibid. 191–2.

attacks on clergy and nuns were exceptional, verbal violence was routine. The militant Milwaukee priest, Fr James Groppi, attracted large amounts of hate mail. From Baltimore, Cleveland, and Philadelphia in 1966, as well as Chicago and Milwaukee, there were reports of priests being abused because of their involvement in civil rights protests or their attempts to mediate in racially based neighbourhood conflicts.[38]

In Chicago anti-clerical abuse was directed not only at young radicals, but at the archbishop, Cardinal Cody. Cody was distrusted by many liberals both because of his highly authoritarian style of leadership and because of his call for a moratorium on marches; but he was equally disliked by conservatives because of his support for integrated schools and housing.[39] There are some parallels with what was happening at around the same time in Britain. In 1968 anti-immigration campaigners marched on Lambeth Palace, Archbishop Ramsey's London residence, to protest against his championing of immigrant rights.[40] It is unlikely that many of the marchers were church-goers—it was more a case of Ramsey being attacked by those outside the church as a symbol of black rights rather than the split within the church community which was taking place in the United States. The nearest to the American situation was maybe in the Sparkbrook district of Birmingham, where immigrants from Ireland, the Caribbean, and Pakistan were moving into an area which until the 1950s had a mainly English-born white working-class population. The clergy at Holy Trinity Anglican parish tried to establish good relations with immigrants, and in doing so incurred the resentment of some of the long-established local population who felt that their own needs were being neglected.[41]

The American conflicts were so explosive because radical priests were seen as betraying their own people. There were plenty of radical priests in Europe too, but they were more likely to be defending the interests of the local community against the state, employers, or those living in other parts of the city. They were most often to be found in working-class parishes or in student chaplaincies, and while often provoking criticism from the press, politicians, employers, and sometimes their ecclesiastical superiors, they often won local popularity by acting as spokesmen for the local community, and playing an active role in local-based organizations. Opposition could, however, come from wider sections of the Catholic community. Thus for instance the fact that

---

[38] McGreevy, *Boundaries*, 183–4, 193, 197–205.   [39] Ibid. 186–91, 221.

[40] Owen Chadwick, *Michael Ramsey* (Oxford, 1990), 177; see also Edson Burton, 'From Assimilation to Anti-Racism: The Church of England's Response to Afro-Caribbean Immigration 1948–1981' (Ph.D. thesis, University of the West of England, 2004), 242–78, 304–19, 357–64.

[41] John Rex and Robert Moore, *Race, Community and Conflict: A Study of Sparkbrook* (London, 1967), 64.

a Dominican worker priest was among the leaders of the worker occupation of the Lip watch factory in Besançon was hardly a surprise, but support for the workers by the archbishop led to criticism from employers and the resignations of laymen who held positions in the diocese.[42]

POLARIZATION WITHIN THE CHURCH

In the mid-1960s it seemed that liberals and radicals were making all the running. But the Dutch Pastoral Council faced two major problems from the start: the fact that in spite of the emphasis on collective decision-making, the final decision still lay with the bishops; and the resistance from Rome to most of their more radical proposals. For instance the council voted overwhelmingly to end the compulsory celibacy rule for clergy, but Paul VI reaffirmed the celibacy rule in an encyclical of 1967, and after that he objected to any further discussion of the issue.[43]

There were also many conservatives in the Protestant churches, as the attacks on *Honest to God* showed.[44] There were critics who complained that the 'new morality' was just a modernized version of the 'old immorality'; that Robinson's modernized language and imagery emptied the old language of essential meaning; or that Christianity could not be separated from 'religion', and that, whatever might be the case with such heroic figures as Dietrich Bonhoeffer, ordinary people needed the sustenance provided by institutions, rituals, and the services of religious professionals. In the Church of England, for instance, the antithesis of John Robinson was Mary Whitehouse (1910–2003), an art teacher in a small Shropshire town and a member of Moral Rearmament, who in 1964 opened her campaign to 'Clean Up TV'. While best known for her attacks on pornography and on the presentation of scenes of sex or violence on television and the stage, she was equally opposed to the liberal 'South Bank' theology—so-called because many of its leading exponents were, like John Robinson, associated with the diocese of Southwark in south London.[45]

Increasingly during the 1960s, as Vatican II brought Catholics and Protestants closer together, both Catholics and Protestants found themselves divided by differences of politics, theology, and ethics. By 1970 the issues

---

[42] Denis Pelletier, *La crise catholique* (Paris, 2002), 243–4.

[43] Coleman, *Dutch Catholicism*, 191–6.

[44] See the reviews, from all angles, in Robinson and Edwards, *Debate*.

[45] Michael Tracey and David Morrison, *Whitehouse* (London, 1979) is an informative (though critical) exposition of her ideas, based on interviews with her.

dividing 'progressives' on one side from 'conservatives' or 'traditionalists' on the other within the Catholic Church and the larger Protestant churches were more fundamental than those which divided Catholic from Protestant or, let us say, Anglican from Presbyterian or Lutheran. This remains true more than thirty years later. Ecumenical links and shared projects were increasingly bridging denominational divides, but it was much harder to bridge the gulf between those deeply committed Catholics or Anglicans or Lutherans who had completely different ideas as to where their beloved church should be going.[46]

Many of the doctrinal issues which had divided Western Christianity from the sixteenth century to the nineteenth no longer seemed so contentious in the later twentieth century. For instance, it is hard to believe that in the later twentieth century many people would have regarded differing doctrines of the Eucharist as a sufficient ground for separating from their fellow Christians; yet in the Reformation era this was one of the most bitterly contested issues, not only between Protestant and Catholic, but between Lutheran and Reformed. The most important development in the modern period has been the emergence of the critical approach to the Bible. In the later nineteenth and early twentieth centuries this caused deep divisions within most Protestant denominations. Although at either extreme of the Protestant theological spectrum, Unitarians were consistently liberal and Pentecostals consistently conservative in their approach to the scriptures, the larger Protestant denominations included a huge range of approaches, from ultra-liberal to fundamentalist, with every possible variation in between. These different ways of reading the Bible fed into the four new sites of conflict which emerged in the 1960s. The first of these was the complex of radical political ideas which in the 1970s came to be known as 'Liberation Theology'. Three other areas of conflict which began to emerge in the later 1960s and which remained of long-lasting significance were sexual ethics; the role of women in the church; and the Charismatic Movement.

Partly because of growing ecumenical contacts, and partly because of sharpening tensions within most churches, denominational identities were weakening. More generally this reflected the move towards a more fluid society in which hereditary identities counted for less, and each individual claimed the right to live his or her own life on a day-to-day basis. One manifestation of this situation was increasing religious mobility. A survey in the United States in 1984 found that a third of the respondents claimed to have a different religious or non-religious affiliation from the one they had had in childhood. A similar survey in 1955 had produced the improbably low figure of 4 per cent admitting to such switching. While part of this increased mobility was due to

[46] This is discussed in respect of the United States in Wuthnow, *Restructuring*, 102–52.

the growth in the number of those refusing any religious label, most of it was caused by movement from one form of Christianity to another. The survey also showed a sharp drop since the 1940s and 1950s in the proportion of those admitting to prejudice against members of other denominations.[47] Moreover, a combination of factors, including greater tolerance, greater indifference, and the weakening of parental and neighbourhood influence, had led to a big increase in inter-confessional marriages, so that more people were growing up with a foot in more than one camp.

CONCLUSION

In the mid-1960s the Western Christian world seemed to be at the beginning of a period of exciting change. Vatican II offered the prospect not only of sweeping reforms in the Catholic Church but also of an end to many of the barriers separating Catholics from other Christians. New theologies, which privileged 'action' in 'the world', an ethic of individual freedom and responsibility and a positive view of modern science, were winning the support of many Protestants. Both Catholics and Protestants were actively involved in many of the social and political movements of the time, and were interpreting their activism as a necessary expression of their Christian faith. Yet in the euphoria of the times, many progressive Christians underestimated the strength both of more conservative denominations (often dismissed as sects) and of the conservative forces within their own denomination. While differences between Christian denominations were losing much of their significance, the ground was being prepared for the battles between liberals and conservatives within both Catholic and Protestant churches which would dominate the ecclesiastical history of the later twentieth century.

[47] Ibid. 88–96.

5

Affluence

In the mid-1960s most Western countries were in the middle of a period of unparalleled prosperity. While the years immediately after the Second World War were principally a time of reconstruction—and in many parts of Europe a time of acute shortages—living standards were unmistakably on the rise by the later 1950s. In Britain this was the era of 'affluence', when former luxuries first became available to the mass of the population. From 1953 real wages were rising steadily in the United Kingdom, and already in 1957 Prime Minister Harold Macmillan was making his famous observation that 'most of our people have never had it so good'. By the later 1950s West Germany's Economics Minister, Ludwig Erhard, was able to boast of his country's 'economic miracle'. In France the years from the Liberation to the oil crisis of 1973–4 are remembered as 'Les Trente Glorieuses'—the thirty glorious years of economic growth. And the United States, the first country to enjoy post-war prosperity, was still in the 1960s and early 1970s experiencing steady growth in per capita income and a fall in the numbers living in poverty.

This chapter focuses mainly on England and France, and looks at the ways in which rising living standards and changes in family life affected religion. The fruits of prosperity were not to be enjoyed all at once, and the relative importance of different forms of consumption varied from country to country. In the UK the first of the former 'luxuries' to become a normal item of household equipment was the television. In 1955 35 per cent of households had a television set, and by 1975 this had risen to 96 per cent. In the same period, ownership of refrigerators rose from 8 per cent to 85 per cent, of washing machines from 18 per cent to 70 per cent, and of telephones from 19 per cent to 52 per cent. But the most characteristically British form of affluence was home ownership: between 1945 and 1976 the proportion of homes which were owner-occupied rose from 26 to 53 per cent.[1] In France the changes were equally rapid, though they started a few years later: 10 per cent of households had a television set in 1959; by 1975 it was 90 per cent.

---

[1] Paul Johnson (ed.), *Twentieth Century Britain* (London, 1994), 365; James Obelkevich, 'Consumption,' in James Obelkevich and Peter Catterall (eds.), *Understanding Post-War British Society* (London, 1994), 141–54.

Ownership of refrigerators rose from 8 per cent to 85 per cent between 1954 and 1972; of washing machines from 8 per cent to 64 per cent in the same period; car ownership rose from 20 per cent to 70 per cent between 1953 and 1973. On the other hand, telephones came more slowly, with only 28 per cent of households having one in 1975.[2]

In France there was a similar tendency for living space to expand, household amenities to increase, including not least improved heating, and for life to concentrate more on the home. Schor describes the typical home, which had a 'living-room', with an 'eating corner' and a 'sitting corner', the latter comprising a low table, a sofa and armchairs, all pointed towards the television.[3] The important fact was that the great majority of the population were benefiting from these changes. There was still a small minority of the rich and a much larger minority of the poor, but the most distinctive feature of the social structure of prosperous Western societies was the emergence of a large middle-income group, comprising the majority of the population, crossing the old boundaries between middle class and working class, embracing people with roughly comparable incomes and lifestyles, dressing in similar ways, living in houses and flats of a similar kind, eating similar food, driving similar cars.

Specific sections of the population were affected by these changes in particular ways. Rural communities were increasingly drawn into a national culture. Women were able to use labour-saving devices which could reduce the time spent in housework. Fathers spent more time at home, while teenagers had a wider choice of entertainment when they got out of the home. Affluence had a wide-ranging influence on people's lives, and sometimes affected their ways of thinking, including their thinking about religion and their religious practices.

YOUTH

The youth culture as it was developing in the later 1950s and early 1960s depended on the rising earnings of working-class and lower middle-class teenagers and young adults. These earnings supported the places where young people met, such as coffee bars (in Britain), milk bars (in Germany), and dancehalls; they paid for the records, the record-players, and the pop concerts, which were their main source of entertainment; for the clothes and cosmetics which emphasized both their attractiveness and their conformity to fashion; for the magazines which kept readers up to date on the latest trends, whether

---

[2] Ralph Schor, *Histoire de la société française au XXe siècle* (Paris, 2004), 305. [3] Ibid.

in music, fashion, or sexual mores; for the motor cycles and scooters which offered a sense both of freedom and of belonging.[4]

For the churches the youth culture could pose an indirect challenge, and sometimes a very direct one. The indirect challenge stemmed from the fact that the churches had long been deeply involved in youth work, but that increasing prosperity meant that young people were able to afford a huge range of alternatives. In England membership of church youth clubs was still considerable at the beginning of the 1960s. In 1960 there were 294,578 members of Anglican clubs, the great majority of whom were aged 14 to 17, with girls slightly outnumbering boys. These clubs were a mainly urban phenomenon, with the thickest concentration being in the Manchester diocese. The 3,574 Methodist clubs had 108,017 members (some of the clubs evidently being quite small).[5] Memories of those growing up at this time frequently refer to church clubs—often with affection, though also often with an emphasis that this represented a phase in the process of growing up. Sometimes there was an explicit statement that its significance was social rather than religious, and in particular that for many teenagers it was the first place where they met members of the opposite sex. One 1960s teenager discovered that she enjoyed kissing when she was 'dragged off to the church youth club' in Burton on Trent by a friend 'who rightly said I was in danger of becoming a swot and letting life pass me by'.[6] A volume of anonymous memories from the 1960s, collected in the 1990s, elicited several references to the importance church youth clubs had played at one point in the respondent's life. One of the contributors wrote: 'My life revolved round the church and its social activities. It provided the youth club, friends, trips: it was a major part of my life.' Another commented:

The Methodist Youth Club was really important to us in the early sixties. It was terribly innocent but we had fabulous times there, just sitting about nattering or playing badminton, cards or table tennis. We weren't interested in religion at all. Going home from the youth club was wonderful, too, because you could walk home with lads. You could call at the chippie on the way.[7]

Church youth clubs were places where gangs of friends went together and where new friendships were made. The extent to which those who went were

[4] For Britain and France, Arthur Marwick, *The Sixties* (Oxford, 1998), 45–80, 101–9; for Germany, Christine Bartram and Heinz-Hermann Krüger, 'Vom Backfisch zum Teenager: Mädchensozialisation in den 50er Jahren,' in Krüger (ed.), *'Die Elvis-Tolle,'* 84–102.

[5] Neuss, *Facts and Figures; Minutes of the Annual Conference of the Methodist Church.*

[6] Carol Dix, *Say I'm Sorry to Mother: The True Story of Four Women Growing up in the Sixties* (London, 1978), 26.

[7] Alison Pressley, *Changing Times: Being Young in Britain in the '60s* (London, 2000), 63.

also interested in the church's religious message no doubt varied greatly—
though I suspect that some of those who now protest that their participation
had nothing to do with religion have either forgotten what they believed as a
teenager or are embarrassed by the memory of it. Michael Thompson (born
1945, Aldershot) belonged to a variety of Anglican youth organizations in his
teens and commented that it was 'a social thing as well as a religious thing'. He
noted that the attractions were multiple: he went with a group of friends, he
enjoyed the sport, met girls, and while sceptical of some aspects of religious
doctrine, argued that religion 'means quite a lot in establishing a basic code of
life'.[8] For some of that generation church activities were the main focus of their
teenage life. 'That was a big day Sunday, it was the best day of the week really',
recalls Jill Bassett (born 1944, north Lancashire), who came from a lower
middle-class family in Lancaster. She met up with friends in the afternoon,
and then went to the Anglican church followed by the church youth club in
the evening.[9] A Lancaster Catholic (born 1933, Liverpool), growing up a few
years earlier, also remembers Sunday evenings as the highlight of the week: 'Oh
drama groups, dancing, outings, just ordinary very calm things to what they
do nowadays. No drinking. . . . Oh it was the life, Sunday night at the youth
club, yes it was.'[10]

But clearly church clubs were vulnerable to the counter-attractions of new
kinds of meeting place and new sources of entertainment. Membership of
Anglican youth clubs had peaked at 308,842 in 1958.[11] Between 1958 and 1960
there had been a 5 per cent increase in participation by over 18s who were
likely to have included a high proportion of the most committed, but this was
more than offset by an 8 per cent drop in participation by those aged 14 to 17.
Membership of Methodist clubs peaked at 114, 211 in 1962. By 1965 membership had dropped to 89,640.[12] For those who had joined simply because it
provided the best place to meet other teenagers, it was easy to move on as they
became more self-confident and perhaps more independent of their parents.
Carol Dix, born in 1947, recalls 'We progressed from dances at church youth
clubs, to the local village-hall hops, and then to the more commercial rock
'n' roll dances in dance halls like Hippodromes and Meccas.'[13] Many found,
as they moved into their mid and later teens, that, without any conscious
decision to leave the church, their free time, and sometimes their energy, was
increasingly taken up with other activities. Michael Thompson became a Mod,
purchased a scooter and all the required clothing, and met up with fellow
Mods in a café. Later he acquired friends who had cars, and would go up to

---

[8] FSMA, interview 32. [9] SFL, interview with Mrs A3L, 22.
[10] SFL, interview with Mrs H6L, 13. [11] Neuss, *Facts and Figures*, 63.
[12] *Minutes of Methodist Conference*, 1963, 1966. [13] Dix, *Sorry*, 45.

London at the weekend for the jazz concerts on Eel Pie Island. Others found they increasingly need a restful Sunday to recover from Saturday night.[14] Barbara Whitworth (born 1958, Oldham) recalls that she was confirmed at 15 and continued going to church regularly for a year or two afterwards, but 'after that I stopped going to church, basically really, because you get to that age where you start going out Saturday might . . . so Sunday morning you don't exactly want to get up at half past nine to start getting ready for church you know. But I do miss it really.'[15]

The youth culture could present a direct challenge to the churches and their values, in so far it was associated with values of hedonism, unlimited experimentation, or the individual's right to live life in their own way without regard for any external moral code. Interviewed by oral historians some twenty-five years later, women who had been teenagers in the 1960s recalled some of the new opportunities of that era. Mrs Horwich, born in 1945, was living with her parents while working in a hospital in Preston in the middle and later 1960s. She recalled the tensions with her mother that stemmed from her 'Swinging Sixties social activities', such as 'enjoying clothes and hairstyles and freedom and sexual freedom', as well as 'the music' and 'a lot of drinking and boozing with friends'. She also mentioned the influence of teenage magazines which 'changed and started advertising contraceptives and all sorts of advice on relationships', and of D. H. Lawrence's *Women in Love*—'I thought this is terrific this, talking about real people and relationships and complications and mental attitudes.'[16]

One important aspect of the widening range of commercial entertainments that became available in the 1960s is that they were open to anyone who could pay. In areas like Lancashire, where the divide between Protestant and Catholic was still deep in the 1950s, church-based youth clubs, dance halls, and football clubs were among the institutions which helped to keep many people within a confessional subculture. As increasing numbers of teenagers could afford to go, or to go more frequently, to coffee bars, pubs, commercial dance-halls, and pop concerts, encounters across the sectarian divide became commonplace. When in the 1980s several hundred English Catholics were interviewed, it was found that from the 1930s to the later 1950s the proportion who had married non-Catholics had remained stable at around 30 per cent, but that there was then a continuous increase. In the 1960s the proportion was 47 per cent, and in the 1970s it was 67 per cent.[17]

[14] FSMA, interview 32.
[15] FSMA, interviews 119 and 16. (Similar comments in interview 46.)
[16] SFL, interview with Mrs H9P, 17–18.
[17] Michael Hornsby-Smith, *Catholics in England: Studies in Social Structure since the Second World War* (Cambridge, 1987), 94.

The booming economy was also among the factors which made the student revolts of the later 1960s possible, since full employment meant that those who failed their exams or were thrown out of university still had excellent prospects of finding a job. As Arthur Marwick suggests, 'The unique ingredient which made it possible for all these movements to develop and expand was ... economic security, which underwrote innovation and daring, and minimized attendant risks.'[18] For similar reasons, working-class youth were tending to be less deferential to parents and employers. The British oral historian, Elizabeth Roberts, quotes a Lancashire woman (born 1947) who walked out of her factory job in the early 1960s after a dispute with the supervisor, and who recalled that 'at that time you could do that. You could leave a job on Thursday and get another job on Monday. Not like now.'[19] Roberts commented on another of her interviewees (born 1944), who had frequent confrontations with his father: 'Mr Rowlandson was different from his working-class, teenage predecessors in several ways: he had his own key, he stayed out far later than was traditional; he saw lots of women, even when he was going out with the girl he eventually married; and he had a car at eighteen.'[20] Roberts also suggests that this less deferential attitude may have affected attitudes to other forces of authority, such as the church. She quotes Mrs Horwich (mentioned above) who came from a lower middle-class family, attended church as a teenager, and recalled that 'I often had to hold back from shouting arguments at the pulpit. It didn't seem fair that you had to be talked to, to be so receptive without saying anything back.'[21]

THE HOME AND THE DECLINE OF COMMUNITY

Growing prosperity enabled increasing numbers of couples to buy a house and to devote a major part of their time and money to improving, equipping, and decorating it. Some of the consequences of this for relationships within the family will be discussed in Chapter 8. Here I will focus on the implication for relations with neighbours and relatives.

The growing centrality of the home and the nuclear family led to a decline in the importance of the neighbourhood and the extended family, which had been central features of working-class life up to the 1950s. Especially in older working-class districts, typically comprising densely populated areas of terraced housing, interspersed with corner shops, pubs, working men's clubs, and

---

[18] Marwick, *Sixties*, 37.

[19] Elizabeth Roberts, *Women and Families: An Oral History, 1940–1970* (Oxford, 1995), 56.

[20] Ibid. 48–9.   [21] Ibid. 49.

churches, tight-knit highly localized communities had long been in existence, with traditions of neighbourly support, but also with clearly defined codes of behaviour and canons of respectability, which could lead to conspicuous deviants being shunned. Concentrations of kin within a small area enhanced the likelihood that those in difficulty would receive rapid help, but also increased the possibility that news of scandal would spread quickly.[22] Many of the rules of expected behaviour were so taken for granted that they were scarcely thought about: when Elizabeth Roberts asked people from Lancashire working-class families why they had done things, they would often reply 'It was the thing to do.'[23] And if anyone forgot what they ought to be doing, mothers, aunts, and grandmothers would often be quick to remind them. Many of these districts were torn apart in the years after the Second World War by slum clearance schemes and dispersal to new peripheral housing estates or satellite towns. But the younger generation were in any case often hoping to get out and buy a house in the suburbs. And some of these areas were changing as a result of immigration. The gradual trend was towards more individualistic lifestyles in which both neighbourly support systems and neighbourly control systems weakened. Dispersal to new housing estates tended to be followed by more fragmented patterns of life. Richard Sykes in a study of the Black Country, the industrial district north-west of Birmingham, found that in the Wren's Nest, a new housing estate established in Dudley in the 1930s, relations with neighbours and with local institutions were never as close as they had been in the older areas of the towns. A survey in the 1950s found that there were still very few people on the estate who had friends or relatives living in the same street. Revd Alan Hayward, who was curate of the Anglican church on this estate in the 1950s, attributed the vandalizing of the church to this sense of detachment from local institutions.[24]

One result was a growing willingness of individuals, and sometimes families, to develop their own codes of behaviour with limited reference to neighbours (whom they might hardly know) or relatives (who were less likely than formerly to live in close proximity). Changes in patterns of family life had some implications for religious practices and relations with churches, since these had been a part of the codes of accepted behaviour which had strongly influenced life in many working-class neighbourhoods. For instance, the churching of mothers after childbirth, the baptism of infants, Sunday School, and eventually marriage in church, all belonged to the realm of expected behaviour. In the 1950s it was still common to refuse entry to the house to

[22] Roberts, *Women*, 199–231.   [23] Ibid. 160.
[24] Richard Sykes, 'Popular Religion in Decline,' *Journal of Ecclesiastical History*, 56 (2002), 299–301.

a new mother until she had been churched. Unbaptized children were considered to be unlucky, and parents who did not send their children to Sunday School were seen as feckless and irresponsible. Registry Office weddings were associated with pregnant brides—a subject of shame not only to the couple but to their families. Most of these rules of accepted behaviour were weakening in the 1950s, and all of them were weakening in the 1960s, though unevenly across the country. Roberts comments that by the 1960s the new cliché was 'Do your own thing', and many people were quickly learning that there were no longer clear-cut rules.[25] Such traditions as the sending of children to Sunday School had gained a lot of their force from the fact that nearly everyone did it. For instance, Margaret Tranter (born 1936, Lancaster), whose parents ran a pub in a village near Lancaster, and were agnostics, recalled that the fact that she never went to Sunday School 'was regarded as quite a scandal in the village because most of the children were forced to go to Sunday School whether they wanted to go or not'.[26] By the 1970s it was much easier for the child who did not want to go to point to a schoolfriend, a cousin, or a next door neighbour who did not go—'So why should I?'

Similar factors may have played a part in the decline of the rite of churching of mothers after childbirth, still very widespread in the early 1950s, but declining rapidly in the 1960s and 1970s. Margaret Houlbrooke argues that one factor was the increasing rarity of the kind of tight-knit highly localized community in which mothers lived close to daughters. 'By insistence, example, powerful expectation, persuasion or occasional threats', mothers had ensured that their daughters were 'done'.[27] The proportion of daughters living close to their mothers was diminishing, and in any case mothers were becoming more reticent about applying such pressures. Oral history suggests that churching was still widespread in north Lancashire in the 1950s and 1960s, and also confirms the important role of mothers. Among ten women who recalled their own churching during the period 1952–71, two said it was 'just the thing to do',[28] two mentioned pressure from their mothers,[29] and one pressure from a great-aunt,[30] one had pressure from the vicar,[31] and one explicitly stated that she had wanted to be churched[32]—though some of those who mentioned the pressures also said that they were glad to have done it. A woman who had a child in 1964 said that her mother was 'disgusted' that she was not

[25] Roberts, *Women*, 160.   [26] SFL, interview with Mrs B4L, 39.
[27] Margaret Houlbrooke, 'The Churching of Women in the Twentieth Century' (Ph.D. thesis, University of Reading, 2006), 264–7.
[28] SFL, interviews with Mr M12B, 25, and Mr B2B, 27.
[29] SFL, interviews with Mrs W6L, 88, and Mrs T2L, 66.
[30] SFL, interview with Mrs A3L, 46–7.   [31] SFL, interview with Mrs W5B, 45.
[32] SFL, interview with Mrs A4L, 26.

churched;[33] in the case of another 1964 mother it was the grandmother who was disgusted;[34] and a few years later it was the father (the only mention in this context of fathers).[35] A woman who was churched in 1971 but not when her second child was born in 1975 was 'disgusted with the service',[36] and right through this period there were some women (a minority), who either refused to be churched or refused to do it more than once, because the service made them feel unclean.[37] This kind of objection was very probably increasing in the 1960s and 1970s. Susan Atkins (born 1947, Preston), a teacher and an active Anglican, recalled that her bookkeeper mother had been churched after losing a baby, but that she herself had read the service, found it 'peculiar', and chose not to be churched.[38] The only evidence of peer pressure *not* to be churched comes from Joan Nicholls (born 1931, Preston), a secretary, who had been an Anglican Sunday School teacher but had not gone to church since marrying a non-church-going husband. She said that the main reason for choosing a christening, but without a churching, when her son was born in 1964 was that her friends were not being churched.[39] However, there is a paucity of evidence (in spite of the assiduous researches of Margaret Houlbrooke, who has carried out the most thorough inquiry on the subject).

Domestic life was changing in very similar ways in France. Morin, commenting on the 'relaxed individualism' that was beginning to emerge in rural France in the mid-1960s, referred to the house, the car, and the television as the three essentials of the new lifestyle. 'The house represents more than ever a need for personal ownership, and for the overwhelming majority in Plodémet it is inconceivable to rent out or even share the ownership of a dwelling':

The domestic revolution has concentrated an enormous emotional investment in the home, shown not only by the capital expended on it but also by the constant attention it receives. The wife focuses her activity on cleaning and furnishing, and the husband on improvement, repairs and decoration. The house is a place of love that arouses, even ensnares, the passion, tenderness, attentions and fetishism of a love that if it does not attach itself to the partner, will certainly attach itself to the child and the house itself.[40]

He also commented that the house had become 'a refuge', 'closed against neighbours'.

Greater prosperity also widened leisure options. Alan Timson (born 1948, Lancaster) noted a big drop in participation in the town's Whit Walks around the end of the 1950s: 'people suddenly started to get affluent and would want to do other things—go down to Morecambe [a nearby seaside resort]

[33] SFL, interview with Mrs H3P, 51. [34] SFL, interview with Mrs W6B.
[35] SFL, interview with Mr R1P, 68. [36] SFL, interview with Mrs G7P.
[37] SFL, interview with Mrs W5B, 45. [38] SFL, interview with Mr B10P, 3.
[39] SFL, interview with Mrs H3P, 51. [40] Edgar Morin, *Plodémet* (London, 1971), 241.

and things like that'.[41] In reflecting on the changes since his childhood in the 1950s, he also commented: 'It's an odd thing about deprivation, but it does actually bring people together, far more than affluence does. Affluence actually, I always feel, divides'.[42] Carol Adams (born 1932, Barrow) had been a church-goer as a teenager and sent her children to Sunday School, but this changed when the family acquired a car:

We would go out for the day on a Sunday when we got the car. . . . In the summer we used to go out on a Sunday, you see, and then I started hiking and quite often I would take one with me and that was Sunday you see, so really it sort of disintegrated and Sunday became a day of leisure, and usually walking somewhere.[43]

Similarly, Roberts notes a declining interest in politics and trade unions. The sharp drop in party membership during the 1950s and 1960s was noted in Chapter 3. Political parties built on powerful class identities suffered from the growing blurring of class lines around the middle of the social hierarchy. Interviews with those brought up in the 1950s and 1960s repeatedly show a pattern whereby a strong inherited political identity was rejected in favour of a different and often more weakly held identity, a strictly pragmatic approach to politics, or even complete indifference. Michael Thompson was born in Aldershot in 1945. His father, an aircraft technician, was strongly Labour, but Michael had 'just got total apathy about politics' and said that he had not voted for years. Brenda Clark was born in 1946 in a Yorkshire working-class family. Her father was a member of the Labour party, but she voted 'on consideration at the time, rather than a sort of deep felt connection either Conservative or Labour'.[44]

The new climate of increasing affluence seems to have been particularly threatening to those institutions, of many different kinds, which were associated with membership of a local community, and gained much of their strength from pressures exerted through the neighbourhood or through kinship networks. Political parties gained a lot of their support in this way, and this could also be true of churches. It was even more true of Sunday Schools, which had for many generations depended on the patronage of parents who were not themselves church-goers, but who felt that 'sending' their children was the right thing to do. Many different factors were combining to make it less clear what the right thing to do was. It was also becoming easier to ignore such rules, even when it could be established what they were. Cars, televisions, and the increasing number of couples buying their own home combined to promote new patterns of family life, at once more mobile, and more focused on

[41] SFL, interview with Mr M10L, 125.   [42] Ibid. 143–4.
[43] SFL, interview with Mrs J1B, 41.   [44] FSMA, interviews 32 and 141.

the home and the nuclear family, and less dependent on the neighbourhood. Full employment and rising incomes meant that neighbourly help of all kinds, including help in finding a job, was less likely to be needed. Keeping one's distance could have its advantages, if it meant less interference from neighbourhood gossips. Slum clearance schemes were disrupting many old-established and relatively homogeneous working-class districts, with well-established local institutions and concentrations of kin, often living in the same street.

THE TRANSFORMATION OF THE COUNTRYSIDE

The social changes of these years were most dramatic—and sometimes most traumatic—in rural areas. The French sociologist, Henri Mendras, reviewing what he calls 'The Second French Revolution', which in his view began in the 1960s and was complete by the 1980s, sees the biggest change as being 'the disappearance of the peasantry'.[45] This was brought about partly by rural depopulation, partly by mechanization, partly by the growing weight of urban influences on rural life—and in the later part of this period, the colonization of the countryside by well-educated urbanites. In 1945, a quarter of the economically active population of France was working in agriculture; by the 1980s this figure had dropped to 6 per cent, but there had been a huge increase in productivity. Up to the 1960s rural cultures had been highly regionalized, or even localized, with pronounced patterns of religious and political allegiance (religion and politics often being closely linked). Some rural areas were strongholds of Catholicism, and others were strongholds of Communism. From the 1960s, however, there was a flattening out of these differences, as regional identities became less significant. And both church and party were having to come to terms with declining levels of militancy.

The story of these years has been told in vivid detail by two French sociologists, Yves Lambert and Edgar Morin. Lambert based himself in Limerzel, a large village in the Morbihan department of Brittany, interviewing many of the inhabitants. He aimed to trace the decline of the 'quasi-Christendom' which still existed in many parts of the Catholic world in the mid-twentieth century. He began around 1900 and finished in the 1980s; he located the period of most rapid change between about 1958 and 1975. The year 1958, when the first television sets arrived in the village, offers one symbolic turning-point; 1965, when, for the first time, less than half the economically active population of the village was working in agriculture, provides another; a third

---

[45] Henri Mendras, *La Seconde Révolution française* (Paris, 1988), 28–34.

came in 1979 when, for the first time, a doctor was resident in the village. Other changes were causing or reflecting Limerzel's gradual emergence from relative isolation: increasing numbers of cars; more people taking holidays; more people finding a marriage partner outside the village; the increasing availability of newspapers and magazines published in Paris.[46]

At the same time, religion was changing rapidly too—partly because of reforms initiated by the church, and partly through changes in popular belief and practice to which the church was forced to respond. In 1958, 92 per cent of the adult population were regularly going to mass; by 1967 this had dropped to 77 per cent; and by 1975 to 55 per cent. Initially the decline in church-going was mainly a phenomenon of young adult men, from whom it spread to teenagers. Farmers remained more devout than factory workers and shopkeepers; and women much more so than men. Even when attendance at mass remained very high, participation in other services was dropping. Vespers was abandoned as early as 1963, as so many families, after going to church in the morning, wanted to go on an outing.[47]

Beliefs and attitudes were changing as much as formal practice. Both at home and in the Catholic school, which most children had attended, the young were trained in attitudes of respect for the clergy, and the priests were used to speaking in a voice of authority. In the 1960s and 1970s, however, they were realizing that if they wanted to be heard, a different tone of voice was needed. A farmer's wife commented in 1976: 'Nowadays they no longer speak much about sin. Earlier they would insist, oh, la, la! But people won't go along with that any more, they won't listen to them any more! Now it's charity, and good relations between families and between neighbours.' And a shopkeeper saw a parallel between developments in religion and in retailing: 'They [the priests] have been forced to adapt too. Once we were there behind our counter, and now people want to serve themselves. Well, it's the same thing in the church: there's no longer a holy table and you can touch the host!' The priest was still the most important person in the village after the mayor, but he was expected to be approachable and tolerant. He no longer stood out from the rest of the community by his level of education, and various specialists had taken over many of the roles previously exercised by the clergy. Even in the church, the shortage of clergy meant that the laity were perforce taking on many tasks from which they had previously been excluded. In a Catholic community such as Limerzel the impact of social and economic changes was compounded by the changes in the liturgy as a result of Vatican II, notably the switch from the mass in Latin to the mass in French.[48]

[46] Y. Lambert, *Dieu change en Bretagne* (Paris, 1985), 231–69.
[47] Ibid. 241–7.　　[48] Ibid. 247–55, 269.

Morin was based in a rural commune that he named 'Plodémet', close to
Brittany's western tip. The commune comprised the *bourg* of that name, with
a population of 1,200 in 1965, and about twice as many people living next
to the sea or in scattered agricultural hamlets. The occupational range was
considerable, including farmers, seamen, factory workers, shopkeepers and
artisans, and the teachers in a large secondary school. The big difference from
Limerzel was that only about a quarter of the population went to mass and
about 40 per cent voted Communist. However, Limerzel and Plodémet had in
common the fact that the dominant tradition was being undermined by social
change. Just as priests were losing in status and authority as the laity acquired a
better education and more confidence in the face of authority, the Republican
'secular priesthood', the schoolteachers, was suffering the same fate. Becoming
a teacher or becoming a priest were two classic routes of social mobility for
bright children in rural families, but now there were many alternatives, most
of them better paid. And parents often had a narrower, more instrumental
view of the purposes of education: the secular school was no longer a rival
church, bringing secular salvation. The teachers were still the mainstay of
the Communist Party, but party activists were dwindling in number and
few were aged under 40. Though many people voted Communist, few were
prepared to take an active part in politics or in the running of the various left-
wing or secularist organizations that had once been mainstays of collective
life. This was partly because, as was suggested in Chapter 2, the ideological
differences which had once split the community in two seemed to have lost
much of their urgency. But growing prosperity and changing lifestyles also
had an impact. From about 1950, a new kind of mentality was emerging,
'focused on individual attainment of well-being and private autonomy', with
its centre in the home, rather than communal organizations. 'Activists feel
isolated in a population where political affinity no longer inspires everyday
loyalty, where television and trips in the car are far more attractive alternatives
than meetings.'[49]

He argued that the drivers in the spread of this new way of thinking were
women. Most women wanted a job, but they continued to see the home as the
principal focus of their lives and the sphere in which they enjoyed power. It was
women who directed their energies to making the home a place of comfort
and modernity and a source of pride—often in the face of the scepticism of
their husbands, who wanted to spend the money on other things. Women,
according to Morin, were 'the secret agents of modernisation', but this had
not brought them into conflict with the church.[50] 'Not yet', we might want
to add, with the benefits of hindsight. However, two points seem significant

---

[49] Morin, *Plodémet*, 180.   [50] Ibid. 163–4.

here. One is that 'tradition', which in many parts of France meant Catholicism, here meant Communism and other forms of left politics: indeed Morin several times mentioned that the church seemed to be more open to new ideas than the political establishment. The second is that the local perception at this time was that Catholicism was actually advancing.

AFFLUENCE AND THE STATE

The fruits of affluence were to be seen not only in the lives of individuals and families, but also in the new possibilities for collective spending. Most countries expanded their education system during the 1960s. Children stayed on longer at school, and more of them went on to higher education. The booming economy of these years permitted a huge expansion in the universities. In the United States the number of students enrolled in institutions of higher education rose from 2.6 million in 1950, to 3.6 million in 1960, and then 8.6 million in 1970. In France, starting from a much lower base, the number of students tripled during the 1960s.[51] In the same decade, nine new universities were established in the United Kingdom. In England and Wales the Albemarle Commission on the Youth Services, reporting in 1960, exuded an expansionist optimism which had never been seen before and would never be seen again. There was a big increase in the number of social workers and in numbers of therapists and counsellors.

The expansion of higher education might at first sight have been good news for religion and the churches. In the United States in the 1950s the college-educated were those most likely to be church-goers; in Britain, as already suggested, students were among the most religiously active groups in the population. However, in the 1960s it would be college-educated Americans who were those most likely to leave the church,[52] and in other respects these new developments presented potential problems for religion and the churches. First the increasing role of the state in areas where the churches had often enjoyed a prominent role meant that there was an increasing demand for institutions and practitioners to be religiously neutral. Second, the increasing stress on professional training meant that 'professional' values tended to be given a higher priority than those derived from religious faith. And third, the intellectual underpinnings of the expanding professions were potentially in conflict with religious assumptions. This was most obviously true of Marxism, which enjoyed a growing prestige during the 1960s and which in the late 1960s and for much of the 1970s had a dominant

---

[51] Wuthnow, *Restructuring*, 155; Schor, *Histoire*, 312.
[52] Wuthnow, *Restructuring*, 157–67.

influence within many university departments, as well as shaping the thinking of many teachers, social workers, youth leaders, and others in the 'caring' professions. It was also true in a more general sense of the most fashionable disciplines of the time, sociology and psychology.

Sociology was embraced by some influential people in the churches as a tool for developing more effective forms of mission. In fact this perception goes back at least as far as Gabriel Le Bras and his school of 'religious sociologists' in France in the 1930s. At the same time, sociology was seen by many of its practitioners as directly challenging religious ways of interpreting human behaviour and religiously based strategies for improving the human condition. The prominent sociologist of religion, David Martin, commented in 1966 that students who are interested in the sociology of religion 'have to "explain" their interest' in a way that would not be expected of those specialising in any other area, and he recalled that a colleague once asked him 'Do you think you have a real subject?'[53] (I remember attending a conference in 1975 at which a sociologist even stated that many of his colleagues regarded religion as something 'unclean'.) In the eyes of many social scientists the emphasis of most religions on individual moral responsibility was at best an irrelevance. It stood in the way of any scientific understanding, based on the identification of key variables; potentially it could divert attention from the structural causes of social ills, and it could lead to the stigmatization of those whose allegedly deviant behaviour was the inevitable consequence of the situation in which they found themselves, rather than the result of any moral failure. Moreover, if science was the key to a more humane and better organized society, the recognition of any factor that was not amenable to scientific investigation—for instance God—meant a return to the pre-scientific dark ages. From this point of view, liberal Christians like John Robinson, with their espousal of situation ethics, were as mistaken as those conservatives who pinned their hopes on a strict moral code. In the 1960s 'scientific' attacks on religion were much more likely to be inspired by the social sciences, rather than the natural sciences.

Sociology was seen by some as having unparalleled radical potential. Sociologists were prominent in most of the student movements of the 1960s. As one far left Turin student explained:

The prevalent idea was that everything could be traced back to social relations. No problem, however mysterious—from God, consciousness, neurosis, to individual responsibility—could not, it was thought, be reduced to a discourse on society. In unveiling and explaining society, you discover the point from which you can begin to transform it. That was certainly the idea in my head and most other people's.[54]

[53] David Martin, *The Religious and the Secular* (London, 1969), 62.
[54] Ronald Fraser, *1968: A Student Generation in Revolt* (London, 1988), 84.

According to Roof, in his study of the 'baby-boom generation' in the USA, 'social science' continued as one of four major 'meaning systems', together with 'theism', 'mysticism', and 'individualism', and was especially influential among the well-educated and among those who had been involved in the movements or the counter-culture of the 1960s. 'Higher education generated new and more secular meaning systems competing with theistic interpretations of the nature of reality. Social scientific modes of explanation, for example, have gained ascendancy, emphasising the role of social forces in shaping people's lives.'[55]

Take the example of the growth of the youth service in England and Wales. When in 1939 the state first decided to get involved in provision of youth services, they did so in conjunction with already existing voluntary organizations. Of the fourteen that were recognized, six were explicitly religious in their basis and there were others which tended in practice to be linked with churches. In the 1950s a combination of increasing national resources with increasing recognition of youth as a 'social problem' led to the establishment of the Albemarle Committee, which met in 1958–9, and which recommended a large expansion of the provision for youth by local authorities, with supporting grants from local government and a big programme of training of full-time leaders. While not directly challenging the religious basis of many of the existing youth organizations, the committee suggested that the use of Christian language or of the language of a Christian-influenced social elite was alienating many of their potential customers and thus reducing their effectiveness, especially as agents in the socialization of potentially delinquent youngsters:

For many young people today the discussion of 'spiritual values' or 'Christian values' chiefly arouses suspicion.... We have been struck by the great number of occasions, in the evidence presented to us, on which words such as the following have been used as though they were a commonly accepted and valid currency: 'service', 'dedication', 'leadership', 'character building' ... [These words] recall the hierarchies, the less interesting moments of school speech-days and other occasions of moral exhortation ... [Young people's] failure to attend youth clubs may be less often a sign of apathy than of the failure of their seniors properly to adjust their forms of language.[56]

In going on to review the results of Albemarle over the next ten years, Bernard Davies concludes that 'the balance of power within the service ... had moved decisively in favour of state controlled forms of secular and professional youth work and, therefore, against the philanthropic and religious motivations

---

[55] Wade Clark Roof, *A Generation of Seekers* (New York, 1993), 53, 124–6.
[56] Bernard Davies, *From Voluntaryism to Welfare State: A History of the Youth Service in England and Wales*, i. *1939–1979* (Leicester, 1999), 47.

which had created this form of practice with young people in the first place'. He adds that the balance had also tipped away from part-timers and volunteers in favour of full-time professionals, especially those with college qualifications.[57] Those working in this as in other 'caring professions' may often have been motivated by their religious beliefs to engage in work that was demanding, often poorly paid, but which could be seen as a direct expression of 'neighbourly love'. However, a variety of factors combined to ensure that these religious motivations tended to stay in the background. As indicated above, in a pluralist society with a range of religious and non-religious beliefs, an emphasis on the religious motives of the providers might risk the exclusion of those most in need. Indeed, religiously based charities were aware of this danger and there was a consequent tendency for them to play down this religious basis. For instance, the Samaritans, the telephone helpline for the suicidal, was founded by an Anglican clergyman in 1954, and counted many Christians, including clergy, among its volunteers, but strictly prohibited any mention of religion by volunteers unless it was explicitly raised by the person at the other end of the line. Moreover, in a class-based society, the fact that the Church of England, and to a lesser extent some of the other churches, was seen as part of 'the Establishment', closely linked with leading figures in politics, business, education, and the armed forces, was likely to alienate the rebel or the outsider. Meanwhile new orthodoxies were emerging which would have considerable influence in the 1960s and 1970s, and would involve the rejection of many of the ideals associated with this 'Establishment'. Some of these will be discussed in the next three chapters.

The same trend towards professionalization and a reduction in the role of priests and nuns could also be seen in countries like West Germany and Belgium, where church-based agencies remained central to the welfare system. For instance, Ziemann notes the huge growth in the 1970s of the Catholic welfare organization, Caritas. During that decade its personnel increased by 48 per cent while the proportion of those belonging to religious orders dropped from 30 per cent to 12 per cent. A major growth area was pastoral counselling, and Ziemann stresses the tension between the need to emphasize Catholic moral norms and the need for a 'scientific' approach, which in practice meant especially adopting the 'client-centred' approach derived from Carl Rogers.[58]

---

[57] Bernard Davies, *From Voluntarism to Welfare State*, 120.

[58] Benjamin Ziemann, 'Zwischen sozialer Bewegung und Dienstleistung an Individuum: Katholiken und katholische Kirche im therapeutischen Jahrzehnt', *Archiv für Sozialgeschichte*, 44 (2004), 379–82; Benjamin Ziemann, 'The Gospel of Psychology: Therapeutic Concepts and the Scientification of Pastoral Care in the West German Catholic Church, 1950–1980,' *Central European History*, 39 (2006), 79–106. Jean-Louis Ormières, *L'Europe désenchantée* (Paris, 2005), 38, comments briefly on similar trends in Belgium.

IMMIGRATION

The booming economies of western and northern Europe were attracting workers from southern Europe, from north Africa, from Turkey, from south Asia, and from the Caribbean. Affluence was transforming the lives of most people in the centres of modern industry, but equally certainly the arrival of millions of immigrants from the poorer 'south' and 'east' would have huge consequences for the cultural and religious life of the prosperous 'north'. Meanwhile many regions of the United States were being transformed by immigration from Latin America, and large-scale Asian immigration to Australia was beginning as a result of the ending in 1966 of the 'White Australia' policy. The religious implications of these migrations were very varied. In some cases the Christian churches were reinforced by the immigration of strongly committed Christians. This was notably true of the United States, where the great majority of immigrants since the 1960s have been Christians. A survey in 1990 found that about 90 per cent of 'Hispanic' Americans were Christians, 61 per cent of Asian Americans, and also the majority of Arab Americans. Of course these immigrants vary greatly in the degree of fervour with which they practise their faith, though they include some, such as the Koreans, who are very active in their churches.[59]

The same could be said of Irish and Caribbean immigrants to Britain, who were much more likely to be regular church-goers than the native population. From the 1920s to the 1960s the largest group of immigrants to Britain was from Ireland, the great majority being Catholic. Then in the 1950s and early 1960s they were joined by large numbers of immigrants from the Caribbean. As with the Irish, their favoured destinations were London and Birmingham. Caribbean immigrants, as well as being more fervent in their Christianity, often practised Christianity of unfamiliar kinds. A large proportion of immigrants joined Pentecostal or Adventist churches, and indeed they formed branches of American Pentecostal denominations, rather than joining Elim, the principal British denomination. Some had started by attending a 'British' church, whether Anglican, Methodist, Pentecostal, or whatever, but had felt a lack of welcome, or even had been made definitely unwelcome—'You can't sit there, that's Mrs Brown's seat', etc.[60] Others simply disliked what they saw as the 'cold' and 'formal' British styles of worship. Between about 1953 and 1960 branches of many Pentecostal denominations

[59] Barry A. Kosmin and Seymour P. Lachman, *One Nation under God: Religion in Contemporary American Society* (New York, 1993), 125–6, 132–42, 147–51.

[60] Edson Burton, 'From Assimilation to Anti-Racism' (Ph.D. thesis, University of the West of England, 2004), 189–91; see also Callum G. Brown, *Religion and Society in Twentieth-Century Britain* (London, 2006), 253–5, 291–3.

were established, and by the 1990s there were said to be no less than sixty-nine different forms of Pentecostalism in Britain. In the 1960s many of them enjoyed a big growth of membership. Then in the 1970s they began to establish closer relationships with the older British denominations, most of which had initially regarded them with suspicion, and in some cases pastors of these churches started to take on community leadership roles.[61] Meanwhile Caribbean and African immigrants and their children were also joining Anglican, Methodist, or Baptist churches, where by this time the welcome tended to be a great deal warmer, and in many parts of London and Birmingham by the later twentieth century the most flourishing congregations were those with a predominantly black membership.

In France, the largest immigrant communities were for long the Italians, Spanish, and Portuguese and in 1974 still about half the immigrants were Catholics. Some Catholic immigrants, like the Republicans fleeing Franco's Spain, brought anti-clerical traditions with them, though others such as those from northern Portugal had received a strongly Catholic upbringing. However, language was a more general problem, with few of the clergy being able to hear their confessions or to preach sermons that they could understand.[62] Sweden had for several centuries been one of Europe's most staunchly Protestant nations, but from the 1960s economic migration and a generous refugee policy brought considerable numbers both of Catholics and of Assyrian Orthodox. However, the biggest religious impact of immigration came increasingly from the arrival of large numbers of Muslims,[63] Hindus, and Sikhs in historically Christian countries. France in particular was by 1974 home to over a million immigrants from North Africa, of whom the great majority were Muslims. In West Germany the two million 'guest workers' in 1970 included large numbers of Turkish Muslims. In Britain the 2001 census, which provided the first reliable figures, would show that there were 1.6 million Muslims, 559,000 Hindus, and 336,000 Sikhs—as well as 152,000 Buddhists, most of whom probably were converts. Naturally, immigrants were mainly attracted to the cities. In Birmingham, in 2001, 20 per cent of the population belonged to religions other than Christianity, in Leicester 27 per cent, and in some London boroughs more than 30 per cent.[64] There were similar trends in Paris, Lyon, or Marseille, in Berlin or Amsterdam. In the last three decades of the twentieth century many of Europe's great cities were

[61] Burton, 'Assimilation to Anti-Racism,' 372–3, 384–401; Leslie J. Francis and Peter W. Brierley, 'The Changing Face of British Churches: 1975–1995,' in Mordechai Bar-Lev and William Shaffir (eds.), *Leaving Religion and the Religious Life* (Greenwich, Conn., 1997), 171.

[62] Gérard Cholvy and Yves-Marie Hilaire, *Histoire religieuse de la France contemporaine 1930–1988* (Toulouse, 1988), 402–7.

[63] For an overview, see Jørgen S. Nielsen, *Muslims in Western Europe* (Edinburgh, 1992).

[64] www.statistics.gov.uk/census2001

being transformed by the increasing presence, usually heavily concentrated in certain districts, of Muslims especially, and sometimes of Hindus and Sikhs. This raised all sorts of issues for the traditionally Christian countries of Europe, whether, like England or the Nordic countries they still had an established church, whether like France they were secular, or whether like most other countries they combined a formal separation of church and state with a mutual supportive relationship between the two. For instance, it raised questions about the place of religion in state schools; about the possibility of state subsidies for Muslim schools; about the role of minority religions in other state institutions, such as prisons and hospitals; about the close continuing ties between state and church when many citizens belonged to other faiths. In time even more intractable issues would arise as a result of different views on marriage and the status of women, and on the right to free speech, including the right to blaspheme.

In Britain the predominant response both of governments, of the Christian churches, and indeed of many secularists, was a multiculturalism which asserted the pluralist nature of a British society in which a range of ethnic groups and religions each had a respected place. In 1975 Birmingham, one of Europe's most religiously diverse cities, was the first to introduce a new religious education syllabus with the emphasis on learning about all of the world's major religions and world-views.[65] Hitherto religious teaching had focused mainly on Christianity, and frequently started from the assumption that children were being educated for membership of a Christian society. Now the emphasis was increasingly on preparation for life in a multicultural and multifaith society, in which knowledge of and respect for a variety of traditions was a paramount virtue. The committee which prepared the new syllabus included noted Christian academics such as the theologian John Hick and the educationalist John Hull, and few of them had a secularist agenda. The need for tolerance and mutual understanding was evident enough, even to the most conservative believer. But increasing contact with other religions was also leading some Christians to rethink important aspects of their faith. A case in point was John Hick, who in the 1970s held a chair of theology at Birmingham University, and who was also deeply involved in All Faiths for One Race, a coalition formed to oppose the influence of the National Front: dialogue with Muslims and later Buddhists converted him to the cause of religious pluralism, which became the central theme of his later theological writings.[66] But even those who did not accept Hick's rejection of Christian

---

[65] Gerald Parsons, 'Education,' in Parsons and Wolffe (eds.), *Religious Diversity*, ii. 175–7; John Hick, *An Autobiography* (Oxford, 2002), 162–8.

[66] John Wolffe, 'Pluralism,' in Parsons and Wolffe (eds.), *Religious Diversity*, ii. 31–5; Hick, *Autobiography*, 159–92.

theological exclusiveness could generally see the advantages of multiculturalism in promoting social harmony. Indeed as religious communities increasingly came to be seen as the basic building blocks of British society, secularists who had originally approved of the dilution of Christian influence began to get alarmed, while Christians increasingly welcomed Muslims and Hindus as allies against secularism.

At the opposite extreme to British multiculturalism was the French reassertion of *laïcité* (the principle of rigorous separation of religion from the state), which came to be focused on the long-running dispute over the acceptability of religious symbols in state institutions, and specifically the right of Muslim girls to wear head-scarves to school. Both Catholic and secularist opinion was divided on this issue. Questions of women's rights were also involved: supporters of the ban argued that the scarves were not so much a religious symbol as a symbol of women's oppression, and that the French state had a duty to protect its young citizens against such violations; opponents of the ban saw this as an example of misguided paternalism. But the eventual government decision that the scarves were an 'ostentatious religious symbol' and therefore unacceptable indicated a determination to defend existing national institutions and values, and to make no compromise, whether in the interests of social harmony or of individual rights.

Questions of the relationship between religion and the state, or religion and society, could now no longer be seen only in terms of Christianity. In the last quarter of the twentieth century, the religious demography of most west European societies, and indeed of Australasia and North America, was increasingly complex, and complicated systems of alliances were developing between adherents of the various religions. In the short term non-Christian immigration weakened the privileged position of the Christian churches. In the longer term the strong religious identities of many immigrants could provide an argument for seeing Europe as 'multi-religious' rather than 'secular', and for giving each of these religions some kind of recognition. On the other hand the 'fundamentalist' nature of much immigrant religion caused widespread anxiety, and provided ammunition for those who were hostile to all forms of religion.

CONCLUSION

The booming economies and the individual affluence of the 'long 1960s' had far-reaching effects on many aspects of life in Western societies, not least including religion. Most obviously, countries that had previously been overwhelmingly Christian and Jewish were pushed in the direction of a growing religious pluralism by large-scale non-Christian immigration. But affluence weakened the position of Christianity and the churches in at least four other ways. Economic change in the countryside undermined the rural cultures which had often been strongholds of Catholicism, bringing villagers increasingly under more secular urban influences. The burgeoning youth culture provided a host of new possibilities for adolescents, often drawing them away from the organizations provided and the values propagated by the churches. Collective identities and communal institutions of all kinds, political as well as religious, were weakened as the life of married couples focused on the home and the nuclear family, and as individuals claimed the right to live in their own way without outside interference. And a more prosperous society could afford to pay a growing number of trained professionals to take over many of the roles previously performed by priests, nuns, or voluntary religious workers. Moreover, prosperity also laid the basis for a mood of innovation, expansive optimism, and sometimes risk-taking. Previously esoteric ideas began to be taken more seriously, and the buoyant economy was able to sustain a variety of subcultures on the margins of respectable society. These experiments will be the subject of the next chapter.

6

New Worlds

Prosperity also allowed the emergence of more exotic cultures, overtly resistant to all established norms of respectable behaviour. The leitmotiv of the 1960s was the drive towards greater individual freedom, and nowhere was this seen as dramatically as in the various counter-cultures which began to emerge around 1965 in California's Bay Area, and then quickly spread eastward, to New York, reaching London and Amsterdam in 1966[1]—and eventually meeting the Pacific again in Sydney and Auckland. Here we meet the 1960s of legend in its fullest flowering—a world in which relatively few people fully participated, but which nonetheless left its mark on the wider society, as it demonstrated new possibilities, previously undreamt of, from which the wider world drew selectively.

THE COUNTER-CULTURE

On 12 November 1966 the luxuriantly bearded San Francisco-based Beat poet, Allen Ginsberg, stood in the pulpit of a Boston church and prophesied. He began by urging that every American aged 14 and above should take the mind-expanding drug LSD at least once. He was particularly hopeful about the beneficial effect that LSD could have on members of the government. He then went on to describe changes already under way in American society and changes that were coming. In cold print his sentences sometime lose coherence, but his vision probably had a mesmerizing effect on many of those present:

There is a change of consciousness among the younger generation, in a direction always latent in Elder America, towards the most complete public frankness possible. As the Gloucester poet Charles Olson formulated it, 'Private is public, and public is how we behave.' This means revision of standards of public behavior to include indications of private behavior heretofore excluded from public consciousness. Thus, new social standards more equivalent to private desire—as there is increased sexual

[1] Richard Neville, *Play Power* (London, 1970), 13–69.

illumination, new social codes may be found acceptable to rid ourselves of our fear of our own nakedness, rejection of our own bodies. Likely an enlarged family unit will emerge for many citizens; possibly, as the Zen Buddhist anarchist anthropologist Gary Snyder observed, with matrilineal descent as courtesy to those dakinis whose saddhana or bold path is the sexual liberation and teaching of Dharma to many frightened males (including myself) at once. Children may be held in common, with the orgy an acceptable community sacrament. . . . America's political need is orgies in the parks, on Boston Common and in the Public gardens, with naked bacchantes in our national forests. . . . I am acknowledging what is already happening among the young in fact and fantasy, and proposing official blessing for these breakthroughs of community spirit. Among the young we find a new breed of white Indians in California communing with illuminated desert redskins; we find our teenagers dancing Nigerian Yoruba dances and entering trance states to the electric vibrations of the Beatles who have borrowed shamanism from African sources. We find communal religious use of ganja, the hemp sacred to Mahadev (Great Lord) Shiva. There's now heard the spread of mantra chanting in private and such public manifestations as peace marches, and soon we will have Mantra Rock over the airwaves. All the available traditions of U.S. Indian vision-quest, peyote ritual mask dancing, Oriental pranayama, east Indian ear music are becoming available to the United States unconscious through the spiritual search of the young. Simultaneously there is a new Diaspora of Tibetan lamaist initiates; texts such as the Book of the Dead and I Ching have found fair-cheeked and dark-browed Kansas devotees. And rumour from the West Coast this season brings the legendary Hevarja Tantra—a document central to Vajrayana Buddhism's lightning-bolt Illumination—into public light as a source book for tantric community rules, LSD structured by ancient disciplines for meditation and community regulation. Ideas I have dwelled on are mixed: there is some prescription for public utopia thru education in inner space. There is more prescription here for the individual: as always, the old command to free ourselves from social conditioning, laws and traditional mores.[2]

The utopias imagined by Ginsberg were already being constructed in the Haight-Ashbury section of San Francisco ('Hashbury' for short) and the new 'counter-culture' was spreading rapidly to most other great Western cities.[3] Denizens of the counter-culture, or the 'underground' as it was sometimes termed in Britain, soon came to be known as 'hippies'. The external signs of the new way of life were beards, long hair for both men and women, colourful and loosely fitting garments, often adorned with beads, flowers, and sometimes bells.

[2] *International Times* (30 Jan.–12 Feb. 1967).
[3] For an overview, see Arthur Marwick, *The Sixties* (Oxford, 1998), 489–98. The former underground journalist Jonathon Green wrote a history of the 1960s with emphasis on the counter-culture, *All Dressed up: The Sixties and the Counter-Culture* (London, 1999), and an oral history, *Days in the Life: Voices from the English Underground 1961–1971* (London, 1998). Among many descriptions of Haight-Ashbury is Todd Gitlin, *The Sixties: Years of Hope, Days of Rage* (New York, 1993), 206–30.

Their styles in hair and clothing were in themselves an affront to the conformist majority. But the hostility of conventional society focused mainly on
three other points. One was their use of marijuana and LSD, the former as a
social drug, the latter because of its mind-expanding potential. Marijuana was
as central to the counter-culture as beer or wine were to mainstream society,
and it had many different roles. It was an essential ingredient for a relaxing
evening (or, indeed, morning, afternoon, or night) with a group of friends. At
least in the early days, the sharing of a joint had a sacramental quality. In the
1968 the Berkeley student paper remarked that:

Marijuana, now a household item in many Berkeley apartments, has lost its mystical
appeal.... The sacred joint, which was once passed from person to person in holy
communion, smoked down until the tip burned one's lips, is left half-used in ashtrays.
Now marijuana is moving from apartments to dorms—though fear of dorm raids
causes paranoia.[4]

Smoking marijuana also had the unusual advantage of combining sensations
of euphoria with feelings of virtue. It symbolized rebellion against mainstream
society, synonymous with materialism, conformism, and support for unjust
wars; unlike alcohol, mainstream society's favourite drug, marijuana did not
lead to violence; it even helped to produce calm, reasonable, well-adjusted
individuals. The British underground paper, *IT*, once told the remarkable
story of Robin C. Essentially it was a conversion narrative, with 'shit' as the
agent of salvation. '[P]rior to smoking he was a nervous depressive, intro-
verted, subject to fits of violence when frustrated. "I lived in a constant state
of tension; I had no friends—no real relationships with anyone—I was con-
stantly holding people away; my career was in a mess and I spent most of my
money on drink." ' He started smoking while working in India, and continued
during a long stay in Kathmandu:

I am now in a permanent state of cool. Don't get frustrated, worried, angry, greedy,
violent, pushy, depressed, lonely, sad, jealous. In fact all the negative states of being
have been totally eradicated. And that I think is progress. I am now able to play music,
sing, write, talk to people without fear of judgement. I just don't get put down. If this
can be the effect on me, why not upon anyone else? I have an understanding of man's
condition, which accounts for my inability to feel frustration, anger, etc., and I believe
I have reached a state which the Buddhists call 'riding the bullock'—controlling the
animal forces rather than letting the animal forces control, and this without tension.[5]

LSD was the key to exploring 'inner space'—offering new possibilities of self-
discovery, and at the same time a sense of oneness with the universe. It owed a
lot of its popularity and prestige to the psychedelic style of the Beatles and

⁴ *Daily Californian* (19 Feb. 1968).   ⁵ *IT* (1–14 Nov. 1968).

many other music groups of the time. 'Sold as everything from a creative aid to a psychotherapeutic panacea', it was, according to Ian MacDonald, 'the dominant influence on late Sixties pop'. Moreover, for some, it was the way to religious experiences of a kind that conventional churches could not offer. Timothy Leary, the former Harvard psychologist, who was the main advocate of drugs as an aid to spiritual experience, founded in 1966 a new religion, the League for Spiritual Development. Each of their 'sacramental assemblings' drew on the traditions and rituals of one of the world's religions:

we hope anyone that comes to our celebrations will discover that each of these great myths is based on a psychedelic experience, a death-rebirth sequence. But in addition we hope that the Christian will be particularly turned on by our Catholic LSD Mass. Because it will renew for him the resurrection metaphor, which for many has become rather routine and tired. The aim is to turn on not just the mind, but the sense organs, and even to talk to people's cells and ancient centres of wisdom.[6]

A second cause of hostility was their advocacy, and often practice, of free love, and their rejection of the nuclear family. The aspect of the counter-culture which most fascinated outsiders was its new approach to sex. Communal living was preferred, and sharing of sexual partners, as well as sharing in the care and upbringing of children, was expected. Jealousy was taboo, and inhibitions were a source of shame. Some tried to shed their inhibitions through public or group sex. Both men, and more particularly women, were under pressure to have sex with anyone who asked for it. Veterans of the British counter-culture, interviewed in an oral history project twenty years later, agreed on the centrality of promiscuous sex, though they differed widely in their assessment of its pros and cons. Women tended to be more critical than men. Hippies believed in free love and also in equality between men and women. This was certainly the theory. But while many of the men who were involved in the counter-culture were enthusiastic at the time or subsequently about the sexual liberation which it offered, some women were more scep-tical. Admittedly these objections were often made retrospectively, and were influenced by involvement in the Women's Liberation Movement, which led them to look much more critically at aspects of their lives which they had previously accepted or even welcomed. The gist of the criticisms was that sex in the counter-culture tended to follow a male agenda and was often exploitative. In particular women were under pressure to have sex with large numbers of different men, and made to feel guilty if they did not want to. When in 1988

---

[6] Ian MacDonald, *Revolution in the Head: The Beatles Records and the Sixties* (2nd edn. London, 1997), 289. Paul Harvey and Philip Goff (eds.), *The Columbia Documentary History of Religion in America since 1945* (New York, 2005), 94. For Leary, see also Jay Stevens, *Storming Heaven* (New York, 1987).

the former underground journalist Jonathon Green published an oral history of the British counter-culture he reported numerous complaints of this kind, by women, and sometimes by men too. As Nicola Lane commented:

It was paradise for men in their late twenties: all these willing girls. But the trouble with the willing girls was that a lot of the time they were not willing because they particularly fancied the people concerned but because they felt they ought to. There was a huge pressure to conform to non-conformity, which left very little room for finding out what your preferences were.[7]

The third, and perhaps most fundamental, source of hostility to the hippies was their rejection of the work ethic. In the eyes of their critics, hippies were 'parasites'; the more articulate propagandists for the counter-culture claimed on the contrary that they were preparing for the day, not too far distant, when the increasing use of computers would render most forms of work redundant, and require a society built round leisure.[8]

As Ginsberg indicated, another major theme, and another important reason for the discomfort which the hippies provoked, was their rejection of the distinction between 'public' and 'private'. Nakedness was a case in point. In mainstream society the pleasure that couples and individuals derived from their private nakedness gained much of its piquancy from the fact that public nudity was taboo. Hippies, on the other hand, while sometimes using nudity as a weapon to embarrass those in authority or to make a political point, wanted to establish the normality of the naked body, and to expel any feelings of shame linked with it. Music was also central to the counter-culture, and this was where 'mainstream' culture and counter-culture overlapped. The most popular musicians of the decade, the Beatles, adopted increasingly unconventional styles of music and messages from about 1966, abandoned their suits and ties, grew moustaches or beards, and made increasingly frequent references to drugs in their songs.[9] If the Beatles were converts to the counter-culture, other musical groups, notably the Los Angeles-based Doors and San Francisco-based Grateful Dead, owed their whole identity to the counter-culture, while also enjoying a wider following.

In Britain the principal organ of the 'underground' was *International Times* (later named simply *IT*), founded in the autumn of 1966. In March 1967 their offices were raided by police in search of obscene literature. Following the raid, and a hostile account of their paper in the mass-circulation *Sunday Mirror*,

---

[7] Green, *Days*, 418. For a totally positive view of sex in the counter-culture, Neville, *Play*, 71–92.

[8] Ibid. 253–78.

[9] MacDonald, *Revolution*, provides a comprehensive analysis of the Beatles' records and the evolution of their music.

International Times published a lengthy editorial outlining the philosophy behind the paper and the movement which it represented:

It is essentially an inner-directed movement. Those who are involved in it share a common viewpoint—a new way of looking at things—rather than a credo, dogma or ideology. Thus it can never be suppressed by force or law: you cannot imprison consciousness. No matter how many raids and arrests the police make, on whatever pretence—there can be no final bust because the revolution has taken place WITHIN THE MINDS of the young.

The editor went on to note some of the characteristics of the new attitude. These included:

a) Permissiveness—the individual should be free from hindrance from external law or internal law in his pursuit of pleasure so long as he does not impinge on others. . . . The search for pleasure/orgasm covers every field of human activity, from sex, art and inner space, to architecture, the abolition of money, outer space and beyond.

b) Post/anti-political—this is not a movement of protest but one of celebration. Although it is futuristic, looking towards the leisure of a computer culture, the new man of the space age . . . those involved in 'the new thing' are for having a good time now. And they are succeeding. This gives rise to envy and creates enemies. Favourite put down words against the new movement are 'frivolous' and 'irresponsible'. The 'pleasure now' attitude ensures, however, that whatever happens this is one revolution that must win one way or nothing. If our ideas are quashed in the future, at least we can look back on the ball-up we had now.

He went on to declare that 'The new movement is essentially optimistic. It has a happy view of man and his potential, based mainly on his creativity. . . . The new approach is to make changes wherever you are, right in front of your nose. The weapons are love and creativity—wild new clothes, fashions, strange new music sounds.'[10]

RELIGION IN THE COUNTER-CULTURE

The editor even hesitated to call 'the new thing' 'a movement', since this seemed to conflict with the sense of individual autonomy which was so important in the underground. For most counter-culturalists it was axiomatic that mainstream religion and churches were part of the conventional society which they had rejected, and some were positively hostile to any kind of religion. Belief in God, adherence to any formal code of morality, or loyalty to any

[10] *IT* (13–26 Mar. 1967).

institution were often seen as ways of abdicating the individual's responsibility for self-realization, without any interference from external authority of any kind. The British underground poet Jeff Nuttall asserted flatly that 'Religious faith and the belief in human freedom just don't mix'.[11] This entirely negative view of religion was commonly presented in the other leading British underground journal, *Oz*, the brain-child of Richard Neville, who had founded a journal with the same name in Australia in 1963. The original *Oz* had 'satirized establishment politicians, the Returned Servicemen's League, the church and the police, defied the existing censorship laws, and was soon charged with obscenity'.[12]

Unlike the often rather earnest contributors to *IT*, *Oz* specialized in provocation and debunking—though the paper's psychedelic style of design sometimes made it difficult to be sure what was being written.[13] Counter-cultural believers—and indeed anyone who failed to adopt Neville's favourite tone of cynicism mixed with black humour—were ridiculed as readily as the members of more conventional religious groups. Successive issues in 1967 each contained at least one contribution attacking believers of one kind or another. A letter to the editor, written in a style similar to that of the paper's own journalists, denounced a mystical group which the writer had encountered, describing a person he had met there as 'the most brainwashed creep I had ever seen (apart from the pope)'. An article by an admirer of R. D. Laing, the radical psychiatrist, often described as the guru of the counter-culture, condemned the Laing cult, arguing that to treat Laing as a guru was to reject his message of individual freedom. An article headed 'Wog Beach Shock' provided a fierce attack on all things Italian, focusing especially on the Catholic Church and its restrictions on adolescent sex. A lengthy, and feeble, parody of the television *Epilogue* featured a vicar talking boringly about a charity he ran. And another letter to the editor by a 17-year-old pupil at St Paul's, an elite London school, attacked the combination of competition, compulsory games, and compulsory prayers, and complained that most of the pupils had been effectively indoctrinated.[14]

The drug prophet Timothy Leary stated unequivocally the tension between the counter-culture and any kind of conventional religion. Writing in the 1980s he recalled:

---

[11] Green, *Days*, 296–7.

[12] David Hilliard, 'The Religious Crisis of the 1960s', *Journal of Religious History*, 21 (1997), 211.

[13] Elizabeth Nelson, *British Counter-Culture 1966–73: A Study of the Underground Press* (Basingstoke, 1989), 50–3, is enthusiastic about *Oz*, but sees *IT* as boring and didactic.

[14] *Oz*, 4–9 (1967—but issues were not dated).

Everything we did in the 1960s was designed to fission, to weaken faith in and conformity to the 1950s social order. Our precise surgical target was the Judeo-Christian power monolith, which has imposed a guilty, inhibited, grim, anti-body, anti-life repression on Western civilization Our assignment was to topple this prudish, judgemental civilization. And it worked! For the first time in 20 centuries, the good old basic paganism got everybody moving again. White people actually started to move their hips, let the Marine crewcuts grow long, adorn themselves erotically in Dionysian revels, tune into nature. The ancient Celtic-pagan spirit began to sweep through the land of Eisenhower and J. Edgar Hoover. Membership in organised churches began to plummet. Hedonism, always the movement of individuals managing their own rewards and pleasures ran rampant....Millions of Americans writing their own Declarations of Independence: My life, my liberty, my pursuit of happiness.[15]

However, there were also many counter-culturalists who saw institutions and dogmas as the problem, rather than religious faith as such. Thus an *International Times* editorial entitled 'The Kingdom is within you' declared: 'Study Marx, the I Ching, pray to Christ, dig Trotsky. Be a provo, don't join anything.'[16] *IT* once included a cover picture of a radical, counter-cultural Jesus, with the caption 'Reward for information leading to the apprehension of Jesus Christ—Wanted—for sedition, criminal anarchy—vagrancy and conspiracy to overthrow the established government...'[17] And later in the same year Theodore Faithfull drew on a range of Christian and other sources, including the Gospel of Thomas, Blake, Teilhard de Chardin, and Wilhelm Reich, in his plea for a higher valuation of the subjective in order to facilitate the fullest development of the human personality.[18] However, religiously minded counter-culturalists were much more likely to take their inspiration from the East. Here it is interesting to compare two interviews by *IT* in 1968 and 1969 with popular music stars. The first was Mick Jagger of the Rolling Stones, who attacked Christianity for making people feel that they were evil. ' "You're so awful that God gave his only son and suffered for you because you are so rotten." Thank-you, well wow! You know, am I really that bad?' The second was the Beatle, George Harrison, who said that 'it was only through India and through Hinduism and through yogis and through meditation that I learned about Christ and what Christ really meant and stood for'.[19] He had found church services 'a bore': 'It's like watching a party political broadcast on television, it's just some guy up there—and it's the sort of attitude that I felt in church...it was "Now this is what it is, and just believe what we're telling you or you'll get your arse kicked"...' But Harrison liked going into churches

[15] Harvey and Goff, *Documentary History*, 94–5.   [16] *IT* (30 Jan.–12 Feb. 1967).
[17] *IT* (23 Aug.–5 Sept. 1968).   [18] *IT* (1–14 Nov. 1968).
[19] *IT* (17–30 Aug. 1968, 29 Aug.–11 Sept. 1969).

when no one else was there, and he declared that 'the Christ-consciousness is like the Krishna-consciousness, which is absolute and it is in every speck of creation'.

THE NEW MYSTICISMS

In fact, *IT* gave a lot of space to spiritual issues and a wide range of views was represented. Writers for *IT* tended to start from the premises that other civilizations had insights that the West had lost; that mind-expanding drugs offered ways to a richer life; and that open-minded people should not dismiss out of hand possibilities which conventional wisdom rejected. While Christianity, and more especially the churches, were often criticized for being too dogmatic or laying down too many moral rules, secular wisdom was criticized for being equally dogmatic and as reflecting too narrow a conception of life and the universe. Hinduism, Buddhism, and Native American spirituality generally received favourable mention, and some *IT* writers also advocated astrology or belief in UFOs. Thus John Michell, in an article containing several characteristic themes, proclaimed that 'the end of the age of Pisces, which coincided with the reign of Christianity, is now at hand'. Recent sightings of flying saucers were 'a portent of the revelations that will attend the opening of the aquarian age'. Calling for a return to older religious beliefs that preceded Christianity, he claimed: 'Earlier religions were concerned above all with understanding the nature of God and the forces which control the rhythm of the universe, whereas Christianity represents a system of ethics rather than an approach to an understanding of the higher forms of life outside the earth.'[20]

Where rationalists had often accepted Christian ethics, while rejecting the theology as being 'unscientific', counter-culturalists were often quite ready to accept the supernatural, while rejecting Christian ethics. They were in a tradition going back to the later nineteenth century of those who wanted a middle way between the dogmas of orthodox religion and orthodox science—a view of life that was spiritual without being exclusive, which would take seriously experiences and phenomena that mainstream science simply rejected out of hand.[21]

The roots of these newly fashionable forms of religion can be traced back to the San Francisco Beats of the 1950s, and beyond them to Aldous Huxley and Alesteir Crowley, to Gerald Gardner, and even further back to figures

---

[20] *IT* (30 Jan.–12 Feb. 1967).
[21] Hugh McLeod, *Secularisation in Western Europe, 1848–1914* (Basingstoke, 2000), 161–4.

like Helena Blavatsky in the later nineteenth century.[22] The Beats, including Allen Ginsberg, Jack Kerouac, and Gary Snyder, pioneered the interest in Zen Buddhism, which was to be the spirituality of choice for 'alternatively' inclined intellectuals, but which also had followers in the popular music world, such as Frank Zappa. Huxley's *Doors of Perception*, published in 1954, reported on his experiments in the use of drugs as a pathway to religious experience. Gardner, the founder of Wicca, and Crowley were the best known of those who wanted to return to a paganism which allegedly was humanity's first religion, and which was based on a closeness to nature that had been lost because of the constricting influence of Christianity. The attraction to Hinduism of Harrison (and for a time of his fellow Beatles) seems to have begun with his interest in Indian music. More generally, Hinduism was valued as being inclusive, as emphasizing individual experience more than dogma, and as having a positive view of sex. Harrison, followed later by the other Beatles, was one of the first of many young westerners in the later 1960s and 1970s who made the pilgrimage to India or Nepal. Meanwhile, various Indian gurus were themselves travelling to the West. The Beatles were followers of the Maharishi Mahesh Yogi, who brought Transcendental Meditation to Los Angeles in 1960. The Krishna Consciousness Movement was founded in New York in 1966, and its headquarters moved to San Francisco in 1967. The Guru Maharaj Ji, Leader of the Divine Light Mission, was brought over from India by American devotees in 1971.[23]

From the mid-1960s a range of previously esoteric ideas began to reach a much wider audience. Most spectacularly in California's Bay Area, but also in many other parts of the Western world, the later 1960s saw a flowering of new forms of religion or 'spirituality' (the term preferred by those who associated 'religion' with an over-rigid body of dogmas and moral rules).[24] In 1975, over 300 of the 3,000 groups listed in the *Spiritual Community Guide to North America* were in the Bay Area. This was a density three times as high as in Arizona, the state which had the highest ratio of 'spiritual communities' to population.[25] When asking Bay Area residents in 1973 about their involvement in the new movements, Wuthnow divided these into three groups: 'Counter-Cultural', 'Personal Growth', and 'Neo-Christian'. Among the 'counter-cultural' he included those that were 'off-shoots of distinctly

---

[22] For antecedents of counter-cultural religion, see Robert S. Ellwood, Jr, *Alternative Altars* (Chicago, 1979), 104–66; Stevens, *Storming*, chs. 4–7; Joanne Pearson (ed.), *Belief beyond the Boundaries: Wicca, Celtic Spiritualities and the New Age* (Aldershot, 2002).

[23] See the following contributions to Charles Y. Glock and Robert N. Bellah (eds.), *The New Religious Consciousness* (Berkeley, Calif., 1976): Gregory Johnson, 'The Hare Krishna in San Francisco', 31–51; Jeanne Messer, 'Guru Maharaj Ji and the Divine Light Mission', 52–72; Donald Stone, 'The Human Potential Movement', 93–115.

[24] See Paul Heelas and Linda Woodhead, *The Spiritual Revolution* (Oxford, 2005).

[25] Robert Wuthnow, *Experimentation in American Religion* (Berkeley, Calif., 1978), 9–12.

non-Western or non-Christian traditions', including Zen Buddhism, Transcendental Meditation (TM), yoga groups and Hare Krishna, all of which drew on Indian or Japanese traditions. He also included Satanism, the roots of which were entirely Western, but explicitly anti-Christian. He found that about 4 per cent of those interviewed had had some involvement with one or more of these counter-cultural movements, yoga and TM being the most popular, while numbers with any experience of Hare Krishna or Satanism were much smaller. Typically they were well-educated, unmarried, and aged under 30.[26] In another study, focused specifically on Bay Area students, Wuthnow found a strong correlation between involvement in the counter-culture and rejection of Christianity. Among those who rejected Christianity were both the 'non-religious' and 'mystics'—the latter being those who were attracted to counter-cultural religions. Both groups were far more numerous in the Bay Area than in most other parts of the USA.[27] As well as the new movements, Wuthnow found certain characteristic ways of thinking, which were widespread in the population generally, but were most common among those alienated from the church. For instance, knowledge of and belief in astrology was quite widespread in the counter-culture, as was belief in extra-sensory perception. As indicated by Ginsberg in his Boston oration, another aspect of the new spiritualities was the discovery of Native American religious practices.

Most of the new movements stressed the need for personal exploration in a way that was consistent with the counter-culture's overriding stress on individual freedom. In contrast to mainstream Christianity, at least as they perceived it, most of these movements highlighted experience rather than doctrine, feeling and intuition rather than rational argument. Thus Gregory Johnson, in his study of Haight-Ashbury's Hare Krishna temple, noted that 'the absolute insight experienced by a devotee could not be interpreted by words or logic. It was something that each person "knows" when he "feels" it.'[28] On the other hand, Hare Krishna imposed a strict ethical discipline—something which most counter-culturalists saw as a harmful legacy of Christianity. According to Johnson, the great majority of converts to Hare Krishna had taken hallucinogenic drugs. Rather as nineteenth-century temperance militants were quite often reformed drinkers, their very strict rules could be interpreted as a means towards rebuilding a life which had been damaged by previous excesses. Temple propaganda invited jaded hippies to '*Stay high for ever....Drop out* of movements employing artificially induced states

[26] Robert Wuthnow, 'The New Religions in Social Context', in Glock and Bellah, *New Consciousness*, 267–93.

[27] Wuthnow, *Experimentation*, 9–12, 156–7.

[28] Johnson, 'Hare Krishna', in Glock and Bellah, *New Consciousness*, 35.

of self-realization and expanded consciousness. Such methods only lead to spiritual laziness and chaos. *End all bring-downs,* flip out and stay for eternity.'[29]

In Europe the biggest counter-cultural centres in the later 1960s and early 1970s were London and Amsterdam. In London the mecca for the alternatively spiritual was Gandalf's Garden in Chelsea, which in 1970 described itself as an 'experimental, spiritually hip community evolving a life-style and producing a mystical scene magazine'. It included a: 'Shop and meeting place selling hand-made goods, occult books, exotic teas and health snacks; also free food and free notice board, yoga classes and weekly mantra meditations, talks, gurus, occultists, yogis, seekers for the miraculous.' Sutcliffe comments that 'The excited jumble of phenomena in this entry from an early directory of multiple religiosity in and on the fringes of the British counterculture reflects the fierce cultural flux of the day, in which multiple realms were flung together in a blitz of cultural mix-and-match.'[30]

The description of Gandalf's Garden came from the *Aquarian Guide to Occult, Mystical, Religious, Magical London and Around*, which began by stating that 'interest in occultism and mysticism is on the increase and there for the taking', declaring that 'there are many paths to the centre, and it is really up to the individual to choose his or her own way, at the same time as having a healthy respect for all the other roads'.[31] In this spirit of openness the guide included some Christian groups, mostly of an unconventional kind. The emphasis on individual seeking meant that Christian retreat centres also gained a mention in this as in some other guides to the 'alternative scene'. In addition to numerous societies, centres, groups, or individual practitioners in these fields, they noted fifteen magazines, including *Zodiac Monthly, Occult Gazette, Flying Saucer Review, The Wiccan,* the Buddhist *Middle Way,* and *Harmony* (devoted to diet reform), as well as those with a more general brief, such as *The Atlantean,* 'which believes in the essential unity of the seemingly diverse aspects of existence. Its contributors deal with subjects ranging from prehistory to metaphysics; from the esoteric sciences to the pros and cons of vegetarianism.'[32]

While many of the new movements of this period started in the United States before they came to Europe, paganism got established in Europe before

---

[29] Ibid. 36.

[30] Steven Sutcliffe, 'Wandering Stars: Seekers and Gurus in the Modern World', in Sutcliffe and Bowman (eds.), *Beyond New Age*, 18.

[31] Francoise Strachan (ed.), *The Aquarian Guide to Occult, Mystical, Religious, Magical London and Around* (London, 1970), pp. ix–x.

[32] Ibid.

crossing the Atlantic. Thus Wicca, described by Pearson as 'a highly ritualistic, nature venerating, polytheistic, magical and religious system', was developed by Gerald Gardner in England in the 1940s, and expounded in his book *Witchcraft Today* (1954). It reached North America in the 1960s and then in 1970s and 1980s developed new and distinctive forms, through the combined influences of Native American spirituality and feminism. Meanwhile, in Britain it initially played a major role in the Pagan Front, established in 1970.[33]

Interviews recorded in a large oral history project[34] conducted by local radio in various parts of the UK in the 1990s suggest that interest in 'alternative' spirituality, other than the well-established faith of spiritualism, was rare among those born before 1935. It increased somewhat among those born between 1935 and 1944, with five out of a sample of seventy-two respondents brought up in Great Britain having beliefs that might be placed in this category. There was then a very marked increase among those born between 1945 and 1954. In a sample of seventy-three people, there were fourteen whose present beliefs might be defined as 'alternative', as well as a few who had been through an 'alternative' phase. The nineteen adherents of 'alternative spirituality' born between 1935 and 1954 included four who described themselves as pagans; four who were Buddhists or sympathetic to Buddhism (including one of the pagans); four who believed in astrology; two who had been influenced in their beliefs by travel to India; one who was influenced by Native American spirituality; and one who had had religious experiences through taking drugs. Those who were attracted to Asian or Native American religion tended to be well-educated and/or middle class, and had been influenced by 'the Sixties', often including the counter-culture, whereas this was less often true of the pagans and believers in astrology, who came from a wider range of social backgrounds. Some of the 'alternative' believers were in decided rebellion against a Christian or Jewish upbringing, but others quite happily mixed 'alternative' and more conventional beliefs—and indeed saw positive virtue in such eclecticism.

Here are a few examples of the kinds of beliefs these people held, and how they got to them. Paul Kenny (born 1947, London) was a folk musician, who had been strongly influenced by the Beatles, and by the 1960s drug culture. He now lived in the country, tried as far as possible to be self-sufficient,

[33] Joanne Pearson, 'The History and Development of Wicca and Paganism', in Pearson (ed.), *Belief*, 32, 36, 39.

[34] Millennium Project recordings held at National Sound Archive, British Library, London (henceforth MPNSA). I have used the summaries of interviews on the National Sound Archive website: www.bl.uk/collections/sound-archive/history.html (accessed various dates in April 2005).

and described himself as a pantheist. Jean Robertson (born 1947 Glasgow), a teacher, reacted strongly against a 'guilt-ridden Calvinistic culture' and a patriarchal father. She travelled to India, and was now influenced by Hinduism, and apparently by forms of 'alternative spirituality' that were not spelt out. Brenda Allen (born 1937, London), a housewife, who had also worked as a machinist, had gone to church regularly when young, but left as a teenager after a dispute with the vicar. Now she described herself as a pagan, and as a believer in tarot cards and in premonitions, though she emphasized that many forms of religious worship are valid—she was not claiming that there is only 'one way'. Brian Coates (born 1947, Dartford), whose jobs had included being a policeman, was a pagan and a keen environmentalist, but also quite sympathetic to Christianity. Angela Orton (born 1945, Hull), who came from a working-class background, was a clairvoyant with extensive knowledge of astrology, who also believed in Jesus. Maureen West (born 1939, Lake District), a counsellor, had been strongly influenced by Germaine Greer's *Female Eunuch*, and was now interested in Native American spirituality. Amanda Waite (born 1952, Black Country), a nurse, had gone to church with an aunt when young, but was now a witch, and had converted her husband to paganism, though as yet her children were not interested. She remarked that paganism was the fastest growing religion because of its closeness to nature.[35]

CHRISTIANITY MEETS THE COUNTER-CULTURE

Where Christianity and the counter-culture met was in the Jesus Movement, which like so many initiatives of the 1960s had its base in California, and never took root so effectively anywhere else. The movement and its Jesus Freaks are a testimony to the adaptability and ingenuity of Evangelical Protestants, chameleon-like in their ability to change their cultural colouring while retaining the essence of their doctrine. Jesus Freaks had often come from the counter-culture and retained hippie tastes in clothes, hair, and mannerisms, while dropping the drugs and the free love. The Movement was a collective name for a variety of Evangelical Protestant groups which from 1967, with a peak of activity in the early 1970s, were appealing to the counter-cultural young by presenting a theologically conservative biblical message in the language of the counter-culture, and without any of the trappings of conventional Christianity. One of the best-known preachers of the movement,

[35] MPNSA, interviews 15118, 15135, 12083, 7570, 7082, 2584, 12559.

Arthur Blessitt, who was originally based in Los Angles, but later walked across America carrying a giant cross, 'wore open-necked flowery shirts, beads, bell-bottoms, and sandals'.[36] The Jesus Movement published Christian underground newspapers and provided a hip translation of the Bible in *Letters to Street Christians*.[37] The main theme of the movement was that countercultural youth, who rejected the church, could relate to Jesus. He too was a rebel, rejected by the respectable citizens of his day. The first issue of *Right On*, the journal of the Christian World Liberation Front, included a 'Wanted' notice in the following terms:

Beware—This man is extremely dangerous. His insidiously inflammatory message is particularly effective with young people who haven't been taught to ignore him yet. He changes men and sets them free.

WARNING: HE IS STILL AT LARGE![38]

But by far the most important of the new forms of Christianity to emerge in the 1960s was the Charismatic Movement. Once again, it started in California. But its worldwide spread far eclipsed anything else emerging from that most fertile of spiritual seedbeds. Charismatic Renewal, as it was called, meant that modern Christian congregations were experiencing the spiritual gifts described in Acts 2 and 1 Corinthians 12. These included most frequently speaking in tongues (glossolalia), but also interpretation of this speech, prophecy, and healing. Since the Los Angeles revival of 1906 these gifts had been seen in the Pentecostal churches, which had been especially popular in Latin America. In North America and Europe 'classical' Pentecostalism appealed mainly to ethnic minorities and those in lower income groups. 'Neo-Pentecostalism', as it was sometimes called, started within the 'mainstream' churches, and attracted the well-educated and the economically successful. The movement began in a Californian Episcopalian congregation in 1959. It reached Britain in 1963, attracting Anglicans, members of the Church of Scotland, Baptists, Methodists, and especially Brethren, a small lay-led denomination of conservative Protestants. By 1967 American Catholics were receiving the gifts of the Spirit, and in 1971 the first groups of Charismatics were formed in France.[39]

[36] Patrick Allitt, *Religion in America since 1945* (New York, 2003), 135.   [37] Ibid. 136.
[38] Donald Heinz, 'The Christian World Liberation Front', in Glock and Bellah (eds.), *New Consciousness*, 154.
[39] Ronald J. Flowers, *Religion in Strange Times: The 1960s and 1970s* (n.pl.: 1984), 71–82; Ralph Lane, Jr, 'Catholic Charismatic Renewal', in Glock and Bellah (eds.), *New Consciousness*, 162–79; David Bebbington, *Evangelicalism in Modern Britain: A History from the 1730s to the 1980s* (London, 1989), 229–33; Gérard Cholvy and Yves-Marie Hilaire, *Histoire religieuse de la France contemporaine, 1930–1988* (Toulouse, 1988), 453–62.

By this time the British movement was splitting in all directions, as many of the pioneers, feeling unwelcome in the established denominations, moved out to form 'house churches'. These in turn were divided among themselves, some being entirely autonomous, while others were part of a 'chain' of similarly minded congregations.[40] David Bebbington, the leading authority on modern British Evangelicalism, emphasizes the links between the Charismatic Movement and the counter-culture.[41] In some respects they were completely different. For instance, the overriding emphasis by Charismatics on the authority of the Bible, usually interpreted in a literalist way, was completely foreign to the spirit of the counter-culture, with its extreme individualism and its repudiation of authorities of whatever kind. On the other hand, the Charismatics freed up Evangelical ethics, getting rid of those taboos which did not have any biblical basis. They saw the good gifts of God as things to be enjoyed, including food, drink, dancing, and sex (as long as it remained within heterosexual marriage).[42] Charismatics were expected to know their Bibles and to base their lives on biblical principles; however, the most important aspect of their contemporary appeal lay perhaps in the extent to which they recognized the role of feelings, emotions, intuition, as well as reason, and the role of the private and the personal at a time when many people were disillusioned with politics. Where they were in clearest conflict with the Zeitgeist was in the primacy that some branches of the movement gave to male leadership.[43] While it is hazardous to generalize about a movement that was so disparate, the affinities of the movement with the counter-culture tended to be in matters of style rather than content. In the longer run the worldwide impact of the Charismatic Movement has been far greater than that of the counter-culture. It is reflected, for instance, in the huge popularity of the 'born again' churches in contemporary Africa, in the strength of Charismatic Catholics in the Philippines, and in the fast-growing house churches in China.[44] However, in the Western world the Charismatic Movement, though one of the liveliest aspects of the contemporary church, still attracts only a small part of the total population.

---

[40] Andrew Walker, *Restoring the Kingdom: The Radical Christianity of the House Church Movement* (London, 1988).

[41] Bebbington, *Evangelicalism*, 233, 240–8.   [42] Ibid. 244.

[43] Joyce Thurman, *New Wineskins: A Study of the House Church Movement* (Frankfurt am Main, 1982), 64.

[44] Allan Anderson, 'The Pentecostal and Charismatic Movements,' in McLeod (ed.), *Cambridge History of Christianity*, ix., 89–106.

CONCLUSION

The 1960s have been called by some historians 'the secularisation decade' and by others a time of 'spiritual awakening'.[45] These contrasting facets of the decade were all vividly manifest in the counter-culture. In the short run the most obvious point was that large numbers of young people, as one aspect of a wider rebellion against conventional society, were breaking away from the churches in which they had been brought up. In the longer term, the more significant fact was that in breaking away they became open to a huge variety of new ideas, many of which were to have a continuing influence in the latter part of the century. Many of these apparently new ideas were actually quite old, but until the 1960s they had not been widely known. However, they attracted many of those in the counter-culture, and from there they spread much more widely through the influence of underground newspapers, books, and especially popular music. Nor were these ideas only influencing those who had rejected the Christian churches. More widespread than explicitly counter-cultural forms of Christianity was a mood of eclecticism which proclaimed the possibility, even the desirability, of mixing elements drawn from different traditions and belief-systems. This was happening within Christianity, with for instance the immense popularity of Taizé, the Protestant monastery in eastern France founded in 1940, which freely drew in its worship on Catholic and Orthodox sources, and in the 1960s became a centre for ecumenical youth pilgrimages; it was happening between traditional religions, as for instance when in the 1960s many Christians started to practise yoga; and many of the newer forms of spirituality emerging in the 1960s and 1970s rejected any kind of exclusivism as a matter of principle. If the respectability of eclecticism was one key legacy of the 1960s, another was the primacy of the individual search. Wade Clark Roof entitled his study of the spirituality of the 'baby-boomer' generation *A Generation of Seekers*. Robert Wuthnow, in a book covering somewhat similar ground, speaks of the shift from a spirituality still dominant in the 1950s, which was based on 'dwelling', to the spirituality typical of the 1990s, based on 'seeking'. The major shift, he suggests took place among the generation born between 1944 and 1960.[46]

[45] Callum Brown, 'The Secularisation Decade: What the 1960s have Done to the Study of Religious History,' in McLeod and Ustorf (eds.), *Decline of Christendom*, 29–46; Robert S. Ellwood, Jr, *Sixties Spiritual Awakening* (New Brunswick, NJ, 2003); for an attempt to balance these two aspects, see Hilliard, 'Crisis,' 227.

[46] Wade Clark Roof, *Generation of Seekers* (New York, 1993); Robert Wuthnow, *After Heaven: Spirituality in America since the 1950s* (Berkeley, Calif., 1998).

7

1968

'There has never been a year like 1968, and it is unlikely that there ever will be again.'[1] Thus begins one of the many books celebrating the political upheavals of that year. 1968 began with the Vietcong's 'Tet offensive' against the American forces in Vietnam. Then came Lyndon Johnson's announcement that he would not stand for re-election as President of the United States. Martin Luther King was assassinated in April, and Robert Kennedy in June. Meanwhile the 'Prague Spring' offered the prospect of 'Socialism with a Human Face'. The best-remembered scenes were those in Paris, where 'the May events' seemed to have brought De Gaulle's government to its knees. Disputes between students and the university authorities had led to occupations of buildings, followed by arrests, demonstrations, and fighting between students and police. This in turn touched off a wave of strikes across France, and demands both for large pay rises and for industrial democracy—the former, though not the latter, being conceded by government and employers. The international wave of student protests did not start in Paris—it had begun with the Free Speech Movement in Berkeley in 1964. But the events in Paris gave radical students all over the world a model which they hoped to reproduce in their own countries. Throughout the year, and continuing in 1969, universities were centres of conflict, in which demands for student power within the university, for better facilities, and changes in methods and content of teaching were mixed with protests on wider issues, most notably Vietnam. In the United States this meant the public burning of draft cards as well as demonstrations and symbolic actions of many kinds; large anti-war demonstrations took place in many other countries. On the other hand, conservative forces soon proved their strength. Already in June 1968, De Gaulle had called an election in France, and won. In August, a Soviet-led invasion of Czechoslovakia ended the 'Prague Spring'. And in November the presidential election in the United States brought victory to the Republican Richard Nixon. In the short run '1968' was a failure. But like the revolutions of 1848, which also ended in defeat, the revolutions of 1968 were not forgotten. The 'Sixty-Eighters', nourished by the

---

[1] Mark Kurlansky, *1968: The Year that Rocked the World* (New York, 2004), xvii.

hopes and ideals of the later 1960s, remained a potent influence throughout
the remaining years of the twentieth century.

German radicals spoke of 'The Anti-Authoritarian Movement'. In the
United States it was simply 'The Movement'. It took distinctive forms in each
country, but there were many ideas and concerns that were common to Sixty-
Eighters in different countries, including above all opposition to the Vietnam
War, which was a universal rallying cry. Ronald Fraser in his study of student
radicals in six countries provides a useful summary of ideas that they shared:

> The attempt to expand the meaning of democracy by increasing people's control over
> their own lives; the notion of people's 'empowerment' by their direct action, which
> in turn radicalises the individual; the concept of organization without leaders or
> led, in which active participation rather than formal membership was the overriding
> criterion; the search for a new political space and the theories to give it content; disil-
> lusionment with liberal or left parties; and a turn away from Parliamentary politics.[2]

The most distinctive theme of the politics of 1968 was the link between the
construction of a truly democratic society and the maximization of personal
freedom. This was explained by a British student activist, Colin Jackson (born
1945), who had led a campaign, in the face of opposition from the university
authorities, to get a contraceptive machine in the gents' toilets. He saw this as
integrally connected with his more obviously political activities, in the same
way that the ostensibly apolitical counter-culture indirectly undermined the
existing society. Commenting on the role of the underground press, he said:

> I felt there was quite a political content to it all and I thought there was a sort of
> rebellion which took all sorts of shapes and forms and one could take one kind of
> rebellion and once people had started to criticise one part of society they could then
> go on and develop a critique of the whole of society...I felt that if you could raise
> people—or their consciousness could be raised—on for example the issue of contra-
> ceptive machines in the gents' loo, you could take them on from that to understand
> why they should support the Vietcong in Vietnam, or indeed why the top hundred
> companies should be nationalised.[3]

THE SPIRIT OF THE TIMES

1968 was also about language, style, ways of living, and above all a distinct
mood and atmosphere. It was a time when everything seemed possible. Every

[2] Ronald Fraser, *1968* (London, 1988), 4.
[3] 1968: a Student Generation in Revolt (henceforth SGR), Transcripts of interviews, National
Sound Archive, British Library, London, C896/39, 21–5, 32.

convention and tradition had been thrown into the melting-pot. A new age was dawning. Participation in a sit-in or a march could produce periods of intense excitement and optimism. Julie Cox (born 1947) remembered the sit-in at the Hornsey Art College (the longest at any British institution) as the happiest time of her life: 'Yes, it was absolutely exhilarating, very liberating, and I felt that it was almost a transcendental experience ... You really felt that you loved people, they were no longer just fellow students. You really did care about people, you really felt you were comrades-in-arms so to speak.'[4]

The feeling of being part of a great movement also fed the belief that real and fundamental change was possible—even inevitable. Renetia Martin, who was president of the American YWCA in 1968–9, writes that:

I would give nearly anything to go back and watch that time all over again, to see those in-your-face powerful women responding to the distinct call of the times. I thought we could just stop the war; I thought we could bring about peace; I thought we could come to mutual understanding; and I thought we women could bring this about in a way no one else could. The sky was the limit.[5]

Moreover, it was a battle between good and evil. Richard Kuper, who had been a student at the London School of Economics in 1967 at the time of the first British university sit-in, commented:

The fact that you were morally superior mattered, people were making a life choice at some level or another. The breaking up of the old world and the searching for a new had some apocalyptic element to it. And people made the choice because they were convinced emotionally as well as on the issues themselves.[6]

Some of the extraordinary atmosphere of the time can be felt by going to the University of California at Berkeley, a world-leader in the field of student protest in the years 1964–70.[7] The main catalyst was the Civil Rights Movement. Some Berkeley students had gone south during their summer vacations, and in 1963–4 the Bay Area saw many demonstrations and pickets directed against racial discrimination by local employers. As a result, a number of future student leaders had their first experience of arrest. When in 1964 the university administration placed restrictions on political and religious activity on campus, the Free Speech Movement was launched, setting a pattern that would be repeated many times in the next six years. Students held mass

---

[4] Ibid. C896/20. 4.

[5] Sara M. Evans, *Journeys that Opened up the World* (New Brunswick, NJ, 2003), 245.

[6] Fraser, *1968*, 113.

[7] This account is mainly based on W. J. Rorabaugh, *Berkeley at War: The 1960s* (New York, 1989); Peter Van Houten and Edward Barrett, *Berkeley and its Students: Days of Conflict, Years of Change, 1945–1970* (Berkeley, Calif., 2003); Jo Freeman, *At Berkeley in the Sixties: The Education of an Activist, 1961–1965* (Bloomington, Ind., 2004).

rallies, occupied buildings, sat down in the street, or boycotted classes. In later years some students turned to burning down buildings. The university authorities responded with arrests and expulsions. Several interlocking issues motivated the protests, including a general objection to the rules which limited student freedom in areas ranging from politics to sex and drug-taking; a specific objection to the persecution of alleged Communists; and demands for better university facilities. However, increasingly one issue overshadowed all others, namely the war in Vietnam. By 1968 many students regarded the war as the clearest indication of the total corruption of American society, and saw active involvement in the anti-war movement as an absolute moral obligation.

Reports and articles in the student paper, the *Daily Californian*, indicate some of the methods and style of their protests. In January there was a march to the Berkeley Draft Board where several young men burnt their draft cards, one wearing the long black robe of Death. Meanwhile campus police raided the room of art student Jane Kochman, confiscating a 'mannequin-like Christ figure' with the facial features of President Johnson, the swollen breasts and belly of a pregnant woman, and a US flag as a loincloth. In February a former student took advantage of the pleasant Californian weather to stage a nude protest with a placard reading 'I am not obscene—The War is'. He was arrested. An article in the paper described Johnson as 'an agent of Satan', and also denounced Cardinal Spellman, the best known pro-war ecclesiastic. Rhetoric that at most other times would have seemed ridiculous became more or less standard discourse. Another article, headed 'The Student as Nigger', accused school and university teachers of fostering a slave mentality, predicted that they would burn in hell, and condemned parents and teachers for interfering with children's 'free unashamed sexuality'. Racial divisions increasingly divided student from student, as well as students from the faculty and administration. After the English department rejected calls for a Black Literature course, one student wrote 'As Black students ... we have learned it most prudent not to address ourselves to every perverted, inane ejaculation that dribbles from the university's several malignant orifices.'[8]

As these examples suggest, the radicalism of these years mixed the prophetic and the playful. The powers that be were alternately denounced in tones of trenchant moralism, and exposed to ridicule or teasing. The moralism often had its roots in Christianity. Mario Savio, the charismatic leader of the Free Speech Movement, came from a strongly Catholic background, and was intended by his parents for the priesthood. This was perhaps reflected in his

[8] *Daily Californian* (8, 17, and 23 Jan., 7, 8 and 17 Feb. 1968).

claim that 'The reason why liberals don't understand us is because they don't realise that there is evil in the world.'[9] The Berkeley Free Church, founded in 1967, combined strong opposition to the war with providing accommodation for homeless youth. The YMCA was one of the main meeting places for radical groups, and the campus ministry seems to have mainly supported the Free Speech Movement.[10] However, it is clear that considerable numbers of students turned away from their ancestral faith during their time at Berkeley, and that those who had either rejected all religion or had adopted a new religion were considerably over-represented among the radical activists.[11] For some, radical politics, sometimes underpinned by Marxism, became a new faith. A survey in 1964 at the time of the first wave of protests found that about half of the most militant section of students claimed no religion. The author, who argued that 'the mainsprings of the rebellion are an optimistic idealism about the kind of society which can be shaped by the new generation and an unwillingness to allow the paternalism endemic to college campuses to extend to the activities necessary for the furtherance of these ideals',[12] raised the possibility that political activism was an alternative to religion. There were also those whose activism stemmed from their religion, but who became disillusioned by the lack of support from fellow-believers. Although clergy were among the most 'dovish' sections of the population and many of them were active in anti-war protests, others were held back by the knowledge that most of their congregation supported the war. Only in the United Church of Christ and in some smaller denominations, such as the Quakers and Mennonites, was there a clear anti-war majority.[13] Both Christian activists and their more secular colleagues tended to be bitter about the fact that there were many clergy who either remained neutral or even supported the war. Cardinal Spellman of New York and Billy Graham were the most prominent of those in the latter category. There was also in these years an immense flowering of new religious movements in the Bay Area, as described in the last chapter. The radicalism of the later 1960s could lead in many different directions religiously. But for a

[9] Rorabaugh, *Berkeley*, 46; Lynne Hollander Savio, 'Remembering Mario', in Robert Cohen and Reginald E. Zelnik (eds.), *The Free Speech Movement: Reflections on Berkeley in the 1960s* (Berkeley, Calif., 2002), 552–4.

[10] Rorabaugh, *Berkeley*, 14, 152; Keith Chamberlain, 'The Berkeley Free Speech Movement and the Campus Ministry', in Cohen and Zelnik (eds.), *Free Speech*, 357–9.

[11] Robert Wuthnow, *Experimentation in American Religion* (Berkeley, Calif., 1978), 155; Rorabaugh, *Berkeley*, 182.

[12] Robert Somers, 'The Mainsprings of Rebellion: A Survey of Berkeley Students in November 1964', 8, Berkeley University Archives.

[13] Mitchell K. Hall, *Because of their Faith: CALCAV and Religious Opposition to the Vietnam War* (New York, 1990), 65–6. For the Catholic case, see James Hennesey, *American Catholics: A History of the Catholic Community in the United States* (New York, 1981), 318–21.

major proportion of those actively involved in the movements of these years it
led away from the Christian churches.

RELIGION IN REVOLUTION

The role of religion in '68' was many-sided and in some respects contradictory.
Some of the most important student leaders of these years were strongly
influenced by Christianity, and in some countries explicitly Christian student
organizations played a major part. On the other hand, many student activists
had little interest in religion, and some saw the rejection of religion as an
integral part of their programme of liberation. Many of the most important
intellectual influences on the student movements were explicitly secular and,
in particular, the various forms of Marxism provided many activists with
a total world-view. Christian student organizations were divided by bitter
political differences, and many Christian radicals found their loyalty to their
churches stretched to breaking-point. Some of these rejected Christianity,
while others developed new forms of Christian community, or maintained
a more private faith. At the same time, 'eastern' religion and 'alternative'
spiritualities provided some militants with a middle path between materialism
and traditional religion.

The role of Christian inspiration and organizations was often most conspicuous in the initial stages. The example of the United States has already been
mentioned. The founders in 1960 of the key civil rights organization, SNCC,
were Christians. But Christian influences gradually weakened as a result of
disillusion with non-violence and with Martin Luther King's emphasis on
working towards reconciliation between black and white.

It was partly a matter of generational differences, with corresponding differences over tactics. The older generation of civil rights leaders were very often
Baptist or Methodist ministers. In the eyes of many students, they were too
cautious, too respectable, and too conscious of the dangers of confrontation
with the forces of law and order. There was also resentment that the high-
profile leaders got the media attention and the credit for movement successes,
while the grass-roots militants were taking the risky initiatives, and were
being rewarded with prison and beatings by police. Some members of SNCC
cultivated an irreverent style. Martin Luther King became 'De Lawd'. Implied
in this was not only the claim that King was a prima donna, who spent too
much time lecturing and preaching to well-dressed white people and not
enough time in prison with the real militants, but also that he belonged to
an old tradition rooted in the days of slavery, and no longer so relevant to the

modern world.[14] Sometimes the alternative answers were sought in Marxism. More often the alternative to Christianity was sought in black nationalism, whether in a Muslim version, or in one that was more secular. By 1966, though Christianity still had a major role in the Civil Rights Movement, it was in competition with a range of other ideological influences. The biblical rhetoric of Martin Luther King still enjoyed immense resonance; but there was now an alternative language of protest, more direct, more idiomatic, angry, and often well-laced with obscenities. King's vision of reconciliation between races seemed less attractive to many than a search for African roots and a bitter denunciation of the corruptions of American society.[15] Non-violence, the 'Soledad brother', George Jackson, would write, amounted to surrender in a country such as the United States, where no one listened to a man without a gun.[16] The emergence of Black Theology in the later 1960s offered a bridge between the church and Black Power.[17] But as in most other periods of revolutionary upheaval, many militants were frustrated by the caution of church leaders, and the priority they often gave to maintaining the unity of congregations, which necessarily included conservatives and those with little political interest. The militants believed that the overwhelming urgency of the political fight required that all other concerns should be moved to the backburner.

A combination of factors placed strain on the religious loyalties of those whose radicalism had Christian roots, especially from 1968 onwards. One was the magnetic attraction of Marxism, and the belief that the scientific understanding of the world offered by Marxism superseded all other kinds of understanding. For many of this generation Marxism provided the essential tools for both understanding and changing the world. Its withering critique of capitalism also appealed to their moralism. And by legitimating political violence and fostering a language of attack and struggle, it was readily compatible with older styles of masculinity. As has often been pointed out, not least by those radicals who later joined the women's movement, there was a strong strain of machismo in the student movement.[18] For some, Marxism simply replaced Christianity, and for others it showed how Christian ideals could become a reality. Those who remained Christian believers often became disillusioned with the church, which seemed too slow to change, and which,

---

[14] Peter J. Ling, *Martin Luther King Jr* (London, 2002), 80.

[15] Gayraud S. Wilmore, *Black Religion and Black Radicalism* (New York, 1972), chs. 7–8.

[16] George Jackson, *Soledad Brother* (London, 1971), 154.

[17] Wilmore, *Black Religion*, ch. 8.

[18] Sara Evans, *Personal Politics: The Roots of Women's Liberation in the Civil Rights Movement and the New Left* (New York, 1979), 108–16; Sylvie Chaperon, *Les années Beauvoir, 1945–1970* (Paris, 2000), 378.

with its varied social and political constituency, was difficult to mobilize for revolution.

A striking illustration of this was the French Catholic student movement, the Mission étudiante, which in 1970 defined itself as an 'association of believers and of communities of believers, situating itself within the revolutionary current'. The movement had been very strongly marked by the events of May 1968 and was increasingly influenced by Marxism. Starting in 1967, but more especially in 1968 and 1969, radical Catholic students formed 'base communities', the members of which met each week to eat together, pray together, and discuss contemporary political issues. According to Hervieu-Léger, these communities were very tolerant in matters of theology, but often quite intolerant in matters of politics: 'orthodoxy' was defined in terms of a shared political stance, so that in practice they could be as dogmatic as the most conservative branches of the church—only the grounds on which orthodoxy was defined had changed. The Mission also became more and more critical of the church, and by 1970 it was not only completely free from any control by the church authorities, but also lacked any internal hierarchy. This was partly because they objected to the church's hierarchical structure and the repression of dissident theologians. But more especially they objected to the fact that the church tried to stay outside the class struggle rather than committing itself to the cause of the proletariat. The students demanded an 'evangelical purity', of which the ideal expression was the sharing of goods by the first Christians as described in the Acts of the Apostles.[19]

The potential tensions between the Christian churches and the student movement were most apparent in West Germany. The outstanding German student leader, Rudi Dutschke, was in the early years of the movement a believing Protestant, and among the strongest influences on his thinking were Dietrich Bonhoeffer, Paul Tillich, and Camilo Torres.[20] In Germany, as elsewhere, student Christian organizations were under strong radical influence. However, the German situation was in one respect unique, and in some other ways distinctive.[21] The unique factor was the major role of Nazism, and especially of the Holocaust, in the political debates of the 1960s. Germany was unusual in the extent to which radical approaches to sex and criticism of the nuclear family were widely seen as integral to political radicalism; and linked with that was the fact that the influence of Marxism was not only especially widespread, but often filtered through the teachings of the Austrian

[19] Danièle Hervieu-Léger, *De la mission à la protestation: L'Évolution des étudiants chrétiens* (Paris, 1973), 106–21.

[20] Gerd-Rainer Horn, 'Christian Students on the Left', paper delivered at the conference on Christian Youth Movements, Birmingham, 19 Feb. 2006.

[21] This paragraph is based on Dagmar Herzog, *Sex after Fascism* (Princeton, 2005).

psychoanalyst, Communist, and prophet of sexual liberation, Wilhelm Reich. From about 1962 there was growing discussion in Germany of the roots of Nazism and the degree to which Nazi crimes were made possible by the support of wide sections of German society. Some critics, with support especially from the liberal magazine *Der Spiegel*, focused on the culpability of the churches, and as mentioned in Chapter 3 these accusations gained widespread publicity in 1963 through Rolf Hochhuth's play *Der Stellvertreter*. In the same year, *Sexualität und Verbrechen* (Sexuality and Crime) was the first major work to claim that Nazi crimes were a product of sexual repression, and would not have been possible in a sexually liberated society. By the later 1960s a new orthodoxy enjoyed great authority among student activists and other supporters of the New Left, according to which sexual liberation and abolition of the nuclear family were necessary preconditions for the building of a socialist society. The sexual conservatism of the churches, it was alleged, had helped prepare the ground for Nazism in the past, and stood as a major barrier to any progress in the future. In 1967 the first *Kinderläden* (centres for the anti-authoritarian upbringing of children) were set up in Frankfurt and from 1969 they spread rapidly, especially in the radical stronghold of West Berlin. Anti-authoritarianism was seen as including a collective upbringing, free from the narrow confines of the nuclear family, together with an open and tolerant attitude to children's sexuality and an absence of strict toilet training. (It was claimed that concentration camp guards had frequently been victims of over-rigorous toilet training in infancy.) A book published in 1969 even claimed that the 'anti-sexual' views of the churches were a form of Fascism. Criticism of the churches was also mixed with the drive to break down the barrier between public and private. Many of Germany's New Left were in reaction against what seemed a claustrophobic upbringing, in which there was an exaggerated emphasis on privacy. The churches had been among the dominant institutions of West German society in the later 1940s and 1950s, so they were now principal targets for all those who wanted radical change. Some of the critics were themselves Christians: in Germany as in most parts of the Western world, '68' had a powerful effect within the churches[22]—and in the years of the *Berufsverbot* in the 1970s and 1980s (when members of far left parties were excluded from public employment) the churches were more open than the state to giving radicals jobs. But more often the critics were liberal or Marxist opponents of Christianity. The liberals had an influential forum in *Der Spiegel*. For the Marxists attacks on religion had a lower priority, but it was taken for granted that the churches were an integral part of the capitalist system.

[22] Angela Hager, 'Westdeutscher Protestantismus und Studentenbewegung', in Hermle *et al.* (eds.), *Umbrüche*, 111–30.

For some Sixty-Eighters the dual requirement for social and personal liberation demanded a direct attack on religion. One of those was Dany Cohn-Bendit, the best-known leader of the Paris students in May 1968. In *C'est pour toi que tu fais la révolution* (It's for yourself that you are making the revolution), he attacked 'hierarchy', 'bureaucracy', and 'all control of information and knowledge', demanding that we 'rid ourselves in practice of the Judaeo-Christian ethic, with its call for renunciation and sacrifice. There is only one reason for being a revolutionary—because it is the best way to live.'[23]

But there were others for whom religion was more or less irrelevant; and for most of the activists of these years, whatever their starting-point, political activity tended to become so all-absorbing as to leave little time and energy for anything else. For instance, Colin Jackson was nominally following a master's course in the late 1960s, 'but in fact what I was doing was organising left-wing movements...and by that time I was a real revolutionary 24 hours a day'. An activist from Essex University, one of the main centres of protest in Britain, recalled that even playing football was suspiciously frivolous in the eyes of the more earnest revolutionaries.[24]

There were also those whose radicalism had Christian roots but who became gradually disengaged from involvement in the church. This seems to have been the case, for instance, with Jim Harrison (born 1949), a libertarian, critical of all kinds of elitism, whether Christian or Marxist. He tried to organize a boycott of exams by his fellow sociology students, on the grounds that exams dominated university life, killing real enthusiasm for the subjects of study, that they were 'competitive not co-operative', and that their main function was to divide people between the 'successful', who go on to well-paid jobs, and the 'failures', who will do the manual work. 'We were talking about co-operative learning, about cheating campaigns, about doing things on the basis of interest rather than by demand of the exams. We were talking about departments that were run more democratically.' When he could not get sufficient support for the boycott, he himself walked out of his final exams, and then staged a public burning of his admission ticket and economics textbooks. He came from a strongly Catholic and Irish radical background, and was influenced by the educational ideas of Ivan Illich, as well as by such other heroes of the Catholic left as the guerrilla-martyr Camilo Torres and the Brazilian archbishop Helder Camara, and by 'liberal/progressive' teachers at his Jesuit school.[25]

[23] Alf Louvre, 'The New Radicalism: The Politics of Culture 1956–73', in Moore Gilbert and Seed (eds.), *Challenge of the Arts*, 62–3.

[24] Fraser, *1968*, 244–56; SGR, C896/39, part I, 26.

[25] SGR, C896/15, 1–3, 9–10, 18–19, 27–30, 40, 43.

Without any conscious rejection of their Christian origins, there were many radicals for whom involvement in 'The Movement' became a complete way of life, in relation to which older beliefs and concerns simply slipped into the background, until they were almost forgotten. There is a poignant passage in Gretchen Dutschke's edition of her husband's diaries. She notes that when they met in 1964 both were believing Protestants and their shared beliefs were part of their mutual attraction. Many years later she and Rudi compared notes on where they now stood religiously. They agreed now that they no longer believed in God and were no longer Christians, but that 'something remained'—yet the remarkable thing is that they had apparently not spoken for years about what might seem to be a very significant change.[26]

REVOLUTION IN THE CHURCH

Alongside the political radicalization of these years there was an equally dramatic religious radicalization, in both the Catholic and the Protestant churches. The Second Vatican Council raised intense expectations among Catholics, including many younger priests and nuns. Ecclesiastical radicals tended also to be political radicals, enthused by the prospects for social revolution both at home and abroad, and increasingly inspired by the emerging Liberation Theology in Latin America.[27] More generally they were out to challenge 'structures' and especially 'authority structures', 'hierarchies', 'elites', and anything 'top–down', or with any hint of the 'closed', the 'exclusivist', or the 'triumphalist'. And they believed that a new Catholic Church could be established, truly based on the gospel, and free from all such traits.

As Paris erupted in May 1968, several groups of radical Christians emerged, representing 'the church in revolution' and also calling for 'a revolution in the church'. This was the culmination of a development over several years, going back to the Algerian War, and beyond that to the worker priest movement. The radicals included members of Christian student and youth organizations and of the CFDT (the non-Communist trade union which, though non-confessional, included many Catholics). There was also a large body of left-wing priests, especially Jesuits, Dominicans, and Franciscans. In late 1968 the

---

[26] Rudi Dutschke, *Jeder hat sein Leben ganz zu leben: Die Tagebücher 1963–1979* (Cologne, 2003), 381–3.

[27] For a highly sympathetic account of the radical Catholics of these years, see John A. Coleman, *The Evolution of Dutch Catholicism* (Berkeley, Calif., 1978); more critical are Gérard Cholvy and Yves-Marie Hilaire, *Histoire religieuse de la France contemporaine, 1930–1988* (Toulouse, 1988), chs. 6 and 7; and for a more neutral account, Benjamin Ziemann, 'Zwischen sozialer Bewegung und Dienstleitung an Individuum', *Archiv für Sozialgeschichte*, 44 (2004), 357–93.

latter formed a group called Échanges et Dialogue (Exchanges and Dialogue) which flourished for a few years as part of an international grouping of radical Catholic priests.[28] They mixed left-wing politics and a strong interest in the Third World with programmes of church reform. There was a divide between those who remained committed to the church and those who saw 'the institution' as more or less irrelevant to real Christianity, but both wings of the movement had certain things in common. They worked towards a maximum of democracy in both church and society, and they included many priests from working-class parishes or engaged with working-class youth. They were seeking a 'declergification' of the church, in which priests could have a job and could marry, in which lay people could take on many of the roles previously reserved for priests, in which the powers of the bishops would be curtailed. They were involved in all kinds of liturgical experiments. They saw no point in the barriers between Christians of different denominations: in May and June 1968 Protestants and Catholics were celebrating the new revolutionary era by holding joint communion services in spite of the disapproval of church authorities.[29] They were strongly attracted to ideas of 'community', and in the years after Vatican II many 'base communities' were formed in Europe, though they were never as influential as their counterparts in the very different context of Brazil and other Latin American countries. In Italy there were already about a thousand such communities by 1967, and there were about a thousand in France in the early 1970s.[30] These sometimes involved communal living, though more often they were small groups who came together at regular intervals, meeting in one another's homes, to perform experimental liturgies, share experiences, and apply their Christian beliefs to contemporary social and political problems. 'Critical parishes' were sometimes formed, often led by a dissident priest who had been suspended by his bishop for marrying or otherwise defying ecclesiastical authority.

Nowhere was Vatican II followed more eagerly than in the Netherlands. Cardinal Alfrink, the archbishop of Utrecht, and Bishop Bekkers of Den Bosch, enjoyed the status of national heroes, feted by Protestants and Socialists, as much as by fellow Catholics in the years after Vatican II. The key event in this period was the Dutch Pastoral Council, which opened in November 1966 and closed in April 1970. As well as the bishops, the council included elected representatives of secular clergy, men's and women's orders, and laypeople, with the latter comprising about half the total membership. The aim was to combine the continuing leadership role of the bishops with collective decision-making. The bishops had the challenging task of holding the balance between

[28] Denis Pelletier, *La crise catholique* (Paris, 2002), 144–67.   [29] Ibid. 34–9.
[30] Gerd-Rainer Horn, 'Christian Students on the Left', conference paper, Birmingham, 2006.

the radicals in their own church, who wanted to speed up the processes of change, and conservatives in the Vatican, who thought change had already gone too far. The Pastoral Council voted overwhelmingly to end compulsory celibacy of the clergy. Since Pope Paul VI, in an encyclical of 1967, had reaffirmed the traditional teaching, he objected to any further discussion of the subject. The bishops were in a delicate position, especially since some Dutch priests had chosen to go ahead and get married anyway. They decided to allow continuing debate, and indeed they called for a general reopening of the debate in the international church. But they rejected the idea that the Dutch church could go it alone, and they consequently condemned those clergy who continued to celebrate mass after marrying. Nevertheless, they allowed married priests to work as teachers or social workers in Catholic institutions— something which bishops in many other countries prohibited. Meanwhile, in a break from the long Dutch history of conflict or, very often, simply separation between confessions, big steps were being taken towards closer relations with Protestants. From 1967 many local councils of churches were set up and a national council followed in 1968, leading to a revision of the rules concerning mixed marriages. A poll of 1970 suggested that attitudes to such marriages had changed radically since 1959. There were also experiments in the sharing of churches and, especially in Amsterdam, new liturgies designed to meet the needs of specific sections of the population.[31]

Support for change was far from unanimous. Indeed a poll of 1967 pointed to a church split down the middle, as 52 per cent of Dutch Catholics were classified as 'liberal' and 47 per cent as 'traditional'. Of course this was a drastic oversimplification, as many people did not fall so clearly into one camp or the other. The important point was that 'progressives' made their voice heard much more readily, since their greatest strength was among the clergy (especially those in elite orders, such as the Jesuits and Dominicans), the professional and managerial classes, and in urban areas. However, the traditionalists were by no means silent. Between 1964 and 1972 a series of militant groups emerged on both wings of the church. These varied from the ultra-conservative Legion of Saint Michael to the Marxist-tending Septuagint, which in 1970 sponsored an international conference of revolutionary Christians in Amsterdam, and which also sponsored 'critical parishes' free of episcopal control. The bishops condemned initiatives of this kind, while resisting demands for the excommunication of those responsible.[32] One of the best known of such 'critical parishes' was the Jesuit student chaplaincy in Amsterdam, which established a reputation between 1965 and 1968 as 'the place where things could be said and done which could not be said or done

---

[31] Coleman, *Dutch Catholicism*, 152–223, 247–61.   [32] Ibid. 224–9, 230–47.

anywhere else'. Relations with church authority had often been tense, and a crisis was reached in 1968 when one of the priests married but continued to celebrate mass. After another priest followed his example in 1970, the student parish was refused use of the Jesuit chapel and moved its services to a Protestant church. They continued to attract large congregations, not only of students, both because of the experimental liturgy and because of the sermons which stressed such themes as 'authenticity, freedom, the social engagement of the faithful, ecumenism'. According to Nuij the situation was one of 'a more or less tolerated disobedience': 'juridically there is a rupture with ecclesiastical authority, but no-one wants a schism'.[33]

Because the Dutch 'progressives' were unusually numerous and influential, and enjoyed more support from the hierarchy than their counterparts in most other countries, the Netherlands was the most visible site of the bitter conflicts within the Catholic Church at this time. The radicals faced powerful opposition from conservatives or moderates, many of them well entrenched in positions of authority. But in Germany too the years 1966–72 were seen as a time of 'civil war', with both sides using sharp language, and both claiming to be the authentic voice of the Council.[34] One major area of conflict was the liturgy. Progressives saw reforms of the liturgy as a way of bringing back non-church-goers, while traditionalists claimed that unpopular innovations were driving people away. For instance, Bishop Graber of Regensburg complained of a loss of mystery—reformed liturgies were too 'horizontal'. In the later 1960s Catholic protest groups multiplied, demanding greater lay responsibility and often focusing on 'Third World' issues. The Katholikentag, an annual mass gathering of Catholics provided a focus for militant groups of all kinds. In the 1950s these had been demonstrations of Catholic solidarity, with the bishops well in control. But the Essen gathering in September 1968 saw unprecedented levels of controversy. Lay Catholics were furious about *Humanae Vitae*, but the clergy also had other reasons for anxiety. Vatican II had removed the protected status of many clergy, making them vulnerable to removal on the decision of their bishop. During 1968 many priest 'Solidarity' groups were formed: their main purpose was defence of their rights *vis-à-vis* the bishop or vicar-general, but they also got involved in other issues, including inter-communion, celibacy, peace, and ecology.

The hopes of these years were captured, with a typical mixture of satire and sympathy, in David Lodge's novel of English Catholicism from the 1950s to the 1970s, *How Far Can You Go?* Several of the leading characters in the novel,

---

[33] Ton Nuij, 'La subculture religieuse de la ville d'Amsterdam', 386–7, in *The Contemporary Metamorphosis of Religion?* Acts of the International Conference on the Sociology of Religion, The Hague, 1973.

[34] Ziemann, 'Zwischen sozialer Bewegung', 357–60.

including Michael and Miriam, a married couple in their mid-thirties, belong to 'Catholics for an Open Church' (COC), a pressure-group formed in early 1969 to organize opposition to *Humanae Vitae*, and to support priests who had been suspended because of their refusal to enforce the papal teaching through the confessional. Their first annual general meeting was followed by a mass, conducted by a suspended priest.

At the mass, real wholemeal bread was consecrated and broken, and handed round in baskets, and the congregation also shared the chalice. At the words, 'Let us give each other the sign of peace', several couples embraced instead of giving each other the customary handshake. Michael and Miriam spontaneously followed suit and because of the novelty of the circumstances, Michael experienced a perceptible erection as their lips touched. He was not abashed, as at a similar experience at the St Valentine's Day mass long ago; after all, that was what they were gathered together here for, to assert the compatibility of *eros* and *agape*, to answer positively the questions, what was love, what was conjugal love, why did God make it so nice? Both agreed that the mass was the most meaningful liturgical event they had ever participated in.[35]

Protestant churches also experienced fierce battles between radicals, moderates, and conservatives in these years, with the reform tide reaching high water mark in the later 1960s, only to recede in the more conservative atmosphere of the early 1970s. Protestant churches differ so much among themselves in their theology, their structures, and in relations with state and society that any generalizations have limited application. In particular, conservative evangelical and fundamentalist churches differed radically from those affiliated to the World Council of Churches and other ecumenical institutions—though the latter also differ widely among themselves. I will return later to look at the more conservative churches, but here I will focus on what is known in the United States as 'the mainline'. The dominant mood in these churches during the later 1960s was one of reform and experiment. The central event of this period was the Assembly of the World Council of Churches at Uppsala in August 1968, with the slogan 'The world sets the agenda'.[36] Martin Luther King was to have given the keynote address but he was assassinated on 4 April. King, fighting injustice 'with Christian weapons', preaching justice and reconciliation in a language rooted in the Bible and the 'Negro Spirituals', and ultimately sacrificing his life for the cause, gave the Protestants of this time their clearest model of Christianity in practice. Dietrich Bonhoeffer was the strongest intellectual influence, reflected in constant references to 'religionless Christianity' and Jesus as 'the man for others'. A third major influence was

[35] David Lodge, *How Far Can You Go?* (London, 1980), 124.
[36] Michael Walsh, 'The Religious Ferment of the Sixties', in McLeod (ed.), *Cambridge History of Christianity*, ix. 314–17.

a growing awareness of the 'Third World' and of 'anti-imperialist' struggles. This all meant action 'in the world', political engagement, and a stress on service rather than defence of the institution, pious practices, or undue attention to theological abstractions. The Assembly mixed sections on 'Worship' and on 'Renewal in Mission' with others on 'Towards Justice and Peace in International Affairs', and a strong ecumenical emphasis. Racism was a major theme of the conference. The most famous and controversial initiative stemming from Uppsala was the Programme to Combat Racism established the following year, which included grants to guerrilla groups operating in southern Africa, as well as projects to raise awareness of racism in European countries experiencing recent immigration.[37]

The World Student Christian Federation (WSCF) went through a gradual radicalization during the 1960s, which accelerated at the end of the decade. Already in 1960, at the world conference of Christian students in Strasbourg, the most popular speakers were those who attacked existing church structures and introduced terminology that would become typical of the 1960s. At the meeting of the General Committee in 1964 the main stress was on 'Christian Presence', with Bonhoeffer and the French worker priests as major influences, and considerable stress on the work of God in secular movements. The legitimacy of political violence was already a major disputed issue. This was the last such meeting for many years at which significant attention was given to worship.[38] A series of regional consultations in 1966–7 revealed distinctive local concerns, such as the need to indigenize theology in Africa and Asia, but also considerable international consensus that the church must be concerned with 'liberation' and 'transforming structures'. In many countries the Protestant student movement was strongly influenced by the events of 1968, and the following five years saw an increasingly deep divide between the revolutionaries and the democratic socialists. (No one was prepared to describe themselves as a liberal, let alone a conservative.) The president, Richard Shaull, an American Baptist who had been radicalized as a missionary in Brazil, belonged to the revolutionary wing, while the Finnish general secretary Risto Lehtonen was a moderate. The executive committee was equally divided. The moderates wanted to maintain good relations with the churches, while the radicals had no time for 'institutions' of any kind; the moderates placed more emphasis on order and procedures, while the radicals saw spontaneity as all-important.

Lehtonen wrote that the Federation's Beirut conference in 1970:

[37] Edson Burton, 'Assimilation to Anti-Racism' (Ph. D. thesis, University of the West of England, 2004), 324–38.
[38] Risto Lehtonen. *The Story of a Storm: The Ecumenical Student Movement in the Turmoil of Revolution* (Grand Rapids, Mich., 1998), 27–36.

marked the entry of a new terminology, a kind of liturgical language of the radical Left, into Federation discussions and documents. It was antithetic to rational argument and analytic style, it was inherently disdainful of institutions and arrogantly assumed a clear-cut and simple judgement of who was for good and who was for evil. 'In' words, which separated the sheep from the goats included 'conscientization', 'new lifestyles', 'education of the masses', 'anti-imperialist struggle', 'system of repression' and the like. Those who did not master the use of this in-language were quickly written off by supporters of the emerging radical left-wing of the Federation.[39]

In an attempt to bring the warring factions together, Lehtonen wrote in February 1971 that there were a number of things that both sides could agree upon, for instance: 'that Christians have to join the struggle against economic injustice, neo-colonialism, racism, authoritarian systems, and militarism, which together blocked the way to a more just society and international order'. But the radicals wanted the WSCF to be part of a 'global revolutionary movement', while the moderates stressed continuity with Christian tradition, links with the churches, and the need of student Christians to respond to the specific situation in their own countries. Lehtonen was critical of the American University Christian Movement (UCM) which was torn apart by internal conflict and closed in 1969. According to Lehtonen, UCM 'reflected an anti-institutional and anti-authoritarian sentiment, directed against the structures of churches, traditional ecumenicity, and higher education, and maintained an uncritical faith in spontaneity and a participatory style'.[40] Charlotte Bunch, president of UCM, dismissed Lehtonen as the leader of 'the more conservative group focused on evangelism and maintenance of the organisation'.[41]

According to Lehtonen's not totally disinterested account, the conflicts of the years 1968–73 had a disastrous effect on the WSCF and many of its affiliated organizations. The New Zealand secretary suggested that they were losing some members who thought them not radical enough. On the other hand they were also losing many moderates, who felt that the movement had been hijacked by a revolutionary elite. By 1971 some commentators in the United States were arguing that liberal and radical Christianity had become so fully identified with 'the movement' that it had lost its own identity, and that the field of student Christianity was increasingly being left to the evangelicals.[42]

The rising strength of the evangelicals would soon be clear for all to see. It was part of a conservative revival which was as evident in the churches as it often was in politics. The growth of more conservative churches in this period will be discussed in Chapter 9. But in American Protestantism the early 1970s also saw a more cautious approach in the 'mainline' churches,

[39] Ibid. 119.   [40] Ibid. 50–6.   [41] Evans, *Journeys*, 135.
[42] Lehtonen, *Ecumenical*, 162–207.

which had tended to support their radical activists in the 1960s. In the Roman Catholic Church conservatives benefited from the fact that, within an ultra-hierarchical structure, conservatives were concentrated in positions of ecclesiastical power. In the Protestant churches, where the most prestigious offices were often held by liberals, wealthy laymen used the power of the purse to put pressure on their clergy. Already in 1960 the oil millionaire, J. Howard Pew, decided that his United Presbyterians had moved too far to the left, and he was organizing other members of the lay elite to oppose ecumenism and social radicalism.[43] In the early 1970s the Episcopal Church, which had been a strong supporter of civil rights and had given a lot of money to African American groups in the 1960s, cut back this support, following criticism from Southern congregations.[44] In the 1960s liberals had supported denominational mergers, which they thought would give the churches a more effective social and political voice, while conservatives, who placed more emphasis on the distinctive doctrines and practices of their own tradition, tended to be hostile. These schemes had flourished in the 1960s but faltered in the early 1970s. According to Hoge, 'One can speak of a more general resistance to ecumenism beginning about 1970 or 1971. During these years the theological climate shifted towards more conservative, individualistic emphases, and the strengthened conservative voices had an effect.'[45]

In the Roman Catholic Church the swing back towards conservatism had begun a few years earlier. Pope Paul VI faced the daunting task of holding an increasingly polarized church together. In most countries there were both clergy and lay Catholics who hated the new liturgy, who wanted nothing to do with Protestants, and remained faithful to all the old devotions which were being swept away in the wake of the Council. Some of them were also ultra-conservative in politics, and this latter group would find a leader in Archbishop Lefebvre, who was locked in battle with the Pope throughout the 1970s.[46] However, in the later 1960s and early 1970s it was the church's progressive wing which suffered a series of body-blows, as the Pope tried to regain control. Already in 1967, Paul VI's encyclical reaffirming the rule of clerical celibacy was a major defeat for the reformers. Still worse was *Humanae Vitae*.

Meanwhile, in the Netherlands, the conservatives may have been a minority, but they had friends in very high places. They used the papal nuncio as a conduit for complaints to Rome, and in December 1970 they were rewarded by the appointment of the relatively conservative Mgr Simonis as bishop of Rotterdam. In fact Simonis soon appeared as a moderate, since in 1972 a

---

[43] Dean Hoge, *Division in the Protestant House* (Philadelphia, 1976), 32–3.
[44] Ibid. 36–40.   [45] Ibid. 32–3.   [46] Pelletier, *Crise*, 173–82.

more extreme conservative, Mgr Gijsen, was appointed bishop of Roermond. Within a few months two-thirds of the active full-time personnel employed by his diocese had signed a statement criticizing their bishop's authoritarian style of leadership.[47]

In the longer term one of the many notable events of 1968 was one which few people noticed at the time. In 1968 Tübingen's Faculty of Catholic Theology boasted two of Germany's best-known progressive theologians, Hans Küng and Josef Ratzinger, the former being dean and the latter Professor of Dogmatics. The year was a turning-point in the latter's career. Ratzinger, like many other German professors at the time (including Küng), suffered the disruption of his lectures by 'anti-authoritarian' students and was involved in disputes with more radical junior colleagues and research students. He also was embroiled in a conflict dividing the Catholic student parish. As well as demanding a more explicit involvement in politics, many of the students claimed the right to elect their own chaplain, whereas Ratzinger defended the traditional rule that the appointment was made by the bishop. Accusing the radicals of exercising a 'real tyranny', 'even in brutal forms', he later claimed that 'anyone who wanted to remain a progressive in this context had to give up his integrity'. He concluded that to remain in Tübingen would mean a life of continuous conflict and he moved the following year to a chair in the new university at Regensburg, which would become a stronghold of ecclesiastical conservatism.[48] Increasingly he argued that Vatican II had been too uncritical in its embrace of contemporary culture with its 'liberal-radical ideology of individualistic, rationalistic and hedonistic stamp'.[49] Having in the 1960s been on the board of *Concilium*, the organ of the conciliar progressives, Ratzinger was a founder in 1972 of *Communio*, its more conservative rival. *Communio* was the voice of those who had been actively involved in the Council but who now argued that the Council documents were being misinterpreted to justify changes far more radical than anything intended by the Council Fathers. He became archbishop of Munich in 1977, and in 1981 moved to Rome as prefect of the Congregation of the Doctrine of Faith, the Vatican office responsible for maintenance of orthodoxy. In 2005 he was elected Pope Benedict XVI.

CONCLUSION

In the later 1960s hopes for speedy and radical changes in both church and society were at a very high level. Christian radicals often suffered a double

[47] Coleman, *Dutch Catholicism*, 262–76.
[48] John L. Allen, *Pope Benedict XVI* (London, 2005), 113–18.   [49] Ibid. 79.

disappointment. Many radicals left their churches, and those Christian organizations that had been most sympathetic to '1968' were severely disrupted.

However, it would be wrong to exaggerate the extent either of the radical defeat or of the conservative resurgence. Many of those who had been influenced by the ideas and movements of that time remained within, or returned to their churches.

The Christian radicalism of the later 1960s suffered many casualties—as in the wider 'movement'. Some dropped out of organized activity of any kind out of disillusionment or exhaustion. But in the church, as in other areas of society, '1968' also left continuing legacies. Even if the utopian hopes of those years faded, many of the radical ideas of the time established a place within the church, albeit a place that was often contested. Anti-racism, 'Third Worldism', ecology, and peace became established parts of the agenda for both Catholic and Protestant churches in the 1970s and 1980s. The World Council of Churches was particularly influenced by concerns of these kinds, most fully embodied in its campaign for Justice Peace and the Integrity of Creation, adopted at the Vancouver Assembly in 1983. Christian feminism rapidly won support during the 1970s, first in the United States and then more widely. The Gay Christian Movement followed soon after. In the years following, both the Catholic Church and many Protestant churches were deeply divided on questions both of theology and of politics, with the two often being related.

8

Sex, Gender, and the Family

No aspect of the 1960s was so much discussed at the time as the 'sexual revolution', none marked such a sharp break from the past as the gay liberation movement, and in retrospect few developments have seemed as significant as the emergence at the end of the decade of 'second wave' feminism. But other, equally important, though much less dramatic, changes were taking place in family life. All of these had implications for religion, and in this chapter I will discuss each of them, beginning with the 'sexual revolution'.

THE SEXUAL REVOLUTION

No one would dispute that there was a huge increase during the 1960s in discussion of sex in the media and depiction of sex in the cinema and on TV, that pop singers (following the lead of Elvis Presley from 1956 onwards) adopted more openly erotic styles in their stage performances, or that women's clothing emphasized the sexual attractions of their wearers in much more direct ways. What is less clear is how far and how fast individual behaviour changed during the decade. The minimalist version points to a gradual increase in pre-marital sex over a longer period, mainly between young people who intended subsequently to marry, and sees the growth of pre-marital pregnancy in the 1960s as a continuation of trends already well-established in the 1950s. The maximalist version would see a qualitative change in the later 1960s, made possible by the availability of the contraceptive pill, and marked both by a reduction of the age at which young people first had sex and by the increasing readiness of young women to have several sexual partners before marriage.[1]

---

[1] For the minimalist view, see Martin P. M. Richards and B. Jane Elliott, 'Sex and Marriage in the 1960s and 1970s', in Clark (ed.), *Marriage*, 44–6, who argue that underreporting in previous decades has led to an exaggeration of the increase in pre-marital sex in the 1960s. Maximalists include Hera Cook, *The Long Sexual Revolution* (Oxford, 2004), 295, who stresses the impact of the pill, and Callum G. Brown, *Religion and Society in Twentieth-Century Britain* (London, 2006), 243–4, who puts more stress on cultural changes.

Both versions agree that in the 1960s the great majority of young people were marrying, and that the average age at marriage dropped during the decade.

An oral history project of the early 1990s which questioned the first generation of pill-users about their contraceptive practices in the 1960s and 1970s provided evidence in support of both versions. The maximalist version was presented by Barbara Smith (born 1942), one of eight children, brought up in a strongly Catholic, mainly immigrant environment in upstate New York. 'We lived in an environment where there was absolutely no question that there would be premarital sex or anything'—mainly because of the scandal which surrounded pre-marital pregnancy, and the limited range of contraceptive methods available. However, there was a lot of heavy petting—and in retrospect Barbara had happy memories of that and felt that she had had more fun than the next generation who lost their inhibitions about 'going all the way'. She married as a student, and soon got pregnant, but her child died in infancy. It was her devoutly Catholic mother who then advised her to go on the pill. Within a year or two, however, everything was changing. Her younger sisters were having sex at 16 or 17:

You know, the world just changed so quickly in those years.... by the time my brothers and sisters grew up it was the days of hippies, it was the days of drugs and sex and rock and roll....I don't think [my mother] liked it very much. I mean all my sisters for instance had abortions. And I mean that would have been unheard of in my period.[2]

Charlotte Hoskins (born 1950 Ilford), who came from this slightly younger generation, though from a very different family background—English, middle class, and with very little religious attachment—painted a similar picture. She said that the pill had done a lot to change attitudes to pre-marital sex:

When I was 15 there was a sort of stigma, but I think towards the end of the '60s and the beginning of the '70s I think that went among the young people. It was, it was almost natural to sleep with your boyfriend...it just seemed natural all the time sort of 'flower power' and 'make love not war' and all the rest of it.[3]

She said that earlier every boyfriend had to be considered in the light of his potential as a future father, but now 'if you fancied him you could just concentrate on "Let's get him in the sack!"' However when she got pregnant at 20 she did marry the child's father, as her sister had done before—though her best friend, when in the same situation, had an abortion.

On the other hand, a number of the women interviewed in this project seem to have married the first man with whom they had sex. Esther Newman, born

---

[2] 'Birth Control' (henceforth BC), transcripts of interviews in the National Sound Archive, British Library, London, C644/012, 5, 8.

[3] BC, C644/09, 28–9.

in 1944 in a north London Jewish family, commented, when asked about the influence of the pill: 'if you had been brought up in a fairly strict and straight-laced way, it didn't of itself turn you into a more uninhibited person'.[4]

It would seem that the maximalist and the minimalist versions each tells a part of the story. The proportion of couples having sex before marriage had been gradually increasing over many years, and the increase speeded up in this period. At the same time a significant minority of young people were having several partners before marriage, some were living with a partner before marriage, and a smaller number were rejecting the whole concept of marriage. The longer term significance of events at this time was that the conventional majority were getting gradually habituated to new ways of behaving that would have seemed beyond the pale ten years earlier. An important role in this was played by women's and teenage girls' magazines, which not only gave increasing attention to sex in the course of the 1960s, but also treated it in new ways.[5] Only a few years earlier contraception had been seen as a rather risqué topic, but by the late 1960s magazines were many people's chief source of information on the subject. As Jenny Blyton (born 1951, Newcastle) recalls: 'the magazine that you read at the time very much were saying , go on the pill, the pill, the pill. That was all what it was, young girls were supposed to be doing, taking the pill.'[6] But equally important was the changing approach to sex—and by implication to ethics more generally—in the advice columns. A study of 'Mary Grant's' advice column in *Women's Own* showed considerable continuity between 1955 and 1964, but major changes between 1964 and 1975. The main theme was an increasing stress on the 'needs and feelings' of the individual, and a growing reluctance to lay down any clear rules. In the former period there was a clear understanding that adultery was wrong, but also an overriding stress on the importance of marriage and the need to take emergency measures to repair marriages which were threatened. By 1970 a wife who was wondering whether she should leave her unfaithful husband was told 'There is really no "should" or "should not" about this'.[7]

Unfortunately for the historian, evidence about the relationship between religious belief and sexual practice, including the influence of each upon the other, is hard to come by. Many people are reluctant to talk about such intimate areas of their lives, and the problem may be especially acute where there is a tension between belief and practice. Some indications come from two surveys carried out by Michael Schofield on the sexual behaviour first of young people, then of young adults. The first of these, based on research

---

[4] BC, C644/01, 11.
[5] Cynthia White, *Women's Magazines, 1693–1968* (London, 1970), 224, 228–30.
[6] BC, C644/04, 2.   [7] Richards and Elliott, 'Sex', 35–8, 44.

carried out mainly in London in 1964 showed that, among older teenagers, boys and girls who never went to church were much more likely to have had sexual intercourse than those who were regular church-goers. For girls, frequency of church attendance was the best predictor of their level of sexual experience. Schofield speculated that sexually experienced teenagers had been alienated from the churches by finding what they were doing condemned by church teachings. However, his data do not provide any explanation of the observed correlation between early sexual experience and non-church-going. It is equally possible that those with no church involvement simply had fewer inhibitions. The later study of young adults aged 23–5, based on research in 1972, suggests that church-goers, though less precocious than their non-church-going peers, were able to reconcile their religious practice with sexual practice that their church might consider deviant. Non-church-goers were indeed somewhat more likely than regular church-goers to have had pre-marital sex, but the difference was not huge—75 per cent of the former and 59 per cent of the latter said that they had done this.[8] It is quite possible that the difference lay not so much in the fact of having had pre-marital sex, but in the way in which it was seen. Very possibly the non-church-goers were more accepting of 'one night stands' and attached less importance to fidelity. However, this is pure speculation, as Schofield provides no evidence on these issues.

The oral history survey quoted above provides some hints, which, sadly, the interviewers totally failed to follow up. Nearly all of the women interviewed had had pre-marital sex, many only with their future husband, but some with a number of partners. At least two had felt uneasy about what they were doing. Amanda Lee (born 1946, Gloucester) was 21 and having sex with her fiancé when she went to her doctor and asked for the pill. She told him a 'cock and bull story' because she felt 'Guilty. Yes, very guilty. Yes, it was guilt. That as a single woman I shouldn't really be doing it.'[9] Pamela Strudwick (born 1950, Southport) felt 'it was wrong... somehow I think it was partly because I didn't ever want to let my parents down. We had a very close feeling for another and it was pretty, slightly religious and quite strict'.[10] On the other hand, Susan Price (born 1947, Rochdale) who was in revolt against her 'very Puritanical working-class household', revelled in the new world of freedom which she enjoyed at university: 'And I was very sexually active at university, this was the swinging sixties! And it was very liberating. . . . I moved away from home, and I moved cultures as well. And I discovered pleasure . . .'[11]

---

[8] Michael Schofield, *The Sexual Behaviour of Young People* (London, 1965), 148–9, 216, 254; Robert Wuthnow, *Experimentation in American Religion* (Berkeley, Calif., 1978), 145; Michael Schofield, *The Sexual Behaviour of Young Adults* (London, 1973), 169.

[9] BC, C644/15, 8.   [10] BC, C644/17, 15.   [11] BC, C644/06, 2–3, 5.

A little earlier, Cressida Willoughby (born 1940, London), who came from a family of agnostic academics, quietly and unostentatiously started sleeping with her boyfriend, and later husband, while a student at Oxford (she contrasted this with two fellow students at her women's college who were 'exhibitionist' about their sex-lives), and appears to have experienced no feelings either of guilt or of exciting rebellion. While her social background was totally untypical—not least in the fact that she derived a lot of her early knowledge of sex from reading her mother's copy of the *Kinsey Report*—she was probably typical in that she married the first man with whom she had sex and that she felt no guilt about their relationship.[12]

A further source of information on this subject is provided by a large number of anonymous questionnaires completed by former students at Girton College, Cambridge.[13] While the principal concern of the questions relating to sex was with the forms of contraception used, the questionnaire also asked when the respondent first had sex. (There is some ambiguity in the answers as some respondents took 'sex' to mean 'intercourse', while others took it to include other forms of intimacy.) Granted that it is not always completely clear what is meant by sex, there is a long-term tendency for the proportion of those reporting sex before marriage to rise, and the age at which they first had sex to drop. Those who said religion was 'important' were less likely to say they had had pre-marital sex, though by the 1970s the gap between the more and less 'religious' had narrowed. In a sample of those coming to Girton between 1950 and 1954, 33 per cent said they had pre-marital sex, including 24 per cent of those for whom religion was 'important' and 57 per cent of those for whom it was not. By 1961 and 1962 the average was 57 per cent, including 30 per cent of those for whom religion was 'important' and 82 per cent of those for whom it was not. In 1971 and 1972 it was 63 per cent, including 50 per cent of those for whom religion was important and 75 per cent of those for whom it was not important. Thus, among the Girtonians, the increasing incidence of pre-marital intercourse from the early 1950s to the early 1970s went in two phases: the initial increase was mainly among the less religious students, who were growing in numbers and also becoming more sexually active; the later increase was mainly explained by higher levels of sexual activity among the more religious students.

Among the early 1960s cohort the respondent whose pre-marital experience seems to have been most extensive, and who also mentioned having had two abortions before her marriage, was also the only one to state that she 'was and is an atheist'. There was also one unmarried respondent who explicitly stated

---

[12] BC, C644/14.   [13] 'University and Life Experience', Girton College Archives.

that 'as a practising Christian I have always believed that full commitment has to come within the marriage bond. I have had normally developed relationships which have stopped short of full sexual relations.' Another stated that her evangelical upbringing had had harmful effects on her sex life and that she had 'felt unfulfilled as a woman', though she, as well as many others who were Christians, had had pre-marital relationships, often though not always, with their future husband; and some of those who said they had no religion had waited until they were married. However, those who said religion was not important to them tended to have had their first experience of sex at an earlier age. For instance, among the early 1960s cohort several of the 'non-religious' but only one of the 'religious' had their first sexual experiences as teenagers—one possible factor, perhaps, being that the 'non-religious' were often also more rebellious. This, and also the ambiguity in some of the categories, is suggested by a church-going respondent who said that she had her first sexual encounter at 17, but added: 'in 1961 this did not extend to intercourse if you were "properly" brought up'. It is likely therefore that religious belief had some inhibiting effect on young people entering their first sexual relationship, but I have seen no evidence that entry into such relationships led to the rejection of these beliefs.

What is clear, though, is that while the churches retained a major voice in public debate in the 1960s—and indeed the 1970s and 1980s—their ability to regulate individual behaviour in what was increasingly seen as the private sphere was diminishing fast. It might appear that the 'new morality' advocated by those like John Robinson was gaining ground, and certainly legalism of any kind was in retreat. But Robinson also laid heavy stress on the fact that doing away with rigidly defined rules left a heavy burden of moral responsibility on the individual. In the 1970s not only were strict moral rules out of favour, but the principal stress tended to be on the need for individual self-fulfilment.

CATHOLICS AND CONTRACEPTION

Both the tensions between religious rules and individual practice and the diminishing power of the church to control sexual behaviour can be seen in the case of Catholics and contraception. The international Lambeth Conference of Anglican bishops had rather cautiously accepted the use of contraceptives in 1930, and had much more enthusiastically endorsed their use in 1958. By that time all the larger Protestant churches accepted the use of contraceptives by married couples. Pope Pius XI had responded to the Lambeth ruling of 1930 with an encyclical *Casti Connubii*, which condemned all use of contraceptives.

As a result of opposition to the family planning clinics which were being established in considerable numbers in the 1920s, this teaching was already gaining a degree of prominence in Catholic teaching which it had not had before. At the same time some Catholic doctors were promoting the 'rhythm method' as a 'natural' form of regulating births which was compatible with Catholic teachings. Pius XII gave a rather qualified approval to the rhythm method when addressing a conference of midwives in 1951.[14]

Meanwhile, at least since the 1930s, Catholic teaching was presenting an increasingly positive view of marriage, and emphasizing the importance of the happy sexual relationship within marriage. In the 1950s Catholic Action groups which prepared Catholic couples for their wedding combined an exalted view of marriage, of its sacramental nature, and of the joys of parenthood, with emphasis on the need for both partners to enjoy sexual rapport and satisfaction, and information about the rhythm method.[15] Barbara Smith learnt about the rhythm method when she went to university in Canada in 1960. She found fellow students taking their temperature to see when they would ovulate.[16] David Lodge, in his novels on middle-class Catholic life in the 1950s and 1960s, describes the earnest attempts of Catholic couples to practise what the church taught—and also the increasing frustration and sometimes bitterness as they recognized the method's unreliability, and suffered the burden of having to confine sex to specific days of the month. Most of the Catholic couples in Lodge's *How Far Can You Go?* remained loyal to their faith, although increasingly distanced from ecclesiastical authority. But one by one in the course of the 1960s they switched to the pill.[17] In the United States and Quebec there is evidence that many church-going Catholics were using contraceptives in the 1940s, 1950s, and even more in the 1960s, and that they were avoiding confession, and consequently were unable to receive communion, because they would have to confess their defiance of the church's teaching. A survey in the United States in 1960 found that 38 per cent of married white Catholic women aged 18–39 were using or had used methods of birth control forbidden by the church, including 46 per cent of those in the 35–9 age group.[18]

Only in 1964 did some devout laypeople start openly to contest the official teaching, and about that time some priests were getting known for their

---

[14] Martine Sevegrand, *Les enfants du bon Dieu* (Paris, 1995), 365–71.

[15] L. W. Tentler, *Catholics and Contraception* (Ithaca, NY, 2004), 136–8; Michael Gauvreau, *The Catholic Origins of Quebec's Quiet Revolution* (Montreal and Kingston, Ontario, 2005), 203.

[16] BC, C644/12, 5

[17] David Lodge, *How Far Can You Go?* (London, 1980), 117–18. See also Lodge's earlier novel, *The British Museum's Falling Down* (London, 1965), which includes a comic treatment of a Catholic couple's attempts to practise the rhythm method.

[18] Tentler, *Contraception*, 132–6.

willingness to grant absolution to those who confessed use of contraceptives. As Tentler says, Vatican II led to 'a further emboldening of the laity, whose willingness to speak publicly on marriage and marital sex grew exponentially in the mid-1960s'.[19] Between 1955 and 1960 well-educated Catholics were still those most likely to adhere to official teaching. Between 1960 and 1965 there was a reversal, with the well-educated leading the drive towards nonconformity.[20] Gauvreau suggests that in Quebec in the later 1950s and early 1960s young married couples were the section of the population most likely to be alienated from the Catholic Church. He cites a survey of 1963 which found that 60 per cent of younger Catholic couples were using contraceptives, and that two-thirds of these couples had given up going to mass. He also quotes a liberal Catholic intellectual who in 1965 was worrying that many of the middle-class elite were leaving the church because it stood in the way of the sexual liberation that was the key to personal well-being.[21] There was a similar story in France, where three confidential documents sent to the bishops between 1960 and 1965 reported that many young couples were giving up the sacraments because they were using forbidden methods of birth control, and that some of them were haunted by a fear of being in mortal sin.[22] Here too, according to Sevegrand, 1964 was a turning-point. The issue was also under intense debate among Catholic moral theologians, and a group headed by Louis Janssens of Louvain had already pronounced in favour of the pill. In February an article by a Catholic feminist in the women's magazine *Marie-Claire* predicted that the Vatican Council would change the church's teaching, and in June the Pope's announcement that the issue was under consideration fed expectations.[23]

It was another four years before these hopes were finally dashed by the publication of *Humanae Vitae*. During those four years many Catholics had started using the cap, the pill, or the condom, often with the connivance of their priests. A survey of American Catholics in 1967 found that 73 per cent wanted a change in the official teaching.[24] When they finally learnt that in the Pope's eyes they had been wrong, few were inclined to return to the rhythm method. How this situation affected their relationship with the church and with the Catholic faith is unclear. Gauvreau believes that it was a major factor in the rapid decline of Catholic practice in Quebec in the later 1960s and early 1970s. It led to 'a rapid and massive erosion of Catholicism's traditional constituency: married couples with families'. He also suggests that the encyclical provided powerful ammunition to those who were hostile to the church on more general grounds: it 'gave credence to those who wanted to

---

[19] Tentler, *Contraception*, 203.   [20] Ibid. 220.
[21] Gauvreau, *Quiet Revolution*, 241–2.   [22] Sevegrand, *Enfants*, 213–18.
[23] Ibid. 218–35.   [24] Gauvreau, *Quiet Revolution*, 245.

excise Catholicism out of a desire to foster an extreme individualism that was based on the exclusive right of the private conscience in all matters pertaining to personal values'.[25] O'Brien suggests that for many Australian Catholics *Humanae Vitae* 'was the beginning of the end of their association with the Church'. She quotes the example of an 'ardently Catholic' woman who was refused communion because she had criticized the encyclical in a television interview and a letter to the press: 'Venetia, like so many, felt abandoned and betrayed and left the Church for several years.' Another woman, who had been told by a doctor to have no more children, was dissatisfied both with the priest who warned her against any use of contraceptives and with the one who told her to do as she thought best: she decided to make the Australian Labour Party 'her religion'.[26]

However, Sevegrand implies, though she does not discuss the issue so directly, that there was less impact in France: most Catholics ignored the encyclical and the bishops were prepared to let them do so. Other issues seemed more pressing both to conservatives and to progressives.[27] The studies by Tentler and Greeley on the United States suggest not so much that many Catholics left the church because of *Humanae Vitae*, but that it led to a change in the ways in which Catholics saw their church and their place within it. According to Tentler, the encyclical was a major reason for the decline of the Catholic subculture, which had still flourished at the time of Vatican II. Individual conscience played an increasingly large role in Catholic thinking, while the authority of the pope and bishops was eroded. Many Catholics felt free to decide for themselves on a range of issues where once the church had given them authoritative guidance. And many of the clergy thought they were right to do so. A survey of American priests in 1972 found that only 13 per cent would refuse absolution to someone who confessed to using contraceptives, while, among several other options, 44 per cent ticked 'accept moral judgment of responsibly formed conscience of users'.[28]

CHANGES IN FAMILY LIFE

The controversy over Catholics and contraception thus first came to a head in respect of married couples who had children, but did not want any more. While the media in the 1960s were fascinated by the rising scale of pre-marital

[25] Ibid. 242.

[26] Anne O'Brien, *God's Willing Workers: Women and Religion in Australia* (Sydney, 2005), 232–3.

[27] Sevegrand, *Enfants*, 334–5, 360–4.

[28] Andrew Greeley, *The Catholic Revolution* (Berkeley, Calif., 2004), 36; Tentler, *Contraception*, 264–9.

sexual activity, they often overlooked the fact that the great majority of these sexually active youngsters would soon marry and would also very soon have children. For a brief period they might be making their contribution to the sexual revolution, but in the longer term their roles as a wife or husband, as a parent and as a householder, would play a more important part in their lives. In this section I will focus on England, as oral history makes it possible to study changes in family relationships in an unusual degree of detail.

Three broad trends were changing patterns of family life in Britain in the years after the Second World War. First, there was the growing influence of the ideal of the 'companionate marriage'. In the inter-war years this had been seen as a mainly middle-class phenomenon. By the 1950s, newspapers, magazines, and marriage guidance experts were all combining to persuade working-class couples that they too should be aiming at a relationship which combined a vigorous sex life with shared leisure activities and a willingness to exchange roles.[29] Second, rising living standards were making the realization of this ideal more practicable by the later 1950s, as increasing numbers of couples were buying their own house, and devoting much of their increased incomes to equipping it and decorating it. And third, there was a gradual increase in the proportion of married women undertaking paid work.

The later 1950s saw a massive increase in television ownership, and though the 1960s is often seen as the decade of 'sex, drugs and rock 'n' roll', it might more accurately be seen as the decade in which the family sat in their pleasantly carpeted, curtained, and wallpapered living-room watching television together. During that decade 'do-it-yourself' (DIY) became a national passion, and when not modernizing the bathroom or eating their supper in front of the TV screen the family was likely to be seen going out together in a motor cycle and sidecar, or the recently acquired motor car. Elizabeth Roberts, whose studies of the working class in north-west England cover both the early twentieth century and the 1950s and 1960s, comments that in the latter period 'few seemed to have experienced a crisis of faith or a dispute with the church—both situations which had been evident earlier in the century. Instead, respondents spoke of being too busy creating a home to go to church, having other things to do.'[30]

---

[29] It is generally agreed that the 'companionate marriage' was a highly influential ideal in the period *c*.1945–70. There is less agreement as to how far it was achieved in practice. Relatively optimistic views include Marcus Collins, *Modern Love* (London, 2003), 167; Geoffrey Gorer, *Sex and Marriage in England Today* (London, 1971), 62. More sceptical views include Elizabeth Wilson, *Only Half Way to Paradise* (London, n.d.), 59–69; Jenny Finch and Penny Summerfield, 'Social Reconstruction and the Emergence of Companionate Marriage', in Clark (ed.), *Marriage*, 7–32.

[30] Elizabeth Roberts, *Women and Families* (Oxford, 1995), 16.

The companionate marriages of the 1960s often became the divorces of the 1970s as reality could seldom match inflated expectations. In the mean time, however, they had important effects on leisure patterns and relations with neighbours and extended family. The later 1950s and 1960s saw a decline in gender-specific activities of all kinds, as couples opted to spend their free hours together. Attendance at football matches, overwhelmingly a male activity, fell by a third between 1946 and 1965.[31] Attendance at cinemas and churches— predominantly, though by no means exclusively, female activities—were also falling.[32] Callum Brown has rightly argued that declining church attendance by women in the 1960s was very important because women had for so long been the majority in most Christian congregations and in particular had been mainly responsible for passing on religious beliefs and practices to the younger generation. He attributes this decline to the impact of 'second wave feminism and the recrafting of femininity',[33] and the significance of these developments will be discussed later in this chapter. However, the oral evidence suggests that the most common reason for women giving up going to church was marriage to a non-church-going man: either she did not want to go to church without him, or they had a shared Sunday activity which they wanted to do together. A typical example was Thelma Jennings (born 1933, Barrow), who regularly attended the Anglican church until she married a non-church-going husband—though she started going again with her children in the later 1960s. (In fact the pattern was repeated in the next generation, as her daughter went regularly to church until she started courting a young man who was not a church-goer.)[34] For some the claims of the home effectively superseded those of the church. Thus Jill Barker (born 1944 in Preston) went regularly to church as a teenager, but 'when we got married we never bothered'. A major reason was that her husband worked most of Saturday and Sunday: 'I think we wanted to buy new things, didn't we, and that were the thing: we wanted carpets and stair carpets and new furniture'.[35] For Mavis Bradshaw (born 1936, Barrow) Sunday was the one opportunity for she and her husband to spend time together. They had both been brought up as Methodists but when they married in 1959 they 'floated away from church', because Sunday was their only free day, and they wanted to spend it going out together on his motor bike.[36]

[31] Richard Holt and Tony Mason, *Sport in Britain 1945–2000* (Oxford, 2000), 3.

[32] Cinema attendance fell by three-quarters between 1946 and 1963: Dominic Sandbrook, *Never had it So Good: A History of Britain from Suez to the Beatles* (London, 2005), 190. Andrew Davies, 'Cinema and Broadcasting', in Johnson, *Britain*, 270, quotes an estimate from the later 1930s that 75% of cinema attendances were by women; however, I have not found statistics for the post-war period.

[33] Callum G. Brown, *The Death of Christian Britain* (London, 2001), 176.

[34] SFL, interview with Mrs W5B, 45–7.   [35] SFL, interview with Mrs G7P, 90.

[36] SFL, interview with Mrs W6B, 25, 39, 58.

In the previous generation it had been common, even normal, especially in working-class families, for husband and wife to have completely separate interests. Thus Edward Martin (born Lancaster, 1937) recalls that his parents never went out together, and that while his mother, who had been a domestic servant before marriage, was a very active Anglican, his labourer father only went to church 'very, very occasionally'.[37] Elizabeth Grant (born 1936, Barrow) also recalled that her parents hardly ever went out together. Her mother, a secretary, belonged to the Anglican parochial church council, and also liked playing badminton and going to the theatre. Her father, a draughtsman, never went to church. His big interest was making model yachts: he spent the winter in the cellar making them and the summer sailing them.[38] Christine Andrews (born 1936, Barrow) also remembers that her father, a shunter, and her mother, a tailor, seldom did things together. She went to the Anglican church, belonged to the Mother's Union, and went to the cinema with a friend. He went to the club for a drink and a game of snooker, listened to boxing on the radio, went to the theatre with his daughter, but did not go to church. Christine followed the standard pattern in that she had been a regular church-goer, but it 'dwindled' after she married a non-church-going husband.[39]

In some cases, though less often, doing things together meant going to church together. Mark Higgins (born 1950, Brighton) came from a completely non-church-going family, but his wife had been brought up as a Catholic. When their daughter was born she wanted her to be baptized as a Catholic, but the priest refused because Mark had never been baptized. However an Anglican clergyman agreed to perform the baptism, and for a time they all attended the Anglican church together.[40] Pauline Ashby (born 1942, Widnes) had converted to Catholicism while engaged to a Catholic.[41] Julie and David Royle, both born in 1950 in church-going working-class families in Barrow, had lost contact with the church as young adults, but had rediscovered their interest in religion at around the same time, and both joined a Methodist church. Becoming parents seems to have been a factor, but she also mentioned a sudden realization of 'who Jesus really was', while he mentioned an anti-nuclear weapons demonstration in Barrow as a catalyst, as it had forced him to think about big questions which he previously ignored.[42] Ian Jones noted how common it was for church-goers in Birmingham in the 1990s to attend as a couple. Among forty-seven married men and women whom he interviewed in his oral history of Birmingham Christianity since 1945, as seen through the eyes of 'ordinary' church-goers, thirty-nine had a church-going spouse. There

---

[37] SFL, interview with Mr G3L, 19–22.   [38] SFL, interview with Mrs R4B, 5–23, 28–9.
[39] SFL, interview with Mrs M12B, 18–25.   [40] FSMA, interview 77.
[41] FSMA, interview 4.   [42] SFL, interview with Mr P5B, 27–8, and Mrs P5B, 30.

were, however, still seven women who went to church without their husband, as against only one man who went without his wife.[43]

The proportion of married women aged under 60 in paid employment rose steadily from 26 per cent in 1951, to 35 per cent in 1961, to 47 per cent in 1971, and 62 per cent in 1981. The implications of this trend for other areas of women's life are less clear. Women continued to do the bulk of housework during this period and, in spite of the increasing availability of labour-saving machinery, time spent on housework did not diminish commensurately with the increased time spent on work outside the home.[44] Resentment at this 'double burden' was one of the factors leading to the rise of the Women's Liberation Movement in the 1970s. There are also hints from oral history that the combination of a job with large amounts of housework meant that mothers had less time and energy to supervise their children's behaviour (including for instance sending them to Sunday School or teaching them prayers) or to belong to organizations. For instance, Susan Atkins, born in Preston in 1947, whose mother gave up her job when she had young children, but returned in 1958, notes that her mother then left the church women's organization she had formerly attended, and eased up on discipline—'I do think mothers who are working do take slightly less notice, they are too fraught trying to get everything done after work'.[45] Certainly this supposition was supported by evidence from the United States in the 1990s where it was found that mothers who had a job were no less likely than mothers who were fulltime homemakers to believe in God or to pray, but they were somewhat less likely to take their children to church, and much less likely to belong to church organizations.[46]

Neither involvement in the 'sexual revolution' as a teenager nor involvement in the labour market as a mother diminished the central importance of marriage, parenthood, and the home for the majority of women of the 1960s generation. There was a significant minority of women, especially those who had gone through higher education and/or the counter-culture, whose outlook changed in more fundamental ways, but for the great majority of working-class and lower middle-class women changes were of a more subtle and limited kind.

---

[43] Ian Jones, 'The "Mainstream" Churches in Birmingham c.1945–1998: The Local Church and Generational Change' (Ph.D. thesis, University of Birmingham, 2000), 139–41.

[44] Pat Thane, 'Women since 1945', in Johnson (ed.), *Britain*, 392–410.

[45] SFL, interview with Mrs B10P, 28. The vicar of a Gloucester council estate parish, where church attendance was low, mentioned as one of the reasons the fact that women who had jobs needed Sunday to catch up at home: letter in *Church Times* (19 Jan. 1962).

[46] Wade Clark Roof, *Spiritual Marketplace: Baby Boomers and the Remaking of American Religion* (Princeton, 1999), 240–3.

Sandra Cook (born 1945, south Lancashire)[47] might be taken as representative, since so many aspects of her life story are typical of her generation. She came from a 'staunch Methodist' and teetotal working-class family. She went to Sunday School, then the church youth club, and continued going to church until she married at 21. She also had a phase as a Young Conservative, to the disgust of her strongly Labour grandfather. Until she met her future husband when she was 19, her social life still revolved round the church, but then she began to live 'a double life' with friends from church and also 'the boozy night life type of life that I'd come to like'. Her fiancé 'didn't go to church', 'liked dancing, liked going to night clubs, liked gambling'. She had already had rows with her parents about her smoking, and now she had more rows, as 'they didn't like me being kept out late, and one thing and another, I liked being kept out late'. Though she had had various other boyfriends, her only sexual relationship before marriage was with her future husband. She worked at the town hall, and part of his attraction was that as an electrician he was a manual worker, and thus 'a real man'. Like so many other young couples at that time, they saved up to buy a house before they were married, and spent their spare time renovating it, so that it would be ready for them to move in immediately after the wedding. Her husband encouraged her to keep her job after they married, and though she intended to stop when their first child was born, she was persuaded by her employers to return part-time. She was later promoted to a position as a staffing officer. Her 'Victorian' father was not impressed:

'I don't know why you want a career. What do you want a career for?' 'I want one!' He sort of thinks I should be at home, you know, and I couldn't have half I've got if I didn't. I've brought up me kids. I've done that bit, it took me what I would say ten years off, I wasn't off ten years, but I took those certain number of years off, and went back to me career. But he's the sort that would belittle a woman having a career.

However, her mother was 'chuffed to death, and quite proud'. When asked what were the best things in her life, Sandra said: getting married, having children and 'getting me independence back again . . . just having a career back'. She no longer went to church: 'And I think it's because it was forced upon me from an early age. I'm still Christian.' In bringing up her children she prioritized good manners, hard work, and ambition. She sent her children to Sunday School, but 'it didn't work', and now their Sunday revolved round sport, which she saw as an alternative means of acquiring the necessary 'discipline'. Thus Sandra had dropped her connection with the church and in other important ways had broken with the values and moral rules inculcated by her parents—with sometimes explosive results. Yet the continuities were as significant as the

[47] FSMA, interview 176.

ruptures, and above all there was still the central focus of life on the family—a focus that had become even sharper as other institutions, such as the church, slipped out of view. In fact, by the time of the interview in the later 1980s, Sandra's parents had also stopped going to church, though in this case it was because they objected to the closure of their own chapel following a merger with another congregation.

Oral history highlights the frequency of changing patterns of religious observance across the life-cycle. Complicated patterns of engagement and disengagement are not uncommon: for instance, strong religious involvement in early adolescence, rebellion in late adolescence, a return to the church when bringing up younger children, a move away as the children grow older, and a return in retirement. As well as changing needs and changing influences, this also reflects the complexity and ambiguity of many people's religious beliefs and their attitudes to the church. Among those who felt that they had been forced to go to church, rejection of God or a totally negative attitude to the church were not uncommon. Among the many people who had been committed church-goers at some point in their lives, but had given it up, there were some who had made a deliberate break on grounds of principle; but much more numerous were those who retained a belief in God, who maybe continued to pray, and in some cases felt regret that something that had been an important part of their lives no longer was.

'SECOND WAVE' FEMINISM

While women like Sandra Cook were modifying and modernizing their roles as wives and mothers, others were questioning the whole basis of their social-ization, their economic position, their relationship with men—and sometimes the impact of religious teachings on their lives. The pioneers of the Women's Liberation Movement in the late 1960s and early 1970s had for the most part studied at university and were eager to use the knowledge acquired there in a rewarding job. They had also very often had one or more of three typically 1960s experiences: marrying and having children while still young; partici-pation in the 'sexual revolution'; and radical political engagement especially in anti-war protests, the student movement, or the American Civil Rights Movement. And in many cases these experiences had brought frustrations: the difficulties of combining a huge volume of childcare and housework with a job, and often a sense that everything was being subordinated to her husband's career; a feeling that the 'sexual revolution' was following a male agenda and was not offering as much as it should to women; and the discovery that in many radical movements women performed essential backroom tasks while men got the glory.

The student movement of the 1960s played an unintended role as a catalyst for the women's movement of the 1970s. Bettina Aptheker, recalling the Free Speech Movement at Berkeley in 1964, noted that although there were plenty of women in the movement, 'Nevertheless it was men who dominated most of our meetings and discussions. Women did most of the clerical work and fund-raising and provided food.' She herself spoke at nearly every rally, but 'It never occurred to me that I was often the only woman speaking at these rallies'.[48] Only around 1968 did radical women begin to question their secondary role in the movement, often in the face of incredulity or ridicule from male colleagues, who feared that the movement was being diverted from more important issues. In that year a Women's Action Council in Berlin reflected tensions between women in the SDS (Social Democratic Student League) and its heavily male leadership. At about the same time the American women began to speak about 'women's liberation', the word 'liberation' being chosen partly to emphasize parallels with anti-colonial movements, but more especially to highlight an agenda much broader than the more narrowly political connotations of women's 'emancipation'.

In Britain the first women's liberation groups (on American models) were formed in London in 1969, and the movement took off in 1970 in the wake of the first national conference at Ruskin College, Oxford. Many of the pioneers had been active in anti-Vietnam War protests, and the movement was partly a reaction against the marginalization of women in many 1960s radical organizations and the sexism prevalent in the counter-culture. Critiques of Christianity and Judaism as legitimators of patriarchy were also standard themes of 'second wave' feminism, with the fiercest criticism usually being directed at the Roman Catholic Church. For instance, two of the articles included in a collection of writings from the British Women's Movement in the years 1969–72 included attacks on Christianity and Judaism—though the version of Christianity that was being attacked seemed to be mainly Catholic, and in some respects medieval Catholic. One of these by Monica Sjoo of Bristol Women's Liberation wrote that 'the Christian religion is centred round an almighty Father-god, his son, and the son's non-sexual virgin mother. The Christian god was serviced by celibate male priests to whom the woman was the creation of the "devil". She alone represented sexuality, her sexual organs were fearsome and unclean, and both were disgusting and unholy.' An article by Pam Whiting on 'Female Sexuality: Its Political

---

[48] Bettina Aptheker, 'Gender Politics and the FSM: A Meditation on Women and Freedom of Speech', in Cohen and Zelnik (eds.), *Free Speech*, 130.

Implications' included a section on 'Religion and the church', which argued that:

Our culture is impregnated with the culture of the ancient Hebrews: the original sin of Eve is still with us, as is the sin of Onan. On this foundation of Hebrew mythology, Christianity erected a superstructure of misogyny. As a direct development of the original sin of Eve myth, the early Christians elevated the 'eunuch priest' cult. Heterosexual intercourse was to become regarded as something common or dirty not to be undertaken by holy men. Christ himself was desexualised.... Throughout the centuries the web of institutions thrown up by Christendom has worked against women's equality and her sexuality.[49]

For the pioneering feminist activist of the 1970s the women's movement was a complete way of life which left little room for other involvements and loyalties. It was a new faith, rather as socialism was in the later nineteenth century. 'Sisterhood' was an overwhelming experience for women who suddenly discovered that other women had suffered the same frustrations and indignities, and who gained strength from knowing that they were fighting together.[50]

However, criticism of religion was less prominent in the literature of the British movement than many other themes. The reasons for this are not entirely clear, though probably a variety of factors were involved. For some feminist activists religion was regarded more with indifference than active hostility, since they perceived Britain as a relatively secularized society, in which other enemies posed more serious problems. Furthermore, the abortion law reform of 1967 and the fact that it had been broadly supported by most churches other than the Roman Catholic Church meant that the biggest bone of contention between churches and the women's movement in many countries was much less of an issue. And the high level of religious pluralism meant that there was no dominant church which could be seen as the enemy: feminists who were no longer active in any religion nonetheless found it possible to retain some degree of identification with the tradition from which they had come. However, many of these pioneers had already left their church or synagogue, or had never had any involvement with it. Reading two volumes of feminist memoirs collected in the 1980s or 1990s, *Once a Feminist*, edited by Michelene Wandor, and *Truth, Dare and Promise*, edited by Liz Heron, one is struck by how many of the contributors either came from non-religious

---

[49] Michelene Wandor, *The Body Politic: Writings from the Women's Liberation Movement in Britain, 1969–1972* (London, 1972), 182–3, 198–9.

[50] See the personal testimonies in Michelene Wandor (ed.), *Once a Feminist: Stories of a Generation* (London, 1990).

families or had given up their religion while teenagers. Particularly poignant is the defensive tone adopted by one of the few professed believers.[51]

Sexism in the church or the implications of Christian theology for women were obviously much bigger issues for those who were still active in their church when they discovered the women's movement. The most spectacular example is the feminist theologian, Mary Daly, who was still a Catholic when she wrote her classic critique, *The Church and the Second Sex* (1968), in which she argued that there was an inherent bias against women in Christian theology. In 1971 she staged a spectacular exit from the church. While delivering a sermon in Harvard's university chapel, she declared: 'Sisters: the sisterhood of man cannot happen without a real Exodus. We can this morning demonstrate our Exodus from sexist religion...we cannot really belong to institutional religion as it exists. It isn't good enough....Our time has come. Let us affirm our faith in ourselves and our will to transcendence by rising and walking out together.'

Descending from the pulpit Mary Daly then led a mass departure from the chapel. This Exodus, modelled on the Exodus from Egypt, the people of God leaving slavery for freedom, was experienced by many women as passionately important and moving. 'I had the feeling of being a whole person for the first time,' someone said afterwards.[52]

The novelist and Christian feminist Sara Maitland, in recounting this story, states that Daly's very public departure was the tip of an iceberg, and that many other women left the church during the same decade either in protest at ecclesiastical sexism or from the conviction that Christianity was irremediably identified with patriarchy: 'Too frequently women find more sisterhood and succour outside the Church and life within it becomes not worth the pain.... There are many women from all denominations who have left, women who once cared passionately and have now withdrawn.'[53]

Jan Griesinger, who got deeply involved in the women's movement in 1969 while studying in an Ohio seminary, thought that 'organised religion', with the exception of Quakers and Unitarians, had not played much part in the early stages of the movement. When she was converted to feminism she did not know any church-based feminists, but 'The feminist movement was contagious and propelled me back into the church-affiliated organizations to reach other women with the good news of liberation to the captives'.[54] Griesinger was ordained in the United Church of Christ, and remained a Christian

---

[51] Alison Hennegan 'did try very hard once' to give up belief in the divinity of Christ, 'but couldn't manage it'. Liz Heron, *Truth, Dare and Promise: Girls Growing up in the Fifties* (London, 1985), 152.

[52] Sara Maitland, *A Map of the New Country: Women and Christianity* (London, 1983), 141–2.

[53] Ibid. 140.

[54] Sara Evans, *Journeys that Opened Up the World* (New Brunswick, NJ, 2003), 195.

radical 'spreading the gospel of feminism and liberation theology as well as a commitment to antiracism, anti-imperialism, and anti-miltarism'.[55] But her experiences, especially in the 1970s, indicate the resistances that the pioneers of Christian feminism could face. Some of the problems were common to many of the movement's pioneers: 'We were unsure what we were doing and unsupported by the men in our lives, as well as most of the women.' But some of the problems were more specific to her situation as a student and later a minister in a male-dominated church. At seminary she had been one of only eight women, beside 167 men, and only one of the teaching staff was a woman. Before the conferences of the National Campus Ministry Association, women chaplains had their own meeting:

We shared our stories: the way men in campus ministry were treating us, the way male church leaders were ignoring us, the way the men we lived with were threatened, the sexism we endured at national campus ministry conferences, the way our jobs were so part time or tenuous or even unpaid, the way we risked our livelihoods by being feminist activists. These stories helped us make sense out of our isolated experiences as women leaders in the church. And we examined the politics of sexism, racism, imperialism and heterosexism in order to move from the personal to systemic analysis of our experience.[56]

She found her work 'both exhilarating and frustrating', and 'was sustained by complaining to my Dayton Women's Liberation friends continually about sexism in the church'. 'It is hard to imagine,' she added, 'how little a feminist perspective was understood at the time. Now, even if people don't agree with it, they are aware that such a perspective exists and have some clue what it is about.' By the mid-1970s 'Change was happening...but the resistance was very strong, even among liberal men who wanted to be our allies but just didn't get it.' She was appalled when one student chaplain was dismissed for being 'an outspoken feminist, a not-very-out lesbian, and an organizer of campus feminist groups and programmes of women's spirituality', and another because 'her women's spirituality programs were labelled as witchcraft'. She was equally angry at the lack of support from her own boss when she got into a confrontation with a conference speaker who had made sexist jokes. In 1977 she would come out as a lesbian, and would become a spokesperson in her church for lesbian, gay, bisexual, and transgendered people.[57]

In Sydney in 1968 Protestant radicals formed a group called Christian Women Concerned (CWC). Initially it concentrated on issues such as racism, poverty, and the war in Vietnam, but, according to O'Brien, 'it became increasingly interested in how Christian teaching contributed to women's oppression'. It founded a journal, *Magdalene*, which combined women's

[55] Ibid. 201.   [56] Ibid. 199–201.   [57] Ibid. 201–2, 206–7.

liberation with language drawn from the Bible—leading to objections from some feminists, who saw no common ground. In 1973 CWC became the Commission on the Status of Women of the Australian Council of Churches. According to its first president, Marie Tulip, it was 'the main centre for the huge explosion of feminist energy and activism in religion in the 1970s and 1980s'.[58]

Feminist discourse had a much wider impact, influencing the thinking of women who never joined any women's group, including those who stayed in their churches. One of the representatives (born 1940) of the 'holistic milieu', interviewed in the Kendal Project, expressed in striking terms this broader diffusion of new critical ideas. She had been brought up as an Anglican but no longer went to church:

> But I have my own kind of beliefs, mostly when I am up a mountain. That's my salvation and spiritual place to be. Where I sort my head out. . . . I wasn't a hippy. I was already married with kids. But it still instilled something into you which is coming out of me again now. The 60s and the start of the 70s were very powerful. All of a sudden it was something different, the way people thought and reacted. And it was more important for women than for men. As well it was the first time they began to think—I know there were suffragettes, but they didn't get that far. When men came back from the war women were still very subservient. But in the 60s women started thinking 'we are the people'. I had been brought up that men came first. A more powerful thing for women than for men. I am a hippy at heart, but externally conventional.[59]

It is rather striking, however, in examining the transcripts of oral history projects which included questions relating to religious change in the 1960s and 1970s that very few of those interviewed gave the influence of feminist ideas or sexism in the church as a reason for leaving the church or rejecting their religion. There is a contrast here with interviews with those brought up in the early twentieth century who quite frequently quoted class discrimination in the church or the influence of radical politics as a reason for leaving. Among the many, mainly working-class and lower middle-class, Lancashire women interviewed by the Centre for North-West Regional Studies who had attended a church as teenagers but ceased doing so as adults, there is only one whose departure had a feminist or partly feminist motive. Elizabeth Grant (born 1936, Barrow) was 'standard Anglican' and apparently continued to be so as a university student, but:

> increasingly through the 1960s I began to feel that there were lots of things about the Anglican Church I didn't like. Like the liturgy where you get carried along with all this

---

[58] O'Brien, *Willing Workers*, 235.

[59] Kendal Project, Department of Religious Studies, University of Lancaster, 'Holistic Milieu', interview conducted 5 Feb. 2002.

wordiness, and you either went along with it and didn't think what you were saying, or you stopped and thought about it and lost the whole thread of the service. And I couldn't cope with their attitude to women. I felt that it was exceedingly chauvinistic, you know women were there to make the parish tea and things, and perhaps do the flowers and that was about it. And I really felt it was very hierarchical and I definitely did not like hierarchical institutions. It wasn't so much the belief I fell out with, it was the whole sort of structure and the liturgy and so on.

The result was not that she rejected Christianity, but that she became a Quaker.[60] In the Millennium Project, a vast oral history survey conducted by local radio stations around the end of the twentieth century, a sample of 167 interviewees born between 1935 and 1954 included 38 people, of whom 19 were women, who gave reasons why they had temporarily or permanently rejected religion or the churches. Women and men gave broadly similar reasons—most commonly either tragic experiences which had led them to doubt the existence of God, or a move to a new environment in which old beliefs and practices seemed less relevant or credible, or where they learnt about new and more attractive beliefs. The only one explicitly to connect her rejection of Christianity with feminist arguments was Jean Barrett (born 1942, Bristol) who said that Christianity had contributed to the bad treatment of women.[61] While the evidence is inconclusive, it seems that the number of women who left their church because of their involvement in the women's movement may have been relatively small—though, as Maitland argues, many of those who did so were exceptionally able and committed. This conclusion also gains support from the Girton project, which included questions about attitudes to feminism and involvement in the women's movement. The cohort arriving at Girton in the first half of the 1950s included one who was, when she completed the questionnaire in the 1990s, a strongly committed feminist, and many who were mildly sympathetic to the movement, but also a considerable number who were critical. As one respondent said: 'I object to discrimination on the grounds of sex, race or disability', but also to 'advocacy of women's rights to an extreme degree'. Among those coming to Girton between 1959 and 1962 the proportion who had become committed feminists was somewhat higher, but there were still many who expressed doubts about the 'strident', 'aggressive', or 'anti-male' character of the women's movement. Among the 1970s cohort the majority described themselves as feminists, but generally of a moderate kind, and only a small number had been actively involved in feminist organizations or campaigns. There were also still some total sceptics.

---

[60] SFL, interview with Mrs R4B, 52.   [61] MPNSA, interview 6099.

In each of these cohorts there were a few women for whom feminism and involvement in the women's movement were central to their identity. One of the questions was about 'ethnic or cultural identity' and while most respondents chose national, ethnic, or religious categories, one wrote 'Feminist', and another 'Gay? Feminist? Confused?' These had generally rejected Christianity, if not religion in general—there are no direct questions about and little information in the responses, relating to 'alternative' spirituality. However, there is no evidence that involvement in the women's movement had been the cause of their rejection of Christianity—this seems to have happened before they became feminists. There are also three larger groups, each of which included both the 'religious' and the 'non-religious'. First there were committed feminists, whose feminism was less central to their identity, and often defined in relation to political or religious beliefs. Second there were a large number who declared support for certain feminist objectives but had no wish to get involved in any organization or movement. And third there were in each cohort a number of respondents who were more or less critical of, or even hostile to, feminism. These included both women for whom marriage and family were central and who felt that feminists were anti-men and anti-family, and also those who were having successful careers, and felt that other women could do the same if they worked at it.

The link between sex, gender, and rejection of the church was much clearer in predominantly Catholic countries, because of *Humanae Vitae*, and more especially because of the confrontations between the Catholic Church and the women's movement over abortion. In France, for instance, abortion was the central concern of the Mouvement de Libération des Femmes (MLF) from its beginnings in 1970. Members of the MLF claimed that the abortion laws were a symbol of all the oppressions suffered by women, starting with 'the obligation to be a mother'.[62] Inevitably this placed the movement on a collision course with the Catholic Church. The same happened in Italy, where abortion was the one issue capable of uniting an otherwise very divided movement and so was the main focus of feminist campaigning from 1975 until the passage of a new law in 1978. Up to 50,000 women took part in demonstrations and 800,000 signed a petition calling for a referendum on abortion.[63] The legalization of abortion in many Western countries in the later 1960s and the 1970s will be discussed more fully in Chapter 10.

---

[62] Danièle Léger, *Le féminisme en France* (Paris, 1982), 24.
[63] Paul Ginsborg, *A History of Contemporary Italy: Society and Politics, 1943–1988* (London, 1990), 369–70, 373, 394.

THE PROUD GAY

The most unexpected and challenging of the new figures to emerge out of the sexual revolution and the radical politics of the later 1960s and early 1970s was the militant gay. The event which marked his arrival was the fighting between police and customers at the Stonewall Inn on Christopher Street in New York's Greenwich Village in June 1969. This led immediately to the foundation of the Gay Liberation Front. An organization with the same name was founded the following year in Britain. The name highlighted the parallels between the campaign for gay rights and Third World liberation movements, and it reflected the Marxism of many of the founders. The Stonewall battle challenged conventional assumptions in several ways. Readiness to fight was one of the signs of a 'real man', and 'real men' were assumed to be 100 per cent heterosexual. Moreover, homosexuals had traditionally responded to prejudice and persecution by concealment—by shunning publicity and by using coded language. The relatively few openly homosexual men tended to be concentrated in certain professions, notably music and the theatre, where creativity and sensitivity counted for more than physical strength. Some homosexuals regarded their orientation as at best a misfortune and potentially a source of shame, and even those who accepted it often saw it as a private matter and were embarrassed by those who 'flaunted' their sexuality. Psychiatrists, while usually condemning the use of the law to punish homosexuality, tended to see it as a form of pathology, often arising from a lack of male role models in families without a father or where the mother was dominant. A major objective of Gay Liberation was to challenge these negative images, to assert 'Gay Pride', and to declare that 'Gay is Good'. Where the older homosexual stereotype focused on fastidious dressing and quasi-feminine looks, the 1970s saw a new image, described by a historian of the gay metropolis of San Francisco as 'assertively proud and aggressively sexual'. Instead of the old tendency towards concealment, the new-style 'liberated gay man' was so keen to declare his sexuality that he tended to adopt a uniform, consisting of 'a body-hugging ensemble—plaid shirt or tight-fitting tee-shirt, tight-fitting 501 (button-up fly) blue jeans, sneakers or construction boots, a hat or cap, an earring, and facial hair, usually mustache'.[64]

The older style of privatized homosexuality had its place in the churches, and especially in the Roman Catholic and Anglican Churches. In the English-speaking world a significant proportion of the many writers and artists who converted to Roman Catholicism in the nineteenth and twentieth century were

---

[64] Les Wright, 'San Francisco', in David Higgs (ed.), *Queer Sites: Gay Urban Histories since 1600* (London, 1999), 183.

homosexual, the most famous example being Oscar Wilde. In the Church of England there had been a homosexual subculture since the later nineteenth century, emphatically identified with the church's Anglo-Catholic wing. It was well-known that Anglo-Catholic priests were often gay, though many of them probably were not practising homosexuals, and an orientation that was understood by insiders was seldom advertised to the general public.[65] Patrick Higgins, in discussing a selection of prosecutions for homosexual offences in 1953–4, includes several where the accused was an Anglican or Roman Catholic priest, as well as one where he was the organist at a fashionable Anglo-Catholic church and another where he was a churchwarden.[66] The new militancy soon had an impact on gay Christians, as well as on more secular gays. But it was more likely than the older styles of homosexuality to come into open conflict with the churches. In Britain the Homosexual Law Reform Society founded in 1958 included a clergyman among its leading members.[67] It was cautious, respectable, and non-confrontational in style, and some of its members were heterosexual. Gay Liberation on the other hand was confrontational, openly hostile to established institutions of all kinds, and emphatically a movement *of* as well as *for* gay men, who were demanding their rights and saw no need for help from well-meaning outsiders. In this respect it was following a path already well-trodden by black and feminist militants. Gay Liberationists were also heirs to the 'sexual revolution' of the later 1960s, which meant that they wanted to talk openly and without inhibitions about sex, and to affirm not only the joys of sex, but the advantages of multiple partners.

Many churches were open to the argument that homosexuals should be freed from discrimination and persecution. In England and Wales, for instance, the Church of England played an important part in initiating the debate on homosexual law reform and supporting the reform movement, as will be shown in Chapter 10. But churches found it hard to accept homosexuality as a legitimate option, every bit as valid as heterosexuality, and even harder to accept sexual promiscuity of any kind. As in the women's movement at the same time, attacks on Christianity and Judaism as legitimators of the oppression suffered by gay people were quite frequent, though the salience of such attacks on religion varied from country to country. In Britain, for instance, the pioneers of Gay Liberation often had a background in student radicalism and the anti-Vietnam War movement, and their main theme tended to be attacks on capitalism and the claim that full gay liberation would

---

[65] David Hilliard, 'Homosexuality', in McLeod (ed.), *Cambridge History of Christianity*, ix. 546–8; David Hilliard, 'UnEnglish and Unmanly: Anglo-Catholicism and Homosexuality, *Victorian Studies*, 25 (1982), 181–210.

[66] Patrick Higgins, *Heterosexual Dictatorship* (London, 1996), 179–231.

[67] Jeffrey Weeks, *Coming Out* (London, 1990), 168–82.

come with the revolution. However, the churches, and especially conservative Christian groups, such as the Festival of Light, were also among their targets, and the latter offered excellent opportunities for counter-demonstrations by the more theatrically inclined Gay Liberationists. This happened at a rally in Central Hall, Westminster, in 1971: 'Thus it was that Malcolm Muggeridge, Cliff Richard and other luminaries gazed aghast as members of the Gay Liberation Front—masquerading as bishops, repenting sinners and can-canning "nuns"—stormed the platform. Others unleashed mice around the auditorium.'[68] Those lesbians and gay men who were active in their churches often found 'coming out' very difficult because of the knowledge that it would lead to hostility and rejection by significant numbers of their fellow members. Some Christian feminists found that more staid church members could cope with their political radicalism, and even their feminism, but lesbianism was more than they could take. Charlotte Bunch, who had been an active Methodist, president of the University Christian Movement, and a prominent member of the radical wing of the World Christian Student Movement, left the church after coming out as a lesbian in 1971:

As a part of the new left and as a feminist, I had become increasingly secular in my orientation, but it was still possible to feel part of the wider Christian community and, indeed, to engage with it on political issues. The more feminist I became, however, the more impatient I was with the phallocentricity of Christianity and with the slowness of the institution to see how it oppressed women. When I came out as a lesbian in the context of the feminist movement, I was simply not willing to be affiliated with an institution that labelled me a sinner or denied me the right to enter its highest callings.[69]

The United States saw the first explicitly gay churches, with the foundation in 1968 of the Metropolitan Community Church in Los Angeles, which then spread to other cities and later to other countries. In Canada the first religiously based gay group was the Unitarian Universalist Gays (1971), followed in 1973 by the first Canadian Metropolitan Community Church and then by groups for gay Catholics, Anglicans, and so on.[70] Britain too had its first Metropolitan Community Church in 1973, at the same time that various denominational groups were being formed, such as the Friends Homosexual Fellowship and Quest, which was Catholic. The Gay Christian Movement (GCM) was founded in 1976, and the hostility encountered by many of the founders reflected the difficulties which openly gay Christians were likely to face. A discreet, half-concealed homosexuality of the traditional kind might

---

[68] *Guardian* (7 July 2006), obituary of Tony Halliday.   [69] Evans, *Journeys*, 139.
[70] Tom Warner, *Never Going Back: A History of Queer Activism in Canada* (Toronto, 2002), 92.

be tolerated, but church leaders tended to agree with Eric Treacy, bishop of Wakefield, who condemned 'those who flaunt their sexuality'. Laypeople were sometimes more openly vitriolic: the bishop of Chelmsford, in resisting calls for action against the vicar of Thaxted, who was president of the GCM, reported that he had been 'horrified and disgusted by the vindictive letters I have recently received which have demonstrated a deep loathing of homosexuals as such, whether they practised homosexual acts or not'. While the letter writers were not necessarily church members, their views seem to have been shared by the Thaxted churchwardens, both of whom resigned.[71]

CONCLUSION

The 1960s and early 1970s were a time of crisis for the churches in most Western countries. The nature, extent, and causes of this crisis are hotly debated, and historians are far from having arrived at any consensus. One of the most influential interpretations of the crisis is that advanced by Callum Brown and Patrick Pasture,[72] which places gender, and specifically changes in women's consciousness and identity at its heart. In as much as women had for at least a century and a half, and probably for longer, played a key role in passing on Christian practices to the next generation, declining religious participation by women in the 1960s and 1970s was certainly of enormous importance, and more important than declining religious participation by men. Right up to the 1960s it had mainly been mothers who had taught their children prayers or made sure they went to Sunday School, and who had hung up crucifixes and pictures of saints or of biblical scenes on the walls of the home. The distancing from religion and the church of many women of the 1960s generation was a key factor in the weakening of the religious socialization of the next generation. However, many of the factors that were distancing women from the church were the same as the factors that were distancing men, and there is no evidence that women were leaving in greater numbers than men. In one of the few cases where the statistics offer a gender breakdown, the statistics of Anglican confirmations in the 1960s and 1970s show a slightly greater rate of decline for males than for females: between 1956 and 1974 the male rate fell by 57 per cent and the female rate by 52 per cent.[73]

[71] Sean Gill (ed.), *The Lesbian and Gay Christian Movement: Campaigning for Justice, Truth and Love* (London, 1998), 3, 8–9.

[72] Brown, *Death*; Patrick Pasture, 'Christendom and the Legact of the 1960s', *Revue d'histoire ecclésiastique*, 99 (2004), 114–15.

[73] Brown, *Death*, 191.

The English church census of 1979 showed that 58 per cent of church-goers aged 15 and above were female and that within each age-band women were more likely than men to be church-goers. When allowance is made for the fact that women were living longer and so there were more old women than old men in the general population, the over-representation of women in church congregations was greatest in the 30–44 age-bracket (which included most of the '1960s' generation).[74]

Of the changes in this period in the field of sex, gender, and the family, those that had an impact on the largest numbers of people were the increasing focus of life on the home and the nuclear family, the influence of the 'companionate marriage' ideal, and the declining importance of the neighbourhood and of customs enforced by pressure from neighbours and extended families. The Women's Liberation and Gay Liberation Movements exercised a powerful influence, but on much smaller numbers of people, revolutionizing the thinking of those who joined, becoming for many of them a complete way of life, and often placing attachments to religion or the churches under severe strain. The most enigmatic aspect of the religious upheavals of this period is the role of the 'sexual revolution'. Except in the specific case of Catholics and contraception, there is no clear evidence that rejection of their teachings on sex was itself a major source of alienation from the churches. Those already detached felt increasingly free to ignore church teaching, while those who remained in the church were claiming a greater freedom to make their own judgements on questions of ethics—and sometimes doctrine too. Meanwhile there were sections of society, including most obviously the counter-culture, where new and unconventional approaches to sex were one important aspect of a wider programme of alternative values and lifestyles, in terms of which all 'respectable' institutions such as the churches seemed alien.

---

[74] Peter Brierley (ed.), *Prospects for the Eighties* (London, 1980), 23.

9

The Crisis of the Church

Around 1967 the statistics of religious practice took a dramatic downward plunge. Nearly every country in the Western world saw a major decline, and the same broad trends were seen both in the Protestant churches and in the Roman Catholic Church. As was shown in Chapter 3, church-going in some countries was falling, albeit slowly, in the later 1950s or early 1960s. But in the later 1960s the fall was more rapid, and it was also hitting countries or religious communities which had hitherto remained immune. In the ten years between 1965 and 1975 large numbers of people lost the habit of regular church-going. Protestant churches saw a serious drop in membership. The Catholic Church saw a mass exit from the priesthood and a large fall in clerical recruitment. Many Protestant churches suffered similar problems, though on a smaller scale. Participation in the rites of passage dropped in some countries, though here there were considerable local differences.

The crisis of these years was experienced most acutely by Catholics and most of all by the Catholic clergy. In the 1950s Catholics still went to church more often than Protestants—though there were some major exceptions to this rule, as, for example, in the 'dechristianized' regions of France. Priests and nuns played a larger part in the lives of the faithful than did their Protestant counterparts, and they tended to enjoy a higher status. Above all, the confessional gave the Catholic priest a unique potential both to control and to support the faithful. By the later 1960s, the behaviour of the faithful was changing rapidly, and equally so was the status and role of the clergy. Many of the clergy had the feeling that the rug was being pulled from under their feet; and laypeople watched with equal bewilderment as more and more priests announced that they were going to get married—often to a former nun.[1]

---

[1] Martine Sevegrand, *Vers une Église sans prêtres: La crise du clergé séculier en France* (Rennes, 2004), 239–41; Andrew Greeley, *The Catholic Revolution: New Wine, Old Wineskins and the Second Vatican Council* (Berkeley, Calif., 2004), 18.

TOWARDS A CHURCH WITHOUT PRIESTS?

In 1968 the French journalist Jacques Duquesne published a book with the title *Demain une Église sans prêtres?* (Tomorrow a Church without Priests?), but his prophecies and prescriptions were dismissed by the French bishops. In 2004, the historian Martine Sevegrand titled her book on 'The crisis of the secular clergy in France' *Vers une église sans prêtres* (Towards a Church without Priests). Armed both with hindsight and with a comprehensive range of statistics, she was able to show that the crisis of the later 1960s was part of a long-term trend, and that it would become even more acute in the 1970s. There were two aspects to this crisis: a fall in recruitment and a rise in the numbers of those who were leaving. Recruitment to the French secular clergy during the twentieth century fell into three phases. Between 1905 (the year of the Separation of church and state) and 1947 there were large fluctuations, with the highest levels being reached in the 1930s and in the period immediately after the Second World War. From 1948 to 1977 there was an almost continuous decline, with a brief respite during the Council years of the mid-1960s. Then from 1978 to 1999 the number stabilized at a very low level. The post-war peak for ordinations to the diocesan clergy was in 1947, when no less than 1,618 men had been ordained. By 1957 the figure was already down to 619. In 1968 it was 469. In 1977 only 99 new priests were ordained. But there was then a slight increase, and the level of ordinations stabilized at between 100 and 150 a year for the remainder of the twentieth century. The year 1947 was also when the number of men known to have left the ranks of the diocesan clergy was smallest—a mere 27. There was then a slow increase until 1966 when the number was 64. In 1967 the number shot up to 105, and in 1972 it was a record 225. In that year, for the first time, the number of those leaving exceeded the number of newcomers.[2]

Sevegrand's wide-ranging analysis shows that the crisis of the French diocesan clergy had many different causes. She easily refutes the idea, popular with some conservative Catholics, that it was 'the fault of Vatican II'—though clearly the impact of Vatican II has to be taken into account when explaining the peculiar atmosphere of the years around 1970. The decline in recruitment was partly due to social and educational changes, which provided alternative opportunities. As Sevegrand shows, by far the biggest drop in clerical recruitment between the 1940s and 1970s was in the traditionally Catholic and predominantly rural west of France, where the priesthood had for long been a means of upward social mobility for ambitious sons of the peasantry.[3] For those from poorer families the first point had been study at the

---

[2] Sevegrand, *Église sans prêtres*, 9–13, 17–23, 69–102.   [3] Ibid. 81.

church-run 'little seminary', which provided a level of education not easily available to poorer students elsewhere, and which offered a stepping-stone to the 'big seminary' and training for the priesthood. By the 1960s, with the expansion of secondary education, the 'little seminaries' were very much in decline. When in the 1950s clerical sociologists studied or bishops commented on the fall in recruitment, they complained that parents were discouraging their sons' vocations, because of the perception that the clergy were poorly paid and had low status. Recruitment to the diocesan clergy also suffered competition from prestigious orders, like the Jesuits and Dominicans, which did carry status, and which attracted the well-educated and those from aristocratic and upper middle-class backgrounds. A second problem was the rule of celibacy. Already in 1943 the archbishop of Cambrai complained that the church's increasingly positive view of marriage and of the sexual relationship between husband and wife was leading to a downgrading of the celibacy which had formerly been presented as the ideal.[4] Questioning of the celibacy rule was sometimes influenced by study of psychology. Sevegrand refers to the 'new perception of sexuality which imposed itself little by little, from the 1950s, among the clergy as well as in the rest of society':

Many priests have said it: celibacy is no longer seen by the people of our time as a witness to faith. With the diffusion of the findings of psychoanalysis, celibacy is more likely to provoke suspicion, and is often lived by those concerned as a deprivation without spiritual value, which is likely to result in an unbalanced personality.[5]

In the 1960s and 1970s both the issue of celibacy and that of the role and status of the clergy would play a major part both in declining recruitment, and more especially in the rising number of departures. From about 1964 American Catholics were speaking of a crisis of clerical morale.[6] Celibacy was one reason, especially in view of the increasingly positive view of sex in Catholic teaching. But there was also a feeling that while Vatican II had plenty to say about both the bishops and the laity, it had not shown much concern with priests. And as always there were complaints about the top–down style of the hierarchy—with the difference that it now seemed out of keeping with the new spirit associated with the Council. Sevegrand's study of the Dijon diocese shows the keen interest in Vatican II and the high hopes for change among the seminarians and younger priests, especially those in working-class parishes. Statements by priests who left during the 1970s indicate that, although most wanted to marry, the majority also had gone through a longer process of disillusionment with the set-apartness of the clergy and the hierarchical nature

---

[4] Sevegrand, *Église sans prêtres*, 24.   [5] Ibid. 279.

[6] Leslie Woodcock Tentler, *Catholics and Contraception: An American History* (Ithaca, NY, 2004), 232–7.

of the church. Around 1968 'declergification' became a popular slogan among the progressive clergy. They wanted priests to be allowed to marry and to work. They wanted the laity to share in many of the roles previously reserved for the priest. They were very critical of what they saw as the authoritarian and inflexible style of leadership provided by the bishops. As the vision of a radically new church faded, many of the reformers married and sought secular employment, though most of them remained Catholics.[7]

David Rice, in an international but mainly American study of priests who left active ministry from the 1960s to the 1980s, found that none of them said they had left because of loss of faith, and the only doctrinal reason mentioned was papal teaching on birth control. Falling in love was mentioned by some as the precipitating factor, but there was also a more general dissatisfaction with the way of life required of the clergy, with the way the church was run, and sometimes with the social and political role of the church. Thus, as well as the celibacy rule, the priests interviewed by Rice mentioned loneliness, resentment of their bishops, failure of the church to speak out sufficiently against the Vietnam War, and dislike of such things as having to wear a cassock.[8] In a society which valued individuality, the clerical uniform seemed to force the free person into a rigid mould—and imposed an identity which seemed not only detached from 'normal' life, but also unmasculine:

A number of priests' wives have told me their husbands have almost a physical revulsion to black, and cannot be made to wear it. I listened to a group of Italian married priests and their wives discussing the wearing of cassocks in the street, compulsory until the mid-1960s...a dreadful custom[,] one of them called it. 'I felt it was a violation of my identity and my personality,' one said. 'I could simply not be totally me while wearing it.' 'You know what they called us?' another priest said. 'The third sex. They mocked us for wearing skirts. And that's why the Church made us wear them.'[9]

Anti-clerical ribaldry was an old theme in some parts of Italy and France, but less so in the United States where, above all in Irish or Polish districts, the cassock evoked respect. But the new theme in the 1960s was the increasing priority given to individual identity and freedom, and the consequent horror of uniforms of all kinds.

Especially from 1968 this also meant a growing willingness of priests to rebel against their bishops. This rebellion was almost sure to fail, because the bishops held all of the trump cards—except for one. At a time when recruitment to the clergy was drying up, bishops needed to keep as many as

[7] Sevegrand, *Église sans prêtres*, 122–3, 165–7, 243, 251–75, 279–80.
[8] David Rice, *Shattered Vows: Exodus from the Priesthood* (London, 1990), 27–45.
[9] Ibid. 31.

possible of the existing diocesan personnel on board. However, many bishops preferred the devastation of their diocese to compromising with challenges to their authority. Rice cites the case of the Texan diocese of San Antonio, where Archbishop Lucey combined militancy on labour and social issues with an ultra-authoritarian style of leadership and a habit of transferring troublesome priests to remote parishes. After sixty-eight priests signed a letter to the pope calling for a Vatican inquiry, and went on to hold a press conference where they publicized their grievances, the ring-leaders were suspended and many others resigned.[10] A more famous case was the archdiocese of Chicago which was embroiled in prolonged conflict between the archbishop and the Association of Chicago Priests, formed in 1966.[11]

Events in Rome also had a major influence on the exodus from the priesthood. Paul VI's more generous treatment of those seeking laicization made it easier for clergy to leave, and also reduced the stigma that they often suffered. At the same time a series of controversial decisions by pope or bishops in the later 1960s and early 1970s bitterly disappointed many of the clergy. Already in 1967, Paul VI's encyclical reaffirming the rule of clerical celibacy dealt a major blow to the reformers. And in 1971 the synod of bishops would reject all proposals for some modification of the rules. Sevegrand attributes the record number of departures by French priests in 1972 to a combination of the bishops' decision on celibacy and the Pope's simplification in the same year of the laicization procedures.[12] Then on 29 July 1968 there came *Humanae Vitae*—not the least of the shocks which hit the world during that fateful year. The pope had appointed a commission, headed by Cardinal Döpfner, archbishop of Munich, to reconsider the church's teaching on birth control. The commission recommended that the use of contraceptives by married couples should be allowed. Paul VI decided to reject this recommendation and his encyclical reaffirmed that only 'natural' methods of birth control, namely the 'rhythm method', were acceptable. The encyclical was doubly shocking: not only had many Catholics begun to use contraceptives in expectation that the official teaching would change, but the Pope's decision to reject the advice of an expert commission, including bishops, as well as theologians and doctors, seemed to make a nonsense of the principle of 'collegiality' promulgated at Vatican II.[13] This was a major factor in the catastrophic movement

[10] Rice, *Shaltered Vows*, 10–21.

[11] Charles Dahm, *Power and Authority in the Catholic Church: Cardinal Cody in Chicago* (Notre Dame, Ind., 1981). One of the disaffected Chicago priests, the sociologist Andrew Greeley, referred to Archbishop Cody as 'a psychopathic paranoid'. Greeley, *Catholic Revolution*, 199.

[12] Sevegrand, *Église sans prêtres*, 78–80.

[13] Martine Sevegrand, *Les enfants du bon Dieu: Les catholiques français et la procréation au XXe siècle* (Paris, 1995) provides a detailed account of teaching on birth control both by the French

of resignations from the priesthood during the following four years. Just as older Americans are said to remember what they were doing when they heard the news of John Kennedy's death, and middle-aged Britons remember what they were doing when they heard of Margaret Thatcher's resignation, older Catholic priests are said to remember what they were doing when they heard the news of Paul VI's condemnation of contraception. In a typical story, an American priest driving along a remote country road heard the news on his car radio and uttered the two words, 'I quit'.[14] Tentler comments that 'It was priests who were that encyclical's principal victims.'[15] Some priests resigned because they would not enforce the papal teaching in the confessional. Some priests were suspended after declaring their opposition, Admittedly bishops varied greatly in their treatment of dissenters. The archbishop of Washington DC suspended a large group of priests, but other bishops, such as Dearden of Detroit, who was thought to have been disappointed by the encyclical, avoided conflict.[16] In London dissidents were treated more severely by Archbishop Cowderoy south of the river, than by Archbishop Heenan on the north side.[17] In France the initial outcry following the publication of the encyclical soon died down, partly because the bishops wanted to avoid a showdown, but also because radical clergy were much more interested in other issues, ranging from a general overhaul of the structures both of the church and of French society, to support for revolutionary movements in Third World countries.[18]

The encyclical did, however, have profound effects on the relations of lay Catholics with their clergy and bishops, even where open conflict was avoided. According to one Detroit priest: 'There was nothing more liberating for Catholic people than that document [*Humanae Vitae*] in the sense that it was so clear that the Church was wrong.' Tentler argues that, as increasing numbers of American Catholics decided to ignore the encyclical, the authority of the bishops was eroded. At the same time, the decline in confession removed what many priests had regarded as their most important role. In Detroit, where the decline in confession, attributed to reluctance to confess the use of contraceptives, had been noted in 1966, the sacrament was said to be in a state of collapse by 1969. In that year one priest commented: 'The once familiar steady flow of penitents has in most places slowed down to a very unsteady trickle.

hierarchy and by successive popes; Tentler, *Contraception*, does the same for the United States, but with more emphasis on the grassroots.

[14] Rice, *Shattered Vows*, 41. [15] Tentler, *Contraception*, 246–7.

[16] Ibid. 257, 264–79.

[17] Adrian Hastings, *A History of English Christianity 1920–1985* (London, 1986), 576.

[18] Sevegrand, *Enfants*, 334–5, 360–4.

Even the big feasts no longer draw crowds to the confessional.'[19] A survey of American Catholics in 1974 suggested a decline that was less dramatic but still very significant. Since 1963 the proportion saying they went to confession at least monthly had fallen from 38 per cent to 17 per cent.[20] In 1968, a young priest from New York state asked: 'Is confession, as some supposedly knowledgeable theologians predict, on the way out? If so, where do I fit in as a priest? How am I valuable to the people? What is my role, my identity in the world?'[21]

Protestant clergymen, and the still small numbers of Protestant clergy-women, took no vow of celibacy, but in the 1960s they were experiencing some of the same pressures and doubts that afflicted their Catholic counterparts. In the Church of England numbers of ordinations had fluctuated much less than in the French Catholic Church: the good years were nothing like as good, and the bad years were not as bad. But here too the later 1960s and early 1970s saw declining numbers, both because of a fall in recruitment and probably because of a rise in the numbers of those resigning their orders or seeking other employment—though here precise figures are not available. Ordinations had hovered around 450 a year between 1950 and 1957, before rising to a post-war peak of 636 in 1963.[22] But then there was a drop to 393 in 1971 and 273 in 1976. A survey undertaken in 1973–4 found that, in a large sample of men ordained between 1951 and 1965, 4.9 per cent had resigned their orders, and 7.1 per cent had found employment outside the church. The authors of the survey commented that most of the latter had left either for financial or marital reasons, 'or because of the tensions and frustrations associated with the Church in general and the clerical role in particular'.[23]

The malaise that many clergy felt in these years was well illustrated in a book on *The Clerical Profession*, written by Anthony Russell, rector of Whitchurch, a small town in Shropshire. Apart from its value as a work of sociological history, the book could also be seen as a poignant statement of how an Anglican clergyman saw his own profession in the 1970s. 'In contemporary society,' he wrote, 'the clergy no longer occupy a position of prominence or centrality in the social, cultural, intellectual, political or any other aspect of national life.' He attributed this situation partly to the fact that contemporary English society 'is work-centred and work-orientated', and that most of what the clergyman does is not seen as work—though this kind of criticism had been equally common in the nineteenth century. The new factor which Russell

[19] Tentler, *Contraception*, 244–5, 258–63, 273.
[20] Greeley, *Catholic Revolution*, 39.   [21] Tentler, *Contraception*, 245.
[22] For ordination statistics, see *Official Yearbook of the Church of England*.
[23] Anthony Russell, *The Clerical Profession* (London, 1980), 265.

identified was increasing competition from the 'caring professions' and from specialized organizations, such as the Samaritans, which had taken over many of the clergy's former roles. Particularly traumatic for the clergy, in his view, were changes in the 1960s. Here he mentioned not only the youth culture but, more unexpectedly 'the emergence of new essentially working-class rather than elitist value patterns and behavioural codes, created and propagated by the media; and perhaps most significant of all, the marked shift of political power away from the professions and middle classes'.[24] In retrospect it is hard to agree with the latter claim. However, it can more convincingly be argued that the 1960s saw the erosion of standards of respectability in matters of dress, language, and manners, which had been accepted not only by most middle-class professionals but by many working-class people, and with which most of the clergy identified themselves. Also hinted at here is the role of the media in subverting the traditional values of which many of the clergy saw themselves as guardians. They felt a particular sense of betrayal when the BBC, with its strongly Christian traditions, seemed to be leading the demolition work, sometimes with the connivance of radical or maverick clergy. Whereas in the 1940s and 1950s most clergy were all too aware that they had to contend with widespread religious apathy, they could at least be reassured that had the support of the BBC, most of the press, and the school system. In the 1960s they often had a feeling of fighting a lone battle with few supporters—hence the often shrill tone of their complaints in letters to the *Church Times*. Analysis of reports and letters in this paper during 1965 suggests widespread concern at the treatment of religion on television and, to a lesser extent, radio. The main subjects of complaint were ridicule of religion on the satirical programme *Not so much a Programme, More a Way of Life*, or in the *Wednesday Play*, undue emphasis on heterodox, atheistic, or anti-church viewpoints in religious programmes, such as *Meeting Point*, and insufficient religious programming at times when such programmes should have been prioritized, such as Sundays or Good Friday. The central issue was whether Britain was still 'a Christian country', with all that this entailed.[25]

---

[24] Ibid. 127–9, 258, 284; see also Paul A. Welsby, *A History of the Church of England 1945– 1980* (Oxford, 1984), 104–5. For critics of the Anglican clergy *c.*1860–1914, see Hugh McLeod, 'Varieties of Anticlericalism in Later Victorian and Edwardian England,' in Nigel Aston and Matthew Cragoe (eds.), *Anticlericalism in Britain c.1500–1914* (Stroud, 2000), 198–220.

[25] For examples of articles or letters criticizing either particular TV programmes or the treatment of religion by TV more generally, see *Church Times* (5 and 26 Feb., 12 Mar., 2, 23, and 30 Apr. 1965), though an article on 1 Jan. welcomed the large audiences for TV religious programmes. In view of Callum Brown's claim (*Religion and Society in Twentieth-Century Britain*, 270) that 'The churches were obsessed with sex in the sixties,' it is worth stressing that few of these complaints focused on the treatment of sex on TV.

SHRINKING CONGREGATIONS

Probably every Western country, with the exception of Ireland, saw a decline in church-going between 1958 and 1974, and in many cases the decline was severe. Protestant attendance was dropping in the later 1950s and early 1960s, while the Catholic decline was mainly concentrated in the period between 1965 and 1975. But when the decline in Catholic church-going came, it was often very rapid.

In the 1950s there were still parts of rural Catholic Europe where the majority of the population went to church every Sunday. By the 1970s such places were rare. The drop in church-going was most severe in such Catholic strongholds as the southern Netherlands, Flanders, Brittany, or Quebec. In the Netherlands 64 per cent of Catholics attended mass on a given Sunday in 1965, but in 1975 it was 31 per cent. In Montreal there was a similar drop from 61 per cent to 30 per cent between 1961 and 1971.[26] In all probability the decline was greatest among those in their teens and twenties. But in view of the scale of the decline, there must also have been many adults who had been regular church-goers all their lives, but who largely or completely gave it up in the 1960s or early 1970s. The causes of this decline continue to be hotly debated. Traditionalists blame the church's problems on the Council, while progressives blame them on *Humanae Vitae*. Even if the Council had never taken place, the church would have had to face many of the same issues, certainly including contraception and a decline in the number of priests. However, the fact that the Council did happen shaped the specific form that the crisis took. It raised hopes very high—often for them to be dashed when it became clear that actual results would fall far short of what seemed to have been promised. At the same time, reforms alienated some working-class and peasant Catholics—not so much the vernacular liturgy as the removal of statues from churches, the discouragement of various forms of folk Catholicism, and the dropping of such badges of identity as the eating of fish on Fridays. In the years following the Council congregations not only became smaller—but following Protestant trends they also became more middle-class.[27]

In retrospect the abandonment of regular church-going could be interpreted as emancipation from an oppressive obligation—and indeed the very high levels of religious practice in many Catholic communities could hardly

---

[26] Jan Kerkhofs, 'The Shortage of Priests in Europe,' in Kerkhofs (ed.), *Europe without Priests?* (London, 1995), 11; Michael Gauvreau, *The Catholic Origins of Quebec's Quiet Revolution, 1931–1970* (Montreal and Kingston, Ontario, 2005), 307–22.

[27] Michael Hornsby-Smith, *Roman Catholics in England* (Cambridge, 1987), 61, 66; Gérard Cholvy and Yves-Marie Hilaire, *Histoire religieuse de la France contemporaine 1930–1988* (Toulouse, 1988), 320–4.

have been maintained without considerable community pressures. Even in England, where Catholic church-going was lower than in for instance the United States, Canada, or the Netherlands, it is noticeable that Catholics who gave up going to church in the 1960s and 1970s often carried a continuing burden of resentment that one seldom finds among Protestants who gave up at the same time. This seems to be because the latter were more likely to feel that going to church was something which they had chosen, and when they stopped they faced fewer social penalties. Catholics often felt that their religious behaviour was under constant scrutiny from their family, and sometimes from priests, nuns, or teachers. This could be especially intense in situations where Catholics had a strong sense of communal identity and loyalty, often bound up with ethnic identity or awareness of a history of persecution or discrimination. Loyalty could thus be seen as the supreme virtue, and to put individual preference or principle first was a form of betrayal.

Anne Kelly, born in 1945 into a working-class family in Preston, can be taken as an example both of the rigour with which a Catholic identity was inculcated and of the bitterness of those who rebelled against it. Her parents were loyal Catholics and one of her uncles was a priest. Priests often visited, and 'It was always, yes father, no father'. She went to church regularly until she married in 1965:

We had to go to church every . . . in fact in Lent we had to go every morning. Yes and it was quite a walk, you know. Then, I think that's what has turned me against it. Now anyway, because I don't force my daughter at all. I only go to church if I have to, which is when there is anything on. I think it has turned us against it completely, you know. . . . So when we got married we just didn't go as much. Occasionally we went, or if we knew that my mum and dad were coming down, and they would ask us about church.

She went on later to complain about how the priests were always asking for money:

It got pretty terrible you know. Every Sunday he was up in the pulpit demanding money more or less, and if you didn't it was hell fire kind of thing. I mean a lot of people actually left the church because of that. And it used to be frightening to go to church, because I got at one point, every time I used to go to church I used to come out because I used to feel sick. I just couldn't stand it any more.[28]

She added that the clergy had changed because they had to: 'I think they would have lost nearly everybody.'[29]

Peter van Rooden, who has conducted an oral history project on changes in Dutch religion, argues that before the 1960s Dutch religious practice was

<hr />

[28] SFL, interview with Mrs R1P, 19–22.   [29] Ibid. 63–4.

to a large extent part of membership of the group, and often accepted in an unreflecting way as something which one had to do. This did not necessarily mean that this compulsion was seen as oppressive: in fact he stresses the ways in which people 'negotiated' the rules, as well as the kinds of comfort and reassurance that these rules could provide. He suggests that the decline in religious practice in the 1960s and 1970s arose not so much from people making a clear break, as from a gradual realization that practices which had once been taken for granted were no longer so important or necessary.[30] In Quebec, where the decline of a once all-embracing Catholic culture was equally rapid, a priest claimed in 1971 that: 'Religious practice is abandoned without drama as one would throw off an old, ill-fitting garment . . . more often, people leave the church without making a sound, sneaking out by the back door.'[31]

Admittedly, major changes in one's personal life or particular experiences could have a catalytic effect. For instance, in the case of women who gave up going to church in middle age, this seems to have often been associated with divorce or a return to study after children left home. For one Catholic woman a turning-point was hearing the song 'Jesus redt' (Jesus saves) by Robert Long in 1974: 'There [the church] was made fun of. I found it embarrassing, but I also thought "that's how it is". It was full of criticism that we felt as well, "God, you have done some strange things", criticism of the Pope. Marvellous.'[32]

Exposure to unorthodox religious ideas or to criticism of the church was coming through television, the press, and popular music, and could no longer be dismissed as coming only from discredited minorities, such as Communists, or from 'bigoted' members of other religious denominations. Responses varied hugely. But a significant number found that their own scarcely recognized doubts were being articulated and authorized.

In countries such as Britain, where church-going was already relatively low, the main cause of declining church membership was a crisis of recruitment. Young people who had gone to Sunday School as children, and in many cases had continued to go to church as teenagers, were leaving in their later teens or early twenties, and were not making the clear commitment of becoming a church member. Historians have often had cause to be grateful for the statistically conscious officials of the Methodist Church of Great Britain who have enabled historians to trace the denomination's rise and decline in unusual detail. Methodist membership was static in the 1950s, but then dropped by 14 per cent between 1960 and 1970, and by a catastrophic 22 per cent between 1970 and 1980. An analysis by Clive Field shows that the proportion of

---

[30] Peter van Rooden, 'Oral History and the Strange Demise of Dutch Christianity,' www.xs4all.nl/pvrooden.
[31] Gauvreau, *Quiet Revolution*, 307.   [32] Van Rooden, 'Oral History,' 22–5.

members resigning rose only slightly in the 1960s; by far the biggest cause of the loss was a 30 per cent drop in the recruitment of new members—which was followed by an even bigger drop in the 1970s.[33] In the 1950s, the numbers of newcomers far exceeded the older members lost through death, though resignations were sufficiently numerous to ensure that total membership remained stationary. By the later 1960s there were even a few districts where the numbers of deaths exceeded the number of recruits. The crisis of recruitment affected all parts of England and Wales with relatively few regional variations. However, it was most acute in the old strongholds of rural and working-class Methodism. Thus the Cornwall district, where only 1.6 per cent of all members at the start of 1967 had joined in the course of the previous year, had the worst record of recruitment, followed in ascending order by Sheffield, Lincoln, and Darlington. At the opposite end of the scale, by far the most buoyant district was Cardiff, where 3.4 per cent of the members were newcomers, followed in descending order by York, London South-West, and Southampton.[34] The religious crisis of the 1960s is too often attributed to gilded youth in capital cities and university towns. But equally significant were changes in villages and small industrial towns, where new free-time activities were becoming available as alternatives to those provided by the churches, where old standards of respectability associated with the Nonconformist chapels were losing their influence, and where the children of chapel-going families were disproportionately likely to go on to higher education and to move away from the home environment.[35]

Three surveys of British university students throw light on the chronology of declining church-going. A survey of students at Oxford and Cambridge universities in 1956 suggested that 63 per cent of women students and 51 per cent of men students were church-goers.[36] At Sheffield University, as already mentioned, 46 per cent of students claimed in 1961 to be church-goers. By 1972, however, this figure had slipped to 25 per cent, and by 1985 it was 15 per cent.[37] A broadly similar trend, but with more detail and some

[33] Clive Field, 'Joining and Leaving British Methodism since the 1960s,' in Leslie J. Francis and Yaacov J. Katz (eds.), *Joining and Leaving Religion: Research Perspectives* (Leominster, 2000), 57–85.

[34] Detailed figures are in *Minutes of the Annual Conference of the Methodist Church*, 1967.

[35] Robert Moore, in a study of Methodism in Durham mining villages, based on research in the 1960s, found that while most of the older male Methodists were miners, none of the younger Methodists was; among the lay leaders of local Methodism in the inter-war years, most of whom were miners, none had a son who had gone down the pit. See his *Pit-Men, Politics and Preachers* (London, 1974), 149.

[36] Ian Jones, 'The "Mainstream" Churches in Birmingham, c.1945–1998: The Local Church and Generational Change' (Ph.D. thesis, University of Birmingham, 2000), 165–8.

[37] David Bebbington, 'The Secularization of British Universities,' in George Marsden and Bradley Longfield (eds.), *The Secularization of the Academy* (New York, 1992), 268.

difference in chronology is shown by the survey of students at Girton, a Cambridge college where at that time all students were women.[38] Here respondents were asked if 'religion was important' to them while they were at Girton. Among students entering between 1950 and 1954, no less than 70 per cent answered 'Yes'. However, for those entering between 1955 and 1959 there was already a drop to 49 per cent, after which, in spite of fluctuations from year to year, the average remained constant for fifteen years. It was 47 per cent between 1960 and 1969, and 50 per cent between 1970 and 1974. The big drop came in the years 1975–9, when the average plunged to 31 per cent. The major decline thus came a little later in Girton than in Sheffield, but the pattern is similar.

The Girton survey also sheds light on the patterns of joining and leaving the church. A significant number of the graduates for whom religion was 'important' in the early 1950s subsequently gave up their involvement, though a very substantial 46 per cent were still involved in organized religion at the time of the survey in the later 1990s. Two gave up going to church soon after graduation and another did so in the 1960s. One, who had been a Catholic, switched in the 1960s to a mixture of Christian Science and Buddhism. It may well be that the high profile which religious groups like SCM, CICCU (the Cambridge branch of the strongly evangelical IVF), and the various denominational societies enjoyed in the early 1950s helped to draw in some of the less religiously committed, who lost interest when they moved to a different environment. Also at this time there were probably some students who came from a class background where attendance at Anglican services was socially expected. In the 1960s and 1970s, though the proportion of students for whom religion was 'important' was lower, most of those who had been religiously active as students remained so in middle age. Of the students entering in 1961 and 1962, where 48 per cent had said religion was 'important' at Girton, 43 per cent were church-goers thirty years later. There had been some changes in between: for instance one woman who gave up church-going soon after graduation returned some twenty years later. None of those for whom religion had been 'unimportant' as a student was now a regular church-goer, though a few were occasional church-goers or described themselves as 'religious' without being attached to a specific faith. Among those entering in 1971 and 1972, 32 per cent said that religion had been 'important' and 32 per cent were involved in organized religion at the time of the survey. A few had switched from one camp to the other in the intervening period, but most remained where they were. Among those entering between 1975 and 1978, 32 per cent said religion had been important; twenty years later 37 per cent

[38] 'University and Life Experience,' Girton College Archive.

were involved in some kind of organized religion. Some of the increase seems to have been due to the return as adults of those who had gone to church as teenagers but had been less involved while at university. Some perhaps liked the increasing availability of more flexible religious identities, such as the respondent who said she was a mixture of Church of England and New Age, or another who had rejected the ancestral Catholic faith but was now a mixture of Anglican and agnostic. Once again, however, most of those for whom religion had been important as a student were still religiously active at around 40, and most of those for whom religion had been unimportant remained uninvolved. Experiences and decisions as a teenager seem to have been of lasting significance for many. All of those for whom religion had been 'important' at university had had some exposure to religious worship as children or teenagers and the majority had been going to church regularly as teenagers; all of the relatively small number of professed atheists had already rejected religion before going to university. It is striking that still in the 1990s this group of highly educated women, many of them occupying prestigious positions in the professions, business, or the civil service, was reporting levels of religious practice well above the national average. Certainly this evidence is often imprecise and sometimes ambiguous. But, until more evidence is available, Callum Brown's contention that the main drivers of church decline in the later twentieth century have been women and members of elites needs to be treated with caution.[39]

In the United States poll data suggested that a dramatic generational divide was opening up in the 1960s. When Americans were asked in 1955 whether they had been to church during the previous week there was hardly any difference between the responses of those in different age-bands. From 1958, however, church-going by the under-30s was in decline, while the habits of older Americans changed much more slowly. Thus between 1955 and 1970 self-reported attendance fell by 15 points for those aged 21–9, and by 7 points for those aged 30–49, while the rate for those aged over 50 remained unchanged. (Admittedly there is the possibility that younger people were readier to *admit* that they had not been to church, and that polls may therefore exaggerate the extent of the generation gaps; but there is no evidence to confirm or refute this surmise.)[40]

Patterns of detachment from the church varied from country to country, but often it took a step-by-step form, with regular attendance at services declining first, and declining participation in the rites of passage coming only

[39] Callum G. Brown, *Religion and Society in Twentieth-Century Britain* (London, 2006), 226–7, 278.

[40] Dean Hoge, *Commitment on Campus: Change in Religion and Values over Five Decades* (Philadelphia, 1974), 168–9.

later. Here one can compare the Dutch-speaking regions of Belgium with England and Wales. Northern Belgium is typical of those regions of Catholic Europe which retained high levels of religious practice, especially in rural areas, up to the mid-1960s, but then saw a severe decline. Thus average mass attendance fell from 52 per cent to 39 per cent in only six years between 1967 and 1973. However, participation in the rites of passage was scarcely affected in that period. In 1973, 94 per cent of infants received a Catholic baptism, 91 per cent of those dying had a Catholic funeral, and 88 per cent of weddings were Catholic. Only in the later 1970s and 1980s was there a large drop in Catholic weddings and a smaller drop in baptisms.[41] In England and Wales, far fewer people went to church regularly, and the drop in church attendance in this period was more gradual.[42] However, the 1960s saw quite a big drop in numbers of baptisms and religious marriages. The proportion of church weddings, which had stood at around 70 per cent from 1934 and 1962, then fell to 66 per cent in 1967 and 54 per cent in 1972. England and Wales were pioneering in the 1960s a trend which hit most parts of western and northern Europe in the 1970s. In the 1960s only Sweden, Scotland, and West Germany saw a similar fall in religious weddings—respectively from 90 to 79 per cent, from 81 to 71 per cent, and from 80 to 72 per cent. In France, Belgium, Switzerland, Italy, Portugal, and most of the Nordic countries the first major drop came in the 1970s.[43]

THE DECLINE OF CHRISTIAN SOCIALIZATION

The proportion of babies born in England to receive an Anglican baptism fell from 55 to 47 per cent between 1960 and 1970. While relatively few figures for baptisms are available, it would seem that England, West Germany, and France were leading where neighbouring countries would follow in the 1970s.[44] The picture is further complicated by differences in the importance attached to

---

[41] Liliane Voyé, 'Belgique: Crise de la civilisation paroissiale et recompositions du croire,' in Grace Davie ansd Danièle Hervieu-Léger (eds.), *Identités religieuses en Europe* (Paris, 1996), 203.

[42] The first reasonably reliable estimate of national church attendance in 20th-cent. England was the Bible Society census of 1979 which found that around 11% of adults attended church on an average Sunday. See Peter Brierley (ed.), *Prospects for the Eighties* (London, 1980), 23. Various local surveys in the 1950s and 1960s suggested that weekly attendance rates of 10–16% were typical. See David Martin, *A Sociology of English Religion* (London, 1967), 45–7; P. D. Varney, 'Religion in Rural Norfolk,' in David Martin and Michael Hill (eds.), *A Sociological Yearbook of Religion in Britain*, iii (London, 1970), 67.

[43] Alfred Dittgen, 'Évolution des rites religieux dans l'Europe contemporaine: Statistiques et contextes,' *Annales de Démographie Historique* (2003–2), 127.

[44] Ibid. 128; Robin Gill, *The Myth of the Empty Church* (London, 1993), 218.

particular rites of passage, whether generally or within specific religious traditions. For instance, in many countries there has been a considerable decline
in the proportion of religious marriages, but a smaller decline in baptisms,
and very little decline in religious funerals. Equally some rites have remained
especially popular within particular traditions, for instance, first communion
in Catholicism and confirmation in Lutheranism.

Fewer children and young people were being socialized into membership
of the church. In the nineteenth and early twentieth centuries, when the
great majority of young people in Western countries received some kind of
Christian upbringing, many went on to rebel as adolescents or young adults.
But by the later 1960s and 1970s an increasing number of young people were
receiving little or no religious upbringing. In Scotland, the proportion of
children enrolled in Presbyterian Sunday Schools halved between 1956 and
1975; the proportion of English teenagers confirmed into the Anglican Church
also halved during the same period.[45]

Oral history illustrates some of the ways in which this was happening. In
the 1960s and 1970s there was an increase in the number of children who
never went to Sunday School at all, but there were also many children who
spent a few years in Sunday School but then left, whether because of lack
of interest, other attractions, or changes in the ways in which their parents
wanted to spend Sunday. The journalist Blake Morrison claims to have been
the only child in Christian history who begged his parents to be allowed to
join a church choir—only to meet considerable resistance from his father, who
said it would 'bugger up Sunday'.[46] From the 1960s, and more especially in the
1970s and 1980s, a wider range of options was opening up both for children
and for parents, and parents were less willing to enforce attendance if the child
showed reluctance. This was partly because of changing styles of parenting,
with greater stress on listening to the child and respecting her or his wishes. It
was partly because as ways of spending Sunday became more varied, it was no
longer possible to say that going to Sunday School was simply what you have
to do on Sundays.

For boys and girls born in north Lancashire in the 1930s, 1940s, and early
1950s it was normal to have at least some experience of Sunday School. For the
next generation, born between about 1955 and 1975 the situation was more
complicated. Some parents remained as strict about Sunday School as their
own parents had been On the other hand, Irene Wells (born 1931, Lancaster),
a factory worker married to a painter and decorator, had a 'quiet Sunday': 'my
three lads have never had anything to do with religion'. Irene came from a
strongly Catholic family but had married a Protestant, and her father blamed

---

[45] Brown, *Death*, 168, 191.   [46] *Guardian* (Weekend Magazine, 1 Apr. 2006), 18.

the boys' bad behaviour on the fact that they had not been to a Catholic school.[47] In the 1950s and early 1960s this was still untypical, at least in north Lancashire—admittedly an area of above average levels of church-going.[48] Among children born in the later 1960s and 1970s there was a growing number of those who never had any exposure to Sunday School. But even then they may have been a minority. Among seventeen parents born between 1941 and 1951 and interviewed in an Essex University oral history project, ten had sent their offspring to Sunday School or taken them to church for at least some part of their childhood.[49]

The survey of women, predominantly from middle and upper middle-class backgrounds, who attended Girton College, Cambridge, showed a decline between 1950 and 1977 in the extent of childhood exposure to organized religion, but the decline was not dramatic.[50] Even the students entering university at the latter date had generally had some involvement in church or Sunday School, usually extending at least to the age of 12 or 13. In a sample of respondents to the survey who had entered between 1950 and 1954, only 8 per cent had not attended religious worship at all as a child and 58 per cent had done so right through their teenage years—sometimes at a boarding school, rather than with their parents. Among the respondents entering in 1961 or 1962, 10 per cent had had no involvement at all in religious worship, while 48 per cent had attended church throughout their teenage years. Of those arriving in 1971 or 1972, 5 per cent had no involvement at all, while 32 per cent attended throughout their teens. And of those entering between 1975 and 1978 there were 14 per cent with no such involvement and 37 per cent who attended throughout their teens. The great majority of children, at least in this largely affluent section of the population, were continuing to attend church or synagogue for at least part of childhood, but the extent of this involvement was tending gradually to diminish. Sometimes this was because of a definite decision by the child: for instance a woman entering in 1976 stated that she 'refused to go' to her parents' Methodist church when she was 13; another, entering in 1977, had been an active Anglican until she 'lost her faith' at 16. In the case of those who stopped somewhere between the ages of 7 and 12 the reasons are not stated but were probably different.

More typical than the families which had no connection with the church were those where the children went to Sunday School for a while and then left,

---

[47] SFL, interview with Mrs H5L, 38, 119–20.

[48] According to Brierley (ed.), *Prospects*, 74, Lancashire, with 16%, as against a national average of 11%, had the highest level of church-going in England in 1979.

[49] These comments are based on the interviews in the Families, Social Mobility and Ageing oral history project.

[50] 'University and Life Experience,' Girton Archives.

or where some of the children went to Sunday School and others did not, or where the parents insisted on Sunday School for a time, but then got interested in doing something else. In many cases one or more of the children lost interest in going to Sunday School and the parents either could not and did not want to force them. Doreen Jackson (born 1936, Barrow) sent her daughters Janet (born 1964) and Rachel (born 1970) to Sunday School and encouraged them to join the Guides, but Rachel 'opted out'. When asked if she brought them up the way she had been brought up, she replied:

No, not really, you couldn't bring Rachel up the way I was brought up. My father was head of the house and what father said was law. My family haven't been brought up that way. They have been brought up to say please and thank-you, but they don't even do that now, because it isn't fashion now, is it? They tend to go with the crowd now, don't they? It's a sad, sad world; no respect.[51]

With growing opportunities for Sunday sport in the 1970s and 1980s, sport often took the place of Sunday School. Indeed some parents saw them as equivalents: wholesome activities which could keep youngsters out of mischief and further their moral development. Doreen Bennett (born Lancashire, 1946) had a daughter in 1968 and a son in 1970. The daughter went to Sunday School for a while but it did not last. Now their Sunday revolved round sport.[52] It was a similar story with Sandra Cook. When asked about how she had brought up her two boys she replied:

I suppose morals is another thing, you know, don't, be careful what you're doing, and, but I think sport helps, you see, we've encouraged them in sport, and I think that gives discipline again, when you're playing a team game, you're disciplined okay. I mean they've both played sport, football, cricket, soccer, tennis, squash, badminton, you name it, in competitive ways since, well, nine. And I think that's it, we haven't, we tried Sunday School, we tried clubs, it didn't work, so we came away from all that.[53]

Again, the weekend meant sport. Roy Wilmot (born 1940, Lancaster) recalled that his wife had taken their son, who had been born in 1960, to the Catholic church until he was about 7 or 8, but by then he was increasingly involved in sport, and before long the parents spent Sunday watching their boy playing football. Roy was himself a fervent footballer, and said that he regarded going to a football match as being as good as going to church.[54]

Not only was there a widening range of activities available on Sunday: many parents felt that their children must make their own choices, and that it would be wrong to force anything upon them. Susan Williams (born 1951, Manchester) was not herself a church-goer, though she had been brought up

[51] SFL, interview with Mrs W6B, 25.   [52] FSMA, interview 81.
[53] Ibid., interview 176.   [54] SFL, interview with Mr W5L, 71–2.

in the Church of England: her daughter went to a Catholic Sunday School 'because she wants to go. It was her idea.'[55] Quite possibly she was spurred on by a Catholic friend, though with diminishing levels of attendance at Sunday Schools the time-honoured pattern of going to church because a friend wants to go was becoming more unusual. Pauline Watson (born 1951, Liverpool), who had never had much interest in religion, said she had asked her daughter if she wanted to go to Sunday School, but she said 'No'.[56] Judith Mann (born 1946, London) sent her children to Sunday School, but became a bit disconcerted by the degree of zeal, especially of her elder daughter. Starting with the Church of England, the daughter had moved on to a Community Church. Judith was grateful that she did not have to worry about drink and drugs, but hoped that 'they're not so influenced that they're not thinking themselves'.[57]

This parental libertarianism was not entirely new. Rose Banton (born 1932, Lancaster), whose first child was born in 1952, said that: 'They never wanted to, so we didn't push them you know.'[58] But by the 1970s it had become a new orthodoxy. Parents who wanted to insist on their children going to church had to find some quite good arguments to justify something that seemed so much in conflict with contemporary ideas of free self-development, and a horror of anything that might suggest 'brain-washing'. Susan Atkins (born 1947, Preston), a former teacher, who at the time of interviews was a full-time housewife with four children, commented: 'I mean we did think about it, whether one ought to sort of let them make their own decisions when they get older, but they make their own decisions when they get older anyway.'[59] A few years earlier, Margaret Tranter, who was herself an agnostic, had reached a similar conclusion. She had an ulterior motive for sending her son (born 1964) to Sunday School, which was that it would help him to get into an Anglican secondary school, which she regarded as the best in the area:

What I intellectualised in my mind was this: that when people talk about giving their child a choice about religion, what they often mean is that there is no choice. Because if the child never goes to a church or Sunday School how can they ever make a conscious choice? So I decided that by sending him to Sunday School I was giving him a genuine choice. In other words he'd be taught all the things he wasn't being taught at home and so he would, you know, have this basic grounding in what the Christian faith was about for two or three years.[60]

The oral history evidence does not suggest any sudden collapse of Sunday School, but rather a gradual decline from the 1950s onwards, caused by a wide range of factors, including a weakening of the social pressures which had

---

[55] FSMA, interview 114.	[56] Ibid., interview 113.	[57] Ibid., interview 155.
[58] SFL, interview with Mrs T2L, 66.	[59] Ibid., Interview with Mrs B10P, 65.
[60] Ibid., interview with Mrs B4L, 86–7.

caused indifferent and even atheistic parents to send their children, the grow-ing availability of other activities on Sundays, and the reluctance of parents to force anything upon their children that was not absolutely required by the law.

The mantra that 'children should be free to decide for themselves' was being heard right across the Western world in the later 1960s and early 1970s, as parents shrank from any 'forcing religion down the throats' of their children. Meanwhile, some of the older generation feared that good habits and essential truths were getting lost in the new atmosphere of freedom. In Quebec one parent was musing in 1970:

I wonder how teachers, educators, and we the parents are going to convince children that the Catholic religion is good. In my time we were forced to line up to go to church on Sunday and then to Vespers. And the good people of that era acquired, by force of habit, a faith which ... they professed. A few wavered, but let's say that the vast majority have remained Catholic. However ... in the young people growing up under the new system, how are they going to acquire the belief that there is a God, a religion to respect, a belief?[61]

BUT CONSERVATIVE CHURCHES WERE GROWING

The crisis of the later 1960s did not hit all churches with equal severity. As I have suggested, its impact on the Roman Catholic Church was particu-larly intense. Established Protestant churches and the more liberal Protestant denominations were also badly hit. Conservative branches of Protestantism weathered the storm more effectively.

In 1972 an American Methodist, Dean Kelley, wrote a famous book entitled *Why Conservative Churches are Growing*. As his readers were well aware, the Methodists and other major 'liberal' and 'moderate' denominations, including the Northern Baptists, the Presbyterians, the Episcopalians, and the American Lutheran Church, were losing members, and many people saw this as a clear illustration of the fact that religion was doomed in the modern world. Yet, he pointed out, it was often overlooked that other churches were growing, including the Southern Baptists, the Missouri Synod Lutherans, the Assem-blies of God, the Mormons, and the Seventh-day Adventists. Some of the growing churches were small but others were big, and all of them were the-ologically conservative. Kelley was not suggesting that his fellow Methodists should convert to fundamentalism, but he did think that they could learn from more conservative Christians: it was not, he argued, the conservatism of these churches that gave them their strength, but their 'strictness'. These

[61] Gauvreau, *Quiet Revolution*, 168–9.

churches offered clear guidelines in matters of faith and morals; they expected a high level of commitment from their members; and they imposed discipline. You might not like what they stood for, but there was no doubt what it was, and this made these churches attractive.[62] As critics pointed out, Kelley was offering a general theory of why some churches prosper and others do not (like the general theory more recently offered by the sociologists, Finke and Stark,[63]) rather than a historical explanation of why churches which had prospered in the 1950s were declining in the 1960s and 1970s. But he had certainly put his finger on an important question. Moreover, the United States was only the most striking example of a wider phenomenon. In the 1960s, liberal and radical Christians had seemed to be making all the running; by the early 1970s it was clear that they had run out of steam and the growth was heavily concentrated among churches or movements that were theologically conservative, though sometimes innovative in style, methods, or organization.

To begin with some of the figures: a study of eight major Protestant denominations in the United States showed that between 1950 and 1960 their membership grew faster than the national population; that between 1960 and 1965 it grew more slowly than the population, and that between 1965 and 1975 it declined. During this latter period only the two most conservative, the Southern Baptists and (marginally) the Missouri Synod Lutherans, continued to grow. However, when these larger 'mainline' denominations were compared with a number of smaller and much more conservative churches a different picture emerged. The Assemblies of God had grown by 37 per cent between 1965 and 1975, the Seventh-day Adventists by 36 per cent, the Mormons by 31 per cent, and the Church of the Nazarene by 29 per cent. Research showed that the growing denominations had a membership which was below average in income and education, had larger than average families, and were more likely to live in the South or, more especially, the Pacific and Mountain states. They were more active in evangelism than most other denominations, but equally important may have been the fact that a higher proportion of their children remained within the denomination where they had grown up.[64]

Several small and three bigger factors seem to have contributed to the contrasting fortunes of 'liberal' and 'moderate' churches on the one hand and 'conservative' churches on the other. The smaller factors were demographic:

---

[62] Dean Kelley, *Why Conservative Churches are Growing* (New York, 1972).

[63] Roger Finke and Rodney Stark, *The Churching of America 1776–1990: The Winners and Losers in our Religious Economy* (New Brunswick, NJ, 1992).

[64] Ruth T. Doyle and Sheila M. Kelly, 'Comparison of Trends in Ten Denominations 1950–75,' in Hoge and Roozen (eds.), *Growth and Decline*, 144–59; Dean Hoge, 'A Test of Theories of Denominational Growth and Decline,' ibid. 179–97.

the more conservative churches happened to be concentrated in regions with growing populations. Between 1965 and 1975, the population of the South grew by 19.5 per cent, and that of the Pacific and Mountain states by 17.7 per cent, at a time when the North-East grew by only 4.2 per cent and the Mid-West by 6.3 per cent.[65] Conservative churches also benefited from the fact that the larger families of their members offered a pool of potential recruits.

There were, however, three larger factors, which were not exclusively American, but also help to explain the relative success of more conservative churches in other countries. First, '1968' had an enormous, and largely damaging effect on the more liberal Protestant churches, as well as on the Catholic Church, while leaving conservative churches and movements largely unscathed. Liberal Christians were deeply influenced by the movements and the ideals of those years—and indeed these movements left their mark on liberal Protestant denominations for the rest of the century. At the same time, many Christian radicals left their churches, whether because they thought them too moderate and insufficiently committed to the struggle or because they wanted to concentrate their energies on political work which seemed to be the top priority. Political differences also proved deeply divisive, especially within Christian student organizations. Meanwhile, liberal Protestant youth, often coming from relatively prosperous families and enjoying a better education, were more likely to be attracted by the counter-culture than their counterparts in more conservative denominations, who were better insulated from the secular world, and who were likely to be under heavy pressure to go out and get a job, usually of a fairly routine kind. In the 1950s, when church-going was the norm in upper middle-class families and widely practised by university students, the sons and daughters of liberal Protestant families tended to stay within the fold; in the 1960s they were the ones most likely to be attracted by the alternatives.[66]

Second, there was a symbiotic relationship between the growth of secularism and of religious conservatism. The apparent secularization of American life in the later 1960s and early 1970s drew a negative reaction from many people, and they found in conservative forms of religion a clear-cut alternative; conversely, growing religious conservatism in the 1970s prompted some secularists to declare their unbelief more loudly. The numbers of Americans with no religion continued to increase at the same time as religion was acquiring a higher public profile and political role.

---

[65] Doyle and Kelly, 'Comparison,' 148.

[66] Wuthnow, *Restructuring*, 157–64; Dean Hoge, 'National Contextual Factors Influencing Church Trends,' in Hoge and Roozen (eds.), *Growth and Decline*, 120–2.

Third, while 'liberal' and 'moderate' churches tended to favour rather formal styles of worship and preaching which appealed more strongly to the head than the heart, some conservative churches were adapting more successfully to contemporary cultural idioms, influenced by the counter-culture and by popular music. In particular the big Christian success story of the 1970s was the Charismatic Movement, an international phenomenon, which soon attracted many Catholics, as well as leading to the formation of many new Protestant congregations. The Charismatics adopted many of the doctrines and styles of worship of the Pentecostal churches, while adapting them to the needs of a relatively well-educated and prosperous, mainly white, and middle-class constituency.

Similar trends were seen in Britain, where the early 1970s brought the rise of the House Church movement. A wave of 'new churches', 'fellowships', 'Christian centres' emerged at this time. Some met initially in private homes, before moving to a school or hall, or acquiring their own premises. Many of the leaders came from a Brethren background; others had tried to introduce Charismatic practices into their Anglican, Methodist, or Baptist church, and had broken away when they met opposition—though some of the largest Charismatic congregations continued to be part of a larger denomination. They appealed especially to young well-educated people, typically employed in schools and hospitals, or as computer specialists, who liked the participatory worship and the emphasis on music, including the attempts to keep abreast of new styles, and welcomed the informal atmosphere and the absence of unnecessary taboos, but who also liked the emphasis on the Bible and the clear guidance on issues which *were* essential. Britain in the 1970s showed a similar pattern to that in the United States with smaller, generally conservative denominations growing, while the larger denominations declined—though admittedly many of the 'small' denominations were much smaller than their American counterparts, and their gains, though impressive in terms of percentages, were too modest in numerical terms to offset the losses by the well-established denominations. Thus in Britain the Mormons, Seventh-day Adventists, and Jehovah's Witnesses were growing in the 1960s and continued to do so in the 1970s and 1980s; the various Pentecostal denominations were growing in the 1970s and 1980s. The House Churches claimed very rapid growth in the 1970s and 1980s, though precise figures are lacking.[67]

---

[67] Brierley (ed.), *Prospects*, 23, found that attendance at Baptist, Independent, Pentecostal, and 'African/West Indian' churches increased between 1975 and 1979, while the Anglican, Catholic, and United Reformed Churches were all losing worshippers. See also Robert Currie, Alan D. Gilbert, and Lee Horsley, *Churches and Churchgoers: Patterns of Church in the British*

The changing balance between liberal and conservatives wings of Christianity can be seen in microcosm in the British universities. In 1960 the liberal and ecumenical SCM was still the largest student Christian organization, with 31 branches and an estimated 3,700 members, but the conservative Protestant IVF and its affiliated Christian Unions (CUs) had 29 branches and about 3,000 members. By the early 1970s the SCM was in severe decline, whereas the Christian Unions were maintaining their numbers—though precise statistics do not seem to be available. Steve Bruce, writing in 1980, claimed that the Christian Unions were then flourishing more than ever before, and were in most universities the largest student-run organization.[68] Some of the reasons for SCM's decline are clear enough. The national organization and many of the local branches were strongly influenced by the political radicalism of the later 1960s, and also by the contemporary critiques of 'structures' and of any kind of hierarchy or discipline. It was difficult to sustain a coherent organization when so many members were opposed on principle to organizations. SCM's Manchester conference in 1969 combined according to Bruce 'strong resolutions on poverty and the need to be prepared to use violence to promote social change' with 'a growing rejection of traditional organisational forms and procedures'. Something of the mood of the time was expressed in an editorial in *Crosstalk*, a broadsheet produced daily at the conference: 'Why are plenary sessions so sacrosanct—no interruptions, no objections, and no spontaneity—and always faced with that bloody great platform? In any event, try the absurd.'[69]

Mary Condren, who had been a leading figure in the early 1970s, later wrote:

The SCM of the late sixties and seventies . . . rejected the divisions between students and others as being capitulation to the norms of a capitalist society; it regarded both the clerically dominated church and the universities as dying institutions which would not be produced in the same form in the new society; it fantasized itself as a revolutionary apocalyptic movement whose priority was to 'live the Truth' rather than make it survive as a growing institution.[70]

The less politically minded were alienated by the militancy of many of the movement's activists, while the radicals were often deciding that they could be doing more elsewhere to hasten the revolution: for instance, many members of the Edinburgh branch joined the Trotskyite International Socialists.[71] The

---

Isles since 1700 (Oxford, 1977), 158; Grace Davie, *Religion in Britain since 1945* (Oxford, 1994), 46.

[68] Steve Bruce, 'The Student Christian Movement and the Inter-Varsity Fellowship: A Sociological Study of Two Student Movements' (Ph.D. thesis, University of Stirling, 1980), appendix II.

[69] Ibid. 315–16.   [70] Ibid. 341.   [71] Ibid. 340.

theological liberalism and political radicalism of the members of SCM made them very open to a wide variety of contemporary cultural and political currents. By contrast, members of the CUs were much better insulated from the anti-institutional, anti-traditional, and often anti-Christian aspects of contemporary culture. Relatively few were strongly politicized. And they belonged to a body which attached a lot of importance to organization and structures.

ATHEISTS 'COME OUT'

Meanwhile, the later 1960s and early 1970s offered a climate in which atheists, agnostics, or those who simply had no religion found it easier to 'come out'. In 1960 the Dutch was the only Western nation to include a substantial proportion of those professing no religion. (In fact, the Netherlands, like France, which also had strong local concentrations of professed unbelievers, was regionally highly varied: in some areas the widespread break from the church went back to the 1880s, while other areas remained solidly Catholic or Protestant in the 1950s.) The proportion of Dutch people belonging to no religion rose from 18 per cent in 1960 to 28 per cent in 1970. But other countries were beginning to join in. In 1966, fewer than 1 per cent of Australians were prepared to tell the census officials that they had no religion; by 1976 the proportion had risen to 8 per cent.[72] One may surmise that some of this growth represented a 'coming out' by sceptics who had previously regarded their religious doubts as a private matter. Some of the increase was certainly due to the greater acceptability of irreligion among the younger generation—encouraged by role models such as the Beatle, John Lennon. In 1966 Lennon claimed in a newspaper interview: 'Christianity will go. It will vanish and shrink. I needn't argue about that. I'm right and will be proved right. We're more popular than Jesus now. I don't know which will go first—rock 'n' roll or Christianity. Jesus was all right, but his disciples were thick and ordinary.'[73] By 1971 the ex-Beatle was pleading for atheism and anarchy in his song *Imagine*. (Actually, Lennon's form of atheism was relatively polite compared with that of the Swedish punk rocker of the 1970s who had a song called *Hang God*.[74])

[72] Hugh McLeod, *Religion and the People of Western Europe 1789–1989* (Oxford, 1997), 146; David Hilliard, 'The Religious Crisis of the 1960s,' *Journal of Religious History*, 21 (1997), 226. See also Peter van Rooden, 'Secularization, Dechristianization and Rechristianization in the Netherlands,' in H. Lehmann (ed.), *Säkularisierung, Dechristianisierung, Rechristianisierung im neuzeitlichen Europa* (Göttingen, 1997), 131–53.

[73] Albert Goldman, *The Lives of John Lennon* (London, 1988), 205.

[74] I owe this information to Daniel Alvunger of Lund University.

Writers and artists, as well as some philosophers and scientists, had for long been associated with unconventional religious beliefs, sometimes going hand in hand with a generally unconventional lifestyle. In the 1960s and 1970s the willingness of popular musicians, television personalities, and even some politicians to declare their unbelief signalled the arrival of a more tolerant and pluralistic society in which norms of respectability and orthodoxy were less clearly defined. Lennon's atheism (as well as the attacks on Christianity by other popular musicians of the time, such as Frank Zappa and Mick Jagger) can be contrasted with the public respect for religion shown by Adam Faith, a leading pop singer of a slightly earlier generation. When in 1962 Faith was criticized by the archbishop of York for presenting sex as the whole meaning of life, he rushed to appear on television with the archbishop in order to make it clear that he had nothing against Christianity, though he did think that the church needed to do more to get in touch with the younger generation.[75] Australia even had a couple of openly agnostic Prime Ministers, starting with Gough Whitlam in 1972 and followed by Bob Hawke.

The ethos of the time favoured openness, plain speaking, and even a deliberate breaking of taboos. The boundaries between what was acceptable in private and what was permitted in public were becoming blurred. As a spokesman for the BBC wrote in 1970, responding to a complaint by the decency campaigners of the National Listeners' and Viewers' Association: 'Whether we like it or not, subjects once regarded as taboo are now discussed openly in the presence of members of both sexes and the range of topics thought of as private has shrunk dramatically.'[76] A striking example of this tendency was the BBC television comedy series, *Till Death Us Do Part*, opening in 1966, which focused on the outrageous behaviour and opinions of an ultra-conservative working-class Londoner called Alf Garnett. The programme provoked frequent complaints because of its ridicule of religion, the royal family, and much else. These complaints reached a climax in 1972 after a programme in which Alf and his family had speculated as to whether the Virgin Mary had been on the pill. The writer, Johnny Speight, had reacted strongly against his Catholic upbringing in the impoverished Canning Town district of east London; he was described by the biographers of his arch-enemy, Mary Whitehouse, as a man consumed by anger. Speight was indeed mildly reprimanded by the Director General of the BBC, but came away promising more attacks on religion.[77]

---

[75] *Church Times* (26 Jan. 1962); Sandbrook, *White Heat*, 433. While Sandbrook stresses the archbishop's attempt to appear trendy, more significant is the pop singer's attempt to establish his respectability.

[76] Michael Tracey and David Morrison, *Whitehouse* (London, 1979), 99.

[77] Ibid. 106–16.

CONCLUSION

The crisis experienced by the Christian churches in the 'Long Sixties' reached a point of extreme intensity between about 1967 and 1972, when there was a mass movement of resignations from the Catholic priesthood and a mass abandonment of church-going—at least in many Catholic communities, where levels of religious practice had often been very high. In England, where church attendance was already low, there was a big drop in participation in the rites of passage in the same period. In the latter instance, a major reason was probably that those who already had little involvement in the church felt under less pressure to conform to the traditions of a church wedding or baptism or, in keeping with contemporary principles of authenticity, felt that they should make a stand. Some of the decline in church-going in staunchly Catholic communities was also due to a feeling on the part of those who had never been very interested that they were now free to drop out. Some of the decline was due to the fact that those who never made a definite decision to leave were now finding themselves drawn into a range of alternative Sunday activities. And there were also those who left because of disagreements with the church authorities, because of conversion to Marxism or feminism, or because of the demands of full-time political activity. There were many different reasons for giving up going to church in this period: it could be called a mass movement in that individual decisions were influenced by the knowledge that friends, neighbours, and family were moving in the same direction; but the motives for these decisions varied widely. At the same time, an increasing proportion of the younger generation were growing up with little exposure to Christianity in childhood and adolescence.

10

From 'Christian Country' to 'Civilized Society'

As was shown in Chapter 2, the Second World War was often seen as a battle for 'Christian civilization' against the 'pagan' Nazis, and the identification of the West with Christianity was confirmed by the cold war against the 'godless' Soviet Union. Practices were generally accepted in schools and other public institutions which assumed that belief in Christianity, or at least in God, was 'normal': for instance, in Britain and in parts of the United States the school day began with prayers and readings from the Bible, and in many predominantly Catholic countries crucifixes hung on the walls of schools, hospitals, and courts of law. The state, in regulating morality, tended to take Christian ethics as normative, though the extent to which and the ways in which they did this differed according to whether a country was predominantly Catholic or Protestant, and how powerful these churches were.

In the 1960s and 1970s most of these laws came under attack and many were modified or repealed. Secularists, naturally resentful of the power exercised by religion and the churches, were often in the forefront of the reform campaigns. But secularists were seldom numerous or powerful enough to effect such changes single-handed. They needed allies, and plenty of these were to be found. In some cases powerful campaigns could be mounted by those most directly affected. For instance, in many countries women's organizations played a key role in campaigns to liberalize the laws on abortion. More generally, however, elite opinion in the 1960s and 1970s, as reflected in the views of legislators, judges, newspaper editors, academics, and many theologians and church leaders, was strongly influenced by ideas of individual human rights, the importance of maintaining a 'private' sphere in which the state had no right to intervene, and the need for equity between sections of the population with different religious and moral convictions.

A first clear indication of this latter trend came in a series of controversial judgments by the United States Supreme Court between 1961 and 1963. The basic concern of the justices was to reconcile the constitutional provision that there should be no establishment of religion with the guarantee of 'free exercise' of religion. Until the 1960s the general assumption was that the United States was a Christian, or at least a 'Judeo-Christian' nation, and that schoolteachers could read from the Bible or affirm belief in God, as long as they did not try to privilege a specific religious denomination. The new rulings effectively declared that atheists, agnostics, and Buddhists had the same rights as Christians and Jews, and that these venerable and hitherto seldom challenged traditions violated the rights of these religious minorities. Thus the Court struck down an inter-faith prayer provided by the state of New York, Bible readings prescribed by a Pennsylvania school board, and a Maryland statute according to which holders of public office must declare a belief in God.[1] The judgment in 1962 which ruled against the inter-faith prayer used in New York stressed that no attack on religion was involved: 'religion is too personal, too sacred, too holy, to permit its "unhallowed perversion" by the civil magistrate', and any privileging, however limited, of one kind of religious belief above another could potentially escalate to the extent of full-blown persecution.[2] 'Christendom' in its nineteenth- and twentieth-century versions had been based on the assumption that public recognition of the Christian beliefs held by the majority (and indeed of the commitment of most people to a specific Christian denomination) could be reconciled with the rights of the minority which did not share these beliefs. In the 1960s new and much more radical interpretations of religious equality and freedom were coming to the fore.

Among the legislators of the period the most consistent advocate of such views was the Canadian Liberal Minister of Justice and later Prime Minister, Pierre Trudeau, described by one commentator as a 'philosopher king'. Trudeau was a liberal Catholic, strongly influenced by the French personalist and advocate of Christian–Marxist dialogue, Emmanuel Mounier. Trudeau's views had been formed in opposition to what he regarded as the over-powerful role of the clergy in his native Quebec. His Omnibus Bill, introduced in 1967 covered divorce, homosexuality, abortion, contraception, and lotteries, in a bid, as he told a journalist to 'get the state out of the nation's bedrooms'. Also in 1967 there was a moratorium on executions, though the death penalty was abolished only in 1976. When presenting his programme to Parliament, Trudeau used a more philosophical language:

We are now living in a social climate in which people are beginning to realize, perhaps for the first time in the history of this country, that we are not entitled to impose the concepts which belong to a sacred society upon a civil or profane society. The concepts

---

[1] Ronald J. Flowers, *Religion in Strange Times* (n.pl., 1984), 141–2.

[2] P. Harvey and P. Goff (eds.), *Columbia Documentary History of Religion in America since 1945* (New York, 2005), 262–7.

of the civil society in which we live are pluralistic, and I think this parliament realizes that it would be a mistake for us to try to legislate into this society concepts which belong to a theological or sacred order.[3]

These changes were supported by the largest Protestant churches, the United Church and the Anglicans, while being opposed by many evangelicals. The Catholic Church accepted most of the package, but strongly opposed the legalization of abortion.[4] These differences partly reflected differences between the teachings of different Christian churches, but also different attitudes to 'Christendom' and the extent to which laws and institutions should be explicitly based in Christianity. A similar package of reforms was enacted in England and Wales, though piecemeal and over a longer period. Most of this chapter will focus on a detailed examination of how, when and why the changes took place in those countries.

THE LEGISLATIVE REVOLUTION

In the 1940s and 1950s reference to Britain as a 'Christian country' continued to be frequently heard. This claim rested partly on the existence of a wide range of laws relating to morality and religion, which were often justified as being an embodiment of Christian principles, or as defending Christianity against its enemies. These included laws prohibiting blasphemy, obscenity, suicide, and male homosexuality, prescribing Sunday observance, censoring films and plays, and restricting drinking, gambling, and abortion. The death penalty, though usually advocated as a deterrent, was also sometimes justified by quotations from the Old Testament. In the 1950s and 1960s nearly all of these laws were under attack, and most were repealed or modified. This section and the two following will examine the role played by religious arguments, by the churches and other religious groups, and by Humanists in these debates, and will consider how far and in what ways the place of Christianity in English and Welsh society was redefined as a result. It should be remembered that Scotland and Northern Ireland have separate legal systems from England and Wales. While some of the changes in this period applied to the whole of the United Kingdom (for instance, the suspension of the death penalty), and some to the whole of Britain (for instance, the abortion law reform),

---

[3] George Egerton, 'Trudeau, God and the Canadian Constitution: Religion, Human Rights and Government Authority in the Making of the 1982 Constitution,' in Lyon and Van Die (eds.), *Rethinking Church, State and Modernity*, 96.

[4] Ibid. 97–8.

others applied only to England and Wales (for instance, reform of the law on homosexuality).

The years 1959–69 saw a legislative revolution. It began under Harold Macmillan's Conservative government of 1957–63, and the pace of change speeded up under Harold Wilson's Labour government between 1964 and 1970. The beginning was the Obscene Publications Act of 1959, which protected works of literary or scientific merit from prosecution for obscenity. Restrictions on gambling were relaxed in 1960 and on drinking in 1961. Attempted suicide was decriminalized in 1961. The death penalty for murder was suspended in 1965 and abolished in 1969. The year 1967 saw the decriminalization of male homosexuality and a major extension of the legally permitted grounds for abortion, and also for the first time contraceptives were made available to unmarried couples through the National Health Service. In 1968 theatre censorship was abolished. And in 1969 the divorce law was liberalized, though attempts to legalize euthanasia and lift restrictions on Sunday entertainments failed. Most of these changes were justified as extending the sphere of individual freedom, though it should be noted that there were also some laws of the 1960s which placed new restrictions on the individual. For instance, the Race Relations Act of 1965 limited freedom of speech by making incitement to racial hatred a criminal offence. Many of these new laws included an element of compromise, and were consequently attacked by more militant groups, such as the Women's Liberation and Gay Liberation Movements, which emerged in 1969 and 1970. For instance the Abortion Act fell some way short of granting abortion on demand, and the Sexual Offences Act defined 21 as the age of consent for male homosexuals.

In contrast to Canada, the British reforms were introduced piecemeal over several years, with many false starts and without any master-plan. Most of the reforming legislation, as is traditional in matters which are thought to be questions of 'conscience' for Members of Parliament, was introduced by backbenchers, with the government being officially neutral. In some cases, the legislation enacted in the 1960s was the culmination of a protracted process. Abolition of the death penalty had first been debated by Parliament as long ago as 1840, and several unsuccessful attempts had been made in the 1950s and 1960s to reform the laws on divorce and homosexuality. In so far as England and Wales had its own Trudeau, it was clearly Roy Jenkins (1920–2003), who initiated the decade of reform by sponsoring the Obscene Publications Act in 1959, and who, as Labour Home Secretary between 1965 and 1967, gave vital support to the proposed reforms of the laws on homosexuality and abortion. He also provided reformers with their most famous slogan. In 1969, when answering accusations that Britain had become a 'permissive society', he responded that as a result of these reforms Britain was now a 'civilised society'.

When Jenkins entered Parliament in 1948 he was an admirer of Aneurin Bevan, hero of the Labour left, and he regarded state planning as the essence of Socialism. After his split with Bevan in the early 1950s his biggest concern became the need to extend the sphere of individual freedom—not, as the Conservatives wanted, in the field of economics, but in the area of personal morality.[5] Jenkins called for the recognition of a 'private' sphere, in which the state should not interfere, and he also subscribed to an implicit progressivism according to which many of the existing laws were 'archaic' or 'barbarous' and so were necessarily out of place in a 'modern' society. It is hard to find any clearly stated philosophical basis for Jenkins's programme. He was in any case said to have an aversion to abstract ideas.[6] It is also hard to discover what relation, if any, his reforming programme had to his views on religion. Jenkins was well known as a *bon vivant*, and the index of a recent collection of essays on his career includes five references to 'champagne' and seven to 'claret', but only three to 'religion'.[7] He seems to have reacted against his Welsh Calvinist upbringing, but to have remained an occasional church-goer in later life.[8] He was evidently no religious zealot, but no secularist zealot either.

Almost as soon as the 1960s were ended, sociologists, political scientists, and journalists were offering their interpretations of the legislative revolution of that decade. In more recent years, historians have joined the debate. Evidently the Labour majority in Parliament from 1964 to 1970 was decisive in allowing the passage of some of the more controversial reforms, since these were supported by a majority of Labour Members of Parliament (MPs) and opposed by the majority of Conservatives. The personal role of Roy Jenkins as Home Secretary was also clearly important. However, commentators are less agreed as to the wider social and religious factors underlying these changes. One popular line of interpretation, namely that these changes were an aspect of 'the Swinging Sixties' or a response to developments in the youth and counter-cultures, can be dismissed out of hand. The reforms were enacted by middle-aged and elderly legislators, who firmly rejected the only demand coming from the youth and counter-cultures, namely the legalization of marijuana. Two areas of serious disagreement among historians and sociologists, however, are the historical context of the reforms, and the role, if any, of religion and the churches. So far as the historical background is concerned,

---

[5] Roy Jenkins, *A Life at the Centre* (London, 1991), 83–98, 120–4, 130.
[6] Andrew Adonis and Keith Thomas (eds.), *Roy Jenkins: A Retrospective* (Oxford, 2004), 277.
[7] Ibid. 344–5.   [8] Ibid. 240.

there is a difference between those who trace the origins of these changes back to the inter-war years, and those who see them as a product of changes in British society after the Second World War. For Haste and Machin, the roots of the 1960s are to be found in the secularization of British society during the inter-war years: the agenda for the 1960s was already prepared in the 1930s, but implementation was delayed in the more morally conservative atmosphere of the war years and their aftermath.[9] Others place the reforms much more specifically in the context of the growing affluence and the cultural revolution of the later 1950s and 1960s.[10] As regards the role of the churches, some writers see them simply as victims of forces beyond their control. Brown, for instance, notes that both liberal and conservative Christians took part in the debates, though he places much more emphasis on the latter, but he sees their contributions as irrelevant to the outcome.[11] Other historians, however, suggest that the churches not only took an active part in the debate, but also influenced the results. Haste in fact describes 'the Church of England's conversion to liberalism' as 'crucial', though she sees it as arising less from conviction than from the need to compromise with 'wider secular and humanist interests'.[12]

My own position is closest to that of Haste and Machin in that I want to put the legislation of the 1960s in the context of longer term social and religious changes. Many of these reforms have a prehistory going back at least to the 1930s. I would go further than either of them in emphasizing the part played by the churches or by religious arguments in making some of these changes possible. The debate going on within the churches was at least as important as the debate between Christians and secularists, and the liberalization of Christian thinking was as important as the growth of humanism and rationalism as a force for reform—nor should liberal Christianity be seen merely as a reaction to rationalism. The social and political (as opposed to intellectual and cultural) influence enjoyed by secularists and Humanists in the 1950s and 1960s has often been exaggerated. Furthermore, those pragmatic Christians who did not belong unambiguously either to the liberal or to the conservative wing of their churches did not simply 'compromise' with current trends, but looked at these questions issue by issue. It should also be stressed that the issues *were* different. Too often the reforms are seen simply as a package,

[9] G. I. T. Machin, *Churches and Social Issues in Twentieth-Century Britain* (Oxford, 1998), 106–7; Cate Haste, *Rules of Desire* (London, 1992), 97.

[10] Christie Davies, *Permissive Britain* (London, 1975), 1–12, 39–40; Callum G. Brown, *The Death of Christian Britain* (London, 2001), 175–80; Andrew Holden, *Makers and Manners: Politics and Morality in Postwar Britain* (London, 2004), 1–2, 27–8.

[11] Callum G. Brown, *Religion and Society in Twentieth-Century Britain* (London, 2006), 267–70.

[12] Haste, *Desire*, 213.

without sufficient recognition of the fact that there were many people who supported some, but not others.

The churches played a significant part in the debates on the four most important of these issues, namely the abolition of capital punishment, and reform of the laws on homosexuality, abortion, and divorce. Religious arguments played a part in the parliamentary debates on all these issues. It should be remembered that the Upper House of the United Kingdom legislature, the House of Lords, was (and, with some modifications, still is) composed in a way unparalleled in any Western democracy. As well as several hundred hereditary peers, life peers nominated by the government of the day, and judges, it included twenty-six Anglican bishops. The Anglican Church thus had a privileged position in the public debate, though in practice most bishops spoke and voted in the House of Lords relatively infrequently. At the same time the religious dimension of public debate on these highly contentious issues was by no means limited to interventions by the bishops.

Though these reforms are often seen as a package, some distinctions should be made. First, the measures introduced by the Conservative government in 1960 and 1961 were relatively uncontentious. There was general agreement with the bishop of Carlisle who, in supporting the bill to decriminalize attempted suicide, declared that the suicidal needed compassion and not punishment.[13] The laws on gambling and drinking were legacies of the 'Nonconformist Conscience'—historically associated with political Liberalism, and so uncongenial to most Conservatives—and in the 1950s and 1960s they could easily be dismissed as 'puritanical', as 'Victorian', and as treating adults as if they were children. Moreover, even those who condemned gambling could not but recognize that the ban on off-course betting while on-course betting was quite legal was a case of one law for the rich and one for the poor. Opposition to reform still came mainly from Nonconformists; but there was much less opposition from Anglicans or Catholics.[14] The Conservative governments of 1951–64 have in fact been described as the most Anglican of the twentieth century, with Macmillan himself, as well as his Home Secretary, R. A. Butler, being among several leading ministers who were committed members of the Church of England.[15] Macmillan was particularly sensitive to church opinion[16] and certainly had no intention of furthering secularization.

---

[13] Mark Jarvis, *Conservative Governments, Morality and Social Change in Affluent Britain* (Manchester, 2005), 95.

[14] Carl Chinn, *Better Betting with a Decent Feller: A Social History of Bookmaking* (London, 2004), 194–5.

[15] Adrian Hastings, *A History of English Christianity 1920–1985* (London, 1986), 425.

[16] Jarvis, *Conservative Governments*, 163.

Second, the death penalty is in some ways an issue apart, since demands for abolition go back to the first half of the nineteenth century,[17] and a Royal Commission heard evidence on the issue in the 1860s, with five of the twelve commissioners declaring their opposition to the death penalty. Christie Davies presents abolition as an aspect of 'permissive Britain', which he defines as the shift from a society based on Christian morality to one with laws guided by utilitarianism.[18] However, the case for capital punishment as it was presented from the 1840s to the 1960s rested principally not on references to the Bible, but on the claim that hanging was a unique deterrent, and that its abolition would therefore lead to a rise in the number of murders. Indeed, Christian arguments always played a bigger role in the arguments of abolitionists than of retentionists.

Capital punishment was the only one of these issues on which in the 1960s public opinion remained clearly and unequivocally opposed to any change; on the other hand, the movement for reform was more widely based and passionate than it was in respect of any of the other issues, and this was reflected in the exceptionally high numbers of MPs and peers who took part in the parliamentary debates. In the nineteenth century, Anglicans and Roman Catholics tended to approve of capital punishment, while Nonconformists opposed it. However, in the 1930s William Temple, then archbishop of York, emerged as a leading abolitionist and in 1956, when the House of Lords voted for retention of hanging, the Anglican bishops were nearly all in the minority. Michael Ramsey, newly appointed archbishop of York, made his maiden speech in favour of abolition. Debates in Convocation in 1962–3 showed that only one Anglican bishop still favoured the death penalty. When in 1965 and 1969 the House of Lords was finally converted to the abolitionist cause, the Anglican bishops overwhelmingly supported the change. It is a sign both of Archbishop Ramsey's own standing and of the importance attached to support from the bishops that he was strongly urged to sponsor the 1965 bill in the House of Lords—though he finally declined this invitation and contented himself with making an abolitionist speech.[19]

Historically, a major role in the abolitionist movement had been played by Nonconformists, especially Quakers, such as Roy Calvert, whose classic critique of the death penalty, published in 1927, was said to have laid down the essential points of the case which finally won through in the 1960s.

---

[17] Hugh McLeod, 'God and the Gallows: Christianity and Capital Punishment in the Nineteenth and Twentieth Centuries,' in Kate Cooper and Jeremy Gregory (eds.), *Retribution, Repentance and Reconciliation* (Woodbridge, 2004), 330–56.

[18] Davies, *Permissive Britain, passim.*

[19] Owen Chadwick, *Michael Ramsey* (Oxford, 1990), 157–62.

Calvert's main achievement had been to assemble statistical evidence from abolitionist countries (and especially from abolitionist states of the USA) to refute the popular belief that the death penalty was a unique deterrent and that abolition would lead to an increase in the number of murders. These statistical arguments played a key role in the parliamentary debates of 1964–5, which focused principally on the question of whether hanging really was a deterrent. However, Christie Davies is mistaken when, in comparing these debates with those in 1948, he claims that there was a switch from 'moralistic' to 'utilitarian' arguments.[20] The statistics had a crucial role in winning over the undecided, but one does not have to scratch far below the surface to appreciate that the strongly committed on either side were still moved by ethical and religious considerations. A characteristic example is that of the Liberal peer, Lord Reay, whose speech consisted mainly of statistics, but who also referred to the fundamental Christian doctrine that all men are redeemable, and concluded by declaring that the death penalty was 'barbarous'. Nor was Viscount Norwich untypical when he combined statistical arguments with the claim that the death penalty was 'the darkest stain' on the statute book, and added 'I can conceive of nothing more totally at variance with Christian morality'.[21]

The Anglican role was most significant in the campaign to decriminalize male homosexuality. The Church of England's Moral Welfare Council, and especially its lecturer, the Revd Derrick Sherwin Bailey, played a major part in opening the public debate on this hitherto taboo topic. The Council's report in 1954 recommending decriminalization was one of the factors influencing the government's decision to set up its own Wolfenden Committee, which reached a similar conclusion in 1957.[22] The Wolfenden recommendations were approved by the Methodist Conference, by the National Assembly of the Church of England (albeit narrowly), and by the Roman Catholic Church's Advisory Committee on Prostitution and Homosexual Offences, but was opposed by the Church of Scotland's Church and Nation Committee.[23] In spite of the government's refusal to respond, the report had a tremendous effect on elite opinion, including some of the younger Conservative MPs.

[20] Davies, *Permissive Britain*, 27–44.

[21] *House of Lords Debates*, 19 July 1965, cols. 502, 509, 519–20.

[22] Experts are divided as to how significant the role of the Church of England Moral Welfare Council was. Peter G. Richards, *Parliament and Conscience* (London, 1970), 63–84, says it was important; Higgins, *Dictatorship*, 35, says it was not. Graham Willett, who is working on an international comparative study of homosexual law reform, says in an email to me (6 July 2006): 'On the churches and homosexuality, their influence on the outcome was, if anything, even greater than you suggest. Derrick Sherwin Bailey seems to have been a powerful force in a behind-the-scenes way; as was St John-Stevas, less behind the scenes...'

[23] Machin, *Social Issues*, 157–8.

Anglican clergy were also prominent in the Homosexual Law Reform Society, set up in 1958 to call for implementation of Wolfenden. Then in 1966, when decriminalization was debated in the House of Lords, seven Anglican bishops, including Ramsey, voted in favour and none against. As a result of the Sexual Offences Act of 1967, homosexual acts 'between consenting adults in private' were no longer illegal in England and Wales, though in Scotland this reform was delayed until 1980, and in Northern Ireland until 1982.[24]

The parliamentary debate was notable for the fact that none of the speakers was prepared to say in so many words that homosexuality was a legitimate option, in no sense inferior to heterosexuality. Lord Annan, the former provost of King's College, Cambridge (which had the reputation of having an unusually high proportion of homosexuals among its fellows and students), perhaps came nearest when he stressed the impact of social change since the Second World War: 'We have moved into a much more pluralist society', where 'many different sections of the community assert the right to live in the way that they see fit, and not to take instruction from those who in days past would have been called their betters'.[25] Most speakers arguing for reform used one or more of the following arguments: that homosexuals were not to blame for their condition (a product, it was suggested, of inadequate parenting or single-sex schools) and that they needed help rather than punishment; that the present laws caused unnecessary suffering, led to homosexuals being blackmailed, and diverted police from the fight against crime; that sex was a private matter in which the state should not interfere; or that gay sex, while morally wrong, was less damaging than other moral irregularities that the law did not penalize. Many speakers referred to the support of the churches for reform, including most notably the Catholic MP, Norman St John Stevas who, in one of the most effective contributions to the debate, declared: 'We are a Christian country and, therefore, it is right to pay attention to the almost unanimous view of the leaders of the churches on the bill.' Almost as frequent, and an important sign of the times, were claims that psychiatrists and sociologists favoured reform. The former Labour Cabinet Minister, George Strauss, dwelt almost exclusively on references to these authorities, mentioning both the churches, 'the moral guardians of the nation', and various kinds of scientist. Opponents of reform frequently claimed that homosexual acts were contrary to Christianity and/or simply 'disgusting' (the term used by Lord Kilmuir, who had been Home Secretary when arrests of homosexuals had peaked in the early 1950s).[26] But their main argument was that many young men who were perfectly

---

[24] Brown, *Religion and Society in Twentieth-Century Britain*, 282.

[25] *House of Lords Debates*, 10 May 1966, col. 623.

[26] *House of Commons Debates*, 19 Dec. 1966, cols. 1121, 1098; *House of Lords Debates*, 10 May 1966, col. 615. For Kilmuir's period as Home Secretary, see Jeffrey Weeks, *Coming Out* (London, 1990), 158–64.

capable of a 'normal' sexual life were being 'perverted' by 'proselytizing' homosexuals.

The Church of England was also centre-stage in the debates over divorce law reform, though in this instance the final outcome was a compromise, which some Anglicans, including Archbishop Ramsey, disliked.[27] The divorce laws, like capital punishment, had been under debate since the nineteenth century. In 1951 and 1963 the Church of England had successfully opposed attempted liberalizations. On the latter occasion, opposition had come from a united front of Anglican, Catholic, and Free Church leaders. However, the Conservative government was in favour of some measure of reform, and wanted to find a scheme which would have the support of the established church. Partly in response to prompting from the government, Ramsey set up a commission which in 1966 produced the report *Putting Asunder*. The key recommendation was that the old concept of 'matrimonial offence', which had been the basis of divorce law since 1857 should be abolished, being replaced by the concept of 'irretrievable breakdown of marriage' as the sole grounds for divorce. This principle then became the basis for the 1969 Act—after a good deal of negotiation between representatives of the church, of the Law Commission (which thought some of the procedures proposed in the church report too complex to be practicable), and interested MPs, who were dissatisfied with the existing law and were mainly anxious to get some kind of reform on the statute book as soon as possible. Here the great bone of contention was the principle of 'divorce by consent', which Ramsey and most other Anglican leaders opposed, although Ramsey was equally opposed to what he regarded as the unrealistic absolutist position of the Roman Catholic Church, which ruled out divorce in any circumstances. Ramsey's view was that marriages did sometimes break down, and that the law had to recognize this fact, but that the law and the church should do everything possible to uphold lifelong marriage as the norm, as well as the ideal.[28] Although the Free Churches were generally more accepting of divorce than the Anglicans—and, in particular, were willing to remarry divorcees, which the Anglicans would not—divorce seems to have been the issue on which 'secular' and 'religious' opinions diverged furthest.[29] Most Christians regarded divorce as an evil, albeit a necessary evil, and in looking at how the laws could be improved, they wanted to maximize opportunities for reconciliation and to avoid making divorce *too* easy. Many Humanists and secularists, on the other hand, took a more relaxed

---

[27] Jane Lewis and Patrick Wallis, 'Fault, Breakdown and the Church of England's Involvement in the 1969 Divorce Reform,' *Twentieth Century British History*, 11 (2000), 308–32.

[28] Chadwick, *Ramsey*, 150.

[29] See the analysis of MPs' voting, correlated with religious affiliation, in Richards, *Parliament*, 183.

view of divorce, seeing it as something unfortunate but often inevitable, and they consequently saw easier divorce not as undermining 'good' marriages, but as a realistic recognition of the fact that there were many 'bad' marriages.

The influence of the churches on the passage of the Abortion Act was less—and indeed it was the Roman Catholic Church which provided the strongest opposition.[30] In fact this was the only one of the reforms of these years to face consistent resistance from one of the major churches. Except on the part of Catholics, there was widespread support from the churches, as well as from members of all political parties, for the principle that some liberalization of the law was needed. The Methodists, the Church of Scotland, and many Anglicans (including Archbishop Ramsey) agreed on this.[31] The disagreement was as to how far this should go. David Steel, the Liberal MP who sponsored the Medical Termination of Pregnancy Bill, was himself a Church of Scotland layman, and used church support as one of the arguments in favour of his bill. In this instance, one cannot say that the churches played a major part in bringing about change; but more widespread church opposition would certainly have made change harder to achieve, and would probably have led to a more restrictive bill than the one actually enacted. The case against reform, argued mainly, though not exclusively, by Catholic MPs and peers (notably Norman St John Stevas, who again made an outstanding contribution to the debate), rested on the principle of the sanctity of life. The killer argument on the other side was that women were dying as a result of the thousands of 'back-street' abortions and that, since abortions would take place regardless of what the law said, it was better that they should be carried out in hygienic conditions by trained medical personnel. Roy Jenkins also made the similarly pragmatic point (graphically underlined in the recent film, *Vera Drake*) that the present situation was a case of one law for the rich and one for the poor, since legal abortions were already obtainable but often very expensive.[32] At this stage no one was prepared to make the argument, which would be forcefully presented by the Women's Liberation Movement a few years later, that women should be free to do as they choose with their own body. Nor did anyone try to assert the 'Wolfenden' principle that abortion belonged to the 'private' sphere.

---

[30] The story of abortion law reform is told in two substantial studies, Keith Hindell and Madeleine Simms, *Abortion Law Reformed* (London, 1971), and Barbara Brookes, *Abortion in England 1900–1967* (Beckenham, 1988).

[31] The most detailed (and most partisan) discussion of 'religion and reform' is in Hindell and Simms, *Abortion Law*, 77–107. See also Richards, *Parliament*, 91–2, 105–6; Machin, *Social Issues*, 200; Chadwick, *Ramsey*, 154–6.

[32] *House of Commons Debates*, 22 July 1966, col. 1142.

THE ROLE OF RELIGION IN THE DEBATE

As well as Christians of many different kinds, Humanists and secularists also took an active part in these debates—usually as proponents of reform. The British Humanist Association and National Secular Society were often among the strongest advocates of change. An analysis of MPs' voting correlated with their religious affiliation showed that atheists and agnostics, and also Jews, voted strongly for the four reforms discussed above, as well as for an unsuccessful attempt to relax the laws on Sunday observance, with Anglicans and those of unknown religion being those most likely to be opposed, while Nonconformists and Catholics had a more mixed record—for instance, they agreed in wanting to abolish the death penalty and decriminalize homosexuality, but Catholics were against divorce and abortion law reform, which most Nonconformists supported, and Nonconformists were much more concerned than Catholics to retain the 'quiet Sunday'. (Incidentally, it would have been helpful if the study had controlled for party: in all probability the majority of Anglicans were Conservatives, while those belonging to the various minorities were all predominantly Labour—in some instances, party membership may have been a bigger influence than religious affiliation.)[33]

Not only did Humanists and secularists vote for reform, they also belonged to important pressure-groups and sometimes played a key role in parliamentary debates. A notable example was the Labour MP, Leo Abse, a secular Jew, who showed impressive stamina in his sponsorship of the homosexual and divorce law reform bills, in spite of many setbacks on the way, especially in respect of the latter. He was also a strong advocate of improved family planning facilities, though much more ambivalent about abortion. Rather strangely—in view of the fact that he was willing at times to speak explicitly as a Humanist in parliamentary debates—he objected to MPs who opposed his campaigns on the basis of their religious views.[34] The one campaign in which Humanists and secularists may have played a decisive role was the one leading to the Abortion Act. The campaign was masterminded by the Abortion Law Reform Association (ALRA), 74 per cent of whose members, according to a survey in 1968, described themselves as atheists or agnostics.[35] A study of pressure-groups active in the 1960s praised ALRA for the effectiveness of its attempts both to influence public opinion and win the support of MPs, and its thorough monitoring of the passage of the bill through Parliament.[36]

[33] Richards, *Parliament*, 183.
[34] *House of Commons Debates*, 22 July 1966, cols. 1147–52. See also Leo Abse's frank and highly idiosyncratic autobiography, *Private Member* (London, 1973).
[35] Hindell and Simms, *Abortion Law*, 120.
[36] Bridget Pym, *Pressure Groups and the Permissive Society* (Newton Abbot, 1974), 156–60.

However, Humanists and secularists were a small minority of the population, and they could only achieve changes if they could find allies. The survey of the religious affiliations of MPs in the 1960s found only 27 out of 630 in the 1964 Parliament who were known to be atheists or agnostics, though in the 1966 Parliament this rose to 48.[37] ALRA attached a lot of importance to support from the churches, and they included John Robinson, bishop of Woolwich, among their vice-presidents. It suited their purposes well that David Steel was a church-goer. The most likely allies in reforming campaigns were to be found among liberal Christians, while there were also many conservative Christians who were likely to be opposed. There was a third group, whom I have termed 'pragmatic' Christians, whose response was less predictable, but who were both numerous and influential. In the next section, I want to look at these three kinds of Christian stance.

To begin with the 'liberal' Christians: John Robinson, Anglican bishop of Woolwich 1959–69, is certainly the most famous and can be taken as representative. *Honest to God* had made him a household name, and he was seldom far from a TV studio in the 1960s. (I can myself remember queuing to hear him preach, and being turned away at the door, because the church was already full.). He was never afraid to speak out on controversial issues: he preached sermons denouncing nuclear weapons and the death penalty, and in 1960 joined the executive of the Homosexual Law Reform Society. He was opposed to censorship, and also passionately believed that Christians needed to take a more positive view of the body and of sex. He was opposed to 'permissiveness', which he equated with irresponsibility. His ethical creed was based on what he called 'Christian freedom', by which he meant acting responsibly and in a spirit of love, in the light of the gospel, but without being dependent on a legalistic code of morality. One implication of this stance was that he not only opposed persecution of homosexuals—which many other Anglican clergy did in the 1950s and 1960s. He was also prepared to say that gay sex was not in itself wrong, and that homosexual relationships should be judged by the same ethical criteria as heterosexual relationships—something that few Anglican clergy were prepared to grant at the time.[38] Perhaps the most influential statement of this viewpoint was *Towards a Quaker View of Sex*, also published in the *annus mirabilis* of 1963, which though written by 'a group of Friends' rather than being an official statement of the Society of Friends was generally understood at the time as the first presentation by a British Christian denomination of homosexuality as something 'normal', rather than being an unfortunate condition, deserving sympathy, but not encouragement.

---

[37] Calculated from figures in Richards, *Parliament*, 183.
[38] Eric James, *A Life of John A. T. Robinson* (London, 1989), 82–3, 85–109, 134–5, 253.

The authors had in fact begun, in the wake of Wolfenden, as a discussion group focusing specifically on homosexuality, but had soon decided that, rather than being separated in this way, it had to be seen in the context of attitudes to sexuality and sexual ethics more generally.[39] The small, but highly active and vocal, Quakers were probably the denomination where support for the 'liberal' position was strongest, but it also had considerable support from Methodists and Congregationalists, the most liberal of the larger denominations, and from Anglicans—who ranged from very liberal to very conservative, with the majority occupying the middle ground. From 1965 until its closure in 1971 *New Christian*, with Robinson as its star columnist, provided an excellent forum for liberal Christians of all denominations.

At the opposite pole to Robinson was Mary Whitehouse, who may be taken as representative of the 'conservative' Christian stance.[40] In 1963 she became concerned at the harmful effects that television programmes on sex and religion were having on the girls in her school. The catalyst was a Sunday evening *Meeting Point*, which, the girls told her, 'was all about premarital sex' and 'ever so interesting'. In 1964 she launched a campaign to 'Clean Up TV'. Her anger was directed mainly against the BBC and its Director General from 1960 to 1969, Sir Hugh Carleton Greene: she had fewer complaints against the various Independent TV channels. Whitehouse was concerned at the graphic presentation of scenes of sex and violence in TV programmes, at the use of bad language by characters in plays, and by the presentation of sexual promiscuity and heavy drinking as 'normal'. She was concerned about religious programmes, especially *Meeting Point*, as she felt that they were slanted towards the liberal theology and 'new morality' associated with figures like John Robinson.[41] The basis of Whitehouse's position was that Britain was a Christian country and the laws and institutions of the nation should reflect that fact. In particular, it was the duty of a national institution, such as the BBC, to promote Christian morality. A decade before Jerry Falwell invented the term 'Moral Majority' to define a similar crusade in the United States, Whitehouse was making the same claim. In her view the great majority of ordinary people wanted Christian standards to be maintained, but they were being undermined by a small clique of Humanists who had gained an influence in Parliament, the media, and the universities that was totally out of proportion to their numbers. Her *bête noire*, Sir Hugh Greene, who, as well as having no interest in religion, had a mission to break taboos of every kind, was

[39] Alastair Heron (ed.), *Towards a Quaker View of Sex* (London, 1963).

[40] The influence of the Moral Rearmament movement on Whitehouse is stressed in Tracey and Morrison, *Whitehouse* (London, 1979). See also Brown, *Religion and Society in Twentieth-Century Britain*, 248–51.

[41] Whitehouse, *Who Does She Think She Is?* (London, 1971), 45–8, 70–2.

a case in point.[42] Ironically Greene's period as Director General was a golden age of religious broadcasting in both quantitative and qualitative terms,[43] though the liberal slant of a lot of those broadcasts meant that they were little appreciated by Whitehouse. Her concerns and her underlying assumptions are well expressed in a petition to Parliament, signed by 365,000 people, and presented by a sympathetic MP in June 1965:

> That the men and women of Great Britain believe in a Christian way of life; Deplore present-day efforts to belittle and destroy it and in particular object to the propaganda of disbelief, doubt and dirt that the BBC pours into millions of homes through the television screen...Wherefore your petitioners pray that the BBC be asked to make a radical change of policy and produce programmes which build character instead of destroying it, which encourage faith in God and bring Him back into the heart of the British family and national way of life.[44]

What particularly frustrated Whitehouse was the relatively little support that she received from leaders of the Church of England, including not only avowed liberals, such as Robinson, but Archbishop Michael Ramsey (who clearly found her an embarrassment).[45] Ramsey (1904–88) may be taken as representative of my third category of 'pragmatic' Christians. Ramsey was probably closer to Whitehouse than to Robinson in his sexual ethics, though his acute sense of pastoral responsibility made him distrustful of absolutes. But he did not share her political conservatism, and he had very different views from hers on the relationship between Christian morality and the law. His insistence on balancing conflicting concerns often led to his espousal of complex compromises, which those (ranging from Mary Whitehouse to Leo Abse) who took more absolutist positions found difficult to understand. Ramsey was broadly in favour of the reforms of the 1960s while having reservations on specific issues—in particular, he supported the principle of abortion and divorce law reform, but had doubts about some details of the legislation finally enacted.[46] These 'pragmatic' Christians had a pivotal position in the 1960s because they were more numerous and influential than either the Humanists, the liberal Christians or the conservative Christians, at least in relation to the relatively small elite groups whose voice was decisive in the making of law. The 1960s

[42] Michael Tracey, *A Variety of Lives: A Biography of Sir Hugh Greene* (London, 1983), 180, 182, 318–19; Hugh Greene, *The Third Floor Front* (London, 1969), 135–7.

[43] Asa Briggs, 'Christ and Media,' in Barker *et al.* (eds.), *Secularization, Rationalism and Sectarianism* (Oxford, 1993), 281, notes the large amount of religious broadcasting by the BBC on television, and especially radio, in the 1960s and 1970s.

[44] Whitehouse, *Who?*, 68–9.

[45] Ibid. 46–7, 145–7; Chadwick, *Ramsey*, 163 (where the archbishop's doubts about the Festival of Light clearly refer especially to the role of Whitehouse, although she is not mentioned by name).

[46] Chadwick, *Ramsey*, ch. 6.

were of course a time of dramatic social and cultural changes, not least among teenagers and young adults, as was shown in earlier chapters. However, the influence of the youth culture on the changes described above was minimal.[47] Similarly the only one of these issues on which it is clear that large numbers of working-class people felt strongly was the death penalty, and on this Parliament chose to override a strongly retentionist public opinion. The reform that seems to have enjoyed the widest public support was the Abortion Act, but all the evidence suggests that it was skilful lobbying by ALRA rather than any overwhelming demand from public opinion that brought about the change in the law.[48]

THE ROOTS OF REFORM

I want to look next at the historical background to the emergence of the groups just described. In doing so I will endorse Machin's view that the roots of many of the changes that came to fruition the 1960s are to be found in the 1930s. Unquestionably many of the campaigns of the 1960s had their origins in the inter-war period. In fact the Divorce Law Reform Union goes back to 1906. But the modern campaign for the abolition of capital punishment began in 1925, ALRA was founded in 1936, and the Voluntary Euthanasia Society (a cause which has not yet achieved its objectives, but which had points in common with some of the movements described here) dates from 1935.[49] The major exception is homosexuality, which remained a taboo subject until after the Second World War, though historians have shown that the ground for later changes in attitude was beginning to be prepared even before the First World War.[50]

What I have described as the 'liberal' Christian and the humanist viewpoints can be traced back at least to the 1920s, and the 'pragmatic' Christian viewpoint to the 1930s. Since the 1860s and 1870s agnosticism had been fashionable in sections of the intelligentsia. The pioneers of this movement had attacked Christian doctrine while largely accepting Christian morality. However, by the 1920s, there were a number of influential writers, of whom the most famous was Bertrand Russell, who were prepared to subject all aspects of conventional morality to scathing critique. This period also saw

---

[47] Andrew Holden, *Makers and Manners* (London, 2004), 161.

[48] For discussion of public opinion on these issues, see Richards, *Parliament*, 57, 84, 108, 156, and *passim*.

[49] Machin, *Social Issues*, 10–11, 97–107; John Byrne, 'A Discussion of Euthanasia since 1935 in British Christianity,' (MPhilB thesis, University of Birmingham, 2007).

[50] Weeks, *Coming Out*, 115–58.

the heyday of the Modern Churchmen's Union (MCU), the bastion of liberal Anglicanism, which had been founded in 1898, and was coming to increasing prominence in the years immediately before the First World War. In 1935 members of the MCU, together with equally liberal Nonconformists, were prominent among the founders of the Voluntary Euthanasia Society, and in 1938 the MCU was the only religious body to declare its support for an extension of abortion facilities in evidence to a government commission on this subject.[51] Another key figure in the liberal Christian camp was the Quaker Marie Stopes, founder of the first family planning clinics and author of the immensely popular *Married Love* (1919), which had a big influence on attitudes to sex and marriage, because of her emphasis on female as well as male sexual desire, and on the importance of the sexual relationship for the emotional richness of a marriage.[52]

If the rationalists and liberal Christians were those most likely actively to promote reform, equally important in making it possible for these reforming efforts actually to succeed was the emergence of what I have called the 'pragmatic' Christian stance. This was already beginning in the 1930s, and was based at the time on the recognition of an increasing pluralism in British society. A good example is Cosmo Gordon Lang, archbishop of Canterbury 1928–42. As a member of the Royal Commission on the Divorce Laws in 1909–12 Lang had opposed any relaxation. However, when a modest reform was enacted in 1937–8 Lang (supported by other bishops) reluctantly agreed, arguing that it was 'no longer possible to impose the full Christian standard by law on a largely non-Christian population'.[53] By the 1950s two other kinds of consideration were increasingly influencing 'pragmatic' Anglicans. One was the idea that the sphere of morality, which encompasses the whole of life, is different from the sphere of law, which includes only those areas in which it is necessary for the state to intervene. This was the basic principle laid down by the Wolfenden Report. Sir John Wolfenden disapproved of homosexuality as much as did the then archbishop of Canterbury, Geoffrey Fisher. But both agreed that there was no reason why it should be a concern of the law—especially since, as was often pointed out at the time, the law did not prohibit adultery, which was equally disapproved of by Christian ethicists, and caused far more pain and disruption to families.[54] The other important development at this time was the increasing respect by Anglican leaders for 'experts', such as doctors, psychiatrists, and sociologists, leading to the view that Christian ethics, rather than being autonomous, had to take account of the latest

[51] Machin, *Social Issues*, 98. On the MCU, see Clements, *Discord*, 85–105.
[52] Marcus Collins, *Modern Love* (London, 2003), 39–48.
[53] Richards, *Parliament*, 134–5; Machin, *Social Issues*, 104.
[54] Richards, *Parliament*, 66–72; Weeks, *Coming Out*, 175–8.

evidence coming from these other disciplines.[55] One example was the report on *The Family in Contemporary Society*, prepared for the Lambeth Conference in 1958, which pointed to the evidence of psychiatrists that a happy sexual relationship was an important ingredient of a successful marriage, and that reliable contraception contributed to this desirable end: it thus prepared the way for the Conference's endorsement of the use of contraceptives by married couples. 'Experts' also played a major role on the committee that produced *Putting Asunder*, which was chaired by a bishop, but also included a lawyer, a psychiatrist, and a sociologist.[56]

The 1960s were a hinge decade, separating the 1940s and 1950s, with their more overtly Christian ethos, from the last three decades of the century, with their more pluralist and also more secular atmosphere. The 1960s shared aspects of both periods. Certainly secularist voices were being heard more loudly and social and cultural changes were weakening the influence of the churches. At the same time this was a period when religious controversy evoked widespread interest, when religious arguments played an important part in public debate, and when legislators took serious notice of the positions taken by the churches. There was considerable variation in the extent and nature of the influence which the churches were able to exercise. The history of race relations and immigration law in the later 1960s indicates both the value that governments attached to church support and their willingness to sacrifice this support when other considerations appeared more compelling. In 1965 Harold Wilson appointed Archbishop Ramsey to chair the new National Council for Commonwealth Immigrants—another indication both of Ramsey's personal standing and of the mediating role which the church was seen as exercising at the time. But in 1968 Ramsey was unable to dissuade the Wilson government from introducing a restrictive Immigration Act (which also led to John Robinson's resignation from the Labour party). By this time Ramsey was in the uncomfortable position of being attacked from both sides: a hate-figure for the far right, and frequently ridiculed by the Conservative press, he was also criticized by some black radicals, who thought him too moderate. The evidence cited above would suggest that the churches were among the leaders in the movements to abolish capital punishment and decriminalize homosexuality, but that their role in the reform of the laws on abortion and divorce was more reactive. In none of these cases is there much validity in the view which sees religion and the churches as passive victims of overpowering secularizing forces.

---

[55] Gerald Parsons, 'Between Law and Licence: Christianity, Morality and "Permissiveness"', in Parsons and Wolffe (eds.), *Religious Diversity*, ii. 243.

[56] Lewis and Wallis, 'Fault,' 320–1.

Nor, as the legislative revolution was completed at the end of the 1960s, did Christians retreat into a privatized religiosity. But in their interventions in public debate they increasingly divided. 'Conservative' Christians, such as Mary Whitehouse, continued to argue that Britain was a Christian country, and that the laws must reflect this fact. They focused mainly on issues such as pornography and the content of sex education in schools.[57] But even more important in Whitehouse's eyes was the suppression of blasphemy, a duty abrogated by a church leadership that had lost the will to fight. Even her worst enemy would hardly have claimed that Whitehouse lacked fighting spirit, and in 1977 she pulled off her most remarkable coup by successfully prosecuting Denis Lemon, editor of *Gay News*, for blasphemous libel, after he published a poem that imagined a homosexual relationship between Jesus Christ and a Roman soldier.[58] An intriguing feature of the trial was the fact that the judge was Jewish, and that he decided that fairness to a religion which was not his own required him to take a hostile view of the offending publication. Meanwhile, 'liberal' and 'pragmatic' Christians, rather than claiming a unique status for Christianity, tried to act as the conscience of a pluralist society by championing values which were Christian, but could also be shared by those of other faiths or none. They focused on issues of poverty, social inequality, and race relations. The conflicts between government and church would become explosive after Margaret Thatcher became Prime Minister in 1979.[59]

COMPARISONS

In Canada, Australia, and New Zealand, British influences were still strong in the 1960s. The regulation of morality in the four countries followed similar lines, as did the reform debate from the 1950s and 1960s. In all of these countries, for instance, the Wolfenden Report was widely discussed and had a big influence on changing attitudes to homosexuality. In New Zealand the debate continued much longer, since the law banning male homosexuality was repealed only in 1986, but otherwise the distribution of forces and many of the arguments used were similar to those in Britain.[60] It was the Methodist church in 1961 which was first to call for decriminalization—though at this

[57] Whitehouse, *Who?*, 139–53.   [58] Tracey and Morrison, *Whitehouse*, 1–21.

[59] See, for instance, Henry B. Clark, *The Church under Thatcher* (London, 1993). A good overview of diverging Christian political approaches is provided by Gerald Parsons, 'From Consensus to Confrontation: Religion and Politics in Britain since 1945,' in Parsons and Wolffe (eds.), *Religious Diversity*, ii. 125–59.

[60] Laurie Guy, 'Between a Hard Rock and Shifting Sands: Churches and the Issue of Homosexuality in New Zealand 1960–86,' *Journal of Religious History*, 30 (2006), 61–76.

stage even the Methodists argued that homosexual acts, while not a crime, were still a sin. But by the later 1960s some Christians, often influenced by situation ethics, were questioning this traditional condemnation. Here too there was an increasingly deep and sometimes bitter division between 'liberal', 'conservative', and 'pragmatic' Christians, with Methodists and Anglicans tending towards the 'liberal' or 'pragmatic' positions, the evangelical churches being mainly conservative, while the Presbyterians were split down the middle. As against the more rigid positions adopted by those in the two more extreme camps, the 'pragmatists' were often influenced by conflicting considerations, among which the humanitarian were often to the fore. For instance, the murder of a homosexual in 1964 in a Christchurch park by a gang of 'queer-bashers', and their subsequent acquittal by the court, was an important influence on those who had doubts about the ethics of homosexuality but could clearly see the evil consequences of the existing laws. The humanitarian argument was countered by an MP who declared in 1967: 'I believe that we must set our face very sternly against it [homosexuality], not because we are not sorry for the poor devils who are caught up in this mess, but because the moral standards of society must be protected.'[61]   This presented very clearly the dilemma that faced those who wanted to weaken the structures of Christendom. On the one hand, shared symbols, values, and moral rules gave the conformist majority a sense of belonging, moral guidance, and a strong sense of identification with a society whose governing principles they had internalized. On the other hand, these all served to marginalize and sometimes to cause the persecution of those minorities who rejected parts of, or even all of, the dominant religion and morality.

The considerable level of support from the churches facilitated the passage in Britain and in Canada of reforms which came a few years later, and often in different circumstances in other Western countries. This was notably true of abortion law reform, which came in 1975 in France, in 1976 in West Germany, and in 1978 in Italy; in the United States several states, beginning with California and Colorado in 1967, had extended the grounds for legal abortion, and the Supreme Court judgment of 1973 in *Roe* v. *Wade* established the legality of abortion. Inevitably, the abortion debate was more highly charged in countries where the main church was Roman Catholic—though in the United States some of the strongest opponents of liberalization were conservative Protestants. However, two new factors made for an essentially different debate. One was the emergence of the women's movement, which became the main protagonist in the cause of liberalization, in a way that had

[61] Ibid. 63.

not happened a few years earlier in Britain. The second was the increasing influence of concepts of individual rights.

In France the legalization of abortion was the central concern of the Mouvement de Libération des Femmes (MLF) from its origins in 1970 up to the law of 1975. According to the MLF 'there can be no individual freedom without free control over one's own body'.[62] Their key tactic was to force this previously taboo topic into the centre of public debate through public declarations. The first of these appeared in the pages of Le Nouvel Observateur, their main supporter in the press, in April 1971: 343 well-known women, including film stars and writers, announced that they had had an abortion. In 1973 there was a similar declaration by 331 doctors who had performed abortions. In spite of the continuing opposition of the Vatican, public opinion evolved rapidly in these years. 'At first limited', writes Pelletier, 'to a militant minority, the fight to liberalise abortion came to symbolise the right of women to control over their own bodies, and even their daily life.'[63] Some Catholic opinion was prepared to see abortion, at least in some circumstances, as a necessary evil, and other Catholics argued that Catholics should not seek to impose their own moral principles on the whole population. The Catholic bishops, while continuing to condemn abortion, were tending to equivocate as to whether a change of the law was justifiable. The decisive arguments in the eyes of wider public opinion seem to have been less ideological than humanitarian. The key episode was the 'Bobigny trial' in the autumn of 1972. This involved the prosecution of a teenage girl from a working-class suburb of Paris for having had a backstreet abortion. Also accused were the girl's mother, the abortionist, and two friends of the mother. The girl and the two friends were acquitted, while her mother and the abortionist received suspended sentences. The main defence counsel, Gisèle Halimi, was a leading pro-abortion campaigner, and used the case skilfully to highlight the human costs of the existing laws, and the fact that middle-class women could afford to go 'to London or Geneva' or pay large fees to qualified doctors in Paris, while working-class women risked their lives at the hands of incompetent amateurs. Prominent doctors testified for the defence, including Paul Milliez, a Catholic who, though personally opposed to abortion, said that he had been 'traumatised for forty years by the drama of the unwanted pregnancies of unaware or uneducated women' and had on at least one occasion performed an illegal operation.[64]

Developments in West Germany, where abortion was legalized in 1976, were in some ways similar. In June 1971 Stern published a list of 374

[62] Danièle Léger, *Le féminisme en France* (Paris, 1982), 25–8.
[63] Denis Pelletier, *La crise catholique* (Paris, 2002), 242.
[64] Ibid. 235–42; Arthur Marwick, *The Sixties* (Oxford, 1998), 703–12.

prominent women who had had abortions, and a wave of similar declarations were published during that summer. The issue was equally central to the early development of the women's movement, and again the
Catholic Church was a leading opponent. A complicating factor was the
prominent involvement in the campaign of the Humanist Union and of *Der
Spiegel*, which tried to use the issue as a handle for a generalized attack
on the churches, although in fact many Protestants supported the proposed
liberalization.[65]

The increasingly influential discourse of individual rights was reflected in
the judgment of the United States Supreme Court in 1973 which established
the legality of abortion. In the United States, where the key decisions were
made by lawyers, they hinged on a woman's right to choose an abortion;
in Britain, where they were made by politicians, they hinged on the potentially harmful consequences of refusing her this choice. *Roe* v. *Wade* struck
down the anti-abortion statutes in Texas and about thirty other states, principally on the grounds that they violated the right to privacy. While denying
that there was an absolute right to 'choose', the justices effectively granted
that right during the first three months of pregnancy. The most substantial
opinion, delivered by Justice Blackmun, referred to various Court decisions
going back to 1891, noting that 'the Court has recognized that a right of
personal privacy, or a recognition of certain areas or zones of privacy does
exist under the Constitution', but that 'These decisions make it clear that only
personal rights that can be deemed "fundamental" or "implicit in the concept
of ordered liberty"... are included in this guarantee of personal privacy.' He
went to argue that 'This right of privacy... is broad enough to encompass
a woman's decision whether or not to terminate her pregnancy.'[66] Justice
Douglas's opinion focused on the meanings of 'liberty' as embodied in the
Fourteenth Amendment to the Constitution. He suggested that it included 'the
autonomous control over the development and expression of one's intellect,
interests, tastes and personality', which must include 'freedom of choice in the
basic decisions of one's life respecting marriage, divorce, procreation, contraception and upbringing of children'. After citing various cases, he concluded
that 'the clear message of these cases' was that 'a woman is free to make
the basic decision whether to bear an unwanted child. Elaborate argument
is hardly necessary to demonstrate that childbirth may deprive a woman of
her preferred life style and force upon her a radically different and undesired
future.'[67]

[65] Simone Mantei, *Nein und Ja zur Abtreibung* (Göttingen, 2004), 108–15, 571–81.

[66] David Garrow, *Liberty and Sexuality: The Right to Privacy and the Making of Roe v. Wade*
(New York, 1994), 590–1.

[67] Ibid. 596.

CONCLUSION

Historians coming from completely different directions have agreed in attributing an apocalyptic significance to the changes in the law of morals in the 1960s and 1970s. Thus Callum Brown claims that:

> The period from 1960 to 1970 witnessed a frenzy of legislation that effectively de-Christianized and liberalised British law and society. The legislation was introduced initially amid great controversy, but latterly was rushed through in 1967–8 with amazing ease. In large part, a crisis of confidence befell Christian conservatism in those years as the landmarks of society started to crumble with disconcerting speed. In a mood of depression, and assailed by liberals within who argued for change, the forces of church reaction largely fell silent during the nation's greatest moral and cultural revolution.[68]

Meanwhile René Rémond, writing as a Catholic, as well as one of France's most famous political and religious historians, writes that:

> Until recently the Decalogue was still the reference to which governments and laws conformed; it enjoyed universal consent. The moral and legal coincided; today they diverge. This is probably the newest and most radical aspect of secularization. After religion it is morality that ceases to be a matter for society, to become only a question of individual conscience. . . . Codes are seeing the gradual disappearance of measures inspired by moral considerations, which were themselves drawn from religious reference.[69]

As this chapter has suggested, these assessments need to be considerably nuanced. For instance, there is no single 'Christian' stance either on the morality of the various practices covered by these laws or on the propriety of making them liable to legal sanctions. Gambling is condemned by Methodists, but not by Catholics; divorce is condemned by Catholics, but not by Methodists—indeed some Protestant states have made provision for legal divorce since the sixteenth century. Similarly, while Catholic moral teaching condemns homosexual acts, these were legal throughout the twentieth century in such predominantly Catholic countries as France, Belgium, Italy, and Spain. And differences within denominations were as significant as differences within denominations: John Robinson, Michael Ramsey, and Mary Whitehouse were all Anglicans, but they often adopted totally different positions in the public debates of the time. Furthermore, Christian moral thinking has always been in a process of development: there is no reason why the conservative positions of those like Whitehouse or Pope Paul VI should be seen as more 'authentic'

---

[68] Brown, *Religion and Society in Twentieth-Century Britain*, 267.
[69] René Rémond, *Religion and Society in Modern Europe* (Oxford, 1999), 199.

than the positions adopted by their liberal or 'pragmatic' Christian contemporaries. To argue such a position consistently would, for instance, mean that the defenders of slavery were the representatives of 'authentic' Christianity in the debates over abolition in the eighteenth and nineteenth centuries. These liberal and 'pragmatic' Christians were key players in many of the debates of the 1960s, and their role needs to be taken seriously. It also should be recognized that the marginalization of the more conservative Christian stances does not mean that legislators were indifferent to questions of morality or that Christians had no influence on the public debate on questions of morality. The clearest example would be the increasing salience of anti-racism in the thinking both of Christians and of wide sections of the general public, especially those on the left. In the 1960s and 1970s, states often shifted their perception of the areas where moral intervention was necessary, but this did not mean that the state was, as Rémond argues, morally 'neutral'. Indeed, in the latter part of the twentieth century, the rights of immigrants and refugees became a central area of Christian moral concern in many Western countries. On this issue, many Christians made common concern with members of the secular left, just as on other issues, such as opposition to abortion, many Christians made common cause with members of the secular right.

It remains true that the legal reforms of the 1960s and 1970s mark an important stage in the decline of Christendom, and the move towards a pluralistic society, in which a range of contrasting moral standpoints have an accepted standing. The precise ways in which this happened varied from country to country. In mainly Catholic countries the issues of abortion, and sometimes divorce, brought an inevitable conflict between the church authorities and the proponents of reform. In mainly Protestant countries the role of the churches was usually more complex and varied. But the overall result was to drop the idea that any one set of moral principles should be regarded as normative, and to seek viable compromises between the requisites of rival moralities.

11

The End of Christendom?

In May 1965 the BBC announced that the early morning radio talk, *Lift up your Hearts*, would be replaced by a new kind of religious programme called *Ten to Eight*. The format would be more varied and there would be a focus on 'finding out what Christianity means to ordinary people'. The Director of Religious Broadcasting explained: 'Twenty-five years ago, when *Lift up your Hearts* was designed, it was possible to assume that most of the listeners would be at least nominally Christian. Designing a new programme in 1965 this cannot be assumed.' There were many protests, with Mary Whitehouse, as often, being first off the mark. Two bishops followed soon after. The bishop of Leicester wrote that this was

part of a general withdrawal of the BBC from its position a broadcasting system of a Christian country. They now want a policy of neutrality instead of a policy of acceptance of a Christian way of life. I regret the reasons given for the change—namely that there is a decline in the number of professed Christians. The real reason is that the non-Christian element has become more militant. Too much weight is allowed to its statements.[1]

The drop in church-going since the mid-1950s was still quite modest. But there had been a revolution in people's perceptions of their society and the place of religion within it. An opinion poll later that year did indeed report that 80 per cent of respondents answered 'Yes' to the question 'By and large do you consider Britain a Christian country?' But the words 'by and large' left a lot of space for qualifications. Christians had in fact often been highly ambivalent about the claim that they lived in a Christian country. For instance, a famous Anglican report published in 1945 had been called *Towards the Conversion of England*. But Christians could become uneasy when secularists, with their own quite different agenda, said things that they would have readily admitted when speaking among themselves. In Britain the shift of the BBC from a declaredly Christian to a neutral stance was perhaps the most important influence on these changing perceptions. While conservative

---

[1] *Church Times* (14 and 21 May 1965).

Christians, such as Whitehouse, suspected a conspiracy, the BBC was trying to reflect a change in public mood which it believed to be already under way. Most importantly this involved a shift towards authenticity, plain speaking, the breaking of taboos, and the removal of many of the demarcation lines between 'public' and 'private'. In so far as formal religious practice was already low in Britain and agnostics had an influential presence in many fields, notably the universities, literature and the arts, journalism, and radical politics, any move towards plain speaking would inevitably include giving greater publicity to the less religious aspects of British life. However, it was television programmes which played the biggest part in this process—and in that respect, Whitehouse had correctly identified the enemy. For instance, 1965 saw programmes with titles like *Is Britain Pagan?*, as well as *The Folklore of Christendom*, 'an agnostic's investigation into Christian beliefs in life after death'. In 1965 the satirical *Not So Much a Programme, More a Way of Life* bitterly attacked Catholic teaching on birth control, and from 1966 the comedy series *Till Death Us Do Part* ridiculed religion in ways that would have previously been impossible on British television. After one such programme in February 1968, Mary Whitehouse called on the Director of Public Prosecutions to institute a prosecution for blasphemy, and the much more moderate television and radio critic of the *Church Times* objected strongly to the use of the obnoxious Alf Garnett as some kind of spokesman for Christianity.[2]

None of this turned believers into atheists. But it established the point that Britain was religiously pluralist, including significant numbers of humanists and sceptics, and that Christianity no longer had a protected position. This had wide-ranging implications, not only for television and radio, but also for the relationship between religion and the law, the role of religion in the education system, and the language of public debate. In Britain the crucial period was the 'mid-1960s', between 1963 and 1966; as was suggested in Chapters 3 and 10, Sweden and, in some respects, the United States may have been a little ahead of Britain in confronting these issues; in most other Western countries this happened slightly later, in the 'late 1960s'. But the shift in public perceptions of the religious identity of Western societies was a fundamental aspect of the 'long 1960s'. Whatever the real extent of change in popular belief and practice, most people *believed* that they were moving into a 'pluralist', 'post-Christian', or even 'secular' society. Some enthused; some were horrified; most simply regarded it as a fact. And this was as true in the United States as in Europe.

---

[2] Ibid. (5 March 1965, 26 March 1965, 23 April 1965, 23 February 1968).

THE NEW PLURALISM

The 'long 1960s' saw changes that would define the patterns of religious belonging and practice in the Western world for the rest of the twentieth century. The most important of these were the sharp drop in attendance at church services by adults and the decline in the Christian socialization of the younger generation. In the long term it was the latter that was most significant. The young adults who left the church in the 1960s could, and sometimes did, return in the 1970s and 1980s—as happened especially in the United States. But the process was broken by which, for many centuries, a basic Christian identity had been transmitted to the great majority of each new generation. The changes in England were described in Chapter 9. But the same was happening in other countries. A survey in 1990–1 found that the proportion of those aged over 18 who claimed to have received a religious upbringing was still as high as 94 per cent in Ireland, 93 per cent in Italy, and 80 per cent in the United States, but the figures for other countries were lower—for instance, 71 per cent in France and the Netherlands, 59 per cent in Great Britain, 43 per cent in Denmark, and 31 per cent in Sweden. It seems likely that in many countries children born in the later 1950s and 1960s were at a turning-point. A series of surveys of students at Sheffield University found that 94 per cent of students responding in 1961 said they had received some kind of religious upbringing, and still 88 per cent in 1971; but by 1985 this had fallen to 51 per cent.[3] This would suggest that in Britain—though probably in some countries the major changes came a little later—important changes in the socialization of the young were taking place around 1970, and that the changes were rapid.

The 1960s brought an explosion of new ways of understanding the world. For those growing up in the 1950s, the main alternatives were Christianity, Scientism and Socialism, or some combination of Christianity and Socialism or of Socialism and Scientism. Other possibilities existed of course for the intellectually enterprising, but those who sought out more esoteric alternatives were likely to be dismissed as eccentrics. Although Socialism and Scientism also had very considerable influence, whether because of the support of powerful political parties, or because of the prestige enjoyed by scientists generally, and the readiness of some to promote science as a completely self-sufficient world-view, Christianity retained a uniquely powerful position, because so many children attended confirmation classes, went to church-run schools, or belonged to religious youth organizations. Many young people rebelled against their upbringing, but for most of them Christianity had to

---

[3] Mattei Dogan, 'The Decline of Religious Beliefs in Western Europe,' *International Social Science Journal*, 143 (1995), p 411; D. W. Bebbington, 'The Secularization of the British universities since the Mid-Nineteenth Century', in George Marsden and Bradley Longfield (eds.), *The Secularization of the Academy* (New York, 1992), 268.

be considered as a major option, and in very many cases they defined their view of the world either in terms of or in reaction to this pervasive Christianity. Autobiographies of those brought up in the nineteenth century almost invariably include some discussion of the evolution of the authors' religious ideas, showing how they adopted, rejected, or modified the beliefs inculcated by parents, church, or school, and this continued in many autobiographies of those brought up in the first half of the twentieth century. Oral history interviews with those born in the 1930s and 1940s show that most respondents have views, whether positive or negative, on Christianity and/or the Christian churches, and are quite able to talk about these views.[4] By the 1970s, however, Christianity was less central, as the options had widened enormously, to include not only many new forms of Christianity and Socialism, but also various non-Christian religions and many kinds of 'alternative spirituality'. Moreover, what had seemed eccentric in the 1950s now seemed to reflect a healthy degree of independent-mindedness.

Within Christianity the biggest new development was the Charismatic Movement, which combined an emphatic supernaturalism with a 'modern' style, attractive to young people bored by more conventional services. Very much in decline, however, was the more low-key style of piety which had flourished in previous decades, which emphasized Christian ethics and membership of the Christian community, rather than the dogmatic or the miraculous. Those who wanted a faith as organized, as intellectualized, and as dogmatic as any form of Christianity, but firmly focused on political action here and now, were attracted to the plethora of Socialist and Anarchist groups that were springing up in the later 1960s and early 1970s, in opposition to the established Social Democratic and Communist parties. For most of them the supreme prophet was Karl Marx, and the more studious discussed the canonical texts as avidly as their evangelical contemporaries discussed the Bible—though Marx was often interpreted in the light of such contemporary gurus as Wilhelm Reich, Herbert Marcuse, or R. D. Laing. The various forms of Socialism that flourished in those years were as much a faith—explaining the world, showing how to change it, and also giving meaning to the individual life—as was any form of Christianity.[5] The passion and the dogmatism with which this faith was pursued was also reflected in the battles between the numerous warring

---

[4] Here I differ from Callum Brown, *Death of Christian Britain: Understanding Secularization 1800–2000* (London, 2001), 182, who argues that interviewees born after the mid-1930s tend to produce short, uninformative answers to questions on religion. While the quality and quantity of responses to questions on religion varies, both in the Families Social Mobility and Ageing project and more especially in the Social and Family Life 1940–1970 project, many of the respondents born in the 1940s and 1950s do provide detailed responses to questions on religion, as I have shown in chapters 2, 5 and 9, where I make considerable use of this material.

[5] Fraser, *1968*, 63–76, 106–7, 143–5, and *passim*.

factions—or *groupuscules*, as they were called in France. The same could be said of the Women's Liberation Movement, which grew rapidly from about 1969, and which became a complete way of life and of looking at the world for many of its most committed members. The movement was also bedevilled by internal conflicts, between, for instance, Socialists, Liberals, and Radicals; between lesbians and straight women; and between those who were already lesbian before the start of the movement and 'political lesbians' whose sexual orientation had changed as a result of their experiences in the struggle.[6]

And then there were the innumerable 'alternative' possibilities offered by the mystics of all kinds, whose ideas were still relatively esoteric, but were gradually acquiring a wider influence. One channel for this influence was the growing interest in ecology during the 1970s, which could be related to the revival of paganism, one of the most important of the new movements of this period. Especially in the United States, feminism and mysticism could merge through worship of the Goddess.[7] Another channel was through interest in alternative therapies, which introduced many people to new religious or philosophical ideas, often of Asian origin. Yoga was rapidly gaining popularity, both among those who saw it as a new form of spirituality and those who just saw it as a way of keeping physically and mentally fit.[8]

American sociologists have highlighted the 'seeker' as a characteristic figure of the 'baby boom' generation.[9] While these 'seekers' might form organized groups, and sometimes even practised collective rituals, and they certainly gained sustenance for their beliefs from others whose quest led them in similar directions, the emphasis was on the right and duty of every individual to follow his or her own 'path' and to reject any rules of belief or behaviour. From the late 1960s the options were rapidly widening. In 1975 a guide was published to *Alternative England and Wales*. It included practical advice on many different subjects, ranging from sex and drugs to establishing a smallholding or a free school, as well as information on radical bookshops and political campaigns. However, the longest chapter was headed 'Mystical', and this overlapped with other chapters on 'Therapy', 'Martial Arts', 'Herbalism', and 'Retreats'. The aim was to list 'all the groups we could find that have regular, open activities and a more or less permanent base except for established churches'—though some of the groups listed were Christian. The largest categories were 'hatha yoga' (40 groups listed), 'hindu oriented' (40), and

---

[6] David Bouchier, *The Feminist Challenge: The Movement for Women's Liberation in Britain and the USA* (London 1985), 60, 64–89, 115–9.

[7] Joanne Pearson, 'The History and Development of Wicca and Paganism,' in Pearson, *Belief beyond Boundaries*, 36–9.

[8] Paul Heelas and Linda Woodhead, *Spiritual Revolution* (Oxford, 2005), 29–30, 43–4, 173–4.

[9] Wade Clark Roof, *A Generation of Seekers: The Spiritual Journey of the Baby Boom Generation* (New York, 1993).

buddhist (36). (The guide had an aversion to the use of capitals). But there were many others, including 'sufi', 'gurdjeff, ouspensky, nicoll', 'occult', 'flying saucers', and 'astrology'. There were also centres open to a variety of alternative activities and groups. Thus Acacia House in the west London suburb of Acton was described as 'A very active, open centre for spiritual healing and esoteric studies'.

Besides daily spiritual healing they teach: Hatha Yoga on Mondays and Thursdays at 6.30 for beginners and 8 for advanced. Meditation and healing on Tuesdays at 8; Buddhist meditation on Wednesdays at 8; clairvoyance on the first Friday of the month; macrobiotic cookery class on the first Thursday of the month....They also have lectures on Saturdays and Sundays, acupuncture, physiotherapy, zone therapy and oriental divination and Tai Chi Ch'uan.[10]

The inclusion of that chapter in a section with the overall heading of 'Self development' reflected the assumption that the reader's main concern should be with individual seeking, rather than with contributing to the life of a community—though of course some of the groups listed did have a strong communal ethos. Many of the groups included 'service to humanity' among their major objectives, but the first step was for each individual to acquire the knowledge and the inner peace that would enable him or her to contribute effectively.

In the 1960s, the growth in the numbers of Muslims, Hindus, and Sikhs, mainly through immigration, seemed less significant than the growth in the number of professed atheists and agnostics. From the perspective of the early twenty-first century both these developments were very important, and both have contributed to the emergence of a religiously pluralist society, in which Christianity has lost a large part (though by no means all) of its privileged position. The result is not entirely the 'secular society' that some have trumpeted and some have bewailed, and not entirely the often celebrated 'multi-faith society'. For divisions *within* religions are as significant as divisions *between* religions, and even secularism can take many different forms. Christianity, Islam, Judaism, and secularism, to take only the four loudest voices in contemporary religious debate, all come in both liberal and conservative, 'open' and 'closed' forms. This has made for complex patterns of *ad hoc* alliances. On some issues, the religious groups may all combine against the secularists, or the secularists may combine with the various minority faiths against the Christians. On other issues, liberal Christians and Jews may have more in common with secularists than with their own more conservative co-religionists. And within the secularist camp there is a difference between

[10] *Alternative England and Wales* (London 1975).

those who simply want complete religious freedom and those who want a war against all religions.

THE PARTING OF THE WAYS?

Between 1945 and about 1972 religious trends in the United States and in western Europe seemed to be moving in the same direction. On both sides of the Atlantic religious practice and the public profile of the churches were rising in the later 1940s and early 1950s, though more so in the United States than in most European countries. From the later 1950s there was a secularizing trend, visible a little earlier in the United States than in Europe, and reaching a climax towards the end of the 1960s. In 1970 the Yale church historian, Sydney Ahlstrom, produced an analysis of American religious trends as apocalyptic as anything in contemporary Europe. In 1960, he wrote, the post-war religious revival had lost momentum, but the rate of change was still slow. However, by 1966, 'it was perfectly clear to any reasonably conscious American historian that the postwar revival had completely frittered out, that the nation was moving rapidly towards a *crise de la conscience* of unprecedented depth'. Words like secular, permissive, and post-Christian had become common. 'The decade of the 1960s was a time, in short, when the old grounds of national confidence, patriotic idealism and even of historic Judeo-Christian theism, were awash.' He noted three broad trends:

(1) a growing attachment to a naturalism or 'secularism' that makes people suspicious of doctrines that imply anything supernatural or which seem to involve magic, superstition, or divine intervention in the natural order;

(2) a creeping or galloping awareness of vast contradictions in American life between profession and performance, the ideal and the actual; and

(3) increasing doubt concerning the capacity of present-day ecclesiastical, political, social, and educational institutions to rectify these contradictions.[11]

But then, about 1972, the American and European paths began to diverge. The decline of church-going continued with little break in many European countries—as well as in Canada, Australia, and New Zealand. In the United States levels of church-going, while still much lower than in the 1950s, stabilized in the 1970s. Gallup Poll data show that the proportion of adults claiming to have attended church during the last week had fallen more or

---

[11] Sydney Ahlstrom, 'The Radical Turn in Theology and Ethics: Why it Occurred in the 1960s', *Annals of the American Academy of Political Science*, 387 (1970), 2–3, 7–8.

less continuously from 49 per cent in 1958 to 40 per cent in 1971. However, the figure then remained at 40 per cent for the rest of the decade, apart from slight fluctuations, and was still 40 per cent in 1980.[12] Other evidence now suggests that the actual rate of church-going was rather lower because of respondents' reluctance to admit that they went to church less frequently than they would like. For instance, a survey in 1975 where respondents kept a diary of their activities during the week found that only 31 per cent mentioned going to church.[13] It is possible that the proportion of respondents who were misreporting their activities was increasing during the 1970s—though there is nothing to suggest that this was so. But other evidence might support the contention that the situation had indeed stabilized. For instance, pollsters regularly asked Americans if they thought the influence of religion was rising or falling: throughout the 1960s a smaller and smaller proportion of respondents said that this influence was rising; but in the 1970s the proportion who said this was again increasing. While money spent on new church buildings had continued to drop between 1970 and 1975, it rose again between 1975 and 1980.[14] And of course the public profile of Christianity, usually in its evangelical forms, rose as a result of the election of America's first professedly born-again president, Jimmy Carter, in 1976, the growing volume, and in some cases popularity, of televangelism, and the emergence at the end of the decade of the New Christian Right as a formidable mobilizing force.

One factor in the stabilization of the church-going statistics was the 'return' to church in the middle and later 1970s of many of the 'baby-boomers' who had left in the 1960s and early 1970s. About 90 per cent of the generation born immediately after the Second World War had been sent by parents to church or Sunday School, but the majority of them gave up going to church as adolescents or young adults. As they in turn began to bring up families, many of them came back to their roots and started going to church again. This pattern was less common among those who had been deeply involved in the counter-culture or radical politics: if they had any interest in religion, it was more likely to be the 'alternative' spiritualities that attracted them. The 'returnees' were likely to be those who had been less influenced by 'The Sixties', and especially those who were economically successful and/or

---

[12] Ronald J. Flowers, *Religion in Strange Times* (n.pl., 1984), 39.

[13] Stanley Presser and Linda Stinson, 'Data Collection Mode and Social Desirability: Bias in Self-Reported Religious Attendance,' *American Sociological Review*, 63 (1998), 143. This article was part of a special number of the *American Sociological Review*, which included rival perspectives on the level of church attendance in the United States and the reliability of various kinds of data.

[14] Flowers, *Strange Times*, 38–40.

politically conservative.[15] By the mid-1970s the Catholics, who had suffered the most severe loss of church-goers in the preceding decade, were also seeing a stabilization. One factor here seems to have been an increasing readiness of Catholics to continue going to church while rejecting aspects of official teaching. *Humanae Vitae* was by that time a dead letter, and many Catholics went their own way in other areas of sexual ethics, while taking a generally relaxed view of the authority of the Pope and bishops.[16]

Since the 1970s it has become common both for sociologists and for journalists to contrast the 'religious' United States with 'secular' Europe (to which Canada is sometimes admitted as an honorary member).[17] These contrasts are exaggerated. The trends mentioned in the earlier part of this chapter are common to western Europe and North America, and the points in common are more important than the points of difference. For instance, 'alternative' spiritualities have grown as prodigiously in the United States as in Europe. The rise in the numbers of those professing no religion in the United States, though much less than in France or the Netherlands, has been close to the European average. For instance in 2001 the 14 per cent of Americans claiming no religion was almost identical to the 15 per cent recorded by the census in Great Britain. In Canada the figure was 16 per cent.[18]

In many parts of the world the most expansive branch of Christianity in the last three decades of the twentieth century was theologically conservative Protestantism, including especially Charismatic and Pentecostal churches of all kinds, as well as Baptists and other more conventional evangelicals, Adventists, and more unorthodox movements with Protestant roots, such as the Mormons and Jehovah's Witnesses. This growth has taken place in Europe (and indeed in other Western countries, such as Australia) as well as the USA.[19] However, the biggest difference between the United States and other Western countries lies in the exceptional strength which conservative and fundamentalist branches of Protestantism already enjoyed before the 1970s. These have been growing in most parts of the world, but in the United States they grew from a base which was much higher then in any other Western country, with the possible exception of Northern Ireland.

---

[15] David A. Roozen and others, 'La génération née après-guerre et la religion instituée', *Archives des Sciences Sociales de la Religion*, 83 (1993), 39; Robert Wuthnow, *After Heaven: American Spirituality since the 1950s* (Berkeley, Calif., 1988), 75–6.

[16] Roozen and others, 'Génération,' 41–3.

[17] For comparison between the USA and Canada, see Mark A. Noll, 'What Happened to Christian Canada?' *Church History*, 75 (2006), 245–73.

[18] Wuthnow, *After Heaven*; Hugh McLeod, 'The Crisis of Christianity in the West: Entering a Post-Christian Era?' in idem (ed), *Cambridge History of Christianity*, ix. 344.

[19] For instance in Britain it is estimated that between 1975 and 1992 membership of all Christian denominations fell by 16%, but that Pentecostalists increased by 52% and members of independent congregations by 42%. Grace Davie, *Religion in Britain since 1945* (Oxford, 1994), 46.

It is wrong to assume that the religious histories of Europe and the United States are fundamentally different, or that Americans have been consistently 'more religious' than Europeans. In the nineteenth century the religious similarities between the United States and Britain were greater than the differences. Though the decline in British religious practice since about 1890 meant that by the 1950s far fewer Britons than Americans were going to church, levels of religious activity in the United States remained close to those in European countries such as Belgium, the Netherlands, Austria, and Italy, and below those in Ireland.[20] The divergence in the 1970s may be attributed to a number of different factors.

First there is the continuing importance of regional differences in the USA. That country is of course vastly greater in area than any European nation and much more ethnically and racially diverse, and its federal system reserves considerable powers to the individual states (these, admittedly, being subject to over-ruling by the Supreme Court). Moreover, strongly defined regional identities are confirmed by the continuing memory of the Civil War which, unlike those in, for instance, Spain or Finland, was fought between two regions of the country. In the UK, by contrast, while regional differences have not yet been obliterated, a process of increasing metropolitan cultural domination has been going on since the later nineteenth century, and one result has been the standardization of levels of religious practice at a rate close to that obtaining in London, and the declining significance of regional differences. These persist in a limited way, but for most purposes there is a single national pattern of religious practice, embracing most of Britain from Cornwall to north-east Scotland.[21] The two regions which stand out by their much higher level of church-going, namely Northern Ireland and north-west Scotland, are peripheral both in a cultural and in a geographical sense, suffer from chronic economic and (in the case of Northern Ireland) political difficulties, and have consequently been depleted by emigration. A similar process has taken place, though much more recently, in France, where large regional differences in religion and politics continued into the 1960s, but had to a large degree been obliterated by the 1980s, partly because of the overwhelming cultural influence of Paris, mediated especially through television, and partly because of changes in the economy and social structure. Mendras described the years 1965–84 as marking the 'Second French Revolution', which saw the completion of the unification of the nation. Major factors included: the influence of the Paris-based media; the decline of the two most locally rooted social

---

[20] Hugh McLeod, 'Dechristianization and Rechristianization: The Case of Great Britain,' *Kirchliche Zeitgeschichte*, 11 (1998), 23–4.

[21] Hugh McLeod, 'Rapports entre la religion et les principaux clivages de la société britannique,' in Hugh McLeod, Stuart Mews and Christiane d'Haussy (eds.), *Histoire religieuse de la Grande-Bretagne* (Paris, 1997), 298–9.

groups, the peasantry and the industrial working class; the rising numbers in more mobile professions, such as managers, technicians, and professionals; the diminishing differences between town and country; and the tendencies towards an extreme individualism, in relation to which local traditions are of little relevance.[22] The same broad social trends can be seen in the USA too, but regional differences have remained greater, and a variety of subcultures have found it easier to withstand the homogenizing tendencies. The secularizing forces have been strongest in the North-East and the West. But the South and the Mid-West, the regions with the highest levels of church-going, have been more successful in retaining a distinctive cultural identity, and especially important, parts of the South have been going through a period of economic revival, and attracting migrants from other regions. At the same time, western states have seen a big growth in the numbers of those with no religion, so that rather than there being an 'American' approach to religion to be contrasted with the 'European' approach, regional differences in religion and irreligion have actually been accentuated in recent years.[23]

Second, there is the relationship between American religion and politics—a subject which has generated a huge literature since the later 1970s, and which has been more responsible than anything else for the enormous growth of interest in American religion by academics and journalists both in the USA and elsewhere. Those who see the correlation between religious affiliation and voting in recent American elections as something distinctively, and often as objectionably, American have short memories. At least up to the 1960s religious variables were the best predictors of a person's voting intentions in the majority of west European countries,[24] though there has generally been a decline in the political significance of religion since then. Britain and West Germany, as well as the USA, saw a swing to the right in the 1980s, but only in the USA was there a significant link between conservative politics and conservative religion. This was partly a matter of sheer numbers—there were more conservative Protestants to be mobilized in the USA. But two other factors also played a part. In the case of Britain, one of these was the lack of any clear identification between particular kinds of religion and particular kinds of politics. Of course in the nineteenth century, and continuing into the early twentieth century, Anglicans tended to vote Conservative and Nonconformists Liberal. But this situation was complicated by the rise of Labour, which drew

---

[22] Henri Mendras, *La Seconde Révolution française* (Paris, 1988), 12–13.

[23] For regional differences in American religion, see Barry A. Kosmin and Seymour P. Lachman, *One Nation under God* (New York, 1993), 49–113. In 1990 the proportion with no religion ranged from 3% in Louisiana to 17% in Oregon, and from 4% in Philadelphia to 20% in San Francisco.

[24] Richard Rose, 'Introduction,' in idem (ed), *Electoral Behaviour: A Comparative Handbook* (New York, 1974), 15–17.

voters from both kinds of church, as well as many Catholics, and by the 1980s most churches contained a mixture of supporters of different parties.[25] There was none that could offer the large bloc of potentially conservative voters that the 'Religious Right' mobilized in the USA. In post-war British politics there have been front-line politicians in all parties who have been strongly influenced by religion[26]—as many, I would guess, as in the USA—but they were not elected because of their adherence to a particular kind of religion, nor, except in quite rare instances, have they been beholden to a bloc of voters belonging to a particular kind of church. The Religious Right in the USA, by contrast, has benefited politically from the fact that conservative Protestants are heavily concentrated in particular states, mainly in the South and Mid-West, and show a very strong preference for the Republican party, so that Republican politicians in those states are forced to take them seriously.[27] What I am suggesting here is that the greater prominence of religion in the politics of the USA than in most European countries is not because (as the European media likes to claim) Americans are 'religious' and Europeans 'secular', but at least in part because of distinctive features of the American political and religious situation which have assisted some religious groups in their attempts to be politically effective.

However, the greatest religious difference between Europe and the United States lies in the degree to which, and the ways in which, religion has penetrated popular culture. There are areas of American life which are as secular as any in Europe. The universities and the media are often cited as strongholds of secularity.[28] If so, there is an instructive contrast with Britain where, in all probability, workers in education and health are the two occupational groups most likely to be church-goers.[29] In the 1950s and early 1960s, as was suggested in Chapter 2, universities may well have been the *most* religious places in British society. In Britain, as in many other parts of Europe, the

---

[25] Bruno Cautres, 'Religion et comportement électoral en Grande-Bretagne,' in Monica Charlot (ed), *Religion et politque en Grande-Bretagne* (Paris, 1994), 165–90, shows a continuing, though relatively weak, correlation between voting and religious denomination.

[26] For instance, to take only the most prominent, Macmillan and Thatcher among Conservatives, and Cripps and Blair in Labour, as well as such leading Liberals as Beith and Hughes, and Williams among the Social Democrats. Wilson came from a strongly Congregationalist background, the continuing significance of which is disputed. His close colleague, the agnostic Crossman, made frequent, sometimes sneering, reference to Wilson's 'Methodism'.

[27] Clyde Wilcox, *Onward Christian Soldiers? The Religious Right in American Politics* (Boulder, Colo., 1996), 75–7.

[28] On journalism, see Grace Davie, *Europe, the Exceptional Case: Parameters of Faith in the Modern World* (London, 2002), 48–9.

[29] While there is no conclusive evidence on this there are many hints. For instance, Jones, 'Churches in Birmingham,' 111, found in 1997 that out of 228 Birmingham church-goers responding to a questionnaire, 22% of those stating an occupation were in education and 9% in health.

ethos of most churches continues to be predominantly middle-class, educated, and respectable, and this has inhibited efforts to appeal to a broader constituency.

American popular Catholicism is not too far different from that found in many parts of Catholic Europe—though with the major difference that the anti-clericalism that has so often accompanied it in Europe has played a smaller role in America. But the USA was and is a country with a Protestant majority, and it is the strength both of popular Protestantism and of a vaguer and more generalized religiosity that is characteristic of modern America. It was reflected in the huge popularity of revivalists like Billy Sunday or Aimee Semple McPherson with styles taken from the world of showbiz, or by the frequency with which Hollywood in the 1940s and 1950s drew on religious themes.[30] In more recent times, one can point to the continuing mixture of evangelism and entertainment, not only on television, but in Christian theme parks, Christian rock music, T-shirts, and bumper stickers with Christian messages, and what might be called Christian science fiction, in the form of novels about the Rapture and other millennial themes.[31] At the same time 'secular' popular culture draws freely on religious motifs, as for instance in the music of Madonna or the cult surrounding Elvis Presley.[32] The intermingling of religion and popular culture is particularly evident in the world of sport, seen by many in America as much as in Europe, as the new religion. Football games frequently begin with prayer. Preachers emphasize their credentials as sports fans by frequent use of sporting metaphors in their sermons. Boxers, in particular, see the hand of God both in their victories and in their defeats.[33] This seems to be particularly characteristic of sports that are both individual and ultra-physical. Thus Paul Anderson, 'The World's Strongest Man', practised 'Lifting to the Lord' and the wrestler Hulk Hogan wore a gold cross in the ring and claimed to bow to no man, except 'the Dude who walked on water'.[34]

The divergence between the United States and Europe is more complex than appears at first sight because the relatively low levels of religious practice in

[30] Peter D. Williams, *Popular Religion in America: Symbolic Change and the Modernization Process in Historical Perspective* (Englewood Cliffs, NJ, 1980), 162–3, 203.

[31] Colleen McDannell, *Material Christianity* (New Haven, 1995), 246–69; William Romanowski, 'Evangelicals and Popular Music: The Contemporary Christian Music Industry,' in Forbes and Mahan (eds.), *Religion and Popular Culture in America*, 105–24.

[32] Mark D. Hulsether, 'Like a Sermon: Popular Religion in Madonna Videos,' in Forbes and Mahan (eds.), *Religion and Popular Culture*, 77–100; Erika Doss, 'Believing in Elvis: Popular Piety in Material Culture,' in Stewart M. Hoover and Lynn Schofield Clark (eds.), *Practicing Religion in the Age of the Media* (New York, 2002), 63–86.

[33] Robert J. Higgs, *God in the Stadium: Sports and Religion in America* (Lexington, Ky., 1995), 9–18; Shirl J. Hoffman (ed.), *Sports and Religion* (Champaign, Ill., 1992).

[34] Higgs, *Stadium*, 10–11.

Europe since the early 1970s contrasted with the continuing links between church and state and the important social role which the churches continued to perform. Admittedly relations between church and state in the USA have been a minefield, with the principle of 'separation' between church and state in continual tension with the principle of 'free exercise' of religion. In Europe there has been less tension, because many forms of relation between church and state that might be deemed unconstitutional in the United States are simply taken for granted by most Europeans. A survey published in 1996 of church–state relations in the countries of the European Union showed how extensive the links were.[35] So, for instance, even the French state, the only one in western Europe which is avowedly secular, has since 1959 subsidized Catholic schools, though France, like the United States, provides no teaching of religion in state schools. All other west European countries provide some kind of teaching of religion in state schools, though the ways in which they do it vary considerably. England and Wales has since 1870 required that teaching be 'unsectarian' (though it may be biased towards Christianity—and at least until the 1970s usually was). Sweden decided in 1962 that religious teaching must be 'objective'. In several others, including Italy, Finland, and most German *Länder*, the teaching is confessional. In the former West Germany the welfare system was mainly based on church provision, and in the 1970s, while church attendance dropped, the Catholic welfare agency, Caritas, was going through a big expansion. It is now said to be the largest non-state employer in Europe. The reunification of Germany in 1990 united the West, with its long traditions of cooperation between church and state, with the formerly Communist East, said to be 'the most areligious part of the world'.[36] But, in spite of the formal separation of church and state, there continued to be 'a constitutionally secured form of co-operation between the two institutions. This is done in order to care in co-operation for the needs of the people.'[37] In Belgium and the Netherlands church institutions of many kinds continued to enjoy state subsidies. The church tax system ensured the churches a regular, and usually generous, income in Germany, the Nordic countries, and Italy.

As well as cooperating with the state in the fields of education and welfare, the churches have been prepared to challenge the state in other areas and to act as a national conscience by articulating values which are Christian,

[35] Gerhard Robbers (ed.), *Church and State Church and State in the European Union* (Baden-Baden 1996).

[36] Thomas Schmidt and Monika Wohlrab-Sahr, 'Still the Most Areligious Part of the World: Developments in the Religious Field in Eastern Germany since 1990,' *International Journal of Practical Theology*, 7 (2003), 86–100.

[37] Gerhard Robbers, 'Church and State in Germany,' in idem (ed.), *Church and State*, 60–1.

but are also assumed to be shared by many non-Christians. Thus the Dutch and German churches took a leading part in the peace movements in those countries in the 1980s, and in Britain the churches were involved in frequent conflict with the Thatcher government, especially following the Church of England's report, *Faith in the City* (1985) which highlighted the dire conditions in 'urban priority areas' and the need for a change of government policies if the conditions of those living there were to be improved.[38] More recently the churches have been the most active supporters of campaigns for fair trade and the cancellation of Third World debts. Perhaps the most striking example of the continuing importance of the churches, even in relatively secularized societies is immigration and asylum.[39] The bleak situation of asylum-seekers and other immigrants would be even worse but for the many church initiatives. Clergy have spoken out against racism and exclusionist asylum policies, and have warned against voting for far right parties. At a more practical level, churches have supported numerous schemes to assist asylum-seekers, and in some cases church people have hidden them in their homes—as happened also in the United States, where, in the Reagan era, church people provided 'sanctuary' for those fleeing persecution by right-wing dictatorships in Central America. In Europe the low levels of religious practice and the secularity of much public discourse contrasts with the essential social role of churches and other religiously based organizations, exercised with the approval or at least the acceptance of the state. The notion that religion has been 'privatized' in Europe is a misnomer. On the contrary: there has been a secularization of many areas of everyday life, yet churches, and indeed mosques and temples, continue to be among the most significant institutions in these countries, with wide-ranging social functions. Far from being 'irrelevant', as some critics claim,[40] they are, whether for good or for ill (according to one's viewpoint), essential to the functioning of European societies.

The differences between Europe and the United States are not so much therefore between the 'secularity' of one and the 'religiosity' of the other, as between different ways of being 'secular' and of being 'religious'. In one area there is little difference between the two sides of the Atlantic: sexual behaviour in the United States no more conforms to traditional Christian teachings than it does in Europe, and the United States were probably a little ahead

---

[38] Andrew Shanks, article on 'Peace' in Adrian Hastings, Alistair Mason, and Hugh Pyper (eds.), *The Oxford Companion to Christian Thought* (Oxford, 2000), 525–6; Henry B. Clark, *The Church under Thatcher* (London, 1993).

[39] For France, see Kay Chadwick, 'Accueillir l'étranger: Immigration, Integration and the French Catholic Church,' in idem (ed.), *Catholicism*, 175–96.

[40] Cf. Brown, *Death*, 191.

of most European countries in the 'sexual revolution'.[41] Levels of religious belief and observance are certainly somewhat higher in the United States than the west European average, though it is often forgotten that there are huge differences in most aspects of religion within western Europe. On the other hand, the acceptance by most Europeans of extensive links between church and state contrasts with the American insistence on maintaining the boundaries between their respective spheres—though each religious or anti-religious group tries to define the separation in a way that would be to its own advantage. The biggest difference between the United States and most parts of western Europe, I have suggested, lies in the degree to which religion continues to be embedded in American popular culture, in spite of the secularization of many elite groups. A second difference is that professions of piety are required of American politicians in a way that seldom happens in Europe, and this probably has done more than anything else to shape perceptions of Americans as an unusually, and perhaps excessively, religious people. These professions are especially expected of presidents, and this is partly because of the dual functions of American presidents as both head of state (and thus as embodying and articulating shared national values) and leader of the government. In Europe these roles are generally separated, so that for instance in the UK, the Queen will talk about religion on television in a way that would be deemed inappropriate if the Prime Minister were to do it (even if he or she happened to be a professing Christian). But it has been an achievement of the American Christian right to make the religious allegiances of even those seeking lesser office a public issue. A questionnaire sent to the 585 members of Congress and governors of states in 1995 revealed that there were only four brave individuals who were prepared to reveal that they had no religious affiliation.[42]

CONCLUSION

The religious, political, and social order known as 'Christendom', which was a defining feature of European life for more than a thousand years, and was exported to the Americas in the sixteenth and seventeenth centuries, was in decline from the eighteenth century. Religious scepticism and alienation from the church began with relatively small numbers of intellectuals and political radicals. But by the later nineteenth century a range of alternative views of the

---

[41] Beth Bailey, "The Sexual Revolution: Was it Revolutionary?' in David Farber and Beth Bailey (eds.), *The Columbia Guide to America in the 1960s* (New York, 2001), 134–42.

[42] Michael Barone and Grant Ujifusa (eds.), *The Almanac of American Politics, 1996* (Washington, DC, 1995).

world were available to the mass of the population. The position of the Christian churches and of Christian beliefs and rituals as socially binding forces were then placed under considerable strain—the more so as radically anti-Christian or anti-church political movements ('political religions', as they are often termed) came to power, beginning in the relatively mild form of French Republicanism, but moving on to Spanish Republicanism, Communism, and Nazism.[43] However, Christendom enjoyed a temporary revival during the Second World War and the cold war.

What appeared to be the final crisis of Christendom came in the 1960s and 1970s, when a variety of developments were combining to undermine existing institutions, values, and moral rules, and to lead towards a society where individual freedom was a central principle, and which offered a much wider range of choices in matters of beliefs, values, and lifestyles. Few people any longer assumed that they were living in a Christian society. The Christian socialization of the younger generation had been substantially weakened. The laws no longer purported to be based on Christianity. Links between religious and secular elites had diminished. In most churches, both clergy and congregations were made up disproportionately of the middle-aged and the elderly. They faced the challenge of adapting to a very different social and cultural environment with depleted resources. Yet, in the pluralist and relatively secular societies of the later twentieth century, the Christian churches continued to have an important role. At a time when many other voluntary organizations had also suffered serious decline,[44] they remained the largest in numbers of active members, and the widest-ranging in social influence.

---

[43] This is the central theme of two recent books by Michael Burleigh, *Earthly Powers* (London, 2005) and *Sacred Causes* (London, 2006).

[44] On this theme an influential text in the USA is Robert Putnam, *Bowling Alone* (New York, 2000).

Conclusion

Most historians and sociologists who have written about religion in the modern West agree that the years between about 1955 and 1975 were a period of decisive change. But they continue to be completely divided in their attempts to explain these changes. I will conclude by summarizing the explanations offered here, and by discussing the similarities and differences between these explanations and those offered by other writers.

Explanations for religious change in the 1960s must operate at three levels: the long-term preconditions, the effects of more immediate social changes, and the impact of specific events, movements, and personalities. In this respect, my methodology is closest to that of Alan Gilbert who, in explaining *The Making of Post-Christian Britain*, integrates a range of factors, some very long-term and others much more recent—though I would disagree with many specific points in Gilbert's argument. However, most accounts have emphasized one of these levels of explanation. For instance, a number of sociologists, including Bruce and Dobbelaere, have placed an overriding stress on the long-term processes of modernization and secularization; Brown is typical of social and cultural historians in stressing the impact of more immediate social changes; and Cholvy and Hilaire, like a number of other church historians, emphasize the role of specific events, movements, and personalities. I have argued that the religious upheavals of the 1960s have to be seen in the context of much longer term developments in Western societies, including notably the growth of religious toleration since the seventeenth century, intellectual critiques of Christianity going back to the eighteenth century, movements of political emancipation since 1789, and changes in thinking about ethics generally and sexual ethics especially since about 1890. I have also noted that the legislative revolution of the 1960s and 1970s, embracing such issues as abortion, contraception, divorce, and homosexuality had its origins in the 1920s and 1930s. On the other hand social changes after the Second World War were decisive in enabling ideas previously limited to an avant-garde or to socially marginal groups to become widely diffused and to become practical possibilities. Here I have emphasized the wide-ranging effects of the unprecedented affluence enjoyed by Western societies in the 'long 1960s'. Almost equally important, however, was the decline of the collective identities which had been central to most Western societies in the second half of the nineteenth century and the first half of the twentieth, and the increasing emphasis on individual freedom. Fundamental changes were also taking place in family life, sexual behaviour, and in the role of women. Again, historians have tended to emphasize one of these dimensions of change at the expense of the others, whereas it was the interaction between social changes of different kinds, as well as the interaction between social change and developments in politics and in the church that made the 1960s such an explosive decade. In this respect it should be noted that the chronology of religious change in the United States and Canada in the period from about 1945 to 1972 was very similar to that in many European countries, although North America was several years ahead in the experience of affluence. The early years of American affluence coincided with the peak of the cold war and with the 'religious revival'. It was in the 1960s that economic and social change interacted with a new mood of political and religious reform, and with the impact first of the Civil Rights Movement, and then of Vatican II, new radical theologies, and above all the Vietnam War to produce a very different kind of religious atmosphere.

The 1960s were a hinge decade, separating the 1940s and 1950s from the 1970s and 1980s, and sharing aspects both of the period before and the period after. The great majority of those coming to maturity in the 1960s had received a Christian upbringing, and in all sorts of ways, both positively and negatively, this continued to be a significant influence on their thinking and behaviour. This was a decade in which interest in religion, and specifically in Christianity, was at a high level, as reflected most obviously in the impact of Vatican II and of books like *Honest to God*, but also for instance in the large audiences for religious programmes on television, and the major role played by the churches and by religious arguments in many of the public debates of the time (as was shown in Chapter 10). However, a lot of this interest in Christianity was of a critical kind, reflecting a dissatisfaction with conventional answers. It was indeed a period when nothing was any longer sacred, and taboos existed only to be broken. But it is a misunderstanding to suppose that it was a period when Christianity, or religion more generally, no longer mattered. Indeed it was precisely because Western societies were still seen as 'Christian' that singers such as John Lennon and Mick Jagger felt the need to state so emphatically their rejection of Christianity, or that the decision of the Beatles to go to India with the Mahirishi Mahesh Yogi provoked so much media interest.

The religious atmosphere evolved rapidly in the course of the decade. So far as Christianity is concerned, it is possible to distinguish between the 'ferment' of the early and mid-1960s and the 'crisis' of the later part of the decade. For instance, Gauvreau notes that in 1964 most Catholic commentators in Quebec were still hopeful about the direction of contemporary religious change, but by 1971 one was stating that 'unbelief' was now the mainstream.[1] The timetable of change varied from country to country, but if one year is to be selected as marking the turning-point it should be 1967. In the early and mid-1960s there were plenty of Jeremiahs (as indeed there have been at most points in Christian history)—but many of them could be dismissed as reactionaries, blind to the need for change. There were also plenty of optimists who believed that they were living through a period of exciting and fruitful reform. Only in the last years of the decade did the scale of the contemporary crisis become clear for all to see.

One of the central arguments of the book is that the crisis did not have any one overriding cause, but that it arose from the cumulative impact of a variety of smaller factors. The change in women's identity and social role, as proposed in Brown's *Death of Christian Britain*, is too specific a factor to provide a sufficient explanation for the crisis.[2] On the other hand, 'modernization', the concept favoured by many historians, and especially sociologists, is too sweeping and generalized an explanation and does not sufficiently account for the fact that so many key changes took place at this specific time. Peter van Rooden, who has conducted a large oral history project on religious change in the Netherlands, provides a subtle and in many respects convincing analysis of the ways in which his interviewees remembered and interpreted changes in their religious beliefs and practice. However, he too sees the many smaller factors feeding into one big factor, namely a fundamental change in mentality, arising from the 'the penetration within mass culture of the ideal and practices of the reflexive self'.[3] This seems to me to overstate the changes in mentality, as opposed to behaviour, at this time. For some 'Sixty-Eighters', activists in the women's movement, and activists in the Charismatic Movement, the 1960s and early 1970s did indeed revolutionize their understanding of the world. But there were also many people whose thinking changed in much more limited ways. For instance, most people's lives remained substantially focused on home and family, on the bringing up of children, on work, and on leisure. Yet as religion, whether for adults or for children, became optional, people responded in many different ways to the choices on offer. Perhaps the biggest change was the weakening of the collective identities that had been so important in the years before 1960s. If collective identities were declining in the face of individual choice, it was partly because the former seemed to have served their purpose and to be now redundant, partly because the mechanisms

---

[1] Michael Gauvreau, *The Catholic Origins of Quebecs's Quiet Revolution* (Montreal and Kingston, Ontario, 2005), 354.

[2] Callum G. Brown, *The Death of Christian Britain* (London, 2001), 176–9.

[3] Peter van Rooden, 'Oral History and the Strange Demise of Dutch Christianity,' 27.

for enforcing adherence to group norms had weakened, partly because a series of new possibilities were opening up, which most people had not imagined before.

I have emphasized changes in at least four areas: the wide-ranging effects of 'affluence', which had major effects on patterns of home and neighbourhood life, but which, if it brought about changes in mentality, did so only very gradually; changes in the areas of gender and sexuality; the impact of new movements and ideals, which can be summed up in the word '1968'; and the conflicts arising from attempts at church reform and theological modernization, and from the resistance which these encountered. Developments within the churches played a major role in precipitating the crisis. However, these have often been described in too narrow and one-sided a way. Thus Alan Gilbert makes the interesting point that a lot of religious belief in mid-century Britain took the form of 'negligible commitment coupled with a nominal acceptance of prevailing beliefs and social habits', and that in this situation, 'anything shaking the kaleidoscope of habit, assumption and received opinions creates a new cultural situation'. He then goes on to claim that John Robinson made the mistake of shaking the kaleidoscope, and that he can therefore be blamed for turning passive believers into active doubters.[4] Yet the evidence for this is scant. Gilbert quotes a letter written to Robinson by one of his critics to illustrate these processes, but does not mention that, according to the editors of the collection from which the quotation is taken, most of the letters written to Robinson were sympathetic. He also quotes as representative of the criticisms by 'theologians and philosophers' two very hostile reviews, without mentioning the many reviews that either were more balanced or were positively enthusiastic. Some conservative Catholics have been equally ready to blame the Catholic Church's problems on Vatican II. Yet, as Damberg and others have shown, Vatican II was a response to already existing problems, including declining numbers of vocations and, in some countries, mass alienation from the church.[5] The reform movements of the early and mid-1960s and the responses to them by ecclesiastical authority did contribute to the crisis of the later 1960s, but the relationship is less straightforward than some of these arguments suggest. First, in the mid-1960s hopes for change in the church were often raised to unrealistically high levels, and especially among Catholics this led to a mood of disillusion as it became clear that these hopes could not be fulfilled. The speedy rise and gradual decline of the 'progressive' Dutch church is a classic example of this phenomenon. Second, the search for

[4] Alan D. Gilbert, *The Making of Post-Christian Britain* (London, 1980), 121–3.
[5] Wilhelm Damberg, 'Pfarrgemeinden und katholische Verbände vor dem Konzil,' in G. Wassilowsky (ed.), *Zweites Vatikanum* (Freiburg, 2004), 9–30.

a more authentic Christianity often led to a discounting of institutional loyalty, confessional identity, rituals, and formal practice. 'Religionless Christianity' may have been more Christian than the conventional forms of faith that it sought to replace, but it weakened the hold of the church, which was often seen as an irrelevance or even a hindrance. In particular the overriding priority given to political action by many radical Christians in the later 1960s left little time for any regular involvement in the church (though some would return there in the 1970s). Third, especially in the Catholic Church, the reassertion by Pope and bishops of traditional teachings in the later 1960s and 1970s alienated even many of those who had much more modest hopes for reform. And fourth, because of a combination of these factors, many churches saw a serious decline in clerical recruitment and the Catholic Church suffered a mass movement of resignations by priests and nuns, which made it impossible to maintain the kinds of pastoral care and control that had previously been normal.

The 1960s saw a great opening up of new possibilities, as previously esoteric ideas and ways of living became widely current. Many of the political hopes of the 1960s faded in the 1970s, and the counter-culture gradually dispersed. Yet some of the movements stemming from '1968' survived and continued to grow, most notably Women's Liberation. Moreover, new ways of living which had taken their most dramatic shape in the counter-culture became more widely diffused in the 1970s and in subsequent decades, including not only those relating to sex and drugs, but those relating to religion and spirituality. The weakening of churches and orthodox Christianity in the 'long 1960s' was due in part to multiplication of alternatives, and the emergence of a climate of thinking in which individual searching and a degree of eclecticism were more approved than strict adherence to any system of orthodoxy. By the end of the twentieth century this trend would have moved so far that the England footballer, David Beckham, when asked if he and his pop-singer wife, Victoria, would christen their son Brooklyn, replied 'I definitely want Brooklyn christened, but I don't know into what religion yet.'[6]

The period of collective emancipation in the nineteenth century and the first half of the twentieth had seen huge divergences in patterns of religious observance in Western societies, as members of different social classes, ethnic and confessional communities, and those living in different regions of each country often adopted widely different religious practices. As the emphasis shifted towards individual emancipation there was a growing convergence, as these differences narrowed. Individual choice played an increasing role in matters of religion and spirituality, and the differences between choices

---

[6] www.insignificantthoughts.com/blog.archives/100412.html (accessed 3 June 2004).

made by those living in different places and social groups became less clear-cut. Peter van Rooden criticizes the stress on 'emancipation' in histories of the 1960s.[7] He emphasizes the continuing force of conformist pressures in Dutch society: the expected forms of behaviour and, he suggests, ways of perceiving the self, have changed, but behaviour and opinions remain highly predictable. While these points are important, it seems to me that a stress on the ethos of individual emancipation in the 1960s is still valid, both because so many people understood what they were doing in these terms, and because the range of areas in which state, church, employers, or even family could prescribe behaviour was diminishing. Equally, the rhetoric of 'freedom' was an important aspect of the growth of 'alternative spiritualities', which claimed to offer possibilities of self-realization which churches denied. It remained true that influences whether from friends and workmates or from the media encouraged some choices and made others much more difficult.

The 'long 1960s' saw a progressive distancing of large sections of the population in most Western countries from Christianity and the churches. But, just as there is no master factor which accounts for this distancing, nor did the process follow any single pattern. At one extreme were those who made a total break from Christianity and the church; and at the other extreme there were still considerable numbers of people who remained both committed members of their churches and accepting of official orthodoxies. Most people were somewhere between these extremes. For instance, one important legacy of the 1960s was the increasing readiness of church-goers to resolve many moral or doctrinal issues in their own way, without direction from church authorities. There were also large numbers of people who had given up regular church-going, but retained some links with Christianity or the church. As was shown in Chapter 9, detachment from the church tended to be a step-by-step process. Those who stopped going to church week by week might still go at Christmas. Those who never attended services might still want to baptize their children and send them to Sunday School. Those who had no involvement in the church often continued to believe in God, to pray, and to call themselves Christians. This is one of the forms of 'believing without belonging', described by Grace Davie.[8] Often the clear break from Christianity and the church came only in the next generation. It might need no moment of decision, as there were increasing numbers of young people who were growing up with so little exposure to the Bible or to Christian language and ritual that all these things seemed strange and were not so much rejected as unconsidered. Maybe this is the best way of seeing the religious impact of the 'sexual revolution'. As was

---

[7] Van Rooden, 'Oral History,' 32–3.
[8] Grace Davie, *Religion in Britain since 1945* (Oxford, 1994), 93–4.

suggested in Chapter 8, there is little evidence that involvement in unapproved sexual activity was in itself a cause of alienation from the church or religious belief. But as contemporary sexual mores moved further and further away from the sexual ethics prescribed by the churches, the distance between those inside and outside the church widened and became harder to bridge. So far as Britain is concerned, survey material from the period 1982–2002 fits better with the model of a gradual distancing from the church across successive age-cohorts than with the model of a revolutionary change compressed within a short period. Crockett and Voas, using a series of surveys during that period, showed a consistent and fairly regular drop in the proportion of those claiming a religious affiliation from the cohort born between 1914 and 1923 to that born between 1964 and 1973. There was a similar decline in levels of church attendance, though here the differences between cohorts were much narrower.[9] However, one should not generalize from the British case. It is very possible that similar surveys in some other countries would show a much sharper drop in church-going among the 1944–53 cohort.

The distancing of individuals from Christianity and the church was a gradual process and is as yet far from complete—still today the majority of people in Western societies describe themselves as Christians, and a significant minority retain an active involvement in their churches. What did change much more quickly was the way in which people in Western societies defined their nation's religious identity. In the 1950s it was still taken for granted by most people that they lived in 'a Christian country'. During the 1960s this definition was increasingly questioned, and by the 1970s it had become common to refer to Western societies as 'pluralist', 'post-Christian', or even 'secular'.

Each of these definitions had its merits, though also its limitations. References to 'pluralism' carry the risk of glossing over differences of power and influence between different religious or anti-religious groups, while definitions of the contemporary world as 'secular' or 'post-Christian' tend to homogenize societies and to gloss over the variations in the extent to which religious or secular forces have influenced different sections of society or areas of life. An example of exaggerated homogenization is Gilbert's definition of a 'post-Christian society' as one in which Christian believers are confined to a subculture.[10] This does not seem to me an accurate description of Western societies in the later twentieth century. While the numbers of Christian believers and of church-goers unquestionably declined, and, in particular,

---

[9] Alasdair Crockett and David Voas, 'Generations of Decline: Religious Change in 20th-Century Britain,' *Journal for the Scientific Study of Religion*, 45 (2006), 571.

[10] Gilbert, *Post-Christian Britain*, ix.

the influence of Christianity on popular culture diminished, church-going Christians continued to be well-represented, probably over-represented, in the higher levels of politics, business, the professions, and even the media (often regarded as the most secular area of contemporary society).

As regards the extent to which Western societies since the 1960s can be defined as 'secular': secularization can mean many different things, as was suggested in the Introduction. There I referred to secularization at the level of individual belief and practice; at the social and political level; and at the cultural level. At the first of these levels, the legacy of the 1960s was mixed. On the one hand there was a drop in church-going and a rise in the number of declared agnostics and atheists. On the other hand, there was also a growth in 'alternative' spiritualities of all kinds—so that those moving away from Christianity could move in a variety of other possible directions, some of which were unambiguously secular, while others were not. (An interesting statistic from the European Value Surveys is that while most specifically Christian beliefs and practices declined between 1981 and 1999, there was no change in the proportion of respondents professing belief in an after-life—a tenet not only of Christianity but of various other religions and belief-systems.[11]) At the second of these levels the legacy of the 1960s was also mixed. As was suggested in Chapter 11, the churches continued to have a major role in the education and/or welfare systems of most Western societies. On the other hand, professionalization and the need to provide for a religiously mixed clientele were often weakening the influence of explicitly religious values within church-run institutions. In Europe the Christian Democratic parties, which had often dominated the politics of the 1940s and 1950s, were losing ground from the 1960s. On the other hand the role of religion in the politics of the United States was increasing by the later 1970s. And, indeed, in Europe as much as America, churches continued to assume the role of national conscience, articulating moral values which were not exclusively Christian, but were often being neglected by the major political parties. The changes in the relationship between law and morality in the 1960s and 1970s are often presented simply as a form of secularization but, as was argued in Chapter 10, this is a crude over-simplification of a much more complex story.

It is at the third of these levels that secularization in the 'long 1960s' was most evident. In *Secularisation in Western Europe 1848–1914* I argued that, in spite of the decline in church-going in England, France, and Germany during that period, religion continued to provide a 'common language', which was to some degree shared by all but the most convinced and committed unbelievers. Even the latter usually continued to regard themselves as

---

[11] Yves Lambert, 'New Christianity Indifference and Diffused Spirituality,' in McLeod and Ustorf (eds.), *Decline of Christendom*, 71.

'Protestant', 'Catholic', or 'Jewish' atheists, and most people, whatever their personal beliefs, continued to participate in the Christian or Jewish rites of passage, which provided generally accepted ceremonies for marking the great turning-points of life. In the 1960s this common language was breaking down. Confessional identities weakened, as did the sense of Sunday, saints' days, or even the major Christian festivals, as 'special'. Those who lacked personal belief were feeling less need to take part in Christian rites—and sometimes they decided that it would be more 'authentic' not to do so. Religious language played less part in political rhetoric, as politicians tried to appeal to an audience that was assumed to include both believers of many different kinds and unbelievers.

These latter changes can be seen as an aspect of secularization, but might more precisely be seen as marking 'the end of Christendom'. I say 'more precisely', both because Christianity is not equivalent to or dependent on the maintenance of Christendom, and because those who reject Christianity do not necessarily replace it with a purely secular world-view. Christendom was a social order in which, regardless of individual belief, Christian language, rites, moral teachings, and personnel were part of the taken-for-granted environment. As the indifferent and the hostile claimed the right to do things differently, one of the pillars of Christendom fell. A related change was the recognition by legislators (and indeed by many church leaders) that they lived in a pluralist society, in which compromises between different religious and moral values were needed. And most important was the decline in the Christian socialization of the younger generation. As Christianity lost a large part of its privileged position, the options in matters of belief, life-path, or 'spirituality' were open to a degree that they had not been for centuries.

Bibliography

1. Archival Sources

Centre for North-West Regional Studies, University of Lancaster

Social and Family Life, 1940–1970: transcripts of interviews conducted in Barrow, Lancaster, and Preston by Lucinda Beier and Elizabeth Roberts.

Department of Religious Studies, University of Lancaster

Transcripts of interviews and other material collected in connection with the Kendal Project on religion and spirituality.

Girton College Archives, Cambridge

University and Life Experience: Questionnaires completed in the later 1990s by approximately 750 former students at Girton College.

National Sound Archives, British Library, London

Transcripts of interviews from the following oral history projects:

Birth Control (interviews mainly with British women, but also with some American and Australian women, about their use of contraceptives in the 1960s and 1970s).

1968: A Student Generation in Revolt (interviews with those who had been student activists in Britain or Northern Ireland in the 1960s).

Families, Social Mobility and Ageing: A Multi-Generational Approach (interviews conducted in later 1980s, sometimes involving several generations of the same family).

University of California Berkeley: University Archives

Somers, Robert H., 'The mainsprings of rebellion: A survey of Berkeley students in November 1964' (1965).

2. Newspapers and Magazines

Church Times
Daily Californian [Berkeley student newspaper]
International Times (later renamed *IT*)
Listener
New Christian
Oz
Radio Times
Redbrick [Birmingham University student newspaper]

3. Contemporary Reference Works

Brierley, Peter (ed.), *Prospects for the Eighties* (London, 1980), giving results of the Bible Society's 1979 census of church attendance in England.
House of Commons Debates.
House of Lords Debates.
Minutes of the Annual Conference of the Methodist Church.
Neuss, Ronald F., *Facts and Figures about the Church of England*, iii (London, 1965).
Official Yearbook of the Church of England.

4. Other Printed Sources

Abse, Leo, *Private Member* (London, 1973).
Adonis, Andrew, and Keith Thomas (eds.), *Roy Jenkins: A Retrospective* (Oxford, 2004).
Ahlstrom, Sydney, *A Religious History of the American People* (New Haven, 1972).
Ahlstrom, Sydney E., 'The Radical Turn in Theology and Ethics: Why it Occurred in the 1960s', *Annals of the American Academy of Political Science*, 387 (1970), 1–15.
Allen, John L., *Pope Benedict XVI: A Biography of Joseph Ratzinger* (London, 2005).
Allitt, Patrick, *Religion in America since 1945: A History* (New York, 2003).
Altermatt, Urs, *Le Catholicisme au défi de la modernité: L'Histoire sociale des catholiques suisses aux XIXe et XXe siècles* (French tr., Lausanne, 1994; 1st publ. 1989).
Alternative England and Wales (London, 1975).
Anderson, Allan, 'The Pentecostal and Charismatic Movements', in McLeod (ed.), *Cambridge History of Christianity*, ix. 89–106.
Annan, Noel, *Our Age: The Generation that Made Post-War Britain* (London, 1990).
Aptheker, Bettina, 'Gender Politics and the FSM: A Meditation on Women and Freedom of Speech', in R. Cohen and R. E. Zelnik (eds.), *The Free Speech Movement: Reflections on Berkeley in the 1960s* (Berkeley, Calif., 2002), 129–39.
Arnal, Oscar, *Priests in Working Class Blue: The History of the Worker Priests, 1943–1954* (New York, 1986).
Auden, W. H., *Collected Shorter Poems, 1927–1957* (London, 1969).
Bailey, Beth, 'The Sexual Revolution: Was it Revolutionary?', in David Farber and Beth Bailey (eds.), *The Columbia Guide to America in the 1960s* (New York, 2001), 134–42.
Ball, Stuart, 'Local Conservatism and Party Organisation', in Anthony Seldon and Stuart Ball (eds.), *Conservative Century: The Conservative Party since 1900* (Oxford, 1994), 261–311.
Bark, Dennis L., and David R. Gress, *Democracy and its Discontents*, 2 vols. (Oxford, 1989).
Barone, Michael, and Grant Ujifusa (eds.), *The Almanac of American Politics, 1996* (Washington, DC, 1995).
Bartolini, S., *The Political Mobilisation of the European Left* (Cambridge, 2000).
Bartram, Christine, and Heinz-Hermann Krüger, 'Vom Backfisch zum Teenager— Mädchensozialisation in den 50er Jahren', in H.-H. Krüger (ed.), *'Die Elvis-Tolle'*, (Opladen, 1985), 84–102.
Baum, Gregory, *The Church in Quebec* (Ottawa, 1991).

Bebbington, D. W., *Evangelicalism in Modern Britain: A History from the 1730s to the 1980s* (London, 1989).

—— 'The Secularization of the British Universities since the Mid-Nineteenth Century', in George Marsden and Bradley Longfield (eds.), *The Secularization of the Academy* (New York, 1992), 259–77.

Beer, D. R., ' "The Holiest Campus," its Decline and Transformation: The University of New England 1946–1979', *Journal of Religious History*, 21 (1997), 318–36.

Berger, Peter L., *The Social Reality of Religion* (Harmondsworth, 1972; 1st publ. 1967).

Berkowitz, Edward D., *Something Happened: A Political and Cultural Overview of the Seventies* (New York, 2006).

Bessell, Richard, and Dirk Schumann (eds.), *Life After Death: Approaches to a Cultural and Social History of Europe during the 1940s and 1950s* (Cambridge, 2003).

Bibby, Reginald W., *Fragmented Gods: The Poverty and Potential of Religion in Canada* (2nd edn. Toronto, 1990; 1st publ. 1987).

Blaschke, Olaf, 'Das 19. Jahrhundert: Ein Zweites Konfessionelles Zeitalter?', *Geschichte und Gesellschaft*, 26 (2000), 38–75.

—— (ed.), *Konfessionen im Konflikt: Deutschland zwischen 1800 und 1970. Ein zweites konfessionelles Zeitalter* (Göttingen, 2001).

Booker, Christopher, *The Neophiliacs* (London, 1969).

Bouchier, David, *The Feminist Challenge: The Movement for Women's Liberation in Britain and the USA* (London, 1985).

Boulard, Fernand, and Jean Rémy, *Pratique religieuse urbaine et régions culturelles* (Paris, 1968).

Briggs, Asa, 'Christ and the Media: Secularisation, Rationalism and Sectarianism in the History of British Broadcasting, 1922–1976', in Eileen Barker, James Beckford, and Karel Dobbelaere (eds.), *Secularization, Rationalism and Sectarianism* (Oxford, 1993), 267–86.

Brillant, Bernard, *Les Clercs de 68* (Paris, 2003).

Brookes, Barbara, *Abortion in England 1900–1967* (Beckenham, 1988).

Brown, Callum G., *Religion and Society in Scotland since 1707* (Edinburgh, 1997).

—— *The Death of Christian Britain: Understanding Secularisation 1800–2000* (London, 2001).

—— *Religion and Society in Twentieth-Century Britain* (London, 2006).

—— 'The Secularisation Decade: What the 1960s have Done to the Study of Religious History', in McLeod and Ustorf (eds.), *Decline of Christendom*, 89–106.

Bruce, Steve, *Religion in the Modern World: From Cathedrals to Cults* (Oxford, 1996).

—— 'The Student Christian Movement and the Inter-Varsity Fellowship: A Sociological Study of Two Student Movements' (Ph.D. thesis, University of Stirling, 1980).

Burleigh, Michael, *Earthly Powers* (London, 2005).

—— *Sacred Causes* (London, 2006).

Burton, Edson, 'From Assimilation to Anti-Racism: The Church of England's Response to Afro-Caribbean Immigration 1948–1981' (Ph.D. thesis, University of the West of England, 2004).

Byatt, A. S., *Babbletower* (London, 1996).

—— *Still Life* (London, 1985).

—— *The Virgin in the Garden* (London, 1978).

Byrne, John, 'A Discussion of Euthanasia since 1935 in British Christianity,' (MPhilB thesis, University of Birmingham, 2007).

Carpenter, Humphrey, *That was Satire that was* (London, 2000).

Carwardine, Richard, 'Religion and Politics in Nineteenth-Century Britain: The Case against American Exceptionalism', in Mark Noll (ed.), *Religion and American Politics from the Colonial Period to the 1980s* (New York, 1990), 225–52.

Cautres, Bruno, 'Religion et comportement électoral en Grande-Bretagne', in Monica Charlot (ed.), *Religion et politique en Grande-Bretagne* (Paris, 1994), 165–90.

Chadwick, Kay, 'Accueillir l'étranger: Immigration, Integration, and the French Catholic Church', in K. Chadwick (ed.), *Catholicism*, 175–96.

—— (ed.), *Catholicism, Politics and Society in Twentieth-Century France* (Liverpool, 2000).

Chadwick, Owen, *Michael Ramsey: A Life* (Oxford, 1990).

Chamberlain, Keith, 'The Berkeley Free Speech Movement and the Campus Ministry', in R. Cohen and R. E. Zelnik (eds.), *The Free Speech Movement: Reflections on Berkeley in the 1960s* (Berkeley, Calif., 2002), 357–61.

Chandler, Andrew, *The Church of England in the Twentieth Century: The Church Commissioners and the Politics of Reform, 1948–1998* (Woodbridge, 2006).

Chaperon, Sylvie, *Les années Beauvoir: 1945–1970* (Paris, 2000).

Chinn, Carl, *Better Betting with a Decent Feller: A Social History of Bookmaking* (2nd edn. London, 2004; 1st publ. 1991).

Cholvy, Gérard, *Géographie religieuse de l'Hérault contemporain* (Paris, 1968).

—— and Yves-Marie Hilaire (eds.), *Histoire religieuse de la France contemporaine 1930–1988* (Toulouse, 1988).

Christian, William, Jr, 'Religious Apparitions and the Cold War in Southern Europe', in Eric R. Wolf (ed.), *Religion, Power and Protest in Local Communities: The Northern Shore of the Mediterranean* (Berlin, 1984), 239–66.

Clark, David (ed.), *Marriage, Domestic Life and Social Change* (London, 1991).

Clark, Henry B., *The Church under Thatcher* (London, 1993).

Clarke, Brian, 'English-Speaking Canada from 1854', in Murphy and Perin (eds.), *Christianity in Canada*, 261–360.

Clements, Keith W., *Lovers of Discord: Twentieth-Century Theological Controversies in England* (London, 1988).

Coleman, John A., *The Evolution of Dutch Catholicism 1958–1974* (Berkeley, Calif., 1978).

Collins, Marcus, *Modern Love: An Intimate History of Men and Women in Twentieth-Century Britain* (London, 2003).

Conway, Martin, 'Belgium', in Tom Buchanan and Martin Conway (eds.), *Political Catholicism in Europe 1918–1965* (Oxford, 1996).

Cook, Hera, *The Long Sexual Revolution: English Women, Sex and Contraception* (Oxford, 2004).

Coupland, Philip, 'Western Union, "Spiritual Union", and European Integration, 1948–51', *Journal of British Studies*, 43 (2004), 366–94.

Crockett, Alasdair, and David Voas, 'Generations of Decline: Religious Change in 20th-Century Britain', *Journal for the Scientific Study of Religion*, 45 (2006), 567–84.

Currie, Robert, Alan Gilbert, and Lee Horsley, *Churches and Churchgoers: Patterns of Church Growth in the British Isles since 1700* (Oxford, 1977).

Dahm, Charles, *Power and Authority in the Catholic Church: Cardinal Cody in Chicago* (Notre Dame, Ind., 1981).

Damberg, Wilhelm, *Abschied vom Milieu? Katholizismus im Bistum Münster und in den Niederlanden 1945–1980* (Paderborn, 1997).

—— 'Pfarrgemeinden und katholische Verbände vor dem Konzil', in Günther Wassilowsky (ed.), *Zweites Vatikanum: vergessene Anstösse, gegenwärtige Fortschreibungen* (Freiburg, 2004), 9–30.

—— 'Das zweite Vatikanische Konzil (1962–1965): Josef Kardinal Frings und die katholische Kirche in Deutschland', *Historisches Jahrbuch*, 125 (2005), 473–94.

Davie, Grace, *Europe, the Exceptional Case: Parameters of Faith in the Modern World* (London, 2002).

—— *Religion in Britain since 1945: Believing without Belonging* (Oxford, 1994).

—— *Religion in Modern Europe: A Memory Mutates* (Oxford, 2000).

Davies, Andrew, 'Cinema and Broadcasting', in Paul Johnson (ed.), *Twentieth-Century Britain: Economic, Social and Cultural Change* (London, 1994), 263–80.

Davies, Bernard, *From Voluntarism to Welfare State: A History of the Youth Service in England*, i. *1939–1979* (Leicester, 1999).

Davies, Christie, *Permissive Britain* (London, 1975).

Dittgen, Alfred, 'Évolution des rites religieux dans l'Europe contemporaine: Statistiques et contextes', *Annales de Démographie Historique* (2003-2), 111–29.

Dix, Carol, *Say I'm Sorry to Mother: The True Story of Four Women Growing up in the Sixties* (London, 1978).

Dobbelaere, Karel, 'Secularization, Pillarization, Religious Involvement and Religious Change in the Low Countries', in Gannon (ed.), *World Catholicism*, 80–115.

—— and Liliane Voyé, 'Western European Catholicism since World War II', in Ebaugh (ed.), *Vatican II and U.S. Catholicism*, 205–31.

Dogan, Mattei, 'The Decline of Religious Beliefs in Western Europe', *International Social Science Journal*, 143 (1995), 405–18.

Doss, Erika, 'Believing in Elvis: Popular Piety in Material Culture', in Stewart M. Hoover and Lynn Schofield Clark (eds.), *Practicing Religion in the Age of the Media* (New York, 2002), 63–86.

Doyle, Ruth T., and Sheila M. Kelly, 'Comparison of Trends in Ten Denominations 1950–1975', in Hoge and Roozen (eds.), *Growth and Decline*, 144–59.

Dutschke, Rudi, *Jeder hat sein Leben ganz zu leben: Die Tagebücher 1963–1979* (Cologne, 2003).

Ebaugh, Helen Rose (ed.), *Vatican II and U.S. Catholicism* (Greenwood, Conn., 1991).

Egerton, George, 'Trudeau, God and the Canadian Constitution: Religion, Human Rights and Government Authority in the Making of the 1992 Constitution', in Lyon and Van Die (eds.), *Rethinking Church, State and Modernity*, 90–112.

Ellwood, Robert S., Jr., *Alternative Altars: Unconventional and Eastern Spirituality in America* (Chicago, 1979).

—— *The Sixties Spiritual Awakening: American Religion moving from Modern to Post-modern* (New Brunswick, NJ, 1994).

Evans, Sara, *Journeys that Opened up the World: Women, Student Christian Movements and Social Justice, 1955–1975* (New Brunswick, NJ, 2003).

—— *Personal Politics: The Roots of Women's Liberation in the Civil Rights Movement and the New Left* (New York, 1980; 1st publ. 1979).

Ferri, Elsa, John Bynner, and Michael Wadsworth (eds.), *Changing Britain, Changing Lives: Three Generations at the Turn of the Century* (London, 2003).

Field, Clive, 'Joining and Leaving British Methodism since the 1960s', in Leslie J. Francis and Yaacov J. Katz (eds.), *Joining and Leaving Religion: Research Perspectives* (Leominster, 2000), 57–85.

Finch, Jenny, and Penny Summerfield, 'Social Reconstruction and the Emergence of Companionate Marriage', in Clark (ed.), *Marriage*, 7–32.

Finke, Roger, and Rodney Stark, *The Churching of America 1776–1990: The Winners and Losers in our Religious Economy* (New Brunswick, NJ, 1992).

Flowers, Ronald J., *Religion in Strange Times: The 1960s and 1970s* (n.pl., 1984).

Forbes, Bruce David, and Jeffrey H. Mahan (eds.), *Religion and Popular Culture in America* (Berkeley, Calif., 2000).

Francis, Leslie J., and Peter W. Brierley, 'The Changing Face of British Churches: 1975–1995', in Mordechai Bar-Lev and William Shaffir (eds.), *Leaving Religion and the Religious Life* (Greenwich, Conn., 1997).

Fraser, Ronald, *1968: A Student Generation in Revolt* (London, 1988).

Freeman, Jo, *At Berkeley in the Sixties: The Education of an Activist, 1961–1965* (Bloomington, Ind., 2004).

Friedan, Betty, *The Feminine Mystique* (Harmondsworth, 1965; 1st publ. 1963).

Frost, David, *An Autobiography: Part One, From Congregations to Audiences* (London, 1993).

—— and Ned Sherrin, *That Was The Week That Was* (London, 1963).

Gannon, Thomas M. (ed.), *World Catholicism in Transition* (New York, 1988).

Garrow, David J., *Liberty and Sexuality: The Right to Privacy and the Making of Roe v. Wade* (New York, 1994).

Gauvreau, Michael, *The Catholic Origins of Quebec's Quiet Revolution, 1931–1970* (Montreal and Kingston, Ontario, 2005).

Gilbert, Alan D., *Religion and Society in Industrial England: Church, Chapel and Social Change, 1740–1914* (London, 1976).

—— *The Making of Post-Christian Britain: A History of the Secularization of Modern Society* (London, 1980).

Gill, Robin, *The Myth of the Empty Church* (London, 1993).

Gill, Sean (ed.), *The Lesbian and Gay Christian Movement: Campaigning for Justice, Truth and Love* (London, 1998).

Ginsborg, Paul, *A History of Contemporary Italy* (London, 1990).

Gitlin, Todd, *The Sixties: Years of Hope, Days of Rage* (New York, 1993).

Glaser, Hermann, *Deutsche Kultur 1945–2000* (Munich, 1999).

Glock, Charles Y., and Robert N. Bellah, *The New Religious Consciousness* (Berkeley, Calif., 1976).

Godin, Henri, and Yvan Daniel, *La France, pays de mission?* (Lyon, 1943).

Goldman, Albert, *The Lives of John Lennon* (London, 1988).

Gorer, Geoffrey, *Sex and Marriage in England Today* (London, 1971).

Greeley, Andrew, *The Catholic Revolution: New Wine, Old Wineskins, and the Second Vatican Council* (Berkeley, Calif., 2004).

Green, Jonathon, *All Dressed up: The Sixties and the Counter-Culture* (London 1999).

——— *Days in the Life: Voices from the English Underground 1961–1971* (London, 1988).

Greene, Sir Hugh, *The Third Floor Front: A View of Broadcasting in the Sixties* (London, 1969).

Greer, Germaine, *The Female Eunuch* (London, 1970).

Greschat, Martin, *Die evangelische Christenheit und die deutsche Geschichte nach 1945. Weichenstellungen in der Nachkriegszeit* (Stuttgart, 2002).

——— 'Kirche und Öffentlichkeit in der deutschen Nachkriegszeit', in Armin Boyens *et al.* (eds.), *Kirchen in der Nachkriegszeit* (Göttingen, 1979), 100–24.

Guy, Laurie, 'Between a Rock and Shifting Sands: Churches and the Issue of Homosexuality in New Zealand, 1960–86', *Journal of Religious History*, 30 (2006), 61–76.

Hager, Angela, 'Westdeutscher Protestantismus und Studentenbewegung', in Hermle *et al.* (eds.), *Umbrüche*, 111–30.

Hall, Mitchell K., *Because of their Faith: CALCAV and Religious Opposition to the Vietnam War* (New York, 1990).

Hanley, David (ed.), *Christian Democracy in Europe: A Comparative Perspective* (London, 1994).

Harvey, Paul, and Philip Goff, *Columbia Documentary History of Religion in America since 1945* (New York, 2005).

Haste, Cate, *Rules of Desire: Sex in Britain, World War I to the Present* (London, 1992).

Hastings, Adrian, *A History of English Christianity 1920–1985* (London, 1986).

——— (ed.), *Modern Catholicism: Vatican II and After* (London, 1991).

Hebblethwaite, Peter, *John XXIII, Pope of the Council* (London, 1984).

Heelas, Paul, and Linda Woodhead, *The Spiritual Revolution* (Oxford, 2005).

Heinz, Donald, 'The Christian World Liberation Front', in Glock and Bellah (eds.), *New Religious Consciousness*, 143–61.

Hennesey, James, *American Catholics* (Oxford, 1981).

Herberg, Will, *Protestant, Catholic, Jew: An Essay in American Religious Sociology* (2nd edn. Garden City, NY, 1960).

Hermle, Siegfried, Claudia Lepp, and Harry Oelke (eds.), *Umbrüche: Der deutsche Protestantismus und die sozialen Bewegungen in den 1960er und 70er Jahren* (Göttingen, 2007).

Heron, Alastair (ed.), *Towards a Quaker View of Sex* (London, 1963).

Heron, Liz, *Truth, Dare and Promise: Girls Growing up in the Fifties* (London, 1985).

Hervieu-Léger, Danièle, *De la mission à la protestation: L'Évolution des étudiants chrétiens* (Paris, 1973).

Herzog, Dagmar, *Sex after Fascism: Memory and Morality in Twentieth-Century Germany* (Princeton, 2005).

Hick, John, *An Autobiography* (Oxford, 2002).

Higgins, Patrick. *Heterosexual Dictatorship: Male Homosexuality in Postwar Britain* (London, 1996).

Higgs, Robert J., *God in the Stadium: Sports and Religion in America* (Lexington, Ky., 1995).

Hilaire, Yves-Marie, 'La Sociologie religieuse du catholicisme français au vingtième siècle', in Chadwick (ed.), *Catholicism*, 244–59.

Hilliard, David, 'Homosexuality', in McLeod (ed.), *The Cambridge History of Christianity*, ix., 546–55.

——'The Religious Crisis of the 1960s: The Experience of the Australian Churches', *Journal of Religious History*, 21 (1997), 209–27.

——'The Religious Culture of Australian Cities in the 1950s', *Hispania Sacra*, 42 (1990), 469–81.

——'UnEnglish and Unmanly: Anglo-Catholicism and Homosexuality', *Victorian Studies*, 25 (1982), 181–210.

Hindell, Keith, and Madeleine Simms, *Abortion Law Reformed* (London, 1971).

Hobsbawm, Eric, *The Age of Extremes* (London, 1994).

Hoffman, Shirl J. (ed.), *Sports and Religion* (Champaign, Ill., 1992).

Hogan, Michael, *The Sectarian Strand: Religion in Australian History* (Ringwood, Victoria, 1987).

Hoge, Dean, *Commitment on Campus: Changes in Religion and Values over Five Decades* (Philadelphia, 1974).

——*Division in the Protestant House* (Philadelphia, 1976).

——and David A. Roozen (eds.), *Understanding Church Growth and Decline: 1950–1978* (New York, 1979).

Holden, Andrew, *Makers and Manners: Politics and Morality in Postwar Britain* (London, 2004).

Holt, Richard, and Tony Mason, *Sport in Britain 1945–2000* (Oxford, 2000).

Home Office, Scottish Home Department, *Report of the Committee on Homosexual Offences and Prostitution* [The Wolfenden Report] (London, 1957).

Hornsby-Smith, Michael, *Roman Catholics in England: Studies in Social Structure since the Second World War* (Cambridge, 1987).

——*The Changing Parish: A Study of Parishes, Priests and Parishioners after Vatican II* (London, 1989).

Houlbrooke, Margaret, 'The Churching of Women in the Twentieth Century' (Ph.D. thesis, University of Reading, 2006).

Howell, David, *British Social Democracy* (London, 1976).

Hulsether, Mark, *Building a Protestant Left: Christianity and Crisis Magazine 1941–1993* (Knoxville, Tenn., 1999).

Hulsether, Mark, 'Like a Sermon: Popular Religion in Madonna Videos', in Forbes and Mahan (eds.), *Religion and Popular Culture in America*, 77–100.

Hutchison, William R., *Religious Pluralism in America: The Contentious History of a Founding Ideal* (New Haven, 2003).

Inglehart, Ronald, *Culture Shift in Advanced Industrial Society* (Princeton, 1990).

Irving, R. E. M., *The Christian Democratic Parties of Western Europe* (London, 1979).

Isserman, Maurice, and Michael Kazin, *America Divided: The Civil War of the 1960s* (2nd edn. New York, 2004).

Jackson, George Lester, *Soledad Brother: The Prison Letters of George Jackson* (London, 1971).

James, Eric, *A Life of John A. T. Robinson: Scholar, Pastor, Prophet* (paperback edn. London, 1989).

Jarvis, Mark, *Conservative Governments, Morality and Social Change in Affluent Britain, 1957–64* (Manchester, 2005).

Jemolo, A. C., *Church and State in Italy 1850–1950* (English tr. Oxford 1960; 1st publ. 1955).

Jenkins, Roy, *A Life at the Centre* (London, 1991).

Johnson, Douglas, *Contending for the Faith: A History of the Evangelical Movement in the Universities and Colleges* (Leicester, 1979).

Johnson, Gregory, 'The Hare Krishna in San Francisco', in Glock and Bellah (eds.), *The New Religious Consciousness*, 31–51.

Johnson, Paul (ed.), *Twentieth-Century Britain: Economic, Social and Cultural Change* (London, 1994).

Jones, Ian, 'The "Mainstream" Churches in Birmingham c.1945–1998: The Local Church and Generational Change' (Ph.D. thesis, University of Birmingham, 2000).

Kahl, Joachim, *The Misery of Christianity* (English tr. Harmondsworth, 1971; 1st publ. 1968).

Kelley, Dean, *Why Conservative Churches are Growing* (New York, 1972).

Kelly, Michael, 'Catholicism and the Left in Twentieth-Century France', in Chadwick (ed.), *Catholicism*, 142–74.

Kerkhofs, Jan, 'The Shortage of Priests in Europe', in Jan Kerkhofs (ed.), *Europe without Priests?* (London, 1995), 1–40.

Kirby, Dianne, 'Religion and the Cold War: An Introduction', in Dianne Kirby (ed.), *Religion and the Cold War* (Basingstoke, 2003), 1–22.

Köhle-Hezinger, Christel, *Evangelisch-Katholisch* (Tübingen, 1976).

Koole, Ruud A., 'The Societal Position of Christian Democracy in the Netherlands', in Lamberts (ed.), *Christian Democracy*, 137–53.

Kosmin, Barry A., and Seymour P. Lachman, *One Nation under God: Religion in Contemporary American Society* (New York, 1993).

Krüger, Heinz-Hermann (ed.), *'Die Elvis-Tolle, die hatte ich mir unauffällig wachsen lassen': Lebensgeschichte und jugendliche Alltagskultur in den fünfziger Jahren* (Opladen, 1985).

Küng, Hans, *My Struggle for Freedom: Memoirs* (English tr. London, 2003; 1st publ. 2002).

Kurlansky, Mark, *1968: The Year that Rocked the World* (New York, 2004).

Laeyendecker, Leo, 'The Case of the Netherlands,' in Roof, Jackson, and Roozen (eds.), *Post-War Generation*, 131–49.

Lambert, Yves, *Dieu change en Bretagne: La religion à Limerzel de 1900 à nos jours* (Paris, 1985).

_____ 'New Christianity, Indifference and Diffused Spirituality', in McLeod and Ustorf (eds.), *Decline of Christendom*, 63–78.

Lamberts, Emiel (ed.), *Christian Democracy in the European Union (1945/1995)* (Leuven, 1997).

Lane, Ralph, 'Catholic Charismatic Renewal', in Glock and Bellah (eds.), *New Religious Consciousness*, 162–79.

Lawson, Tom, *The Church of England and the Holocaust: Christianity, Memory and Nazism* (Woodbridge, 2006).

Léger, Danièle, *Le féminisme en France* (Paris, 1982).

Lehmann, Hartmut, *Säkularisierung* (Göttingen, 2004).

Lehtonen, Risto, *The Story of a Storm: The Ecumenical Student Movement in the Turmoil of Revolution* (Grand Rapids, Mich., 1998).

Lewis, Jane, *The End of Marriage? Individualism and Intimate Relations* (Cheltenham, 2001).

_____ *Women in Britain since 1945* (Oxford, 1992).

_____ and Patrick Wallis, 'Fault, Breakdown, and the Church of England's Involvement in the 1969 Divorce Reform', *Twentieth Century British History*, 11 (2000), 308–32.

Ling, Peter J., *Martin Luther King Jr* (London, 2002).

Lodge, David, *Changing Places* (London, 1975).

_____ *How Far Can You Go?* (London, 1980).

_____ *The British Museum's Falling Down* (London, 1965).

Louvre, Alf, 'The New Radicalism: The Politics of Culture', in Moore-Gilbert and Seed (eds.), *Cultural Revolution?*, 45–71.

Luckmann, Thomas, *The Invisible Religion* (English tr. New York 1967; 1st publ. 1963).

Lyon, David, and Marguerite Van Die (eds.), *Rethinking Church, State and Modernity: Canada between Europe and America* (Toronto, 2000).

McDannell, Colleen, *Material Christianity* (New Haven, 1995).

MacDonald, Ian, *Revolution in the Head: The Beatles Records and the Sixties* (2nd edn. London, 1997).

MacDonald, Michael, 'The Secularisation of Suicide in England 1660–1800', *Past and Present*, 111 (1986), 50–100.

McGreevy, John T., *Parish Boundaries: The Catholic Encounter with Race in the Twentieth-Century Urban North* (Chicago, 1996).

Machin, G. I. T., *Churches and Social Issues in Twentieth-Century Britain* (Oxford, 1998).

MacKinnon, D. M., *et al.*, *Objections to Christian Belief* (Harmondsworth, 1965; 1st publ. 1963).

McLeod, Hugh, (ed.), *The Cambridge History of Christianity*, ix. *World Christianities, c.1914–2000* (Cambridge, 2006).

McLeod, Hugh, *Class and Religion in the Late Victorian City* (London, 1974).

—— 'The Crisis of Christianity in the West: Entering a Post-Christian Era', in McLeod (ed.), *Cambridge History of Christianity*, ix., 323–47.

McLeod, Hugh, 'Dechristianization and Rechristianization: The Case of Great Britain', *Kirchliche Zeitgeschichte*, 11 (1998), 21–32.

—— 'God and the Gallows: Christianity and Capital Punishment in the Nineteenth and Twentieth Centuries', in Kate Cooper and Jeremy Gregory (eds.), *Retribution, Repentance and Reconciliation* (Woodbridge, 2004), 330–56.

—— 'Introduction,' in McLeod and Ustorf (eds.), *Decline of Christendom* (Cambridge, 2003), 1–26.

—— *Piety and Poverty: Working Class Religion in Berlin, London and New York, 1870–1914* (New York, 1996).

—— 'Rapports entre la religion et les principaux clivages de la société britannique', in Hugh McLeod, Stuart Mews, and Christiane d'Haussy (eds.), *Histoire religieuse de la Grande-Bretagne* (Paris, 1997), 287–314.

—— *Religion and the People of Western Europe 1789–1989* (Oxford, 1997).

—— *Secularisation in Western Europe, 1848–1914* (Basingstoke, 2000).

—— 'Varieties of Anticlericalism in Later Victorian and Edwardian England', in Nigel Aston and Matthew Cragoe (eds.), *Anticlericalism in Britain, c.1500–1914* (Stroud, 2000), 198–220.

—— and Werner Ustorf (eds.), *The Decline of Christendom in Western Europe, 1750–2000* (Cambridge, 2003).

McRoberts, Kenneth, *Quebec: Social Change and Political Crisis* (3rd edn. Toronto, 1998).

Maitland, Sara, *A Map of the New Country: Women and Christianity* (London, 1983).

—— *Very Heaven: Looking back on the 1960s* (London, 1988).

Mantei, Simone, *Nein und Ja zur Abtreibung: Die evangelische Kirche in der Reformdebatte um Paragraph 218 St GB (1970–1976)* (Göttingen, 2004).

Martien ten Napel, Hans, 'Christian Democracy in the Netherlands', in Lamberts (ed.), *Christian Democracy*, 51–65.

Martin, Bernice, *A Sociology of Contemporary Cultural Change* (Oxford, 1981).

Martin, David, *A General Theory of Secularization* (Oxford, 1978).

—— *A Sociology of English Religion* (London, 1967).

—— *The Religious and the Secular* (London, 1969).

Martin, William, *The Billy Graham Story: A Prophet with Honour* (London, 1991).

Marwick, Arthur, *The Sixties: Cultural Revolution in Britain, France, Italy and the United States, c.1958–c.1974* (Oxford, 1998).

van Melis, Damian, ' "Strengthened and Purified through Ordeal by Fire": Ecclesiastical Triumphalism in the Ruins of Europe' in Bessell and Schumann (eds.), *Life After Death*, 231–41.

Mendras, Henri, *La Seconde Révolution française* (Paris, 1988).

Messer, Jeanne, 'Guru Maharaj Ji and the Divine Light Mission', in Glock and Bellah (eds.), *The New Religious Consciousness*, 52–72.

Mol, Hans (ed.), *Western Religion* (The Hague, 1972).

Moore, Robert, *Pit-Men, Politics and Preachers* (London, 1974).

Moore-Gilbert, Bart, and John Seed (eds.), *Cultural Revolution? The Challenge of the Arts in the 1960s* (London, 1992).

Morgan, D. Densil, *The Span of the Cross: Christian Religion and Society in Wales 1914–2000* (Cardiff, 1999).

Morin, Edgar, *Plodémet: Report from a French Village* (English tr. London, 1971; 1st publ. 1967).

Murphy, Terence, and Roberto Perin (eds.), *A Concise History of Christianity in Canada* (Don Mills, Ontario, 1996).

Nelson, Elizabeth, *The British Counter-Culture 1966–73: A Study of the Underground Press* (Basingstoke, 1989).

Neville, Richard, *Play Power* (London, 1970).

Nielsen, Jørgen S., *Muslims in Western Europe* (Edinburgh, 1992).

Noll, Mark, 'What Happened to Christian Canada?', *Church History*, 75 (2006), 245–73.

Norman, E. R., *Secularisation* (London, 2002).

Nuij, Ton, 'La Subculture religieuse de la ville d'Amsterdam', in *The Contemporary Metamorphosis of Religion*, Acts of the International Conference on the Sociology of Religion (The Hague, 1973), 377–91.

Nurser, John, *For All Peoples and All Nations: Christian Churches and Human Rights* (Geneva, 2005).

Obelkevich, James, 'Consumption', in James Obelkevich and Peter Catterall (eds.), *Understanding Post-War British Society* (London, 1994), 141–54.

O'Brien, Anne, *God's Willing Workers: Women and Religion in Australia* (Sydney, 2005).

Ormières, Jean-Louis, *L'Europe désenchantée: La fin de l'Europe chrétienne, France, Belgique, Espagne, Portugal* (Paris, 2005).

Osgerby, Bill, *Youth in Britain since 1945* (Oxford, 1998).

Parsons, Gerald, 'Between Law and Licence: Christianity, Morality and "Permissiveness"', in Parsons and Wolffe (eds.), *Religious Diversity*, ii. 231–66.

——— 'From Consensus to Confrontation: Religion and Politics in Britain since 1945', in Parsons and Wolffe (eds.), *Religious Diversity*, ii. 125–59.

——— 'How the Times they were A-Changing: Exploring the Context of Religious Transformation in Britain in the 1960s', in John Wolffe (ed.), *Religion in History: Conflict, Conversion and Coexistence* (Manchester, 2004), 161–89.

——— and John Wolffe (eds.), *The Growth of Religious Diversity in Britain from 1945*, 3 vols. (London, 1993).

——— 'There and Back Again? Religion and the 1944 and 1988 Education Acts', in Parsons and Wolffe (eds.), *Religious Diversity*, ii. 161–98.

Pasture, Patrick, 'Christendom and the Legacy of the Sixties: Between the Secular City and the Age of Aquarius', *Revue d'histoire ecclésiastique*, 99 (2004), 82–117.

Pearson, Joanne (ed.), *Belief beyond Boundaries: Wicca, Celtic Spiritualities and the New Age* (Aldershot, 2002).

——— 'The History and Development of Wicca and Paganism', in Pearson (ed.), *Belief beyond Boundaries*, 15–54.

Pelletier, Denis, *La crise catholique: Religion, société et politique en France (1965–1978)* (Paris, 2002).

Porterfield, Amanda, *The Transformation of American Religion: The Story of a Late-Twentieth-Century Awakening* (Oxford, 2001).

Presser, Stanley, and Linda Stinson, 'Data Collection Mode and Social Desirability: Bias in Self-Reported Religious Attendance', *American Sociological Review*, 63 (1998), 137–45.

Pressley, Alison, *Changing Times: Being Young in Britain in the '60s* (London, 2000).

Preston, Ronald, 'The Collapse of the SCM', *Theology*, 89/732 (1986), 431–40.

Prévotat, Jacques, *Être chrétien en France au XXe siècle de 1914 à nos jours* (Paris, 1998).

Prittie, Terence, *Germans against Hitler* (London, 1964).

Putnam, Robert, *Bowling Alone* (New York, 2000).

Pym, Bridget, *Pressure Groups and the Permissive Society* (Newton Abbot, 1974).

Rawlyk, George A. (ed.), *The Canadian Protestant Experience 1760–1990* (Montreal, 1994).

—— and Mark Noll (eds.), *Amazing Grace: Evangelicalism in Australia, Britain, Canada, and the United States* (Montreal and Kingston, Ontario, 1994).

Rémond, René, *Religion and Society in Modern Europe* (English tr. Oxford, 1999).

—— (ed.), *Société secularisée et renouveaux religieux* (Paris, 1992).

Rex, John, and Robert Moore, *Race, Community and Conflict: A Study of Sparkbrook* (London, 1967).

Rice, David, *Shattered Vows: Exodus from the Priesthood* (London, 1990).

Richards, Martin P. M., and B. Jane Elliott, 'Sex and Marriage in the 1960s and 1970s', in Clark (ed.), *Marriage*, 33–54.

Richards, Peter G., *Parliament and Conscience* (London, 1970).

Robbers, Gerhard (ed.), *Church and State in the European Union* (Baden-Baden, 1996).

Robbins, Keith, *History, Religion and Identity in Modern Britain* (London, 1993).

Roberts, Elizabeth, *Women and Families: An Oral History 1940–1970* (Oxford, 1995).

Robinson, John A. T., *Honest to God* (London, 1963).

—— and David L. Edwards, *The Honest to God Debate* (London, 1963).

Rolph, C. H., *The Trial of Lady Chatterley* (Harmondsworth, 1961).

Romanowski, William, 'Evangelicals and Popular Music: The Contemporary Christian Music Industry', in Forbes and Mahan (eds.), *Religion and Popular Culture in America*, 105–24.

van Rooden, Peter, 'Secularization, Dechristianization and Rechristianization in the Netherlands', in Hartmut Lehmann (ed.), *Säkularisierung, Dechristianisierung, Rechristianisierung im neuzeitlichen Europa* (Göttingen, 1997).

Roof, Wade Clark, *A Generation of Seekers: The Spiritual Journey of the Baby Boom Generation* (New York, 1993).

—— *Spiritual Marketplace: Baby Boomers and the Remaking of American Religion* (Princeton, 1999).

—— Jackson W. Carroll, and David A. Roozen (eds.), *The Post-War Generation and Establishment Religion: Cross-Cultural Perspectives* (Boulder, Colo., 1998).

Roozen, David A., Jackson W. Carroll, and Wade C. Roof, 'La génération née après-guerre et la religion instituée: Un aperçu sur 50 ans de changement religieux aux États Unis', *Archives des Sciences Sociales de la Religion*, 83 (1993), 25–52.

Rorabaugh, W. J., *Berkeley at War: The 1960s* (New York, 1989).

Rose, Richard, 'Introduction', in Richard Rose (ed.), *Electoral Behaviour: A Comparative Handbook* (New York, 1974), 3–25.

Ruff, Mark Edward, *The Wayward Flock: Catholic Youth in Post-War West Germany, 1945–1965* (Chapel Hill, NC, 2005).

Russell, Anthony, *The Clerical Profession* (London, 1980).

Sandbrook, Dominic, *Never had it So Good: A History of Britain from Suez to the Beatles* (London, 2005).

——— *White Heat:A History of Britain in the Swinging Sixties* (London, 2006).

Savio, Lynne Hollander, 'Remembering Mario', in R. Cohen and R. E. Zelnik (eds.), *The Free Speech Movement: Reflections on Berkeley in the 1960s* (Berkeley, Calif., 2002), 552–6.

Schmidt, Thomas, and Monika Wohlrab-Sahr, 'Still the Most Areligious Part of the World: Developments in the Religious Field in Eastern Germany since 1990', *International Journal of Practical Theology*, 7 (2003), 86–100.

Schofield, Michael, *The Sexual Behaviour of Young Adults* (London, 1973).

——— *The Sexual Behaviour of Young People* (London, 1965).

Schor, Ralph, *Histoire de la société française au XXe siècle* (Paris, 2004).

Schwarz, Egon, 'Rolf Hochhuths "Der Stellvertreter"', in Walter Hinck (ed.), *Rolf Hochhuth: Eingriff in die Zeitgeschichte* (Reinbek bei Hamburg, 1981), 117–45.

Sevegrand, Martine, *Les enfants du bon Dieu: Les catholiques français et la procréation au XXe siècle* (Paris, 1995).

——— *Vers une Église sans prêtres: La crise du clergé séculier en France* (Rennes, 2004).

Shanks, Andrew, 'Peace', in Adrian Hastings, Alistair Mason, and Hugh Pyper (eds.), *The Oxford Companion to Christian Thought* (Oxford, 2000).

Shellard, Dominic, *Kenneth Tynan: A Life* (New Haven, 2003).

Silk, Mark, *Spiritual Politics: Religion and America since World War II* (New York, 1988).

Smith, Mark, *Religion and Industrial Society: Oldham and Saddleworth 1740–1865* (Oxford, 1995).

Snape, Michael, *God and the British Soldier: Religion in the British Army in the First and Second World Wars* (London, 2005).

Sohn, Anne-Marie, *Age tendre et tête de bois* (Paris, 2001).

Stevens, Jay, *Storming Heaven: LSD and the American Dream* (New York, 1987).

Stone, Donald, 'The Human Potential Movement', in Glock and Bellah (eds.), *New Religious Consciousness*, 93–115.

Strachan, Francoise (ed.), *The Aquarian Guide to Occult, Mystical, Religious, Magical London and Around* (London, 1970).

Sutcliffe, Steven, 'Wandering Stars: Seekers and Gurus in the Modern World', in Sutcliffe and Bowman (eds.), *Beyond New Age*, 17–36.

——— and Marion Bowman (eds.), *Beyond New Age: Exploring Alternative Spirituality* (Edinburgh, 2000).

Sykes, Richard, 'Popular Religion in Decline: A Study from the Black Country', *Journal of Ecclesiastical History*, 56 (2002), 287–307.

Sykes, Richard, 'Popular Religion in Dudley and the Gornals, c.1914–1965' (Ph.D. thesis, University of Wolverhampton, 1999).

Tavard, George H., 'Ecumenical Relations,' in Hastings (ed.), *Catholicism*, 399–421.

Tentler, Leslie Woodcock, *Catholics and Contraception: An American History* (Ithaca, NY, 2004).

Thane, Pat, 'Family Life and "Normality" in Postwar British Culture', in Bessell and Schumann (eds.), *Life After Death*, 193–210.

―― 'Women since 1945', in Johnson (ed.), *Twentieth-Century Britain*, 392–410.

Thurman, Joyce, *New Wineskins: A Study of the House Church Movement* (Frankfurt am Main, 1982).

Tomasson, R. F., *Sweden: Prototype of Modern Society* (New York, 1970).

Towler, Robert, *The Need for Certainty: A Sociological Study of Conventional Religion* (London, 1984).

Tracey, Michael, *A Variety of Lives: A Biography of Sir Hugh Greene* (London, 1983).

―― and David Morrison, *Whitehouse* (London, 1979).

Turner, Frank M., *Contesting Intellectual Authority: Essays in Victorian Intellectual Life* (Cambridge, 1993).

Turner, John Munsey, *Modern Methodism in England, 1932–1998* (Peterborough, 1998).

Van Houten, Peter, and Edward Barrett, *Berkeley and its Students: Days of Conflict, Years of Change, 1945–1970* (Berkeley, Calif., 2003).

Varney, P. D., 'Religion in Rural Norfolk', in David Martin and Michael Hill (eds.), *A Sociological Yearbook of Religion in Britain*, iii (London, 1970), 65–77.

Voyé, Liliane, 'Belgique: Crise de la civilisation paroissiale et recompositions du croire', in Grace Davie and Danièle Hervieu-Léger (eds.), *Identités religieuses en Europe* (Paris, 1996), 195–213.

Wain, John, *Sprightly Running: Part of an Autobiography* (London, 1962).

Walker, Andrew, *Restoring the Kingdom: The Radical Christianity of the House Church Movement* (London, 1988).

Walsh, Michael, 'The History of the Council', in Hastings (ed.), *Catholicism*, 35–47.

―― 'Pius XII', in Hastings (ed.), *Catholicism*, pp 20–26.

―― 'The Religious Ferment of the Sixties', in McLeod (ed.), *Cambridge History of Christianity*, ix. 304–22.

Wandor, Michelene, *Once a Feminist: Stories of a Generation* (London, 1990).

―― *The Body Politic: Writings from the Women's Liberation Movement in Britain 1969–1972* (London, 1972).

Warner, Tom, *Never Going Back: A History of Queer Activism in Canada* (Toronto, 2002).

Weeks, Jeffrey, *Coming Out: Homosexual Politics in Britain from the Nineteenth Century to the Present* (2nd edn. London, 1990).

―― and Kevin Porter, *Between the Acts: Lives of Homosexual Men 1885-1967* (2nd edn. London, 1998).

Weldon, Fay, *Female Friends* (London, 1975).

Welsby, Paul A., *A History of the Church of England, 1945–1980* (Oxford, 1984).

White, Cynthia L., *Women's Magazines 1693–1968* (London, 1970).

Whitehouse, Mary, *Who Does She Think She Is?* (London, 1971).

Wickham, E. R., *Church and People in an Industrial City* (London, 1957).

Wilcox, Clyde, *Onward Christian Soldiers? The Religious Right in American Politics* (Boulder, Colo., 1996).

Williams, Peter, *Popular Religion in America* (Englewood Cliffs, NJ, 1980).

Williams, S. C., *Religious Belief and Popular Culture in Southwark, c.1880–1939* (Oxford, 1999).

Wilmore, Gayraud S., *Black Religion and Black Radicalism* (New York, 1972).

Wilson, Elizabeth, *Only Half Way to Paradise: Women in Postwar Britain 1945–1968* (London, n.d.).

Wolfe, Kenneth, *The Politics of Religion in Broadcasting* (Canterbury, 1984).

Wolffe, John, 'How Many Ways to God? Christians and Religious Pluralism', in Parsons and Wolffe (eds.), *Religious Diversity*, ii. 23–53.

Wright, Les, 'San Francisco', in David Higgs (ed.), *Queer Sites: Gay Urban Histories since 1600* (London, 1999), 164–89.

Wuthnow, Robert, *After Heaven: Spirituality in America since the 1950s* (Berkeley, Calif., 1998).

—— *Experimentation in American Religion: The New Mysticisms and their Implications for the Churches* (Berkeley, Calif., 1978).

—— *The Restructuring of American Religion* (Princeton, 1988).

—— 'The New Religions in Social Context', in Glock and Bellah (eds.), *The New Religious Consciousness*, 267–93.

Ziemann, Benjamin, 'Zwischen sozialer Bewegung und Dienstleistung an Individuum: Katholiken und katholische Kirche im therapeutischen Jahrzehnt', *Archiv für Sozialgeschichte*, 44 (2004), 357–93.

—— 'The Gospel of Psychology: Therapeutic Concepts and the Scientification of Pastoral Care in the West German Catholic Church, 1950–1980', *Central European History*, 39 (2006), 79–106.

5. Internet Sources

The Millennium Project, summaries of interviews conducted in the later 1990s with several thousand people in all parts of the UK, available through website of National Sound Archive, www.bl.uk/collections/sound-archive/history.html (accessed on various dates in Apr. 2005)

Religious affiliation in Canada, as reported by Canadian Census, 2001, http://www.12.stat.can.ca (accessed 28 Sept. 2004)

Religious affiliation in England and Wales, as reported by UK census, 2001, www.statistics.gov.uk/census2001 (accessed 10 Mar. 2004)

Religious affiliation in the USA, as reported by a survey in 2001, www.gc.cuny.edu/studies/key_findings/htm (accessed 28 Sept. 2004)

van Rooden, Peter, 'Oral History and the Strange Demise of Dutch Christianity', www.xs4all.nl/pvrooden (accessed 14 Apr. 2005)

Wikipedia article on Ingemar Hedenius, http://sv.wikipedia.org/wiki/Ingemar_Hedenius (accessed 4 December 2006).

6. Conference and Seminar Papers

Alvunger, Daniel, 'A Secularised Lutheran Kingdom of the Swedish Nation?', paper at the Modern History Seminar, University of Birmingham, 19 May 2004.
Brown, Callum G., 'Secularisation, the Growth of Militancy, and the Spiritual Revolution', paper at the Anglo-American Historical Conference, London, 6 July 2006.
Horn, Gerd-Rainer, 'Christian Students on the Left', paper at the conference on Christian Youth Movements, Birmingham, 19 Feb. 2006.
Willett, Graham, 'Homosexuality in the "British" World, 1945–1970', paper at the conference on 'Empires of Religion', Dublin, 22 June 2006.

Index

abortion 2, 42, 215
  in Britain 45, 53, 165, 177, 216, 217, 218,
    226, 227, 230, 231, 233
  in Canada 216
  in France 182, 235–6
  in Germany 236–7
  in Italy 182
  in USA 235, 237
Abse, Leo 227, 230
affluence 14–15, 29, 102–23
agnosticism 2, 12, 41–2, 71, 72, 109, 206, 227,
  231, 241, 245–6
Ahlstrom, Sydney 246
Alfrink, Cardinal 82, 95, 152
Algerian War 56, 81
Allegro, John 86
'alternative' spiritualities 2, 18, 25, 133,
  135–7, 146, 180, 243, 244–5, 262
Annan, Noel 42, 224
anti-clericalism 26–7, 50, 53, 76, 191
anti-Semitism 16
Aptheker, Bettina 176
astrology 135, 136, 137, 245
asylum 254
atheism 2, 20, 55, 72, 165, 212–13, 227,
  245–6
Attlee, Clement 34
Auden, W. H. 28, 35, 42
Australia 1, 6, 22, 36, 49, 51, 57, 90 n.20, 96,
  124, 169, 212, 213, 234, 246
Austria 44, 51, 249

Bailey, Revd D. Sherwin 43, 223
baptism 1, 62–3, 172, 202–3
Baptists 23, 38, 62, 65–6, 87, 248
base communities 148, 152
BBC 31–2, 40–41, 71–2, 195, 213, 229–30,
  240–1
Beatles 79, 87, 126, 128, 133, 136, 258
  see also George Harrison, John
    Lennon
Beats 79, 132–3
Bebbington, David 139
Beckham, David 261
Beier, Lucinda 47
Beith, Alan 251 n.26
Bekkers, Bishop 82, 95, 152

Belgium 33, 44, 50, 51, 73, 74, 76–7, 202,
  249, 253
Berger, Peter 16
Berrigan brothers 97
Bevin, Ernest 34
Bezzant, Revd J. S. 83
Blair, Tony 251 n.26
blasphemy 45, 217, 234, 241
Blavatsky, Helena 25, 133
Blessitt, Arthur 138
Böll, Heinrich 69
Bonhoeffer, Dietrich 80, 84, 88, 91, 99, 148,
  155, 156
Booker, Christopher 60
Bowlby, John 45
British Broadcasting Corporation
  see BBC
British Council of Churches 86, 88
Brown, Callum 7, 8, 13–14, 38–9, 60–1,
  84 n.2, 89, 171, 186, 201, 220, 238, 259
Bruce, Steve 7, 211, 257
Buddhism 1, 70, 79, 125, 126, 132, 134, 135,
  136, 200, 245
Bunch, Charlotte 157, 185
Butler, R. A. 221

Calvert, Roy 222–3
Canada 1, 22, 36, 44, 185, 216–17, 234, 235,
  246, 248, 258
  Quebec 6, 56, 59, 69, 75–6, 167–8, 207,
    258–9
capital punishment 43, 53, 216, 217, 218,
  222–3, 227, 228, 231, 233
Caritas 253
Carter, Jimmy 247
Catholic Action 55, 76, 167
censorship 20, 42, 45, 67–8, 76, 217
Charismatic Movement 100, 138–9, 210, 243
Cholvy, Gérard 8, 11, 13, 257
Christendom 18, 31, 58–9, 60, 216–17
  'Christian country' 39, 40, 41, 42–6,
    215–41
  decline of 18–30, 112–13, 240–56
  'quasi-Christendom' 46–7
Christian student organisations
  Christian Unions 38, 211–12
  Inter-Varsity Fellowship 38, 211–12

Christian student organisations (*cont.*)
  Jeunesse étudiante chrétienne 56, 81
  Mission étudiante 148
  Student Christian Movement 38, 90,
    211–12
  Student Volunteer Movement 81
  University Christian Movement 157
  World Student Christian Federation 156–7
church-building 35–6, 247
church-going 21, 26, 36, 38, 48, 51–58, 54,
  164
  decline of 60–1, 65, 113, 188, 196–202, 214
  statistics 2–3, 25, 38–9, 46, 51–2
church-membership 38–9, 65, 198–9, 207–10
church-state relations 20–4, 33–4, 44–6,
  75–6, 121–2, 215–39, 252–5
Church of England 38–41, 43, 45, 62–6, 70,
  79–80, 83–7, 88, 89, 90, 99, 104–5, 118,
  185–6, 194–5, 206, 221–34, 240, 254
Church of Scotland 223, 226
Churchill, Winston 31, 70
churching 47, 64, 108–10
cinema 42, 51, 57–8, 171, 252
Civil Rights Movement 3, 30, 81, 91–2, 97–8,
  143, 146–7, 158
  Student Non-Violent Co-ordinating
    Committee 81, 146, 258
class and religious practice 52, 58–9, 196
clergy
  celibacy 13, 94, 99, 153, 190, 192
  clericalism 15, 75, 81
  conflicts with bishops 154, 159, 191–3
  marriage of 153–4, 188, 191
  ordinations 1, 64, 89, 189–90, 194
  radical 97–9, 145, 151–2, 154, 178–9
  resignations 1, 4, 188, 189–90, 192–3, 194,
    261
  shortage of 12, 56, 113
  status and morale 47, 113, 188, 194–5, 197
  worker priests 53, 99, 156
  see also anti-clericalism
Cody, Cardinal 98, 192
Cohn-Bendit, Dany 150
Cold War 31, 33–4, 45, 215
communion 38, 64–5, 100, 152
  first communion 47, 203
confession 169, 188, 193–4
confirmation 38, 64, 186, 203
Congar, Yves 55
Congregationalists 23, 38, 62, 66, 229
contraception 57, 106, 216, 218, 227
  and Anglicans 166, 233
  and Catholics 44, 45, 70, 95, 166–9

Humanae Vitae 13, 154, 155, 168–9, 182,
  192–4, 248
  the pill 3, 161–4, 167
Cook, Hera 57
Coplestone, Fr Frederick 40
Cowderoy, Archbishop 193
Cox, Harvey 11, 87
Cripps, Stafford 251 n.26
critical parishes 152, 153
critiques of Christianity or the church 16, 20,
  37, 54–5, 68–9, 176–7, 178, 212–13
critiques of Judaism 176–7
Crockett, Alasdair 263
Crossman, Richard 251 n.26
Crowley, Alesteir 132–3

Daly, Mary 178
Damberg, Wilhelm 12, 260
Daniel, Yvan 52
Davie, Grace 262
Davies, Bernard 117
Davies, Christie 222–3
Davis, Charles 88
Dearden, Archbishop 94, 193
dechristianisation 10, 14
  see also secularization
Denmark 2, 44
divorce 2, 33, 44, 216, 218, 225–6, 227, 230,
  232, 233, 238
Dobbelaere, Karl 7, 9, 257
Doodeward, Bishop van 82
Döpfner, Cardinal 192
drugs 3, 79, 134, 144, 206
  alcohol 106, 126, 139, 174, 217, 218, 219,
    221
  LSD 124–5, 126, 127
  marijuana 125, 126, 219
  and spiritual experience 127, 132, 136
Dutschke, Rudi 148, 151
Dylan, Bob 25

Échanges et dialogue 152
eclecticism 2, 140, 261
ecumenism 2, 87–8, 89, 93, 95–6, 100, 101,
  140, 152, 153, 154, 158
education 23, 32, 74, 75–6
  church day schools 47, 113, 206, 253
  religion in schools 32, 35, 78, 216, 253
  secular schools 114
  teachers 27
  see also students, Sunday Schools,
    universities and colleges
Edwards, David 85, 89

Eisenhower, Dwight 35
England 4, 6, 8–9, 12, 14, 21–2, 26, 37–44,
    46–9, 51, 53–4, 61–6, 79–80, 83–6,
    103–12, 117–18, 121–2, 162–6, 180–2,
    196, 198–202, 203–7, 244, 253
    Birmingham 62, 98, 119, 120, 121, 172–3,
      251 n.29
    Black Country 64–5, 108
    Lancashire 46–51, 104–6, 109–10, 170–5,
      180–1, 203–6
    London 62, 63, 90, 99, 119, 120, 124, 135,
      164, 199, 213, 244–5
euthanasia 218, 231, 232
Evans, Sara 90

Faith, Adam 213
Faithfull, Theodore 131
Falwell, Jerry 229
family 45–9, 107–15, 123, 127, 148–9,
    169–76, 203–7
    see also marriage
fforde, Arthur 71
Field, Clive 198
Finke, Roger 208
Finland 77, 249
Fisher, Archbishop Geoffrey 68, 79, 232
Fletcher, Joseph 11, 87
Forster, E. M. 41
France 2, 6, 8, 10, 20, 21, 25, 27, 33, 44, 45,
    46, 51–3, 55–6, 60, 66, 73, 75, 81, 99,
    102–3, 110, 113, 122, 148, 151–2, 168,
    182, 191, 193, 202, 236, 242, 248, 253
    'May events' 141, 148, 150, 151–2
    Brittany 46–7, 74–5, 78, 112–15, 196
    Paris 249–50
Fraser, Ronald 142
freethought 27
Freud, Sigmund 16, 28, 57
Friedan, Betty 58
Frost, David 70, 86–7
funerals 202–3

gambling 174, 218, 221, 238
Gardner, Gerald 132–3, 136
Gaulle, Charles de 141
Gauvreau, Michael 76, 168, 258–9
gender
    and private/public divide 44
    and religious practice 52, 186–7
Germany 10, 14–15, 16, 20, 23–4, 25–6, 33,
    44, 51, 54, 57, 59, 66, 68–9, 148–9, 154,
    159
Gielgud, John 43

Gijsen, Bishop 159
Gilbert, Alan 7, 8, 12, 14, 257, 260, 263
Ginsberg, Allen 79, 124–5, 133, 134
Godin, Henri 53
Goethe, J. W. 25
Graber, Bishop 154
Graham, Billy 9, 35–6, 145
Great Britain 31–2, 39, 41–2, 44, 45, 57,
    58–9, 67–8, 69–72, 78–9, 86–90, 98,
    102–3, 115, 119–22, 127, 128, 136–7,
    139, 142–3, 169–78, 183–6, 195,
    210–13, 217–34, 240–1, 242, 255, 263
    see also England, Scotland, Wales
Greene, Hugh Carleton 71–2, 229–30
Griesinger, Jan 178–9
Griffith Jones, Mervyn 68
Groppi, Fr James 98

Haeckel, Ernst 24
Haley, William 40
Halimi, Gisèle 236
Hamilton, William 87
Hardy, Thomas 28
Hare Krishna 134–5
Harris, Ruth 81, 92
Harrison, George 131, 133
Haste, Cate 220
Hawke, Bob 213
Hedenius, Ingemar 55
Heenan, Cardinal 193
Helder Camara, Archbishop 150
Hennegan, Alison 178 n.51
Herberg, Will 34
Heron, Liz 177
Hervieu-Léger, Danièle 148
Hick, John 121–2
Hilaire, Yves-Marie 8, 11, 13, 66, 257
Hilliard, David 11, 60
Hinduism 1, 3, 25, 120–2, 125, 131–2, 133,
    137, 244, 245
Hochhuth, Rolf 69
Hoge, Dean 158
homosexuality 15, 41–5, 53, 78, 80, 228
    Gay Christian Movement 185–6
    Gay Liberation Movement 183–6,
      218
    and law 78–9, 89, 216, 217–8, 223–5,
      227, 233, 234–5, 238
    see also lesbianism
Houlbrooke, Margaret 109
House Churches 210
Huddleston, Fr Trevor 84 n.2
Hughes, Simon 251 n.26

Hull, John 121
Huxley, Aldous 132–3

Ibsen, Hendrik 27
identities 73–8
  class 77–8, 111
  confessional 47–50, 74–5, 99–101, 177
  political 73–9, 111
  regional 249–50
immigration 119–22, 239, 254
individual freedom 106–7, 109, 110, 114,
    123, 129–31, 140, 166, 237, 245, 250, 256
Ireland 2, 4, 20, 22, 24, 39, 44, 51, 196, 217,
    224, 249
  see also Northern Ireland
Islam 1, 3, 70, 120–2, 245
Italy 2, 24, 34, 44, 51, 77, 117, 182, 191, 202,
    249, 253

Jackson, George 147
Jagger, Mick 131, 213, 258
Jehovah's Witnesses 210, 248
Jenkins, Roy 218–19, 226
Jesus Movement 137–8
Jews, Judaism 20, 163, 227, 245, 265
Johnson, Lyndon 87, 141, 144
'Judeo-Christian' religion and culture 51, 73,
    131

Kahl, Joachim 16
Katholikentag 154
Kelley, Dean 207
Kennedy, J. F. 73
Kerouac, Jack 79, 133
Kilmuir, Lord 224
King, Martin Luther 81, 91–2, 141, 146–7,
    155
Kinsey, Alfred 28, 57, 165
Knight, Margaret 40, 41
Köhle-Hezinger, Christel 49

Laeyendecker, Leo 10
Laing, R. D. 130, 243
Lambert, Yves 46
Lane, Nicola 128
Lang, Archbishop Cosmo Gordon 232
LaPorte, Roger 97
law and morality 42–6, 78–9, 215–39
  Lady Chatterley's Lover 67–8, 89 n.18
Lawson, James 81
Leary, Timothy 79, 127, 130–1
Le Bras, Gabriel 51, 116

Lefebvre, Archbishop Marcel 94
Lehtonen, Risto 156–7
leisure 110–11, 113, 128, 172, 252
Lemon, Denis 234
Lennon, John 212–3, 258
lesbianism 89, 179, 185, 244
Lewis, C. S. 37
Lewis, H. D. 41
liturgy 153–4, 155, 156
Lodge, David 154–5, 167
Lubac, Henri de 55
Lucey, Archbishop 192
Luckmann, Thomas 52
Lutherans 50, 100, 203, 207–8

Machin, G. I. T. 220, 231
MacKinnon, Donald 83–4
Macmillan, Harold 44, 102, 218, 221, 251
    n.26
Maharishi Mahesh Yogi 133, 258
Maitland, Sara 178, 181
Marcuse, Herbert 243
marriage
  church teaching on 190
  civil weddings 109
  'companionate' 170–5
  guidance literature 57–8, 163, 232
  'mixed' 49, 50, 95–6, 101, 106, 153, 203–4
  religious weddings 202–3
  see also divorce
Martin, David 17, 116
Martin, Renetia 143
Marwick, Arthur 1, 14, 60, 107
Marx, Karl 16
  Marxism 11, 115–16, 145, 146–51, 153,
    243–4
McCurdy, M. S. 91
McPherson, Aimée Semple 252
media 14, 35, 249–50, 251
  magazines 105, 149, 163, 168, 236–7
  newspapers 55, 69, 84, 233
  radio and television 69–72, 80, 86–7, 89,
    99, 170, 195, 213, 229–30, 240–1, 247,
    258
  see also BBC, cinema, religious press,
    underground press
Mennonites 145
Methodists 22, 23, 38, 44, 62, 65–6, 104–5,
    198–9, 207, 223, 226, 229, 235
middle class 15, 26, 52, 54, 75–6, 153, 196,
    201, 204, 209, 210
Middleton, Neil 87
Milliez, Paul 236

Modern Churchmen's Union 232
Montgomery, Field Marshal 31
Mormons 207–8, 210, 248
Morrison, Blake 203
Mounier, Emmanuel 216
Muggeridge, Malcolm 171
Munch, Edvard 27

Native American spirituality 132, 134, 136
neighbourhood 107–12
Netherlands 2, 6, 9, 14, 20, 24, 33, 49, 50, 51,
    59, 74, 77, 82, 95–6, 99, 152–4, 158–9,
    196, 197–8, 212, 248, 249, 253, 254
    Amsterdam 124, 152–4
    pillarisation 9, 21, 56, 74
Neville, Richard 130
'new morality' 72, 84, 85–6, 166
New Zealand 1, 22, 44, 51, 124, 157, 234–5,
    246
Niebuhr, Reinhold 35
Nietzsche, Friedrich 16, 28
Nixon, Richard 36, 141
Northern Ireland 217, 224, 248, 249
Norway 44, 60
Norwich, Viscount 223
Nuij, Ton 154
nuns 92, 95, 97, 188
Nuttall, Jeff 130

O' Brien, Anne 169
obscenity 67–8, 218
Ormières, Jean-Louis 7

Paganism 136–7, 244
    see also Wicca
Pasture, Patrick 6, 186
Peale, Norman Vincent 35
Pearson, Joanne 136
Pelletier, Denis 236
Pentecostalists 100, 119–20, 138, 207–8, 210,
    248
Pew, J. Howard 158
pluralism 1–2, 21–2, 73–9, 122–3, 177,
    232
political parties 111
    Christian Democrats 24, 34, 73, 76–7,
        264
    Communists 29, 34, 45, 53, 56, 70, 73,
        74–5, 114–15, 144, 256
    Conservatives 77, 79, 218, 221, 225, 227,
        250
    Labour 73, 77, 111, 218–19, 227, 250
    Republicans 251

Social Democrats 24–5, 29, 45, 50, 73,
    251 n.26
politics and religion 20–4, 26–7, 30–4,
    141–60, 250–1
    see also church-state relations
Popes
    Benedict XVI 11, 159
    John XXIII 74, 82, 83, 93
    John Paul II 11
    Paul VI 12, 13, 69, 93–4, 96, 97, 99, 153,
        158, 192–3, 238
    Pius XI 166
    Pius XII 34, 55, 69, 167
popular culture 251–2
popular music 103, 106, 125, 126–7, 128,
    131–2, 210, 212–13, 252
popular religion 6, 12, 196
Portugal 4, 20, 120, 202
Presley, Elvis 161
private and public 42–6, 67–72, 124–5, 149,
    166, 213, 219, 226, 237, 241
professionalization 115, 117–18, 123
Protestants
    conservative 158, 207–12, 235, 248,
        250
    evangelical 157, 217, 235
    liberal 158, 207–12
    revivalist 252
    *see also under names of specific
        denominations, movements and
        organisations*

Quakers 87, 145, 178–9, 222, 228–9, 232

race 88–9, 98, 121, 156, 157, 160, 218,
    233
    anti-racism 179, 234, 239, 254
    see also Civil Rights Movement,
        immigration
Ramsey, Archbishop Michael 79, 87, 98, 222,
    225, 226, 230, 233, 238
Ratzinger, Cardinal Josef, *see* Pope Benedict
    XVI
Reagan, Ronald 254
Reay, Lord 223
rechristianisation 32–3
Reich, Wilhelm 28, 131, 149, 243
Reith, Lord 40
religious orders
    Dominicans 94, 96, 99, 151, 153, 190
    Franciscans 96, 151
    Jesuits 94, 151, 153–4, 190
    see also nuns

religious press 87–90, 96, 138
  Church Times 89, 241
  Frères du monde 96
  Maintenant 96
  New Christian 87–90, 229
Rémond, René 238–9
Rice, David 191–2
Richard, Cliff 171
Roberts, Elizabeth 47, 107, 170–1
Robinson, Bishop John 3, 11, 38, 53, 68, 83, 84–6, 99, 116, 166, 228, 229, 230, 233, 260
  Honest to God 3, 11, 12, 84–6, 99, 228, 238, 258
Roey, Cardinal van 74
Rogers, Carl 118
Roman Catholic Church
  In England 44, 48–9, 65, 70, 71, 87, 106, 150, 167, 196, 226
  In France 46–7, 51–3, 55–6, 74–5, 81, 97, 99, 112–15, 120, 151–2, 189–90
  In Germany 56, 68–9, 154, 159
  In Netherlands 82, 95–6, 99, 152–4, 158–9, 196, 260
  In Quebec 56, 59, 69, 75–6, 167–8, 207, 258–9
  In United States 73, 92, 97–8, 167–9
  see also clergy, nuns, Popes, religious orders, Vatican II
Rooden, Peter van 9–10, 197–8, 259, 262
Roof, Wade Clark 117, 140
Ruff, Mark 10, 14–15
rural areas 26, 46–7, 51, 63, 112–15, 196, 249
Russell, Revd Anthony 194–5
Russell, Bertrand 40, 231
Rynne, Xavier 93

Samaritans 88, 118, 195
Satanism 134
satire 60, 69–71
Savio, Mario 144–5
Schiller, Friedrich 25
Schofield, Michael 163–4
science and religion 24, 26–7, 45, 72, 87, 242
  social science 115–17
Scotland 38, 51, 61, 62, 202, 211, 217, 224, 249
Second Vatican Council, *see* Vatican II
secularity 2, 3, 19, 254–5
secularization 7, 8–9, 13–14, 16–18, 23–4, 24–30, 96, 177, 209, 254–5

Sevegrand, Martine 12, 168, 189
Seventh-day Adventists 210, 248
'sexual revolution' 15, 56–8, 161–6, 175–6, 184, 229, 254–5
  sexual ethics 27–9, 47, 80, 89, 100
  sexual freedom 106, 125, 127–8, 129, 149
  see also contraception, homosexuality, lesbianism, 'new morality', situation ethics
Shaull, Richard 156
Shaw, Bernard 27
Sheen, Bishop Fulton 35
Sherrin, Ned 70
Sikhism 120–1, 245
Silk, Mark 35–6
Simonis, Bishop 158–9
situation ethics 11, 84, 87, 117
  see also 'new morality'
Sjoo, Monica 176
Slack, Rev Kenneth 88
Snyder, Gary 125, 133
socialization 46–51, 113, 202–7, 242–3, 256, 262–3, 265
Solzhenitsyn, A. 68
Spain 4, 20, 26, 45, 120, 249
Speight, Johnny 213
Spellman, Cardinal 144, 145
sport 171, 174, 205, 252
Stacey, Revd Nick 90
Stark, Rodney 208
Steel, David 226, 228
Stevas, Norman St John 223 n.22, 224, 226
Stopes, Marie 232
Strauss, George 224
Strindberg, August 27
students 107, 115
  and politics 56, 81,141–2, 146, 150, 151
  and religion 11–12, 15, 36, 37–8, 39, 52, 53, 61, 83–4, 85, 115, 117, 165–6, 199–201, 204
  and sex 164–6
  see also Christian student movements, universities and colleges
suicide 217, 218, 221
  see also Samaritans
Sunday, Billy 252
Sunday observance 217, 218, 227
Sunday Schools 30, 47–8, 61, 62, 109, 111, 174, 203–7, 247
Suzuki, D. T. 79
Sweden 2, 44, 50, 55, 78, 202, 253

Switzerland 14, 20, 49, 51, 54, 202
Sykes, Richard 108

Taizé 140
Teilhard de Chardin, Pierre 55, 131
Temple, Archbishop William 32, 222
Tentler, Leslie Woodcock 168, 193
Thatcher, Margaret 234, 251 n. 26, 254
theological concepts
  biblical interpretation 100
  Black Theology 147
  church as 'People of God' 93–4
  death of God 11, 87
  declergification 152, 191
  dialogue 73, 76, 93, 96
  hierarchy of truths 93
  Liberation Theology 100, 151
  religionless Christianity 89–90, 99, 151,
    261
  social action imperative 89–92, 96,
    101
Tillich, Paul 91, 148
Tingsten, Herbert 55
Torres, Fr Camilo 148, 150
Toulmin, Stephen 41
trade unions 73, 111, 151
Treacey, Bishop Eric 186
Trudeau, Pierre 56, 76, 216–17
Truman, Harry 35
Tulip, Marie 180
Tynan, Kenneth 88

UFOs 132, 135, 245
underground press 126, 128–9, 130–2, 138,
  142
Unitarians 178
United Church 217
United Church of Christ 145, 178–9
United Kingdom, *see* Great Britain, Northern
  Ireland
United States 6–7, 8, 15, 22, 34, 36, 50, 51, 57,
  61, 73, 80–1, 87, 90–2, 95, 97–8, 115,
  119, 124–5, 130–1, 137–8, 141, 143–7,
  157–8, 162, 166–9, 173, 175–6, 178–9,
  183, 185, 191–2, 193–4, 201, 207–9,
  215–16, 235, 237, 242, 244
  comparisons with Europe 3, 22–3, 246–55,
    258
  relations between denominations 50–1
  religious mobility 100–1
  'religious revival' 8, 34–6, 61, 258
  separation of church and state 215–16,
    253

Bay Area and San Francisco 79, 124, 125,
  132, 133–5, 143, 183
Chicago 97–8, 192
the South 91, 208, 209, 250
see also Civil Rights Movement, Vietnam
  War
universities and colleges 115–6, 251
  Berkeley 126, 141, 143–6, 176
  Cambridge 37–8, 77, 79–80, 83–4, 165–6,
    199–201, 204, 224
  Essex 150
  Hornsey 143
  LSE 143
  Michigan 36
  Oxford 37, 84 n.2, 199
  Regensburg 159
  Sheffield 39, 199–200, 242
  Tübingen 159
  Vanderbilt 80
urban areas, urbanisation 26, 52, 54, 62–3,
  153

Varah, Revd Chad 88
Vatican II 2, 3, 6, 10, 11–13, 30, 82, 92–101,
  151, 159, 189–90, 192, 196
Vidler, Revd Alec 79–80, 83–4
Vietnam War 3, 10, 15, 30, 88, 97, 141–2,
  144–5, 191, 258
Virchow, Rudolf 24
Voas, David 263
Voyé, Liliane 7, 9

Wain, John 37
Wales 20, 38, 51, 219
Wandor, Michelene 177
Watts, Alan 79
Weber, Max 7
Wedekind, Frank 28
welfare 23–4, 75–6, 118, 253
Whitehouse, Mary 89, 99, 213, 229–30, 238,
  240–1
Whiting, Pam 177
Whitlam, Gough 213
Wicca 133, 135–6
Willett, Graham 223 n.32
Williams, Revd Harry 80, 83–4
Wilson, Harold 218, 251 n.26
Wolfenden, John 43, 232
  Wolfenden Report 43–4, 78–9, 223–4
women
  and family 33, 109–10, 173–5
  oppression of 16, 64, 122, 176–8
  paid employment 173–5

women (*cont.*)
 and religion 9, 100, 171–83, 186–7,
  199–201
 and secularization 13
 Women's Liberation Movement 127, 171,
  173, 175–82, 185, 218, 226, 235–6, 244,
  261
 see also gender
working class 14–15, 42, 52, 54, 62, 64, 113,
  231, 249
 changes in 1960s 107–12
World Council of Churches 155–6, 160

World War II 31–3, 37, 42, 44, 45, 55, 61, 62,
  77, 215
Wuthnow, Robert 15, 140

YMCA 145
YWCA 91, 143
yoga 244–5
youth 14–15, 64, 103–7, 123, 201, 219
 youth clubs 47, 66, 75, 104–5, 117–18, 174

Zappa, Frank 133, 213
Ziemann, Benjamin 118

Printed in Great Britain
by Amazon